Conflict and Stability in Europe

This reader is one part of an Open University integrated teaching system and the selection is therefore related to other material available to students. It is designed to evoke the critical understanding of students. Opinions expressed in it are not necessarily those of the course team or of the University.

Conflict and Stability in Europe

Edited by Clive Emsley

CROOM HELM LONDON

in association with

THE OPEN UNIVERSITY PRESS

Selection and editorial material
copyright © The Open University 1979

Croom Helm Ltd, 2-10 St John's Road, London SW11

British Library Cataloguing in Publication Data

Conflict and stability in Europe.
    1. Europe — History — 1789-1900 — Addresses, essays, lectures
    2. Europe — History — 20th century — Addresses, essays, lectures
    I. Emsley, Clive II. Open University
    940.2'08   D299

    ISBN 0-7099-0154-2
    ISBN 0-7099-0155-0 Pbk

Printed in Great Britain by offset lithography by
Billing & Sons Ltd, Guildford, London and Worcester

CONTENTS

EDITORIAL NOTE

Since the readings in this book have been specially selected for the Open University course *Conflict and Stability in the Development of Modern Europe, 1789-1970*, some passages from them which are not discussed in the correspondence texts of the course have been deleted. A few large abridgements have been made. All abridgements are indicated thus: [. . .]. All editorial insertions, such as explanatory footnotes, have also been placed within square brackets. Some of the readings are very short extracts from the original publications and are labelled 'extract' on the contents page. For reasons of space, footnotes have unfortunately had to be deleted.

INTRODUCTION

Clive Emsley

The articles and extracts in this collection were assembled for use with the Open University history course, *Conflict and Stability in the Development of Modern Europe, 1789-1970*. They were selected by members of the course team at the university, and by external consultants, who together prepared the correspondence material for the course. They do not present a definitive statement on conflict and stability in the development of modern Europe; indeed in some cases their relevance to the course title may, in the absence of the correspondence teaching material proper, appear tenuous. It would require tortuous reasoning to draw them all into a unity in an introduction, but then so too would any introduction to the variety of articles and books recommended by a dozen or so lecturers planning a one-year course at any conventional institution of higher education.

The form and title of the course were hammered out during lengthy course team meetings. The title was a compromise. 'Conflict' and 'stability' are not opposites. In some ways they may be seen as reflecting two separate but parallel polarities: on one hand a Marxist school of historians which sees conflict as central to change, and, on the other, a non-Marxist school which, unwittingly perhaps, has absorbed the tenets of functionalist sociology and assumes social systems to be in a state of equilibrium, readjusting when under pressure. But we made no conscious effort to sit on the fence between these two schools, and indeed ideological divisions and theoretical assumptions were not central issues in our discussions. The choice of words was pragmatic; it was recognised that 'conflict' and 'stability' could co-exist — either could be used to describe aspects of, for example, the Cold War. We chose them simply because they seemed to raise the issues which we want students to consider in looking at Europe during the last two centuries.

Change has been both rapid and dramatic over this period. The wars and revolutions, the manifestations of class conflict through strikes and lockouts, have received much attention from historians, and much emphasis has been put on them when discussing changes and/or developments in societies. But there have also been significant periods during these two centuries for which 'stability' seems the key word. There was no major, lengthy international war in Europe between 1815 and 1914; diplomats generally looked to conferences to resolve conflicts and restore an accepted balance of power. Victorian Britain appeared to many contemporaries, and continues to appear to many today, as a fundamentally stable society — stable, but by no means stagnant. Then again, where conflict was, or threatened to be, major and catastrophic, an underlying stability may be detected. Professor Georges Dupeux has demonstrated the remarkable similarity in French voting patterns during the elections of 1849, following revolution and the creation of a republic, and those of 1936, which resulted in the victory of the Popular Front. It has been argued that the *Sozialdemokratische Partei Deutschlands* of Wilhelmine Germany — the largest socialist party in the years preceding the First World War, and a party which believed in the inevitability of revolution — actually created a subculture and a bureaucracy largely similar to those of the state within which it existed and that it thus, paradoxically, became a force for cohesion and stability.

The articles and extracts that follow contribute to the controversies which have arisen out of the last two centuries of European history and which we are exploring in the course with our overall concepts of 'conflict' and 'stability'. Did urbanisation and the impoverishment in nineteenth-century cities breed crime? Was nineteenth-century imperialism the product of capitalism? Was one country specifically to blame for the holocaust of the First World War? Or for the Cold War? Why was it one of the most backward countries of Europe that experienced Marxist-inspired revolution at the beginning of the twentieth century? Was there any significant difference between totalitarianism of the Left and that of the Right? Some answers are suggested in these papers, grouped here as teaching material to be read, amplified, and criticised.

1 THE IMAGE OF THE JOURNALIST IN FRANCE, GERMANY, AND ENGLAND, 1815-1848*

Lenore O'Boyle

Source: *Comparative Studies in Society and History*, vol.X, 1967-8 (Mouton, The Hague), pp.290-317.

The growth of the professions in the nineteenth century occurred as a process of specialization; distinct functions separated out of certain broad categories of activity. The church, the law, and medicine were the matrices from which new professions emerged and became differentiated in response to the growing needs of an increasingly complex society. The reasons for that complexity were in the main economic and stemmed from the industrialization of the first half of the century.

Within the limits of this pattern, however, the development of individual professions varied from one country to another, and the history of journalism demonstrates how an occupational group could have a different function and importance depending on the kind of society in which it operated. In general, the history of journalism conformed to the Western European pattern of professional development, insofar as it was a response to the increasing literacy, growing wealth, and improvements in communications and printing techniques that came with industrialization. Everywhere the emergent figure of the journalist had to be differentiated from a stratum of educated men with pretensions to social leadership, a group comprising the artist, the teacher, and the political leader. In France, Germany, and England, however, the process of separating journalism from related activities took rather different forms. While in each country the occupation combined *belles lettres*, reporting, and political agitation, still in each case these component elements were combined in different proportions; the variation is explicable only in terms of dissimilarities in economic and political systems.

The economic system was determinative in that a certain kind of newspaper press could emerge only at a certain stage of industrial society. That is, only an economically advanced society could produce a newspaper press that supported itself completely from sales to a mass reading public and from paid advertisements. Without such an economic basis the newspaper

*The author is grateful to the American Association of University Women for financial help provided during the work on this essay.

press was either ineffectual or had to rely on political subsidy. Likewise journalism as a full-time occupation with its own standards of performance and moral integrity, and at least a degree of social status, could appear only when the newspaper press had become a profitable business enterprise. Still the economic factor is by itself not enough to explain the position of the newspaper press. The economic situation in France and Germany in the early nineteenth century, for example, was different, but hardly different enough to account for the striking contrasts in the press of the two countries. Account must therefore be taken of the political factor: the nature of the press in each country was crucially affected by the existing distribution of political power. In France, where the middle class increasingly monopolized power, newspapers were essentially instruments of party, weapons used by one section of the middle class against another. The German press reflected the conflict between absolute governments, employing censorship and subsidies, and an emergent middle class demanding a share in government. In England an advanced middle class achieved political compromise with the aristocracy and devoted its chief energies to economic matters, so that the great dailies concentrated on advertising and news rather than politics. In contrast to France and Germany, however, England had a laboring class strong enough to produce a newspaper press devoted to social grievances, and as such was an acutely felt threat to the upper classes.

The interaction of political and economic factors can be analyzed through a comparative study of journalists in the first half of the century in France, Germany, and England. The study can best be focussed through comparison of the attitudes towards the newspaper press, and the image of the journalist in these societies: what was the newspaper press judged to be, how did the journalist see himself, and how was he viewed by other social groups?

France

In France the journalist was slow to define a role distinct from that of the artist, politician, and financier, and to lose a reputation for venality and social inferiority. The chief reason for this was doubtless the relatively backward state of the French economy, which remained predominantly agrarian, with a small business community not much inclined to innovation and dominated by finance rather than industry. There was little paid advertising, nor was there a mass reading public, and in consequence French newspapers could not build up the kind of revenue that would have made them a profitable or even self-supporting business. They remained financially dependent on the various political parties, and thus highly politicized and partisan. The critic Alphonse Karr wrote that 'There are only two kinds of newspapers: those that approve and support the government, whatever it does, and those that blame and attack it, whatever it does.'

To successive governments, accordingly, the newspaper press appeared as a political force requiring regulation. Preliminary censorship was abandoned in 1819, but other means of control were always in use. There were burdensome stamp taxes, and in 1819 a system of caution money was instituted. Under this system the owner of a newspaper was required to deposit a fairly large sum with the government as surety for the payment of any fines that might be levied in the future. The aim was both to restrain individual owners by the threat of loss and to ensure that newspapers were controlled by the prosperous classes opposed to revolution. Such financial measures, however, probably only accentuated the political character of the press, since ownership was thus confined to the wealthy middle class who already dominated political life and who regarded the press chiefly as a means to political influence. The highly successful if controversial press-magnate Émile de Girardin, a strong critic of the system, argued that this kind of control only prevented independent individuals from setting up newspapers while it did nothing to hinder the political parties or the rich; the parties could always raise enough money to establish a newspaper. The effect, in Girardin's words, was 'to create for the benefit of some great feudatories a privilege by which the exclusive exploitation of public opinion is delivered to them as a monopoly, and thus to create in the state an aristocracy the more redoubtable in that it is unrecognized.' In a situation in which no writer could express views that differed from those of the newspaper owners, to the German poet Heinrich Heine it seemed that the French press suffered from an unofficial censorship more oppressive than the government censorship of Germany.

Opponents of caution money further claimed that it resulted in reducing the number of newspapers so that all varieties of existing opinion were not reflected in the press. Moreover the papers that did survive naturally gained in importance, and a naïve observer might easily believe that these newspapers represented a small number of powerful, unified parties. 'Twelve newspapers that divide France among them', wrote Honoré de Balzac, 'are twelve powers as strong or even stronger than the seven ministers, for they overthrow the ministers but themselves remain in existence; whereas a hundred newspapers are no longer to be feared. . . ' Girardin suggested that the government abandon caution money and permit free entry into the newspaper field, then make up for the resulting revenue loss by dropping subventions to the government-supported press. The government would be stronger in the end, since it would find that it could always count on a certain amount of voluntary press support. In any case Girardin thought caution money ineffective as a restraint since newspapers preferred to pay fines to losing subscribers, and they found that the best way to keep subscribers was to play up political and social dissensions; given a steady diet of such journalism, the most objective reader was bound to end a political sectarian. Girardin concluded that the basic solution to the unhealthy condition of the press was to reduce to a minimum the financial burdens attached to starting a paper, so that anyone who seriously wanted his own newspaper could have it. Then more newspapers would be established and more views and interests find a hearing. In this variety, opinions would neutralize each other, and the average reader would be freer to form his own views.

In time the extreme political orientation of the press was modified, though only partially as the result of economic growth. Change came about because of the increase in literacy and the formation of a new reading public that was no longer so engrossed in politics, and because of the increase in paid advertising that lessened the financial dependence of the press on the political parties. In 1836 Girardin started the *Presse*, a major venture in the newspaper field that he hoped would inaugurate a new type of journalism. The paper sold at forty francs, exactly half the usual price of the time. Girardin calculated that the revenue lost through the lower price would be made up by an enlarged body of subscribers attracted by the paper's cheapness, and by an expansion of advertising. Advertising and circulation would react favorably òn each other, as business men would want to advertise in a paper of mass circulation, and readers would prefer a paper with many advertisements. The project was Girardin's answer to the difficulties of the political press, which had to rely on political subsidy because circulations were too small to attract advertisers. It was also aimed at the *petit journal*, the small paper that did not deal with politics and consequently was exempt from the stamp tax and caution money, but was at least as meretricious and certainly more offensive than the political newspapers. Directors, actors, and actresses were compelled to pay to avoid bad reviews in the *petit journal*, tradespeople paid to have their wares 'puffed'; politicians and other prominent figures were victimized by ridicule and imputations of misbehaviour; books were damned or praised at the discretion of the paper's owner. Such dubious practices were necessary because the financial basis of the *petite presse* was so precarious. Increased income from sales and advertising would at once enable the newspapers to win independence from political groups, to abandon blackmail, and to cater less to a taste for scandal. Girardin hoped to arrive at a newspaper press like the English; in England, he pointed out, newspapers were read primarily for their news and their advertising and only secondarily for their political doctrine and opinions.

Actually the system of paid advertisements had existed in France since 1827, and the *Journal des Débats*, despite a large number of subscribers and policies designed to attract advertising, had achieved no results that could be compared to those of *The Times*. Girardin did not in fact find advertising as important a source of revenue as he had hoped, and he also learned that the extensive sales which were so necessary to attract advertising could not be maintained by cheapness alone. Girardin accordingly concentrated on amusing the mass public — though he preferred to speak of educating it. The *Presse* dropped the regulation long political articles and substituted gossip, fashion, and journalistic stunts. Undoubtedly the greatest stroke was the introduction of the serial, an innovation caught up with tremendous enthusiasm by the new reading public that was anxious for diversion but not very interested in politics. Girardin was willing to do what was necessary to change the press from a political to a business enterprise, less a matter of principle than an *affaire*. He 'was odious to all those who dated from the time in which the press was only a means to propagate opinion. He was an admired figure to all those for whom the press is a business . . .' Political agitation was subordinated to news, advertising, and entertainments, with the aim of building up the largest circle of readers; after 1835 newspapers seem to have been successful to the degree that they played down politics. With this partial commercialization of the press journalism could become more of a distinct profession, a full-time career with defined procedures, rather than an easy way temporarily to earn a living for people whose main hopes and interests lay elsewhere.

Yet the evolution of the journalistic profession, as measured by developments in England and in Germany, seems to have been somehow incomplete. French newspapers remained political and venal to a surprising degree throughout the century, as if the political character of the French press had become inveterate. Probably the main reason was the obvious one of France's limited industrialization; there was also a failure to exploit advertising resources effectively. But there was also a political factor, and perhaps a limited explanation of the lasting characteristics of French newspapers should be sought in the pattern of political strife typical of modern France and never more so than in the period after 1815 in which the French newspaper press took shape.

The years 1815-1830, and to a lesser extent 1830-1848, were characterized by intense political absorption and discussion, as Frenchmen tried to think through basic problems of government and to develop satisfactory institutions. On the deepest level their problem was to define the sovereign power, to locate the final authority in French society. Did sovereignty reside in the monarch, the Chambers, the people, or in all three together? Or did it lie outside of any group of men? Even when men wished to avoid the problem they found they could not. The Revolution had destroyed consensus on fundamental matters, and now every specific issue seemed inevitably to lead back to the question of the respective rights of government and people, monarch and Chambers. Nothing created more difficulties of this sort than the subject of press regulation, so that the doctrinaire Charles de Rémusat wrote in his memoirs that liberty of the press was perhaps the great question of the century, and that anyone who wished to understand modern politics should study in detail the discussions on the subject from 1814 to 1830 in the press and the Chambers.

The newspaper press was important, new, and little understood. Article 8 of the Charter seemed to grant liberty of the press, but it was not originally clear that this would extend to newspapers; Beugnot, one of the authors of the Charter, later wrote that no member of the Committee preparing the Charter had intended the article to apply to newspapers. It was by no means obvious what social forces the newspapers represented. It was frequently said that the newspapers represented public opinion, and as such contributed as directly as the Chambers or the monarch to the formation of public policy. René de Chateaubriand explained the relationships between public opinion and government by asserting that the Chambers existed to judge the particular interests of France, while the nation itself rendered its judgments through the medium of the press apart from the representative bodies. Pierre Royer-Collard thought of the press as a fourth power in the state, exercising some of the functions once associated with the corporate bodies of the *ancien régime*; the newspapers checked the power of the central government just as the *parlements* had formerly done. In this view freedom of the press was not only a liberty but also a power, inasmuch as the press balanced the other powers in society.

A free press appeared to be a necessary part of representative government. Without it government and people would not understand each other. 'In the discussions that necessarily arise between the ministry and the Chambers, how could the public know the truth if the newspapers were under the censorship of the ministry, that is, under the influence of one of the interested parties? How could the ministry and the Chambers know public opinion, that constitutes the general will, if that opinion could not be freely expressed?' Free elections required a free press. Only the press could provide a check on government in periods in which the Chambers were not in session. Newspapers were at all times indispensable as a medium for exposing the wrongdoing of individual officials.

Even the firmest defenders of the press, however, had in the end to admit that the simple identification of the newspaper press with something called public opinion would not altogether do. Why in any case assume that newspapers rather than the Chambers expressed public opinion? 'A hundred persons in France would have the right that has been at times contested to the Chamber, to the king, and to his government, that of representing public opinion! What more menacing oligarchy could ever have been put together for the enslavement of peoples. . . .' It was obvious moreover that the newspapers did not reproduce some opinion common to all elements in French society, but rather different and often sharply opposed points of view. 'The fifty, sixty, hundred men who edit newspapers', said Jean Villèle, 'and who express a variety of thoroughly conflicting opinions, neither represent nor express public opinion.' Nor did newspapers represent the opinions of individual citizens, since their columns were not habitually open to any one at all who wished to express his views on politics. The journalists were a group of self-selected men who assumed a political function; 'they arrogate a kind of magistracy in the state. . . .' Duvergier de Hauranne summed it up thus:

> Several persons form an association, establish a periodical publication, and, depending on the degree of recognition accorded their talents, the party that they follow or the passions they flatter, gain a more or less substantial number of subscribers. At one stroke certain individuals have acquired the right to speak every day to all of France, to condemn or approve the acts of government, to inflame or appease passions: certainly the exercise of such a right requires some rules to prevent abuses; for, notice gentlemen, a newspaper is not a register in which all citizens are entitled to insert their claims; it is open only to the editors and those sharing their opinions.

Thus newspapers were revealed as the organs of political parties, and it was this connection with party that made them seem so dangerous and their control so important. In an age that wanted nothing so much as peace and stability, the idea of party revived all the fears left by the factionalism of the Revolution. The prevailing fear of disorder inevitably colored men's thinking about the press, as the realization grew that newspapers offered a new and potentially very dangerous means of political agitation. Every age, Baron Pasquier told the Chamber of Peers, has its own fanaticism. In past ages this had been political in character, but in the present time 'another fanaticism is dominant — that of political opinions. Where are the organs of this fanaticism found? By whom is it encouraged, cultivated, upheld, exalted? Who can deny, gentlemen, that it is by the newspapers and periodicals of every kind?'

The potential danger of the newspaper press was made even greater by the fact that newspapers were not only political weapons but also business enterprises. 'A journal is sometimes an affair of conscience, more often an affair of party, and nearly always an affair of money.' The obvious danger was that political discussions in the press would be conducted ever more recklessly in an attempt to gain readers by providing excitement, novelty, and scandal.

> The interest of the newspapers . . . is in agitation, in the successions of events, in a permanent state of inquietude and expectation; curiosity lives only from events and uncertainty, and for the newspapers the principle of existence and the elements of success lie in curiosity; the monotony of order and peace is fatal to them; the day when the reign of passions will end, when concord, so long exiled, will return to men, newspaper enterprises will no longer have nourishment or life.

To the argument that the newspapers as business enterprises were entitled to the rights enjoyed by other forms of property and that government regulation would hurt their commercial prospects, proponents of press regulation answered that if newspapers were property, they were property of an unusual kind; '. . . the journalists do not possess property; they have only a concession, a privilege, or at least their property, if one can call it such, is comminatory and conditional.'

The image of the journalist revealed in these debates was that of a man either himself a political fanatic or willing to exploit the fanaticism of others for his own ends. The picture was overdrawn but not unjustified. The French press was undeniably factious and revolutionary. In a country where political life was confined to the wealthy and literate, newspapers could exercise significant influence, and where the mechanisms of parliamentary government were as imperfectly understood as they were in France political opposition could easily slide over into revolution. Very often the aim of journalists was simply to gain office for themselves, and they threatened and blackmailed the men in power, with the menacing implication that if jobs and influence were not forthcoming peaceful intimidation might be succeeded by forceful overthrow of the government.

The aspirations of the journalists must be viewed in relation to the struggle for political office on the part of all sections of educated society in nineteenth-century France. Alexis de Tocqueville called the desire for office 'the great, chronic ailment of the whole nation . . .' The royalist Joseph Fiévée once wrote that if there were only two men living in France one would be soliciting the other for a place; Duvergier de Hauranne commented that Fiévée could have gone on to say that if there were three men in France the first would be soliciting the second for the place of the third. In 1815 the returning Bourbons immediately found the demand for office a major problem. There were fewer offices than before because much of the administrative and military machinery needed to run the Napoleonic empire had become superfluous — Chateaubriand remarked that under Napoleon half of France had been supported by the other half. There were more applicants because the Revolution had opened new opportunities to the sons of workers and peasants, and because the restored nobility now needed and wanted jobs and so competed for positions they would formerly have been ashamed to hold. 'I expect', wrote Stendhal in a letter of 10 April 1814 from Paris, 'that M. le comte d'Artois is finding it most embarrassing to reconcile all conflicting claims. Thirty thousand noblemen with nothing better to do are flooding into the city in all the diligences to demand everything.' And the Duke de Richelieu, returning to France after a twenty-five-year absence, was appalled by the change in the national character and the coarsened manners of the upper classes. 'The upper classes think of nothing but to push themselves forward, to enrich themselves, to get good jobs; all means are permissible to achieve that end. . . .' With the accession of Louis-Philippe fifteen years later there took place a purge of government personnel so extensive as to shock even the most sophisticated. Saint-Marc Girardin was caustic in an article in the *Journal des Débats*:

A fortnight ago there was the popular uprising, hours of courage and enthusiasm, hours of virtue and self-sacrifice. Today there is quite another insurrection: it is the insurrection of the petitioners, the mass uprising of all the office-seekers; they run to the antechambers with the same fervor with which the people ran to face the firing.

This exaggerated desire for office was nothing new in France, where the evolution of bureaucratic government had for a long time led men to associate government positions with wealth, status, and security. What was new after 1815 was the conjunction, which was peculiar to France, of a relatively undeveloped economic system with the democratic and egalitarian tendencies inherited from the Revolution. The Revolution had sanctioned the goal of upward social mobility and rewarded the most aggressive personal ambitions. Comparable opportunities did not exist for the post-revolutionary generation. Certainly business offered opportunities and many young men did succeed in making fortunes, yet it was not easy to start with little or nothing; some capital, and much courage, talent, and hard work were usually required for success in business. And the educational system was not one calculated to orient the young towards business careers. The lycée offered a course grounded in the classics and almost entirely literary and theoretical in character, designed to prepare for careers in law, administration, and the liberal professions. The professions themselves required long and expensive preparation, and there is considerable evidence that they were overcrowded.

In such circumstances writing for the press must have seemed a godsend to many. It gave some of the prestige of an intellectual profession, since it required a literary education, but it did not demand a long and costly period of preparation. Nor did it require a man's full time and so was the ideal way for a poor law student or artist to make out temporarily. The same situation could be observed elsewhere in Europe. Everywhere men who were, in Girardin's phrase, victims of a university education, men who had not succeeded in becoming lawyers, doctors, or professors, turned to journalism.

What was unique about the French press was the intimate association between journalism and politics; writing for the newspapers was regarded as a normal step in a man's political career and an accepted means of gaining political office. The English were always impressed by this feature of French society because it contrasted so sharply with English practice. In England, wrote Walter Bagehot, a coalfitter's son looks to the bar and hopes to emulate Lord Eldon, whereas in France the pale young aspirant from the provinces goes to Paris and hopes to emulate Thiers. 'Just consider for a moment what a difference this one fact shows between France and England. Here [in France] a man who begins life by writing in the newspapers, has an appreciable chance of arriving to be Minister of Foreign Affairs.'

The part played by the press in the overthrow of Charles X and the profit the journalists drew from that event were obvious to all observers. Rémusat later recalled that the press was almost the sole instrument for the intellectuals in opposition during the Restoration: 'All of us who fought in those wars . . . whatever we are we were made by the press.' The royalist Alfred Nettement in a book published in 1842 judged with considerable bitterness that the war waged by the *Journal des Débats* against the Bourbons had been motivated solely by self-seeking vanity. 'For these men it was not a matter of ensuring that affairs were handled in this or that manner, but of ensuring that affairs were handled by themselves.' He drew up a partial list of members of the staff rewarded by the new government: one of its founders now in the Chamber of Peers and four editors in the

Chamber of Deputies; one given a chair in the Collège de France; one made aide-de-camp to M. le duc d'Orléans; one in the Council of Ministers; one first secretary in the London embassy; a number made prefects.

The July Monarchy in its turn found that it had to defend itself against the press. Chateaubriand, not without satisfaction, said of the new regime, 'it lives by the press and the press is killing it . . .' but he noticed also that the opposition did not want to overthrow Louis-Philippe but rather '. . . it makes a disturbance in order to gain places . . .' The Tory *Quarterly Review* described the 1848 revolution as arising from 'the accidental audacity of a dozen obscure agitators, the spawn of two printing offices. . . .' and William Nassau Senior, having described how the journalists turned to Alphonse de Lamartine for a decision between regency and republic, noted that neither Lamartine nor anyone else seemed to have thought it odd that a handful of journalists should dethrone a king and themselves decide on a new form of government.

Much about the journalist's role can be explained by the restriction of political life to a single class. Newspapers were written by and for the middle class; they were, in effect, weapons used by one part of the middle class against another. The opposition in these years wanted office, not mass uprising and a radical overthrow of existing society. Given the number of governments France had enjoyed, or suffered, since 1789, there was certainly no excessive reverence in the face of any particular existing government, and factions of the ruling class were willing to use extra-parliamentary methods to oust their opponents. Provided that violence did not go too far, street fighting could be useful. Politics, however, was intended to remain strictly a middle-class affair, and this exclusion of the lower classes had much to do with the character and importance of the press. The professor and *littérateur* Éduard Alletz saw a connection among the representative forms of government, the importance of the press, and the degree of education enjoyed by the common people:

> Constitutional government establishes the reign of journalism . . . under this form of government the lower classes are excluded from all partici-pation in sovereignty, and there remain, to exercise political rights, only the classes capable of deliberating through the written word. . . . In a country where there is more liberty than education, the press, instead of repeating what everyone thinks, attempts to determine what everyone thinks . . . you can be sure that in a country where the lower classes are quite ignorant the press will exercise too much influence. . . .

Thus the political importance of the journalist was the result of a number of factors. In the absence of a mass press journalism was seen less as a profession in its own right than as a stepping-stone to other careers. Given the comparatively unprogressive French economy career opportunities were limited and the desire for political office accordingly remained very strong. At the same time new institutions of self-government offered the individual increased opportunity for political advancement, and the unsettled state of political opinion and practice gave scope to intellectuals to judge political events in the press.

Germany

The most striking feature of the German newspaper press was its mediocrity, which fact seemed the more remarkable in view of the high standards of German education and the vigor and productivity of German intellectual life.

An English observer, writing in the *Foreign Quarterly Review* in 1844, could dismiss Germany's political press as being 'without interest – without influence – without character – without sympathy'. Made twenty years earlier the judgment would no doubt have been even more severe. After a brief period of growth in the immediate post-war years, German newspapers were reduced in the 'twenties to a condition of almost unrelieved nullity by the repressive policies in the Karlsbad decrees. The 'thirties and 'forties brought a somewhat freer political atmosphere and this was reflected in journalism, but the general level of the newspapers remained far below that of England and France during the whole period before 1848.

Germany did produce one great newspaper, Johann Cotta's *Augsburger Allgemeine Zeitung*, which, next to *The Times*, was probably the foremost paper in Europe. About a half-dozen others were of superior quality. The great mass of newspapers, however, were at best no more than respectable local productions, few of which could attract men of talent, or afford staffs large enough for adequate news coverage and varied writing. Uninteresting and uninformative, they rarely reached more than a very limited public, and the fact that most existed at all was due less to their merits than to the extreme localism of German life; every town thought it should have its own newspaper and other types of periodical, and so insipid publications proliferated.

The state of the economy helps to explain the weakness of the newspaper press. Germany was still an agrarian country, considerably less advanced than France. Even by 1848 there was relatively little industrial production, few great capitalists, and a proletariat only beginning to take shape as a class. The middle class was composed of professional men, academics, state officials, and a business group made up largely of small shopkeepers and artisans. Obviously anything like the heavily capitalized newspaper based on advertising revenue and mass sales was economically and technologically impossible.

Economic backwardness, as in France, contributed to produce a large number of journalists of that ill-defined type characteristic of a beginning profession. The appearance of such a group was an index of the lack of career opportunities. In contrast to England or even France, ambitious members of the middle class showed little enthusiasm for business. This fact can be accounted for both by the absence of exciting business opportunity and by the inordinate prestige of the professions and the bureaucracy; it seems safe to say that nowhere in Europe did the state official enjoy such respect as in Germany. In consequence, career expectations were narrowly focussed on state employment. The professions themselves were dominated by the state, since in most instances positions in teaching, the church, and the law were state appointments. English observers marvelled at the extent to which the government managed social and commercial as well as political affairs, and some thought that the result was that 'the young, the aspiring, the clever, and the small capitalists in particular, look for success in life to government employment, to public function, not to their own activity and industry in productive pursuits.' There were many Germans who agreed. The writer Karl Gutzkow, looking back to his days as a student in the late 'twenties and early 'thirties, calculated that for every three independently-minded students there were 97 who wanted only to be pastors or officials. His contemporary, Heinrich Laube, wrote that 'a position connected with the state, and only such a position, was desired; every free activity that depended only on one's own independent strength was considered adventurous, even suspect.'

As in France, the educational system was geared to the production of officials and professional men, and in Germany higher education was so cheap that large numbers of poor students managed to attend a university. There is evidence, as there is for France, of overcrowding in the learned professions and the bureaucracy. Various state governments, for example, tried during the 'twenties to discourage young men from studying for the civil service. Foreign observers and Germans of various occupations and ranks agreed that Germany suffered from an over-production of intellectuals; the conservative novelist and sociologist Wilhelm Riehl asserted that the intellectual proletariat constituted a permanent problem in German society: 'Germany produces a greater intellectual product than it can use and support.'

This abundance, or surplus, of intellectually trained men, would help to explain why the literary field was as crowded in Germany as it undoubtedly was; literature offered the poor university graduate the best of both worlds, the prestige of an intellectual profession without the expensive preparation for one of the established professions. Foreign observers seldom failed to be impressed by the number of books published in Germany. In the period 1820-1840 the production of books in the country rose about 150 per cent, with a similar increase in the number of booksellers, an increase proportionally greater than the rise in population during the same years. 'If authorship goes on in a similarly progressive ratio to that which it has lately done', speculated the English writer John Strang in the 'thirties, in what can be taken as partial seriousness, 'it may be safely assumed, that in a few years the names of German authors will exceed the number of living German readers.'

The economics of German publishing made it easy to get into print. Prevailing market practices made it possible for German publishers to avoid risk. Publishers paid low prices for manuscripts, used cheap materials, and could publish without much discrimination because the lending libraries offered a safe outlet and because there was little respected literary criticism to be feared. The absence of a German copyright law before 1837 made pirating easy, and in addition an immense number of very cheaply prepared translations were issued.

German writers were poor not because it was difficult to publish but because it was too easy; Gutzkow noted that many of the small journals would accept anything provided that they did not have to pay for it. An 1846 article in the *Revue des deux mondes* described the *Literat*, the type figure of Leipzig, center of the German book trade. The *Literat* made translations, corrections, annotations, and was badly paid for them all. He was ordinarily the child of a village schoolmaster, sent without money to a university, and driven by misery to attempt to support himself by writing. Sometimes he earned the doctor's title, sometimes he simply appropriated it. He was always in the front of radical social movements. In short, he was the product of what Laube called Germany's 'universal literary conscription'. Established writers were not in a much better position, and Germans were always amazed by the prosperity of successful French writers. 'A poor German scholar', wrote Ludwig Börne, 'turns yellow with vexation and envy when he sees how good life is for French men of letters.'

Thus limited career opportunities combined with a relatively large number of educated men resulted in too many poorly paid writers supplying indifferent publications. Yet these factors in themselves do not seem sufficient to explain the low level of the newspaper press. Political disunity, as already indicated, certainly stood in the way of improvement. Above all the blame would seem to rest, as contemporaries judged, on the system of censorship common to the German states. William Howitt described the newspaper press to his fellow Englishmen:

> The newspapers present a conglomeration of dry facts, relating generally far more to other nations than their own. . . . All those great questions which involve the political progress and development of a people form no part of their topics, these are reserved for the sole consideration and management of the government. . . . For over all the heads of such journals hangs the iron pen of the censor, and fills every writer with terror.

The question of press regulation brought into focus, as it did in France, the problem of political sovereignty. In Germany the prevailing political system was absolutism, and between absolutism and censorship there is an evident connection. If subjects have no natural right to participate in political affairs then public opinion can have no authority over government, and government consults the public, if at all, at its own convenience. What can be printed becomes a matter solely of government's decision as to what discussion is useful or harmful. The previously quoted critic in the *Foreign Quarterly Review* summed up the matter neatly: 'The political journal, which is in England but ancillary, and in France the parent of a political party, may be regarded in Germany as one of the *regalia* of the crown. The preparation, manufacture, and sale of political intelligence, are as much a royal monopoly in Germany as those of tobacco in France. . . .'

The logic of censorship was irrefutable if absolute government was accepted as legitimate, but in post-1815 Germany such acceptance was no longer complete. The example of revolutionary France, the impact of the late wars, and the real if slow growth in economic life, had led to a new spirit among the growing middle class. Monarchs and nobility were uneasy and defensive. In South Germany moderate constitutions were granted, and even in Prussia the king did not repudiate, although he did ignore, his war-time promise of self-government. German society was in a condition of equilibrium, with power so distributed that no one social group was strong enough to have its way completely, and each group retained some freedom of action as against the others. Rulers became increasingly hesitant to insist on their full power and to demand complete control of the press. To decide in principle, however, on the permissible limits of public discussion proved next to impossible, and in practice the question of what could or could not be said in the press was left to be settled according to what expediency and the relative strength of journalists and government dictated. Censorship lacked guiding principles, with the result that any limit

set up by government seemed arbitrary and any advantage taken by news-
men seemed revolutionary.

Journalists put themselves forward as the spokesmen of public opinion,
and claimed to represent the different interests within society that should
be taken into account by governments. Thus they appeared to be something in the order of officials elected by the people to state popular wants
to government; the radical Johann Wirth thought that journalists should
actually be elected and paid by the people. Governments, however, believed
that the journalists manufactured public opinion rather than expressed it.
In their eyes journalists were primarily subversive political figures, a handful of unprincipled men who stirred up social unrest for base motives of
economic gain and personal advancement. Thus Metternich in 1819 could
state that 'all the German Governments have arrived at the conviction that
. . . the press serves a party antagonistic to all existing governments.' It is
such attitudes that are reflected in the special style of official pronouncements: the press 'brings about unspeakable evil, by denigrating all authority,
questioning all principles, attempting to reconstitute all truths . . .'; 'these
papers serve as organs of a party that works undisturbedly for the overthrow of all that exists in Germany . . . 'the activity of these papers cannot
be better indicated than by the name of open conspiracy . . .'; 'the daily
increasing mischief of the press. . . .'

This attitude of the governments involved a certain paradox, for the
journalists were feared as dangerous revolutionaries but at the same time
despised as second-rate writers who represented no one. The Baden liberal
Ludwig Häusser attributed the failure to create effective pro-government
newspapers directly to the governments' unwillingness to take the press
seriously. Governments hired journalists to defend their policies but then
treated these men without respect or consideration, as if they were mere
hack writers, and the natural consequence was that the official press was
usually so dull and unintelligent as to be unreadable. Likewise governments
refused to meet seriously the arguments used by opposition journalists,
dismissing them as the ravings of Jacobins or subversives.

The governments' fear is perhaps more understandable if it is remembered
that formally constituted political parties were not permitted within the
German Confederation and that journalism seemed to offer a means by
which parties could be created. Newspapers could not be instruments of
party in the same way as in France, but they could prepare for party life
and serve as a substitute. In Germany the political press did in fact precede
political association. The situation and some of its implications were
analyzed by Marx:

See, they say, what firm, lasting, defined policies *English* and *French* newspapers have. They are based on actual life, they give the appearance of an *existing formed* power, they do not indoctrinate the people but themselves are the real doctrines of the people and its parties. You [the German newspapers] , however, do not express the thoughts, the interests of the people, you first *create* them or rather you impute them to the people. You create party spirit. You are not its *creations*. Thus it is made a matter of reproach to the press first that *no* political parties exist, then that it tries to *correct* this deficiency and to create political parties. But this is obvious. Where the press is *young* the popular intelligence is *young*, and the political thinking of an awakening popular intelligence as expressed *day-by-day* will be less finished, less formed, more precipitate than that of a popular intelligence that has grown great and strong and self-conscious in political battles.

It is accordingly clear why governments clung to censorship, and equally why censorship became a prime target of the liberals. The writer Gustav Freytag later wrote that no feature of the old regime was more frequently denounced than the censorship, and that the sharpest attacks did not express the true degree of bitterness felt. In practice liberals did their best to make the censor's life difficult. His position was almost impossible to fill to everyone's satisfaction, and no one, as a rule, wanted the job. The governments could not afford a large enough staff at adequate pay, so often the duties of censor were added as an extra burden to an already fully occupied official, with predictable results – he either neglected his duties as censor or was badly overworked. Censors were always insecure, particularly those in subordinate positions, since they could never be perfectly sure what could or could not be allowed. Theodor Mundt, when being prosecuted by the Prussian Government as a member of the literary group Young Germany, was relieved to learn that a special censorship for the group was being established; he wrote to his friend Gustav Kühne that 'higher officials are entrusted with it, from whose anxiety one suffers less than when one deals with the regular censors who are themselves under strong control.' Karl Varnhagen von Ense noted disapprovingly that the Prussian censors cared very little about conscientiously excluding unfit material and were careful only with publications they thought the king might see.

Discussion of censorship gave liberals the opportunity to present their political program. The arguments for press freedom usually started from the premise that man has the right to express his thought, that the exercise of this right is necessary if man is to attain his full human stature, and that denial of the right is accordingly immoral. Argument then moved to the political sphere. In the South German assemblies speakers claimed press freedom as a necessity of constitutional government.

> Active participation in public affairs is the foundation of a representative constitution. But without a certain degree of free communication of thought such participation is not possible. . . . Therefore it has long been recognized by all enlightened and thinking men that without freedom of the press every representative constitution is only a shadow without body which the first breath blows away.

Speakers pointed out that the German people lacked experience in self-government, hence needed the education in constitutional life that a free press could provide; without the press the people could not understand what their representatives were doing. Karl von Rotteck claimed freedom of the press as the foundation of all other freedoms, and quoted Sheridan, '"Better no Parliament than no freedom of the press!"' Rotteck went on:

> It [the press] guarantees the nation a parliament always in session, in its larger part incorruptible, always sincere. It assures certain victory for truth and justice, without force, solely through the divine judgement of unfettered public opinion, through the directing authority of human reason.

It was argued that a free press was also important for governments. Without it governments could not learn the true state of public opinion and so risked ruling against the wishes of the people. By forbidding discussion governments simply discredited themselves, because their subjects believed that the prohibition stemmed from fear, and they sacrificed efficiency and reputation when they failed to check subordinate officials whose wrongdoing could have been exposed through the press.

Liberals insisted that impartial censorship was an impossibility, if only because the members of modern society did not share a set of common values. The censor did not represent right as against wrong or truth as against error, but merely his own or his government's opinion. Thus by its very nature censorship had to be arbitrary. To the argument that only censorship prevented the dissemination of lies, slander, and immorality, liberals replied that the solution lay in giving the newspaper press more rather than less freedom, so that responsible writers could refute unworthy colleagues. The press would provide its own best corrective; '. . . the true and indispensable political court of censorship today consists solely in complete legal publicity and in complete legal freedom for the public opinion of the Fatherland. . . .'

In their advice to their governments the liberals managed a rather fine balance between reassurance and threat. On the one hand they benignly assured the rulers that revolution would not result from the grant of press freedom since German subjects were peaceable and devoted to their princes; the grant of press freedom would only confirm their devotion. On the other hand there were more ominous references to the wisdom of forestalling revolution by timely concession. The people, it was said, revolted when they were forced to stifle their criticism, not when they were free to express it.

Governments were urged to submit to the inevitable. 'What is ripe in the life of the people happens, however much a shortsighted policy may strive against it.' Freedom of the press, said Adam von Itzstein in the Baden assembly, had become a magic word to the people, and it would avail misguided princes nothing to try to withhold it. 'A spring, gentlemen, can be stopped up, but it breaks out again on all sides with more destructive force.' The liberals rightly sensed that governments were on the defensive. Rotteck pointed out that the governments conceded the virtues of a free press in the preambles of the very laws issued to restrain it. The political climate had changed: 'No king, no prince of the present day would permit himself the observation, I am the state.'

On pragmatic grounds opponents argued that censorship was ineffective, or did more harm than good. The foreign press was not and probably could not be kept out of Germany, so Germans could read all that could not be printed at home, and worse. Moreover people believed nothing they read in the censored press, particularly praise of the government, so governments got no credit even when deserved. In reaction to the official press readers sought out another kind of newspaper, exciting and vulgar; German speakers sometimes distinguished between the *schlechte* press and the ordinary press, somewhat as Englishmen of the time talked of the 'respectable' and the 'unstamped' press. Liberals pointed out that German writers frequently had only the choice between displaying servility in the government press and catering to vulgarity in the sensationalist press, so that self-respecting men often avoided journalism altogether. Karl Welcker, denouncing the irresponsible journalists, commented that this was the 'essential misfortune of censorship, that only that kind of people make themselves heard in the newspaper, while a really honorable man seldom undertakes the important business of speaking to his people'. By leaving the newspaper field to the worst representatives of journalism the evils that censorship was designed to reduce were actually increased; governments 'thus encouraged the darkness in which they [revolt, tumult, conspiracy] ripen to destructive outbreak'.

Meanwhile governments, knowing what reserves of irresponsibility and even criminality had accumulated in certain circles, became increasingly committed to censorship because they dreaded the excesses that might follow its suspension.

Censorship was also intimately connected with the question of German unity. Speakers usually placed the main blame for harsh press regulations on the German Confederation rather than the state governments. It was felt that the Confederation had taken the lead in repression, and that individual state governments had either had reluctantly to comply, or had been able to defend their repressive policies by pleading the necessity of submission to the Confederation. Accordingly much of the criticism of censorship regulations attempted to prove that the Confederation had exceeded its legal competence. This line of attack led straight to the central problem of German unification, and many speakers who argued for a free press did so on the grounds that only a free expression of opinion could bring about the moral and intellectual unity of the German people. Nationalist sentiment expressed itself also in resentment over the humiliating contrast between the treatment of the press in Germany and elsewhere: 'The Germans feel the shame of being the only one among the educated peoples of Europe who lacks freedom of the press.'

Was the typical journalist the committed fighter for freedom pictured by liberals and feared by governments? In actuality many journalists wrote indifferently for whatever side paid best. Many, however, were principled liberals, and certainly the journalist himself stood to gain from a freer, more open society. He came as a rule from a relatively poor family and had probably made sacrifices to attend a university. He had prepared himself for one of the professions or for state service, and sometimes had practised his profession or worked for a government before turning to journalism. In many cases he would have found his progress blocked because of his poverty, or because the good positions were monopolized by the wealthy, or because he resented the reactionary governments and in turn was distrusted by them; the state, fearful of liberalism in the universities, at times expelled the students it suspected, and such expelled students were natural recruits for opposition journalism. For this kind of frustrated intellectual journalism offered a career of sorts, probably in many cases intended to be only temporary. At best it was not a career that brought great rewards in German society. Given the restricted sale of newspapers and the conditions of publishing, the journalist could not earn very much money and his social status was low. Learning in itself did not provide direct entry into higher social circles; the German nobility had never cultivated artists and men of learning as had the French. There is then nothing surprising in finding that the image of the journalist was so often associated with liberalism.

Insofar as the journalist played a political role it had to be, in Germany's political conditions, that of a teacher rather than a political leader. The point becomes clear through comparison with France. Börne in 1830 noted that Thiers, who had come to Paris as an unknown and who was barely thirty years old, had just been appointed Under Secretary of Finance, and he commented, 'It is just as if Heine or Menzel or I had become a minister. And what are we?' In the absence of representative institutions and free party life the German journalist had nothing like the political power of the French. Nevertheless he could play a political role, that of liberal theorist and prophet of the middle class.

The respect in which the German journalist most resembled his French counterpart was in the imprecise definition of his occupation. Journalism seems to have been a refuge more often than a choice. Towards the end of the century the liberal Karl Biedermann wrote of this earlier period:

> The proverbial description of the writer for the daily press as a 'man who had failed' was far truer then than today. Preparation for the profession of journalism by deliberately adopting an appropriate plan of study ... which is increasingly the rule today, was very rare at that time. A certain widespread desire 'to have one's say' seemed sufficient to enter upon the career of publicist.

Writers of the press frequently moved from journalism to another occupation and back again, or attempted to combine journalism with creative writing or scholarship. The representative figure of the eighteenth-century newspaper had been the reporter who passes along facts without comment, and the typical figure of the second half of the nineteenth century was to be the powerful editor of the great daily. The journalist of our period was typically the *Schriftsteller*, the man of letters, at once artist, professor, and political thinker.

England

English journalism in this period came close to attaining full development as a profession. By mid-century it was a socially respectable, full-time occupation, distinct from other occupations, and with its own code of professional ethics. This development came with the growth of what was commonly designated the 'respectable' press, the great daily newspapers typified by *The Times*. The 'respectable' press was itself a product of English industrialization. The new middle class formed a wide literate public that wanted both political and economic news, so that for the first time it became possible for a daily newspaper to attract enough readers and enough advertisers to be self-supporting, without reliance on either political subsidies or unworthy methods of journalism.

The commercialization made it possible for the journalistic profession to mature. The wealth of the press was the chief factor. The great papers, led by *The Times*, began to pay high salaries so that better men were attracted to the field, and the reporter could live on a social level not too out of line with that of the established professions. The wealth of the press also made possible improvement in professional ethics; when the financial rewards of honest reporting were so high, blackmailing individuals and selling one's convictions to politicians seemed unnecessary. The idea became established that the primary function of a newspaper was to report the news accurately and not to slant it for political purposes; *The Times* from 1803 on refused political subsidies. In addition, writing for the press became increasingly a full-time occupation rather than accessory to another or a step on the way to something better. The journalist could now be more readily distinguished from the printer, the law student, and the professional man of letters. It took some time, certainly, before reputable men were willing to associate themselves openly with journalism. Even the first great editor of *The Times*, Thomas Barnes, a university graduate and one of more than average culture, met with considerable social discrimination, and a man like Thackeray for years thought it necessary to use a pseudonym for his writings in the press. Similar cases could be multiplied. By mid-century, however, journalism had in general attained a measure of respectability.

It was important that the development of industry in England made it easier than elsewhere to separate journalism from politics. A commercialized press made it possible and profitable for the journalist to devote himself permanently to his job without being tempted to use it as a means to political office. Moreover the general abundance of career opportunities in business and the professions diverted men from preoccupation with political office, and thus militated against repetition of the French pattern of revolutionary politics. The contrast was remarked by the French historian Élie Halévy who, writing of England after the passage of the 1832 Reform Bill, observed that there was nothing 'of that fury with which in France the classes new to power stormed the citadel of government and when once installed in power disputed among themselves the precarious tenure of office'.

The character of English politics, moreover, precluded the journalists' assumption of a political role comparable to that of the German or French writer. The English journalist, operating within long-established institutions of representative government, could certainly not be a type of political prophet, as the German journalist tended to be. The French model was also unlikely because of the greater stability of English political life, which rested on consensus as to what constituted legitimate government, and on agreement as to the way in which power was to be transferred from ministers who had lost public confidence to an alternative group of leaders. In the absence of a fully developed party structure the system was imperfect, but it worked well enough so that the French kind of revolutionary politics, in which the press took so large a part, could be avoided.

There was, however, a newspaper press in England that must be recognized as essentially political. This was the 'unstamped' press, quite distinct from the 'respectable' press, and with an even larger circulation. Written by and for the lower classes, it expressed the discontent of a large, wretched laboring class suffering the full impact of rapid industrialization; this press was described by a knowledgeable French observer as 'nothing more than a weapon of war'. It did not have the same function as the political press in France, since there political conflict was largely confined to one class, nor was it equivalent to the kind of thing seen in eighteenth-century England when elements of the governing class intermittently used the press to win support from the lower orders. Rather the radical press spoke for the emerging proletariat, the laborers who were becoming conscious of themselves as a group with common economic interests and were attempting to organize as a class. The press assumed particular importance for the working class, since there were heavy restrictions on labor's right to organize, violence was self-defeating, and periodical publications offered practically the only means of protest and organization. Hence freedom of the press became one of labor's chief demands. Faced by oppressive libel laws and taxes designed to keep up the price of newspapers, the lower class defined freedom of the press quite differently from writers for the 'respectable' press. For men like Barnes it meant chiefly economic independence and freedom from political subsidy. For the workers, freedom of the press came to mean immunity from prosecution for criticizing the government, and freedom from taxes that made newspapers too expensive for the laborer to buy.

In the circumstances it was natural that leadership of the working class fell very largely to the journalists. Frequently they combined a number of callings; a man like William Cobbett, for example, was not permitted to be only a journalist, but was forced by events to be a political leader and organizer as well. Comparison can perhaps be made with German journalists of the same period, but the Germans were not revolutionaries; they wanted to liberalize society and government so that they might benefit from the resulting freedom to advance themselves in the world. English journalists of the working-class press stemmed mainly from the class of artisans and skilled laborers, and they were in the main a group seriously committed to the cause of the workers and involved in the struggle in the most direct way.

The radical press owed its existence to the conditions of early industrialization; eventually it declined as industry developed, and many of the evils prevalent in the first part of the century proved to be transient rather than permanent features of the capitalist system. Earlier workers had responded with incomprehension, violence, and bitter attacks on the social order in their press. To the governing class the working-class journalists had seemed the most desperate revolutionaries; as German governments thought any questioning of their political monopoly a threat to civilization itself, so the wealthy in England tended to regard criticism of their traditional social privileges as no less than criminal subversion of religion and morality. As the century progressed the laborers adjusted to the new conditions and began to develop peaceful means to win reforms, and this change was reflected in their press. Accordingly the governing class, reassured as well by having held the line at moderate suffrage reform in 1832, grew less alarmed at working-class agitation. After 1832 there was a growing conviction, particularly among the Radicals, that the working class needed to be educated politically, and the stamp tax came to be opposed as a 'tax on knowledge'. Working-class and Radical agitation led to a reduction in the stamp tax, and the 'unstamped' press proved to have been only a temporary feature of working-class politics.

The profession of journalist by mid-century, then, was in general characterized by respectability. What it lacked was prestige. One reason for this was that in the process of freeing themselves from direct reliance on political subsidy the great dailies had become dependent upon the public; it was obvious that, with sales and advertising crucial, no newspaper could long sustain a position that led to loss of readers. This aspect of the press led to serious criticism by the Radicals, they saw that newspapers were too commercialized to fulfil the function of educating the mass of the people.

Against this background judgments like that of John Stuart Mill become understandable:

You know in how low a state the newspaper press of this country is. In France the best thinkers and writers of the nation, write in the journals and direct public opinion; but our daily and weekly writers are the lowest hacks of literature, which when it is a trade, is the vilest and most degrading of all trades, because more of affectation and hypocrisy, and more subservience to the baser feelings of others, are necessary for carrying it on, than for any other trade, from that of a brothelkeeper upwards. . . .

In France the newspapers, for all their venality, long remained the forum for a political discussion pitched at a comparatively high level, often written by men of intellectual distinction who knew themselves to be addressing a small, educated public. Thus the French journalist retained a kind of eminence and importance denied his English counterpart. The price of this eminence was incomplete professionalization; the French journalist was politician and artist as well as a writer for the daily press. In England journalists in the main continued to have only an indirect relationship to government. The support of *The Times* was important for any ministry, as Barnes had good cause to know from the attentions paid him by major political figures. *The Times* nonetheless was a commercial paper dependent on sales and consequently very limited in the extent to which it could hope to form rather than reflect opinion; there seems no reason to doubt Barnes' sincerity when he wrote of *The Times'* opposition to the Poor Law of 1834: 'Having never myself been impressed with the idea of that enormous power of the Times to which you refer I never for a moment supposed that we could prevent a measure from being carried which Parliament had thru a thousand channels been prepared to support.' While safe seats in Parliament were sometimes given to deserving newspaper supporters, the press never became a stepping-off place for a political career to the same extent as in France. Barnes himself never entered politics in a formal way, and he strongly disapproved of journalists who did.

This limitation of political activity and influence on the part of English journalists, partly self-assumed and partly imposed by society, had as its effect the isolation of newspaper men from the social circles where important political decisions were made. Edward Bulwer Lytton wrote that the journalists were 'a peculiar and separate body . . .'

> They live more separated from sympathy with aristocratic influences than any other class: belonging, chiefly, to the middle order, they do not, like the middle order in general, have any dependence on the custom and favour of the great; literary men, they are not, like authors in general, courted as lions, who, mixing familiarly with their superiors, are either softened by unmeaning courtesies, or imbibe the veneration which rank and wealth personally approached, instil into the human mind, as circumstances at present form it.

The great and esteemed profession of England was the law, and there can be little doubt that the prestige of the man of law came largely from his traditionally close link with politics. Some of the social prestige that seems always to come with the exercise of political power attached to the English lawyers, as, in quite different ways to be sure, it did to the French journalists of our period. This consideration, suggestive of the intricate connections among politics, economics, and professional growth, helps to explain why, at the very time that in France men like Girardin were trying to modify the political character of the French press by creating commercial newspapers based on sales and advertising, in England critics like Mill were judging the emergence of the commercialized press and the professional journalist as loss rather than gain.

2 THE 'PREINDUSTRIAL' WORKER MOVEMENT: THE *CANUTS* OF LYON

Robert J. Bezucha

Source: R.J. Bezucha (ed.), *Modern European Social History* (Lexington, Mass., D.C. Heath, 1972), pp.93-123.

The working class was born in the workshop, not the factory. It is one of the cherished dogmas of social history that artisans, their status and jobs threatened by economic change, fathered the labor movement. Outside of the capital cities such as Paris and Berlin, there was no more important European incubator than Lyon. Twice within three years, in November 1831 and April 1834, the second city of France was the scene of bloody insurrection. These uprisings of the Lyon silk workers, or *canuts* as they were called, presented the rulers of Metternich's Europe with a frightening spectacle. The young Karl Marx believed that the *canuts*, with their motto 'Live Working or Die Fighting', had launched the inevitable class warfare.

Riot and revolt hold a constant fascination for students of modern European history, but until recently much of the work on these subjects has been methodologically crude, so that simple, value-laden terms such as 'the mob' and 'the people' have passed as descriptions of complex phenomena. All this is now changing. Some of the most significant contributions to social history have dealt with the study of crowds and the role of collective violence. As historians have learned new ways to do their work, they have also come to recognize that violence registers only that moment when a volatile social compound has reached the flash point. But what elements made up this formula? What sorts of antagonisms heated it to explosion? The answers to questions such as these seem critical for understanding the context of violence, whether in Lyon or elsewhere.

The present essay is meant to serve a triple purpose. First, to trace the operation of the Lyon silk-weaving industry about the year 1830 and to indicate the economic and social antagonisms that developed as it changed in the half-century after 1789; from this will emerge a definition of the term *'preindustrial' worker movement*. Second, to describe the *canuts'* attempt to organize their community and break the economic power of the silk merchants. Third, to explain the uprisings of 1831 and 1834 within the particular Lyonnaise context of violence. We shall discover along the way that the *canuts* were a unique community of workingmen, whose organization and ideology were remarkable for their time. Nevertheless, this

37

essay should not be consigned to that unjustly denigrated corner of the profession called local history. Social historians must go 'inside' a number of worker communities and examine how their members perceived themselves, their work, and their future in order to understand better exactly how and why artisans fathered the labor movement.

I

As Detroit is linked with the automobile industry in the minds of modern Americans, so nineteenth-century Europeans associated Lyon with the production of silk cloth. More than a quarter of her nearly two hundred thousand residents were employed by the *Fabrique*, the traditional name for the local silk industry. In 1830, there were approximately twenty-five thousand looms in Lyon, and silk and silk-related products accounted for almost half of the city's total commercial income and a third of the value of all French exports. Lyon, in other words, was one of the largest and most important manufacturing centers in the world.

Textiles were in the vanguard of the Industrial Revolution. The production of silk cloth, however, was an exception. In 1830, the structure of the Lyonnaise *Fabrique* appeared on the surface to be essentially the same as in 1730. Although manufacturing was concentrated in an urban environment, there were no large-scale factories. The hand production was divided between three basic groups: the merchants (popularly but inaccurately called *fabricants*), who purchased raw silk, let it out for weaving on contract, and marketed the finished cloth; the master weavers (*chefs d'atelier*), who owned the looms and wove the cloth in their workshop in return for payment from the merchants; and the journeymen (*compagnons* or *ouvriers en soie*), who labored at the looms under the masters' supervision and received half of the contracted payment for the cloth. This archaic system seems simple and static in description, but in reality it was highly complex and fluid. The social and economic antagonisms produced by precisely these complexities, moreover, generated the worker movement in Lyon. Let us move 'inside' the *Fabrique* as it was around 1830, and follow the three basic groups through the manufacturing process. Our purpose will be three-fold: to learn how the industry was changing over time, to see how each group perceived its own role and those of the others, and to understand how they defined the problems of the industry and their possible solution.

The silk merchants were commercial capitalists seeking to market goods of high quality at the lowest possible cost. Most of them, however, were not French counterparts of the infamous Mr Bounderby in Dickens' novel *Hard Times*, grinding out large profits by the ruin of the weavers. Silk, unlike cotton cloth, was a luxury product constantly at the mercy of the sensitive mechanisms of world trade. One report on economic prospects issued by the local chamber of commerce noted the cholera epidemic in Paris, revolutions in Latin America, the banking crisis in the United States, tariff debate in England, and the growth of Swiss and German competition, as all directly affecting Lyon. The vicissitudes of the market caused rapid fluctuations in the state of the local economy. Between 1824 and 1826, for example, the amount of raw silk purchased and registered for weaving fell by 25 per cent. The result was recurrent financial crisis for many merchants and unemployment or lower rates for the weavers. 'The *canuts*', wrote one observer, 'pass rapidly from excess of misery to prosperity and back again to distress.' The merchants were puzzled that the worker movement began to develop at a time when the *Fabrique* was emerging from half a decade of stagnation. From their point of view a relative abundance of contracts should have spelled general satisfaction.

Market fluctuations alone do not explain the precarious position of the average silk merchant. Equally important was the fact that there were too many firms. During the late Empire and the Restoration (roughly 1810-1830), the annual value of cloth production doubled while the number of *fabricants* grew tenfold. While the major firms were able to withstand a temporary crisis, around them were clustered literally hundreds of small houses with little capital margin. The result, in the words of a spokesman, was 'a continual war of merchant against merchant'. Such intense local competition made the average *fabricant* understandably hostile to demands for higher weaving rates. While publicly he would reject them out of a statesman-like concern for liberal principle and the health of the national economy, privately he might be attempting to prevent his business from going under.

In the merchants' minds, the future of their industry depended on maintaining high quality in the ornate, brocaded cloth called *façonnes,* and developing cheaper production methods for the plain cloth called *unies*. All of their innovative efforts pointed toward the achievement of these two goals. Firms that specialized in the sale of *façonnes* had their own designers who patented their intricate and beautiful creations. The municipal government supported an art school where local children were trained for employment by the merchants; a student with exceptional ability might even be offered a partnership in a firm. Despite the fact that the mounting and weaving of *façonnes* required the work of a skilled artisan operating a special loom, the merchants considered these functions to be of secondary importance. As their newspaper stated, 'The merchants compose the intellectual portion of the industry. The difference between a merchant and a master weaver is that between an architect and a construction worker.'

Such a condescending attitude toward the work of all weavers severely poisoned relations between masters and merchants.

The market price of *façonnes* was also an important consideration in the merchants' minds. For this reason they applauded the introduction of the semi-mechanical Jacquard loom (named after the local master who invented it in 1804), which cut weaving time and production cost. Later in this essay we will examine how these iron frames altered the social structure and geography of the worker community. It is sufficient to say here that by 1830, only a quarter of the looms in the *Fabrique* were Jacquard models, and their owners constituted an élite group.

The vast majority of the *canuts* continued to work the simple, wooden *unies* looms. Their livelihood was threatened by the fact that cheap foreign cloth used for handkerchiefs, hats, and simple clothing, was cutting deeply into what had previously been a secure Lyonnaise market. The merchants believed that the local *unies* houses could only survive by radically reducing production costs. Not only were all resolved to resist paying higher weaving rates even in the best of times, but many were also convinced that *unies* production no longer had a future within the existing structure of the *Fabrique*. A sensible solution from their point of view was to seek cheaper hand labor outside the city. Between 1825 and 1840, the period of the making of the worker movement, the percentage of rural looms out of the total number employed by the merchants rose from 21 to 52 per cent. The worker uprisings of 1831 and 1834 accelerated, but did not initiate this outward migration. With cottage industry growing at their expense the *canuts* in Lyon itself did not appreciate the irony of the fact that their fate at the hands of 'economic progress' was the opposite of most nineteenth-century handloom weavers.

The factory system had only begun to be anticipated in the Lyonnaise *Fabrique*. Mechanization (for winding thread) and large workshops (for printing designs on plain cloth) had been introduced, but in 1830 there was little weaving done outside the masters' shops. An important exception was the so-called *Grand Atelier* (literally, *large workshop*) established in a chateau on the edge of the city, where perhaps as many as five hundred men and women lived in model dormitories, ate meals in a common restaurant, and operated the owner's looms in shifts under the supervision of foremen. When this innovative, paternalistic experiment failed, the employees mourned their loss, but the master weavers were encouraged that theirs was a critical function, and the merchants concluded that the owner had been too 'liberal' with the *canuts*. Nonetheless, many *fabricants* were convinced that factories and machines were the wave of the future.

The silk merchants believed themselves to be the central figures of the

Fabrique. Commercial considerations dictated their decisions, whether to pay minimum weaving rates, to disperse, or eventually to mechanize the looms. From their point of view the existing structure of the *Fabrique* was archaic and the destruction of the traditional workshop form of production was to be desired because the master weavers had become little more than 'parasites' and 'useless intermediaries' between themselves and the journeymen. The *canuts*, on the other hand, saw matters another way.

'The *canuserie*, or class of weavers, is divided and subdivided like society', wrote the master weaver, Pierre Charnier. 'It has its rich and its poor, its aristocrats and its humble subjects.' While the fundamental distinction among those who worked the looms was between journeymen and master weavers, significant differences existed within the latter group itself. Among Lyon's eight thousand *chefs d'atelier*, the 'aristocrats' were the handful of masters who owned several looms. Acting as virtual subcontractors for the merchants, in theory nothing prevented them from amassing enough capital to become *fabricants* themselves. Although such a step was far more difficult than it had been during the boom years of the late Empire and Restoration, the merchants continued to employ the prospect of social mobility as a scourge with which to chastise the *canuts* for their 'idleness'.

The middle rank of master weavers was composed of those (less than one in eight) who owned four or more looms. Eligible for election as representatives on the board of labor conciliation (the *Conseil des Prud'hommes*), these men were the 'active citizens' of the worker community.[1] The average *chef d'atelier*, on the other hand, owned one to three looms, which he operated in his home workshop with his family and perhaps one or two journeymen. Socially proud and fiercely defensive of the fact that he was not an *ouvrier*, a simple worker, his absolute dependence on the merchants' rates brought the 'humble subject' close to the economic position of a piece-work laborer. The ambiguous role of the master weaver – the threatened loss of his independent economic and social status – was to be a critical element in the formation of the worker movement in Lyon.

An important theme weaves itself persistently through contemporary descriptions of the Lyon silk industry around 1830: the 'typical' *canut*, a colorful, docile, and diligent sort of local character, had disappeared. In his place was to be found a belligerent idler, spouting political slogans (supplied him by the meddlesome Republicans, since the 'typical' *canut* presumably never had a thought in his head), and declaring himself at war with the merchants. Local writers enjoyed slumming in the worker neighborhoods in search of some toothless old wreck whom they could proudly unveil to their readers as (the quote here is remarkable) 'the last of the Mohicans'. Since worker strikes and riots had actually been a part of Lyonnaise life for more than a century, in one sense these observers were seeking to paint over the harsh present with a mythical golden past. In another sense, however, they were correct. At the same time that the mode of production remained constant, the nature of the worker community had significantly changed. The *canut* of 1830 was different from the one of 1789.

This transformation was produced by two interwoven sets of pressures: legal and institutional on the one hand, technological and demographic on the other.

The Revolution swept away the traditional corporate structure of the silk industry that had been called the *Grande Fabrique*. A series of new laws and institutions gave the silk merchants greater power, and the master weavers less, than they had enjoyed under the Old Regime. The chamber of commerce (1802), the *Condition Publique* (1804), and the commercial court (1791) were all special institutions through which the merchants regulated the quality of the cloth and promoted trade. The *Conseil des Prud'hommes* (1804) was theoretically a restoration of the traditional board of labor conciliation; whereas merchants and masters had formerly been equally represented, the new statutes awarded a permanent majority to the merchants. Such inherent inequality reflected the general character of post-Revolutionary French law with regard to the workingman.

The labor legislation of the Revolution and the Empire, written according to the principles of individual and economic 'liberty', remained intact until 1848. The law of 14-17 June 1791, better known as the *loi le Chapelier*, denied all citizens the right to strike or associate in any manner in order to advance 'their pretended common interests'. That the interpretation of this law blatantly followed class lines may be seen in the fact that while workingmens' associations were forbidden as obstacles to a free economy, employer organizations such as chambers of commerce were permitted. Napoleonic legislation also made a series of specific distinctions between the rights of workers and employers. The Penal Code (1810) forbade all 'coalitions' to raise or lower wages; penalties for workers, however, were more severe than for employers. The Civil Code (1803) permitted courts to accept an employer's word in a wage dispute, while a worker was obliged to produce some evidence to support his claim. Articles 291 through 294 of the Penal Code prohibited all unauthorized associations of more than twenty members for 'religious, literary, political, or any other purpose'. Armed with these measures, the authorities were able to prevent the legal formation of effective worker associations. Finally, each worker was obliged to carry with him an identification booklet called a *livret*, in which his employer noted the terms of his service, his conduct, and his debts. In France as a whole, these laws were commonly used by master tailors, cobblers, and other artisans to regulate the activities of their journeymen. The unique structure of the Lyonnaise *Fabrique*, however, meant that they applied to the master weavers as well as journeymen. Each *chef d'atelier*, for example, had a special book called a *livret d'acquit*, in which the terms of his weaving contracts were recorded. If upon reading it a merchant determined that a man was rebellious or a poor risk he would simply refuse to give him work. Such were the Lyonnaise merchants' weapons for social control.

The cumulative effect of this legislation was to deprive the *canuts* of the protection, frequently exaggerated in their minds, that they had enjoyed under the Old Régime, and to send them legally defenseless into the world of *laissez-faire*. In 1830, their community and their nation were still in the midst of a conflict-ridden transition from traditional to modern society. Little wonder that the preindustrial worker movement was Janus-like: looking backward toward the supposed 'moral order' of the world that had been lost; searching at the same time for the collective means of survival in the new competitive age.

The fundamental demographic alteration of the Lyonnaise worker community between 1789 and 1830 was produced by the interaction of technological innovation (principally the Jacquard loom) and the legal, social, and economic effects of the Revolution. In order to state matters as simply as possible, let us begin by describing the physical transformation itself, and then briefly discuss its causes.

As Lyon and the silk industry grew in the half-century following the Revolution, a strong centrifugal force was in operation in the worker community. In 1789, the majority of the looms were concentrated in the five old quarters spread along the right bank of the Saône river (marked *A* on the map and today called *Vieux Lyon*). Workshops were also scattered throughout the city so that the weaver, the merchant, and even the aristocrat often lived side by side. There were virtually no looms in the immediate suburbs (*faubourgs*) or rural areas outside Lyon. If we discount for the present discussion the development of peasant weaving and cottage industry we described earlier, by 1830 Lyon had approximately twice as many looms as in 1789, but the majority were to be found either in the suburbs or in new areas within the city itself. Nearly a quarter of them were still housed in *Vieux Lyon*, but these were overwhelmingly the old, outmoded *unies* frames; out of 1,956 looms in the Gourgillon quarter, for example, only 39 were Jacquard models. Furthermore, the *canuts* were no longer familiar faces in the bourgeois neighborhoods. As late as 1825, for example, 128 looms remained in the wealthy Orléans quarter; by 1834, there were only two, and these were likely operated by widows. As the workshops moved out from the urban center, Lyon was becoming socially and economically

Map 2.1: Lyon, 1834

LYON, 1834
A. Vieux Lyon
B. Les Brotteaux and La Guillotière
C. The Croix Rousse Hillside
D. The Croix Rousse Commune

Vaize

FAUBOURG DE VAISE

COMMUNE DE LA CROIX ROUSSE

CHAMP VERT

Cimetière de Loyasse

St.
Irenée

A

C

D

Jardin des
Plantes

Place de
Louis XVIII

Place
de
Louis
le Grand

Place
Louis
XVI

LES BROTTEAUX

B

LA GUILLOTIÈRE

0   200   400   600
Meters

polarized. Perhaps the most obvious and fundamental way in which the 'typical' *canut* of 1830 differed from his pre-Revolutionary counterpart was that he lived neither in *Vieux Lyon* nor as the neighbor of the silk merchant.

Four factors seem to have caused this demographic transformation. The first was the manner in which the Revolution stimulated urban growth and opened new land for development. In 1789, for example, the broad plain (marked *B* on the map) that lay directly across the Rhône river from the center of Lyon was governed from the city of Grenoble, 60 miles away. The Revolutionary reorganization of local and national administration brought this area into the new Rhône department, with Lyon at its center, and thereby stimulated the growth of the suburbs of Les Brotteaux and La Guillotière. Similarly, the confiscation and public sale of church property enabled private real estate speculators to construct entire neighborhoods with buildings specifically designed to accommodate silk workshops. In 1789, the land on the slopes of the steep Croix Rousse hill (marked *C* on the map) was the property of religious orders. In 1834, for example, the 1,427 residents of the *rue Tolozan* operated 678 looms where the orchards of the Capuchin monastery had stood forty years earlier. Finally, the rapid expansion of the city up this hillside made the independent Croix Rousse commune at its peak virtually a contiguous part of Lyon (marked *D* on the map). On the eve of the Revolution, the total population of all of the city's suburbs had been around six thousand persons; in 1830, the Croix Rousse commune alone had 17,475 residents and 6,763 silk looms.

The second factor was an indirect response to the introduction of the Jacquard loom. Many of the buildings of *Vieux Lyon* had been constructed in the sixteenth and seventeenth centuries and were physically incapable of housing the new looms. Apartments in the new buildings outside the central city, on the other hand, were specifically designed to have tall ceilings and reinforced floors. The result was a steady migration of the best-equipped *façonnes* workshops into those neighborhoods that had been opened since 1789. In 1829 (a year for which we have complete fiscal census information), over 40 per cent of the 5,035 looms on the Croix Rousse hillside were Jacquard models as compared with less than 10 per cent of the 5,847 looms in *Vieux Lyon*. Much of the industry's muscle remained in the old quarters, but its heart had been transplanted.

The cost of living was the third factor that explains the centrifugal pressure felt by the *canuts*. The central quarters of Lyon were undoubtedly the most expensive place for a workingman to live in all of France. Contemporary observers agreed that Lyonnaise rents were high, particularly when compared with the situation of silk weavers elsewhere (double those in Avignon, for example), and fuel and food far too expensive. The principal reason for high prices was the *octroi*, the municipal tax on all goods that entered the city. The *octroi* was so strictly collected that workers returning to Lyon after a Sunday afternoon in the country had their market baskets inspected at the toll barriers. While only a successful *chef d'atelier* could afford to install a Jacquard loom in a new building on the Croix Rousse hillside, even a poor *unies* master was able to move to the suburbs, where he not only escaped the *octroi* but also was able to cultivate a green garden for his family. Only the poorest of the *canuts* remained trapped in the old city. As the Prefect of the Rhône reported in 1833: 'The suburbs are in the midst of prosperity; the town suffers. People are leaving the sober, humid, stuffy town and seeking breathing space.'

The fourth and final factor resulted from the abolition of professional requirements, which disappeared along with the Old Régime. The *chef d'atelier* of 1830 was no longer a person who had been admitted to the select circle of the masters' guild after years of apprenticeship and training. In the age of *laissez-faire*, anyone who could afford to purchase or rent a loom might call himself a 'master' weaver. To the horror of many older *chefs d'atelier*, the idea of apprenticeship itself was fast dying out. In its place came the era of the journeymen weavers, who arrived in Lyon by the thousands when the *Fabrique* flourished and abandoned the city when it languished. Often untrained and with few roots in the community, the journeymen were called 'the floating population' by the local authorities. Most of them came from the rural regions of France, but a considerable number came from abroad; according to statistics compiled by the Prefect in 1833, among the 3,297 journeymen living in the Croix Rousse commune only 547 had been born there, and 1,100 were foreigners. The *canuts* themselves, or at least their leaders, sensed the fact that their community had become less stable and more fluid than it had been in 1789. One key to understanding the significance of Lyon during this traditional, preindustrial period of European history lies in the fact that much of the initial energy of the worker movement was internally directed, aimed at the self-regulation of masters and journeymen and defining the relations between the two groups. In this physically and socially transformed atmosphere, the complex result of a nexus of revolutionary, technological, and demographic change, the master weaver of 1830 plied his trade.

Conflict was a by-product of the daily operation of the *Fabrique*. The master weavers were constantly made aware of the legal and customary control the merchants held over their lives. Here is a dramatized conversation that appeared in the worker newspaper, *L'Echo de la Fabrique*. A poor *unies* master has just delivered a rush order to a merchant, who is sitting behind the iron grill (the cage, as the *canuts* called it) of his warehouse:

Chef d'atelier. Here is the piece I've brought you.

Fabricant. Well, it's about time. It was due at eight o'clock this morning and it's already noon. Because of you I won't be able to send the order out today.

Chef. Please excuse me, Monsieur, but my wife and I have worked on nothing else for the last twelve days. We haven't even left the loom to eat. We had many problems because the thread was so poor and the weave so fine. And my wife, who is pregnant, intended to weave all night, but she fell asleep at the loom. That is why I am late.

Fabricant. That's all well and good. Nevertheless you've caused my order to be late. [Looks over the cloth.] Here's a stain. What did you do, eat your stew over the loom?

Chef. Oh, Monsieur! If it's there it's because we were so pressed for time. My wife didn't even have time to make soup. We haven't eaten anything but bread while we worked on your order.

Fabricant. Ah, here's a thread out of line. [To his clerk] Monsieur Léon, mark this man down ten centimes per *aune* for waste.

Chef. But Monsieur, have you no conscience? After we worked all night with such poor thread there are bound to be mistakes. It isn't fair to mark us down for that.

Fabricant. Fair or not, that's the way it's going to be. When I pay good money I expect good work. And if you're as poorly paid as you claim, let me remind you that you didn't have to take the job. You could have refused it.

Chef. But you know very well that I haven't worked for three months and that I took it because my savings are gone. I couldn't refuse it because my wife is pregnant.

Fabricant. That is not my affair. I'm in business to make money, not to give you charity. What you are saying means little to me.

Chef. Will you give me another order?

Fabricant. Give you another order? After the way you made me late on a commission! You dare ask for another order. No, my dear man. We only give orders to those who appreciate what we give them. Here is your payment.

Chef. Dog of a merchant! If good times come you'll hear from me again.

Fabricant. [To his clerks] Messieurs, you will be heads of commerce some day. I cannot recommend more highly such severity with the workers. . . . It is the only way to force them to weave well. It is the only way that our industry can prosper.

Such a confrontation was not pure fiction. We know, for example, that the harsh treatment given Pierre Charnier by a clerk of the Bouila silk firm in 1827 led directly to the founding of the masters' secret Society of Mutual Duty.

Secure inside 'the cage', the merchant was on guard against all of the familiar abuses and petty crimes of domestic manufacture, sloppy work, the theft of thread (in Lyon called *picquage d'once*), the artificial weighting or stretching of the cloth. From the *canuts*' point of view, however, the abuses the *fabricants* themselves built into the system were far more serious. Among the more vexing were the refusal either to permit the master to write the weight of the thread he received and the terms of the specific contract in the merchant's books or to weigh the finished cloth in his presence, although both were required by law, the failure to return bobbins that were the property of the master, and the rejection of the request for higher rates for rush orders necessitating nighttime weaving — work which cost the *canuts* extra oil for their lamps and coal for their stoves, as well as their sleep. Furthermore, because the warehouses dispensed orders and received cloth only within fixed hours, masters who chose to dispute a merchant's decision risked angering their fellow weavers standing impatiently in line behind them.

Owners of Jacquard looms had a special set of grievances against the merchants. By custom, the *chef d'atelier*, not the *fabricant*, bore the cost of mounting *façonnes* patterns on the loom. This was an operation that not only could idle the loom for a week or more, but also required a considerable investment; in the case of an important order, an outlay of 100 francs in materials and special tools was not unknown; yet, should the merchant cancel the contract, the master was unprotected and simply lost his investment. Risks such as these reduced competition for the newest *façonnes* contracts. Not only did the merchants fine them severely for any damage to the cardboard forms (*cartons*) that transferred the pattern to the cloth, but the masters also knew that working with a new pattern increased the likelihood of unexpected mounting costs and problems. Little wonder that some with the skill and equipment to work *façonnes* wove *unies* instead because the latter promised them more working days at less financial risk. These long-forgotten grievances may strike the reader as less than burning issues. Nevertheless, they lay at the heart of the conflict between merchants and masters in Lyon.

The master weavers were not a naturally homogeneous class. The 'aristocrat' who owned several Jacquard looms was united, however, with the 'humble subject' who owned only two or three *unies* frames by the conviction that they performed the critical function in the manufacturing process. The growth of the worker movement after 1830 rested on their ability to convince the journeymen that it was the merchants and not themselves who were the real 'parasites' of the *Fabrique*.

The fluid world of the journeymen weavers is difficult to recapture in simple terms. The image of the true *compagnon*, a young bachelor who lived in the shop, worked for half of the rate for the finished cloth, and slept in the same room as the loom, simply does not work in the case of Lyon. In a large workshop housing four or five looms, one might find the master and his wife operating two looms, an apprentice being trained under a four-year contract, an experienced journeyman renting a loom from the master by the month, and an unskilled weaver signed on for the preparation of a single order. In this hypothetical example, the apprentice could have lived with the master and his family, the experienced journeyman with his wife in a rented attic room, and the unskilled weaver in a boarding-house with other new arrivals from his rural region or country. In the case of the latter, moreover, he was as likely to take a job for the next week on a construction project as to move to the shop of another master. The critical question concerning the complex 'floating population' is why the journeymen, despite the separation of social status and economic interest that potentially existed between the two groups, did not see masters as 'useless intermediaries', but instead recognized a sense of solidarity with them against the merchants.

The answer revolves around the negative and positive poles of a single problem. Seeking to explain the relative absence of industrial conflict among immigrant laborers in nineteenth-century Boston, Stephan Thernstrom has observed that unskilled workers who had the greatest grievances 'are precisely those who never stayed put very long in any one place'. So it was with the *canuts* of Lyon. While the journeymen weavers came and went, strangers to one another and often not speaking the same language, the masters remained to define and articulate the problems of the community. The *chefs d'atelier*, always concerned by the alleged 'licence' and 'insubordination' in their shops, were to use their secret society to enforce rules and regulations on the journeymen. Later in this essay we will learn that the journeymen initially modelled their own association after that of the masters. It is appropriate to note here, however, that as their society matured — as the journeymen gained a sense of institutional continuity — they began to formulate demands on the masters. The fact that all worker associations were abolished by the government in 1834 prevents us, however, from learning whether or not the solidarity between masters and journeymen would have survived.

A more positive explanation lies in the fact that the *canuts* not only experienced mutual hardships, but also shared social goals to a remarkable extent. If one were to regard the workshop roles in crude economic terms, the master would seem a petit bourgeois craftsman whose property, in the form of his looms, placed him in constant conflict with the journeyman, a sort of preproletarian, who had only his labor to sell. Yet, both men worked daily side by side and their income was determined by the weaving rates set by a third party, the merchant. Although the journeyman might complain about the irregularity of his work or even demand a portion greater than the traditional half of the established rate for the work he had done, he could not accuse the master of idleness at his expense. It is significant that Joseph Benoit, a journeyman elected to the Chamber of Deputies from Lyon after the revolution of 1848, should refer to the *chef d'atelier* as 'a worker [an *ouvrier*, a term which the masters themselves rejected as demeaning] and one of the most mistreated in our economic society', and describe the plight of the journeyman by saying that 'his life, like that of the master weaver, is a continual struggle, a constant fear for the future'. To the merchants' charge that the masters were 'parasites' who unjustly deprived the weavers of half of their earnings, the masters responded that the journeymen were satisfied with this traditional arrangement and that with hard work they could rise to become masters themselves. If the latter argument has the same air of unreality about it as the merchants' contention that any *chef d'atelier* might become a *fabricant*, the fact remains that the journeymen held no set of social goals or values other than those articulated for them by the master weavers. So far as generalization is possible concerning such a diverse group, the journeymen reflected the masters' perception of the problems of the industry. And that view, as stated by the *Echo de la Fabrique*, was that 'without contradiction, the most direct and scandalous [abuse] is *the immoral and arbitrary exploitation of the master weaver by the merchant*, . . . who by virtue of the laws which rule us . . . exploits the industry as he chooses'.

We have completed our trip 'inside' the Lyon silk industry around 1830 and followed the merchants, masters, and journeymen through the manufacturing process. Equipped with some sense of the economic and social antagonisms that were present within the *Fabrique*, we can come to grips with the term 'the "preindustrial" worker movement'. A careful reader may already have wondered why 'preindustrial' has been set apart by quotation marks, and 'worker movement' has generally been used instead of 'working class'. At the risk of belaboring the obvious, let us consider these questions in reverse order.

First, when applied to traditional or transitional (that is, nonmodern) society, Harold Perkin has noted that 'the concept of class is a bludgeon rather than a scalpel, and it crushes what it tries to dissect'. Considering the occupational triad of the *Fabrique*, it seems obvious that to apply the familiar sociological or economic definitions of *class* to the case of Lyon in 1830 would likely confuse more than clarify any explanation of why the city became synonymous with labor agitation. If one adopts the looser, working definition offered by E. P. Thompson, that

> class happens when some men, as the result of common experience (inherited or shared), feel and articulate the identity of interests as between themselves, as against other men whose interests are different from (and usually opposed to) theirs. The class experience is largely determined by the productive relations into which men are born — or enter involuntarily. Class consciousness is the way these experiences are handled in cultural terms: embodied in traditions, value systems, ideas and institutional forms. . . . [*The Making of the English Working Class*, Gollancz, 1963; Penguin edn, 1968, pp.9-10]

we see that the *canuts* did develop something akin to class consciousness, a clear sense of 'us' against 'them'. But to refer to their activities as those of a working class tends to obscure the fact that they were not a class, but members of a hierarchical community of artisans. The term 'worker movement' serves to remind us of this distinction.

Second, although it spills from their pens with regularity, historians have yet to agree on a definition for the term 'preindustrial' (hence the quotation marks). In part, this is a result of the fact that there is little consensus as to the meaning of 'industrialization' as a historical process rather than a sociological concept. The *canuts* did not operate power-driven looms in factories under the supervision of the merchants or the foremen, but it would be semantic torture (to use E. P. Thompson's phrase) not to call the massive, highly developed, and technically alert *Fabrique* an industry. And while the relations between the merchants and weavers were not those of a traditional artisan society, they cannot be accurately described as either modern or industrial; 'preindustrial', for all of the problems it raises, seems the best term. Modern industrial relations are characterized by the institutionalization of conflict, the channelling of grievances into (usually) nonviolent strikes and/or their resolution through negotiated settlement. In the following section, we shall see that the *canuts'* attempt to organize their community clearly pointed in this direction. That the route before them was blocked and they twice resorted to a violent uprising suggests that they were a social group caught in transition. This is not to say that there was a single road that all workingmen took on the way to modern industrial relations, but to suggest why the *canuts*, on a continent that had scarcely

begun to feel the effects of heavy industry, anticipated so much of the
ideology and tactics of the future labor movement.

II

Economic and social antagonisms exist in every industrial setting. The
worker movement in Lyon was not generated, therefore, solely because of
the conflict between the merchants on the one hand and the masters and
journeymen on the other. The principal explanation must be found in the
cumulative effect of four factors: community continuity, occupational
concentration, relative worker affluence, and a high level of literacy. We
shall discuss each of them briefly since they go far toward telling us what
was unique about the *canuts*.

First, Lyon was not a new industrial town like Manchester or other cities
commonly associated with the origins of the working class. The city and the
silk industry had been associated for centuries with the result that customs
and traditions existed in the *Fabrique*. In a rapidly changing world, the
canuts lived with a sense of the past. Second, not only did the entire local
economy revolve around a single industry, so that the crises of the *Fabrique*
were shared by all workers, but also the continued dominance of shop production gave a rhythm and quality to the *canuts*' work that was far different
from that of the factory system. Other historians have suggested that conflict
of interest between rival artisan groups on the one hand, and the strangeness
of factory life on the other severely retarded the development of an organized worker movement. Neither case applies to Lyon. Third, although their
future was uncertain, the *canuts* nevertheless constituted an elite among
French workingmen in 1830. Contemporary writers were fond of noting that
at the same time the cotton weavers of Lille wore wooden clogs and lived
in caves, the silk workers of Lyon wore boots and lived in furnished rooms.
'They believe themselves unfortunate', wrote the economist Villermé, who
had observed conditions throughout France, 'because they have created new.
habits for themselves, new needs. . . .' But recognizing that the worker
movement was a product of the *canuts*' relative affluence is to grasp only
part of the answer; that the fulfilment of their social and economic goals
was threatened also suggests that it resulted from what sociologists call
'relative deprivation'. Fourth, at a time when three quarters of all Frenchmen
were illiterate, a remarkably high percentage of the *canuts* were literate.
Illiteracy bore a social stigma among the master weavers; one member of the
Executive Council of their secret society resigned because his opinion was
ignored due to his inability to read or write. That there were two worker
newspapers in Lyon at a time when there were no others on the entire continent testifies to the important role literacy played in the lives of the *canuts*.

Building on the four factors cited above, the attempt to organize the worker community essentially followed three lines: the newspaper press, secret associations, and plans for the reorganization of the *Fabrique*. What bound them together were the shared goals of winning for the *canuts* (particularly the master weavers) the respect that they felt due them, and of wresting from the merchants the social and economic power that they wielded by their absolute control over the weaving rates.

In our age of electronic communications, we often underestimate the role newspapers played in the past in imparting information, identifying issues, and molding both opinion and values. Nineteenth-century Frenchmen, however, were aware of the power of the press, as the history of official attempts to censor or control it attests. In Lyon, every faction seemed to have a journal of its own. The silk merchants quoted the *Courrier de Lyon*, while the *canuts* read the *Echo de la Fabrique* (founded shortly before the uprising of November 1831) or its rival, the *Echo des Travailleurs* (begun in November 1833). Debated in the cafes, workshops, and meetings of the secret associations, the worker press helped establish the norms of their community.

The weaver, said the *Echo de la Fabrique*, seeks 'to live by the fruit of his labor and not be subject to the humiliations of a Helot or a Muscovy serf'. Pride and humiliation were like magnetic poles in the self-conscious development of community solidarity. In 1832, for example, the paper promised a free subscription to the person who suggested the best word to describe all silk workers. Other 'classes' had an 'honorable' word for themselves, it explained, and because *canuts* was used by the merchants many weavers considered it insulting. Forty-one words were entered in the contest, most of them disappointingly pretentious ones with Greek or Latin roots, such as *textoricarien* and *bombixier*. Language, nevertheless, is central to group identity and it is significant that soon after the contest terms such as 'proletarians' and 'laborers' (*travailleurs*) began to be employed for masters and journeymen alike.

The themes of pride and humiliation extended also into discussion of the problems of daily life. 'Who has never seen', asked the *Echo des Travailleurs*,

> these houses of seven or eight stories, veritable hives of activity. . . .
> Thousands of men, women, and children are crowded into these narrow,
> airless, dirty buildings and it is a pity to see in what holes live these in-
> genious workers, who produce velours, satins, gauzes . . . and all the other
> magnificent cloths. the nation does not know . . . how many men of
> genius are hidden in this glorious and unfortunate town of Lyon.

The public water supply, a matter of serious concern to the teeming neighborhoods on the Croix Rousse hillside, serves as another example. During the summer months the hundreds of residents of the *rue Tolozan* drew water from a single fountain that delivered only forty litres an hour. In addition to the inconvenience, the danger of fire was always present when oil lamps were used around the looms. The Municipal Council promised that the money it charged for the use of these fountains would go for the construction of more wells and pumps. The worker community was outraged, therefore, when the *Echo de la Fabrique* informed them that the funds were actually financing a new theatre where the merchants could enjoy the opera. Little wonder that the *Echo des Travailleurs* should proclaim,

> Our goal . . . is *social* equality. . . . a uniform condition of well-being . . . an integral development in all men of their moral and physical abilities; this does not yet exist.

The worker press also led the campaign to break the economic power of the silk merchants. In an industry as diffuse as the *Fabrique*, where there were hundreds of merchants, eight thousand workshops, and countless varieties of cloth, each woven according to a different rate, a central source of information was an essential step toward organization. Which merchants paid the highest rates? Which treated the masters like dogs? What were economic prospects for the coming month? Had the *Conseil des Prud'hommes* decided what should be done with an apprentice who broke his contract, a master caught stealing thread, or a merchant who refused to pay the agreed rate? The *canuts* learned the answers from their own journals. A letter to the editor of the *Echo de la Fabrique* was a weapon frequently used by disgruntled masters to attack the merchants.

The worker press not only presented the *canuts*' view of the problems and abuses of the *Fabrique*, but it also stated time and again their demand for a *tarif*, a fixed minimum weaving rate for every type of cloth. While the concept of a *tarif* was rooted in the 'just wage' tradition of the Old Régime, the inconsistency of the post-Revolutionary governments made it a burning issue in Lyon. A *tarif* had twice been established by the Emperor Napoleon, but under the Bourbon Restoration it was alternately enforced or ignored, its legality seemingly resting on administrative whim. The establishment of the July Monarchy, born on the barricades in 1830, raised the *canuts*' hopes. The government's subsequent decision to side with the merchants and to oppose the *tarif* as an obstacle to a free and competitive economy caused the workers to become quickly disillusioned with the rule of Louis-Philippe. When their campaign for a *tarif* was officially frustrated, they resorted to other means of guaranteeing their future.

While the *Echo de la Fabrique* and the *Echo des Travailleurs* were in serious disagreement over the future scope of the worker movement, they were united by the manner in which they articulated the benefits of secret associations and justified the illegal action that membership entailed. The weaver could no longer 'resign himself to suffering and dying while singing psalms to the Virgin and praying that She will send him work'. He must realize that his work was a form of property, it was 'the *capital* of the proletarian', and that all men had a 'right to work'. Since the *canuts* had a 'moral obligation' to protect their property and rights, the human laws that forbade unauthorized associations and strikes were superseded. In an article with the suggestive title 'On the Industrial Revolution in France', the *Echo de la Fabrique* inquired whether another revolution was necessary to raise the 'property' of work to a status equal with those of land and money. And the *Echo des Travailleurs* proclaimed that 'all advanced men . . . profess their agreement on this point: that their only strength lies in association'.

Adolphe Thiers, a government minister centrally concerned with political order and economic development after the Revolution of 1830, acknowledged the accuracy of this statement when he lamented, 'Associations are one of the maladies of our epoch.' Indeed, a characteristic of the times was the manner in which dissenting groups throughout France held the term 'association' as a kind of messianic formula, the means of attaining all goals, of solving all problems. In Lyon it became part of the ideology of the militant worker movement. But only after a struggle. The *canuts'* societies were not launched by 'advanced men', rather by conservative master weavers; the founder of the Society of Mutual Duty, for example, was a monarchist who owned several Jacquard looms and believed that the demand for a *tarif* was a less appropriate issue than restoration of order and respect in the workshops. The attempt to organize the worker community by means of illicit associations was marked, therefore, by internal conflicts from which the militants emerged with a fragile (and ultimately ephemeral) victory.

The structure of the worker associations was determined by the law that forbade unauthorized groups of more than twenty members. Although the government tolerated a few organizations that it considered little threat (principally the ancient fraternity of artisans called the *compagnonnages*), all others were obliged to form around small lodges that were secretly united in a single association.

The master weavers' Society of Mutual Duty had a pyramidal structure with the individual lodges at its base. Two men from each lodge served on a central lodge composed of twenty-two delegates. The presidents of the central lodges formed the Grand Council, or Council of Presidents, of Mutualism. Although democratic in theory, in practice the latter was an oligarchy, which acted as a constant brake against the more aggressive rank and file. Membership requirements were strict, in keeping with the founders' intention that Mutualism should be a force for social restraint in the community. Not until 1833 did unmarried masters become eligible and even then they had to be proposed by two married members and have their moral conduct come under scrutiny at four meetings. An initiation fee of five francs and monthly dues of one franc further served to exclude the riffraff.

The journeymen weavers' association, called the Ferrandiniers, after a mixed cotton and silk cloth, mirrored the Mutualists' structure and social concern; in fact, they referred to themselves as 'the sons of Mutualism'. The local authorities feared what might result from the organization of the volatile weavers and actually sent Pierre Charnier, the founder of Mutualism, to buy off the Ferrandiniers with 6,000 francs. To his delight the conservative master found they were not bent on violence and described them as 'true and good journeymen'.

The Mutualists and Ferrandiniers played professional, social, and educational roles in the attempt to organize the worker community. The original purpose of both groups was to provide mutual aid. Their regulations permitted treasury funds to be used in the form of small loans (to allow masters to rent special tools or purchase an additional loom) and to help sick, injured, or temporarily unemployed members. Deceased members received dignified funerals (at which attendance was required of lodge members) and their widows were given a small pension. Dissension arose when militants sought to use the treasury as a strike fund or to turn funeral ceremonies into a public show of strength. Three days before the uprising of April 1834, for example, 6,000 *canuts* marched in the funeral procession for a master weaver.

The Sunday meetings of the Mutualist and Ferrandinier lodges were important events for their members. Although the discussion of politics and religion was formally barred (not only to avoid a crackdown by the police, but also because the members strongly disagreed on the former topic), the worker newspapers were read aloud in these sessions, the decisions of the *Conseil des Prud'hommes* debated, banquets and dances were planned, the visit of Saint-Simonian 'missionaries' announced, and collections taken for the striking coal miners of Anzin. For many *canuts*, socialization was achieved by means of their associations.

Yet from within and without came the criticism that these societies were too exclusive and conservative. The *Echo des Travailleurs*, for example, ridiculed those who believed 'there is no salvation outside Mutualism'. In 1833, a campaign was begun to expand their influence and goals in order to improve the condition of all *canuts*. While the prefect deplored 'this spirit of egotism . . . so fatal to our industrial class', the merchants' newspaper predicted that 'when the organization of the workers into lodges is completed . . . they will be the masters of the *Fabrique*'.

The aggressive campaign had four stages. First, the Mutualists established a body of overseers called *Syndics*, whose task was to be informed of current rates offered by each merchant house in the several branches of the *Fabrique*. Second, a small number of firms notorious for their low rates were selected for a strike in July 1833, a period when the *Fabrique* was flourishing. Perhaps a thousand looms were idled. While members of the Ferrandiniers visited the workshops to convince their fellow weavers of the justice of this action, representatives of the Mutualists called on the merchants and demanded higher rates. The latter refused to talk with anyone but those masters with whom they had contracts. The local authorities privately advised the merchants to make no concessions, and after ten days sent the police to raid the office of the *Echo de la Fabrique* and to arrest the fourteen men identified as leaders. The strike was broken, but there was widespread official frustration over the lack of a legal way of suppressing the worker associations themselves. 'The Government has decided on repression', wrote the Minister of Commerce, 'and the only hesitation is as to the means. . . .'

The third stage was reached in December 1833, when an open rebellion against the conservative leadership of the Council of Presidents was staged by the Mutualist rank and file. An ad hoc Executive Council, elected by two delegates from each lodge, was created and its members, who represented a younger generation of master weavers, pledged themselves to a program of action. The older Council of Presidents continued to function, but power had passed to the new body.

The final stage of the worker associations' shift toward militancy occurred in February 1834, when the Executive Council called for a general strike in a demand for a *tarif*. The Mutualists endorsed the decision by a vote of 1,297 to 1,044, and the Ferrandiniers followed their lead. Resorting to threats of smashed looms and slashed cloth where necessary, they were able to idle all of the 25,000 looms in Lyon and its suburbs. On February 14, the Mayor wrote to the Prefect: 'I walked today in the St Just quarter [*Vieux Lyon*] and the northern part of the town [the Croix Rousse hillside] where the workshops are found and I failed to discover a single loom in operation.'

Alarmed by the 'occult power' that the Mutualist leaders wielded over the *canuts*, the government refrained from arresting them for fear of triggering violence; the only recourse was to promise the merchants protection and hope that the strike would collapse under its own weight. It did not take long, for the worker associations had far exceeded their means. On February 19, despite the Executive Council's declaration that 'our cause is that of the entire city, of all France, even of the universe', the Mutualists voted to end the general strike. The militants' victory had been a Pyrrhic one.

The general strike marked both the success and the failure of the attempt to organize the worker community by means of secret associations. On the one hand, the Mutualists and Ferrandiniers had extended their influence, albeit only for a moment, over all the *canuts*; on the other hand, their failure to win concessions from the merchants caused many to lose faith in militant action. The government took steps to assure that a general strike would not occur again. After arresting the members of the Mutualist Executive Council, it introduced a bill to make illegal all unauthorized associations, whether or not they were divided into lodges.

Plans for the reorganization of the *Fabrique*, the third part of the attempt to organize the worker community, were often discussed as a solution to troubled industrial relations in Lyon. We have already learned, for example, that the merchants considered either dispersing the looms into the countryside or concentrating them in factories; their intention was to undercut or abolish the role of the master weavers. The latter, on the other hand, proposed a plan designed to destroy the economic position of the merchants. Each group fundamentally believed that the other's destruction would guarantee future prosperity for themselves. Economic conflict can run no deeper.

The master weavers' plan called for the formation of a series of cooperative associations called central commercial houses, one for each of the principal branches of the *Fabrique*. Formed with the belief that it would permit the *canuts* to 'battle against the inhuman merchants, who enrich themselves on our suffering and privation', each house was to be headed by an 'active *fabricant*' (presumably an experienced master weaver), elected by the employees' association and charged with supervising both the manufacture and sale of the cloth. The employees associated with each house were to work for a fixed daily wage and also receive a percentage of the annual profits.

The plan for a central commercial house was an expression in positive terms of the *canuts*' perception of the problems of the *Fabrique*. The radical centralization of production would not only eliminate competition between merchant houses, but also increase efficiency and hold manufacturing costs to a minimum for the weavers. This, in turn, would have a twofold result: it would permit a lower market price, enabling Lyonnaise cloth to compete with foreign products; and it would allow the weavers a fixed rate, the equivalent of a *tarif*, for their work. In addition, the principles of self-administration and profit sharing would not only serve as incentives to the masters and journeymen, but would also furnish public proof that the *canuts* were not idlers, rather honest artisans trapped inside an exploitative system. Finally, the elimination of the merchants from the manufacturing process would end class conflict and restore tranquility to the city and the industry. The central commercial house would be 'the simplification of the industrial mechanism . . . in the collective name of the master weavers'.

Such hopes may appear as pie-in-the-sky dreams of threatened artisans, implicit proof of the way 'association' had become their messianic formula, but the idea of a central commercial house itself was no fantasy. In July 1833, nine master weavers from the Croix Rousse wrote to the newspapers to announce plans for such a project. By November they had published its statutes and had begun to seek worker-stockholders at 25 francs per share. There are indications, moreover, that the Mutualists were contemplating using the funds in their treasury to found a model house. A related project called the Commercial Society was actually launched by a group of master weavers in October 1834, but with the worker movement in a state of collapse following the April uprising, it saw little success. Its failure, however, should not be read as a judgment on the idea of a central commercial house. One can only speculate as to its fate had the worker newspapers and associations continued to flourish.

The *canuts'* attempt to organize their community did not pass unnoticed elsewhere; the general strike, in particular, was the subject of widespread discussion. But it was their violent uprisings that riveted all attention on the second city of France.

III

'The barbarians who menace society are no longer to be found on the Tartar steppes; they are presently in the suburbs of our manufacturing towns.' This comment by the *Journal des Débats* accurately reflects the reaction of most Frenchmen to the events of November 1831 and April 1834. But the *canuts* were not a wild horde suddenly descended from the hills. As we explore the Lyonnaise context of violence, it will be clear not only that the resort to arms grew directly from the economic and social antagonisms of the *Fabrique*, but also that there are discernible patterns in the uprisings that reflect the structure and organization of the worker community.

The November 1831 uprising resulted from the perfidious treatment of the *canuts'* demand for a *tarif*. In October, a worker group (with the Mutualists, although still in their conservative phase, taking the lead) successfully used a combination of mass rallies and petitions to pressure the Prefect to convene a commission to negotiate a *tarif*. On October 25, while several thousand *canuts* waited outside the Prefecture, a panel of merchants and masters reached a general agreement with regard to weaving rates. But the *canuts'* apparent victory was short-lived. The merchants ignored the date of implementation and complained to Paris about the Prefect's intervention. On Thursday, November 17, the announcement came from the capital that the agreement had been only 'an engagement of honor' and was not legally binding. The *tarif* was thereby annulled.

Tension mounted during the weekend. A general work stoppage in the shops and a protest march from the Croix Rousse to the Prefecture in the center of the city were called for Monday, November 21. The Prefect responded by sending National Guard units, largely composed of silk merchants and clerks, to bar the *canuts'* descent. A column of weavers began to march down the hillside. Shots rang out and they retreated with their dead and wounded, crying 'To arms! Vengeance! They have killed our brothers!' The November uprising had begun.

News of the skirmish on the Croix Rousse hillside spread quickly. Fighting soon broke out in the other worker neighborhoods. The garrison was totally unprepared for such a revolt and by midnight of the next day the municipal council recommended that the Army evacuate the city. A band of insurgents seized the undefended Hôtel de Ville. The Prefect was a prisoner in the Prefecture. On November 23, 1831, the *canuts* controlled Lyon.

They had no idea what to do with their unexpected triumph, however. Grasping this fact, the Prefect appointed a commission of sixteen wealthy and influential masters to govern the city. This act successfully defused the power of a radical group seeking to proclaim a Republic at the Hôtel de Ville. Under the supervision of these conservative masters, order was restored in the city; squads of workers were sent to guard the silk warehouses and the municipal treasury. And when the army returned, led by the Minister of War, Maréchal Soult, and the King's son, the Duc d'Orléans, the city gates were open for their arrival. The November uprising ended with a whimper. But its implications were staggering. As one of the merchants' spokesmen wrote:

> The moral influence of the November insurrection will be immense: their victory, so singularly the result of a succession of accidents and the incapacity of the authorities, will make them [the workers] more demanding. . . . Perhaps for a hundred years the marvelous tale of the defeat of the National Guard and the garrison of Lyon by the unarmed workers will charm the leisure of the workshop; this tradition will pass from generation to generation; a son will say with pride . . . , 'My father was one of the conquerors of Lyon.'

As we have seen in our discussion of the July 1833 and February 1834 strikes, the lessons drawn by the government and merchants were vigorously applied during the next three years: official intervention in economic disputes only spelled trouble, all worker attempts to press their demands by means of collective action must be resisted, and never again be militarily unprepared. The rejection of negotiation and the evolution of confrontation as a conscious policy at the precise time the *canuts* set about organizing their own community went far toward making a second uprising inevitable.

On April 5, 1834, a crowd of weavers awaiting the verdict in the trial of the leaders of the February general strike disarmed a squad of troops guarding the courtroom. The authorities responded with a firmness that belied their panic. The *Fabrique* had been caught in an unexpected crisis; unemployment was widespread among the *canuts*. In addition, the government in Paris, whipped by the hysterical conviction that the Republicans had infiltrated the worker societies and were prepared to use them as the cutting edge of another revolutionary upheaval, had steered passage of a special law giving the police the power to suppress any undesired association, no matter what its structure or professed goals. Seizing this unexpected opportunity for alliance with the workers (something which, I have argued elsewhere, they had failed to accomplish as a result of their own efforts), the Lyonnaise Republicans called for massive demonstrations to protest the law on associations on the day the trial reconvened. Unemployed, their demand for a *tarif* rejected, their strikes broken, their leaders on trial, and their associations in mortal danger, many *canuts* heeded the call. The government, meanwhile, prepared to meet this challenge with a show of force.

On the morning of April 9, 1834, thousands of troops patrolled the streets of Lyon. Fighting broke out when soldiers were twice provoked into firing on the unarmed crowds. Once the demonstrators had been dispersed, resistance was confined to isolated pockets; all but one were in distinctly worker neighborhoods. Although fighting continued for six days, there was never any doubt as to the outcome; the difficulties of street fighting and the military's mistaken belief that the rebels were well armed largely explain the delay. Eventually the uprising was crushed under the weight of 1,729 artillery rounds and 269,000 musket shots. The Army suffered almost three hundred and fifty casualties (civilian casualties are impossible to calculate, but certainly were higher), but the Minister of War's personal investigator proudly proclaimed that the garrison of 1834 had avenged the humiliation of 1831.

News of the second Lyon uprising — the largest domestic rebellion between the revolutions of 1830 and 1848 — sparked minor troubles in a number of other towns. The government, believing (or claiming to believe) itself the victim of a national conspiracy, made thousands of arrests and later tried hundreds of radicals for sedition. Because Lyon was associated with the 'April events', a myth was born that while the uprising of November 1831 had been economic in character, that of April 1834 was a political insurrection. A few Republicans did play a role in the second uprising, but to accept this interpretation is to distort seriously the Lyonnaise context of violence.

Three significant patterns emerge from a comparison of the two Lyon uprisings. First, both revolts were triggered by a government decision to deny the *canuts* precisely that protection they believed would guarantee their future. The rejection of the *tarif* is related to November 1831 in the same manner as the threatened suppression of the worker associations is linked to April 1834. Those who have argued that the latter was political fail to ask the critical question: Would the *canuts* have rebelled if their leaders had not been on trial and only the Republican associations had been threatened? Both uprisings sprang directly from the particular antagonisms of the *Fabrique*.

Second, the critical personnel in both uprisings was essentially the same: the journeymen weavers. The warning that they would close their shops and turn the *compagnons* loose in the streets was the masters' ultimate threat in their struggles with the merchants and local authorities. This tactic was often used in the troubled decades before 1789, during the local revolutionary events in 1830, and again in 1831 and 1834. We do not have accurate documentation concerning the composition of the crowd in November 1831, but the dossiers of the hundreds of persons arrested in April 1834 make such an analysis possible for the second uprising. They reveal that over 90 per cent of the insurgents were members of the local worker community. Nearly four out of every ten persons arrested were silk workers, a clear refutation of the government's contention that only a handful of *canuts* participated in the fighting. The fluid world of the journeymen is further reflected by the fact that only one in three of all persons arrested was born in Lyon or the Rhône department, two-thirds were bachelors, and nearly 90 per cent were under the age of forty. Only two men out of the hundreds arrested confessed they had no trade or occupation and only a handful (2.5 per cent) admitted having a previous criminal record. One must conclude that the insurgents of 1831 and 1834 were young, mobile, and employable, men who had come to Lyon seeking work. Far from constituting a mob of barbarians or revolutionaries, they fought only when their future appeared gravely threatened.

Third, the worker neighborhoods formed the backbone of resistance in both uprisings. By means of illustration, let us focus our attention on a single street already mentioned for its concentration of *canuts*. The *rue Tolozan* was a center of worker militancy on the Croix Rousse hillside. A placard was displayed there announcing the mass meeting of November 21, 1831, and when the National Guard fired on the marching weavers its residents took up the cry 'To arms! Death to the merchants!' In the period between the two revolts, M. Falconnet, the editor of the *Echo de la Fabrique*, lived in the *rue Tolozan* along with many members of the Mutualist and Ferrandinier societies. During the general strike in February 1834, the Mayor was obliged to send a squad of soldiers there to protect the life of a master weaver who had announced his intention to resume work. And in April 1834, the street exploded. According to the official government report, the fighting in this area of the city was the most highly organized of all the rebel strongholds. Nonetheless the resistance was a neighborhood affair. A majority of the persons arrested on the entire hillside lived in a four-block area around the *rue Tolozan*. Typical of these insurgents was Claude Clocher, a young native of Savoy, who worked as a journeyman in a shop directly above the cafe that served as rebel headquarters. When he was arrested and charged with having manned an observation post at the end of his block, Clocher's only weapon was a sword given him by a neighbor who was a former member of the National Guard. When asked by the police to explain the uprising, he replied that 'misery caused it all'.

The intentionally limited scope of this essay prohibits an extended discussion of the *canuts*' resistance. This brief account of the two uprisings and their common patterns, nonetheless, should have revealed the Lyonnaise context of violence. November 1831 and April 1834 mark the moments when the complex social and economic compounds of the *Fabrique* reached the flash point. Hopefully the reader now understands the particular antagonisms that caused the explosion.

By way of an epilogue it is important to note that the *canuts* did not remain in the vanguard of the worker movement throughout the nineteenth century. As the railroad arrived (ironically the line connecting Lyon with the coalfields of Saint Étienne was completed in 1834) bringing the metal and chemical industries in its wake, the *Fabrique* lost its overwhelming importance in the local economy. The emigration of *unies* continued and *façonnes* production fell victim to the 'democratization' of taste after mid-century. The era of the journeyman weaver came to an end, replaced over the next decades by that of the industrial factory worker. The master weavers remained, but the Revolution of 1848 was their last hurrah, a final fling at violence. Increasingly preoccupied with protecting their artisan status and contemptuous of the slavish proletarians, the *chefs d'atelier* became solidly conservative. During the Lyonnaise Commune in 1871, the factory workers belonging to the First International sent out the call to arms. The neighborhoods of the Croix Rousse, the *canuts* of the *rue Tolozan*, failed to respond.

Note

1. Under the July Monarchy all men had equal social rights, but only those who paid 100 francs direct taxes annually had the right to vote. The latter group were called active citizens.

3   CHURCH AND REVOLUTION: ASPECTS OF THE SOCIAL HISTORY OF THE TRIER PILGRIMAGE OF 1844

Wolfgang Schieder

TRANSLATED BY RICHARD DEVESON

Source: 'Kirche und Revolution: sozialgeschichtliche Aspekte der Trierer Wallfahrt von 1844', *Archiv für Sozialgeschichte*, vol.14, 1974, pp.419-54.

The pilgrimage to the so-called 'Holy Coat' of Trier in the year 1844 is one of the events of the German *Vormärz*[1] the negative relevance of which to the German revolution has so far scarcely been adequately recognised. The only historians really to have paid attention to it have been Catholic ecclesiastical scholars, since pilgrimages, like other forms of veneration of relics, belong on the margins of Catholic worship. It is worth asking, however, whether pilgrimages, and the great Trier pilgrimage of 1844 in particular, may not deserve a much more wide-ranging kind of attention from historians than is offered in denominationally based ecclesiastical history. The Trier pilgrimage has a social-historical dimension that bears interestingly on the central question of the *Vormärz*, namely the relation between social and religious activity. If it is seen as more than simply an expression of old or revived popular religious custom, questions can be raised as to the relative importance of spontaneity and organisation. What set the hosts of travelling pilgrims on their way? What political strategy of the church's underlay the whole pilgrimage movement? Finally: was the pilgrimage, for the church leadership, merely an instrument of internal church revival, or should it be seen, pre-eminently, as a thoroughly concerted display of political power on the church's part?

I

The occasion for the pilgrimage of 1844 was the putting on public display of a relic that was normally kept under lock and key: a piece of clothing purportedly worn at His death by the historical figure of Christ. The Trier affair − the processions of the pilgrims and the events in the city itself − was described many times by contemporary supporters of the pilgrimage, most memorably by the old Joseph Görres,[2] in his publication *The Pilgrimage to Trier*, though this was admittedly a product of 'Romantic science poetry' and not of direct testimony. Despite conflicting assessments of the affair, contemporary observers proved to be in accord in being impressed by the great number of pilgrims. It was clear, above all, that the pilgrimage was a mass phenomenon. Since mass movements were no everyday occurrence in the German *Vormärz* police state, the Trier pilgrimage was seen as sensational in virtue of the high level of participation alone. Seen from today's perspective, it can be called the largest organised mass movement of the *Vormärz* period as a whole.

In 1832, in Hambach and elsewhere, the liberal democratic middle class of south-west Germany organised large public demonstrations for the first time. Tens of thousands took part. In 1844 the Catholic Church mobilised, not tens, but hundreds of thousands. In a detailed advance estimate, the church authorities in Trier arrived at a total of 152,875 pilgrims, with those, indeed, coming from external dioceses reckoned at only 8,850. In May 1844 the Lord Mayor and Chief Administrator of Trier calculated that 300,000 people would come to the city. In fact, many more came.

The church leadership had the results of a 'Special Demonstration' circulated, according to which a total of 1,050,835 pilgrims had seen the relic exposed in Trier Cathedral. This figure came from counts made in the cathedral by the voluntary security force of the Trier citizenry, the so-called 'Guard of Honour'. Jakob Marx, the pilgrimage propagandist, regarded the figure as the most reliable. The *Triersche Zeitung* of 8 October 1844 also mentioned a total of 1,100,000 visitors to the cathedral. The figure of a million was taken over into the contemporary literature from these Trier sources and transmitted down to the present day. It is, however, pitched far too high. For one thing, the cathedral counts were quite inexact. Furthermore, on 19 out of a total of 50 days no counts were made in the cathedral and figures were estimated afterwards. Despite all security measures, too, a considerable proportion of pilgrims seems to have gained admittance into the cathedral on more than one occasion. On the basis of contemporary statistics, we arrive at about half the number of pilgrims calculated by the over-eager assessors in the cathedral. These statistics give the following picture (see Table 3.1).

The figures of Marx and Delahaye shown here indicate a round total of 450,000 pilgrims; Bechtold's incomplete data point in the same general direction. Both Marx and Delahaye, for different reasons, added in a further 100,000 not included in church or police lists respectively. Even if these unconfirmable additions are thought over-generous, a total estimate of about 500,000 pilgrims does not seem to be set too high.

This is, in any event, a quite remarkable figure, on two counts: first, these half a million people flocked to Trier in the space of only 50 days (from 18 August to 6 October); secondly, according to the census of late

Table 3.1: Contemporary Statistics on the Number of Pilgrims

Line	Place of origin	Number of Pilgrims			Population	
	Trier diocese, by deaneries, 20.8 – 14.9	M.Bechtold	Jakob Marx	A.Delahaye	by *Kreis* (local district) Total	Catholic
1	Bernkastel	16,776	17,776	18,231	44,116	29,699
2	Bitburg	24,144	27,344	29,244	40,914	40,810
3	Daun	10,400	11,000	10,300	23,912	23,857
4	Ehrang	26,739	29,239	24,539 ⎫	57,169	55,550
5	Hermeskeil	28,500	19,700	31,500 ⎭		
6	Merzig	22,286	22,286	22,286	31,709	31,279
7	Ottweiler	11,000	11,000	11,000	28,693	19,215
8	Prüm	9,485	11,265	8,380	30,226	30,147
9	Saarbrücken	3,500	3,500	4,000	38,779	19,143
10	Saarburg	26,164	26,325	28,624	29,961	29,679
11	Saarlouis	19,385	18,670	13,610	45,648	44,190
12	St Wendel	5,600	6,800	6,800	37,449	19,524
13	Wittlich	26,455	27,005	26,455	34,816	34,301
14	Adenau	7,100	7,100	6,650	22,995	22,945
15	Ahrweiler	4,700	5,500	6,260	31,687	30,421
16	Cochem	14,558	15,821	15,950	32,434	31,975
17	Engers	5,250	6,200	6,690	57,015	20,526
18	Koblenz	3,540	6,920	4,800	51,855	45,950
19	Kreuznach	2,317	1,810	7,000	52,508	29,377
20	Mayen	11,250	13,400	11,250	44,464	43,372
21	St Goar	4,348	5,408	5,478	34,283	27,926
22	Simmern	3,100	4,300	3,400	36,759	14,668
23	Zell	9,230	9,230	9,230	28,158	18,628
24	Birkenfeld	1,620	2,020	1,720	(20,000)	?
25	Meisenheim	–	110	80	(10,000)	?
26	Trier diocese, 20.8 – 14.9	297,447	309,729	313,477	(865,550)	(663,182)
27	Trier diocese, 15.9 – 6.10	?	42,000	37,480		
28	Trier diocese	(297,447)	351,729	350,957		
29	Cologne diocese	(960)	22,000	27,700		
30	Limburg diocese	(2,000)	14,000	15,300		
31	Luxemburg diocese	(6,040)	24,000	33,050		
32	Mainz diocese	–	4,000	2,450		
33	Metz diocese	–	18,000	11,910		
34	Münster diocese	–	150	–		
35	Nancy diocese	–	3,000	900		
36	Speyer diocese	(2,650)	8,000	7,480		
37	Verdun diocese	–	–	200		
38	Alsace and Belgium	–	–	200		
39	Total	?	444,879	450,147		

Sources:

M Bechtold, a priest, had responsibility within the cathedral provostry for registering processions. A manuscript (probably Bechtold's), containing incomplete statistical data, is in the Trier Diocesan Archive.

Jakob Marx, *Die Ausstellung des h. Rockes in der Domkirche zu Trier im Herbste des Jahres 1844*, Trier, 1845.

Anton Delahaye, *Statistische Uebersicht der während der Ausstellung des heil. Rockes im Herbste 1844 zu Trier gewesenen Fremden und Beschreibung der Feierlichkeiten, welche dabei stattgehabt*, Trier, 1844.

Note: Typographical errors in the original table have been corrected.

1843, the city had only 24,554 inhabitants, of whom, moreover, 7,798 lived in 16 suburbs and villages on the outskirts, some of them quite far from the centre. Thus, for seven weeks an average of 10,000 people a day came into a city of which the main buildings, within the medieval walls, housed only 15,064 inhabitants. It is not surprising that contemporary descriptions speak of the 'almost daily over-crowding' of the city.

It is obvious that the vast majority of pilgrims came from the diocese of Trier, within the administrative boundaries of which lay the two Prussian government districts of Trier and Koblenz as well as the Oldenburg enclave of Birkenfeld and the Hesse-Homburg rural district of Meisenheim on the left bank of the Rhine. As Table 3.1 shows (line 28), they constituted over 350,000 of the 450,000 recorded pilgrims. If we assume that the government districts of Trier and Koblenz together had at least 663,182 Catholic inhabitants (line 26), then, ignoring the tiny Catholic minorities in Birkenfeld and Meisenheim, over half of the Catholics in the diocese of Trier would have responded to Bishop Arnoldi's appeal. Admittedly, multiple pilgrimages per person are included in that figure. They should in the main be assigned to the local districts and deaneries immediately surrounding Trier. Let us compare Catholic population figures in the table for the deaneries of Bitburg, Ehrang and Hermeskeil, Merzig, Saarburg and Wittlich with their respective numbers of pilgrims (lines 2, 4 and 5, 6, 10 and 13). Assuming only single pilgrimages per person, between 60 and 95 per cent of the Catholic populations in these deaneries would have had to come to Trier. Since, however, effectively only adults travelled to Trier, these percentages must be rejected, even if we include non-Catholics, negligibly few in these particular districts. Noticeably fewer pilgrims came from the more distant deaneries of the Hunsrück and the Eifel, and in the Koblenz government district only Mayen and Cochem exceeded 10,000 at all. In other words, the frequency of pilgrimages declines significantly with increasing distance from Trier.

The Trier pilgrimage would presumably have created much less of a stir if it had been merely a local event arranged by the Trier diocese. The exposition of the cathedral relic, however, also exerted considerable drawing-power outside the narrow confines of the diocese. Fairly large groups of pilgrims came, in particular, from the historical areas of the former Trier archbishopric, from the diocese of Limburg in one direction and the dioceses of Luxemburg, Nancy and Metz in the other (cf. lines 30, 31, 33 and 35 in the table). The high number from the Cologne archbishopric is also worthy of note (line 29). Smaller groups came from the dioceses of Mainz and Speyer (not Prussian), bordering Trier on the south (lines 32 and 36). The Trier exposition, then, kindled a popular movement that not only was incomparably large but also extended widely across regions. It constituted, in fact, a 'pilgrimage of the peoples of the Rhine', in Görres' celebratory words — words, it is true, of poetic licence and exaggeration. Both in numbers of participants and in size of catchment area, the Trier pilgrimage outstripped all comparable ecclesiastical ventures in Germany in the first half of the nineteenth century.

II

Pro-church journalism was unanimous in hailing the Trier pilgrimage as a festival of unity that breached all political barriers and class divisions. It has rightly been said that 'unity' was the 'great watchword of the supporters of the pilgrimage'. At the foundation of this cult of unity was the ecclesiastico-religious symbolism of the supposed seamless garment, the tunic of the dead Jesus of Nazareth, regarded from earliest times as a symbol of the unity of the church. Thus Görres, invoking Augustine, called the pilgrimage a 'symbol of the infrangible unity' of the church. This traditional justification, however, ideologised by Görres in a Romantic sense, was overlaid, in apologies for the pilgrimage, by socio-political argument. Jakob Marx spoke of the 'brotherly union and equality of people of all stations'. He saw the pilgrimage as abolishing the 'differences among men in civil society' and their splintering into 'particular classes'. With a characteristic blending of the socio-political dimension and ecclesiastical dogmatism, he dissociated himself from a class-based concept of the common people according to which 'simple town and country folk are to be regarded as antitheses of the respected, the rich, the polite, the so-called educated'. 'The church', he noted, 'knows only clergy and people, and the latter contains, in an ec-clesiastical sense, all of the faithful, be they rich or poor, polite or humble, governors or governed, learned or unlearned, nobility or commoners.' In his view, and in the view of other propagandists for the pilgrimage, the Catholic Church had thus, via the route of an active unity of belief, founded a new unity of the people. And this was by no means intended in a merely spiritual and symbolic sense. A Würzburg pilgrimage pamphlet said: 'The edifice that fraudulent freedom seeks to achieve, as its greatest object, by means of smoking ruins and corpses — that, religion has attained; fraternal equality held sway among the thousands.' Here, then, is an appeal on the pilgrimage's behalf for revolutionary *égalité*, conjoined with *fraternité* and *liberté* — but all to be taken in a counter-revolutionary sense. The class harmony claimed for the pilgrimage proves to be less a social reality than a socio-political programme. The social physiognomy of the Trier pilgrimage movement must therefore be examined more closely.

In contradiction to the church's notion that it had mobilised all levels of society for the pilgrimage, contemporary opponents of the pilgrimage complained that only members of the lower social strata had taken part. Those critics of the pilgrimage venture whose views are recorded said, for example, that the pilgrims belonged 'almost exclusively to the lower classes', that they looked 'truly poor and wretched', that the 'majority of pilgrims' consisted of 'destitute, uneducated people, who brought their last farthings with them to Trier'. An anonymous writer points out that the pilgrims should be reckoned among the 'poor classes', classes 'whose need and misery grow from day to day and threaten to bring us to the edge of that abyss which has already begun to manifest itself in the instances of English pauperism and the French proletariat'. The same charge is made in the open letter to Bishop Arnoldi of Trier by the Silesian ex-priest Johannes Ronge, first published in the *Sächsische Vaterlandsblätter* in Leipzig on 15 October. In this powerfully worded pamphlet Ronge provided the first impetus for the religious and political 'German Catholicism' movement, which, dogmatically and ideologically, and in virtue of its initially mass character, constituted the most noteworthy reply to the Trier pilgrimage movement. Ronge's attack, however, also caused the attention of a wider public to be directed to the question of the social origins and composition of the hosts of Trier pilgrims. The crucial sentences in Ronge's proclamation run: 'Five times one hundred thousand people, five times one hundred thousand Germans of good sense have already hastened to a piece of clothing in Trier, to venerate it or merely to see it! Most of these thousands of people are from the lower classes, very poor in any event, oppressed, ignorant, dull-witted, superstitious and, some of them, degenerate.' Thus did Ronge inaugurate the debate concerning the social character of the Trier pilgrimage.

What is particularly striking about this controversy is the fact that many of the pro-church writers on the subject of the pilgrimage, having been driven onto the defensive, fully confirmed the pilgrimage's class character. 'To be sure, most were from the lower classes', a Breslau pamphlet says, for example, 'simply because in the region of the Rhine, as everywhere, such people are by far the most numerous.' A Rheingau priest, in an 'open letter' to Ronge, explicitly defends the 'hundreds of thousands of pilgrims' on the grounds that they come from the 'healthy core of the German nation: from the common people'. Others conceded that the bulk of the pilgrims were peasants and small artisans, but sought to defend them against the reproach of poverty and ignorance. The pilgrims were 'poor country folk', but not 'rabble'. Even though Jakob Marx and others stood fast by the unification ideology of the pilgrimage, contemporary polemics made it clear that the great mass of the pilgrims were members of the lower social strata, i.e. peasants (especially winegrowers), small artisans and tradespeople. It was also repeatedly reported that a large number were women.

It must be borne in mind that the economic position of this lower stratum was severely threatened. At the beginning of the 1840s the Mosel area was, with Silesia, the poorest region of the whole Prussian state. As in Silesia, the above-average level of pauperisation of the Mosel population was quite recent in origin. Back in the first decade of Prussian rule, the Mosel region had experienced a perceptible economic upturn. That this upturn veered immediately into a crisis had to do with the special economic structure of the area, which was largely based on a monoculture of wine. After incorporation into the Prussian state, the Mosel winegrowers had won themselves a quasi-monopolistic preference arrangement, which gave them cause to extend their vineyards and undertake corresponding capital investment. The signing of the Prussia-Hesse customs treaty in 1828 put paid at a stroke to this preference arrangement, since the Prussian government took no account of the customs policy's immediate social consequences for its subjects. The accession of Nassau to the German Customs Union in 1835 intensified the wine-trade crisis in the Prussian Rhineland. By 1836 about 49,000 winegrowers had been affected by it. The misguided taxation policy of the undiscerning financial authorities in Berlin further exacerbated the hardship of the winegrowers. Since the 1830s the plight of the Mosel had been regularly discussed in the Rhenish provincial parliaments, along with all its side-effects, such as the wood-stealing which moved Karl Marx to publish his first social critiques, in the *Rheinische Zeitung*, in 1842. These impoverished winegrowers, and the tradespeople dependent on them, made up the central core of the Trier pilgrims.

The lower-class pilgrims were not, certainly, left to themselves. In line with previous church plans, numerous clergy were to be found among them, as procession leaders. In the notes made by Bechtold, the bishop's representative, there are names of 283 priests for the period up to 14 September. One Mainz procession alone was accompanied by 15 priests. But the higher clergy came too, including no fewer than ten bishops. It was no coincidence that among them were the heads of the church in the dioceses from which most of the pilgrims came: the bishops of Limburg (Blum), Luxemburg (Vicar Apostolic Laurent), Nancy (von Menjaud), Verdun (Rossat), Cologne (Coadjutor von Geissel) and Speyer (Weis). Conversely, the bishop of Mainz, Kaiser, from whose diocese relatively few pilgrims went, did not attend. Kaiser, indeed, is said to have instructed his priests not to make propaganda on behalf of the Trier exposition. In his stead, however, Arnoldi was able to welcome to Trier a Belgian bishop (Vicar Apostolic von Wykersloot from Leyden) and three bishops from Westphalia: the bishop of Münster (Maximilian von Droste-Vischering), his suffragan bishop (Vicar Apostolic Lüpke) and the bishop of Osnabrück

(Melchers). The rare appearance of so many high church officials shows how much importance the Rhenish church leadership placed on the pilgrimage. In addition, their presence in Trier was heavily emphasised. Arnoldi shared with the bishop of Verdun, for example, the duties at the closing ceremony of the exposition. He informed the Metropolitan of Cologne, Geissel, of his plans for the pilgrimage as early as the end of May, and kept him up to date, in further letters, with the progress of the enterprise right up to Geissel's arrival in Trier on 28 September. He worked particularly closely with the head of the Luxemburg church, Laurent. The latter not only had publicised the pilgrimage in one of his own pastoral letters but also crossed the frontier on foot himself, with a procession from Luxemburg. Arnoldi travelled out from Trier to meet him.

The Westphalian bishops brought no mass processions with them. Their presence in Trier, however, produced another social-historical conjuncture. In the radical *Mannheimer Abendzeitung* during November 1844 there were arguments whether only the 'mob, polite and common' had taken part in the pilgrimage or whether other social ranks had also attended. The class here described in unspecific, polemical language as the 'polite mob' – a phrase which at once aroused fierce criticism and counter-criticism – was the aristocracy. It is known, in fact, that the Westphalian Catholic nobility, in particular, travelled to Trier during the period when the 'Holy Coat' was exhibited. The most sensational case of an alleged miracle cure brought about by the relic was that of a Countess von Droste-Vischering. Baron von Andlaw of Baden, who wrote to the *Mannheimer Abendzeitung* on 14 November, was also a pilgrim in Trier. On the other hand, the educated and prosperous middle class was almost entirely absent: that is to say, academics, civil servants and members of the Rhenish bourgeoisie or, in the parlance of the time, the *Mittelstand* (middle class) or the *gebildete Klassen* (educated classes). The Trier pilgrimage can thus be seen, from the viewpoint of social history, as a mass movement of the lower social strata, with staging and accompaniment provided by the Catholic clergy and nobility. Contrary to the ideology of unity promulgated by church propagandists, the middle class played practically no role. Rather, it rejected and stood apart from the 'close alliance' between 'ultramontane priesthood' and 'high nobility' that emerged in the pilgrimage. Consistently with this position, many middle-class spokesmen at first ranged themselves with the German Catholic counter-movement, and against the pilgrimage.

This stance had already become evident from the fact that Ronge first published his celebrated letter to Arnoldi in the *Sächsische Vaterlandsblätter*, edited by Robert Blum: the most influential anti-pilgrimage declaration was thus issued, by the former priest, in an organ of the middle-class liberal left. The *Deutsche Allgemeine Zeitung* reported soon afterwards that Ronge's article was being read and discussed in Silesia 'in most public gatherings of middle-class citizens'. The *Mannheimer Zeitung* reported from Baden that it was the 'middle classes' that had been 'especially electrified by this essay'. In Saxony, too, Ronge's appeal won the sympathy of the middle-class opposition. Apart from the *Sächsische Vaterlandsblätter*, Karl Biedermann's *Herold* and other journals also took Ronge's side. The most influential vote for German Catholicism, however, probably came from the liberal historian Gervinus, in his publication 'Die Mission der Deutschkatholiken' ['The Mission of the German Catholics']. Gervinus saw the German Catholic movement as arising from the 'heart of the middle classes'. He interpreted it, in accordance with his liberal philosophy of history, as a political movement of the historically educated middle class. He contraposed a programme of rallying of middle-class opinion, on a supra-denominational religious basis, to the alliance of Catholic Church and preindustrial proletariat that had come to the fore in the Trier pilgrimage.

By contrast, middle-class radicals admired German Catholicism precisely for its mass character: as a 'movement of the people in the mass' that was taking seriously the 'social idealism of Christianity'. And in 1849, in a critical retrospect, Bruno Bauer still spoke of Ronge as the 'hero of the middle class'. He had articulated the middle class's 'horror' at the 'spectacle in Trier'. True, the social reality of the German Catholicism movement, to the best of our present knowledge, lived up to the wishful thinking of neither the liberal nor the radical middle-class intelligentsia. German Catholicism did not remain a middle-class movement, nor did it build a political bridge between the middle class and the emergent proletariat. What is certain, however, is that Ronge's attack created a national awareness that the middle class had been excluded from the Trier pilgrimage.

III

Despite its mass character, the Trier pilgrimage would doubtless not have been thought sensational if it had been merely one pilgrimage within a regular cycle — like, for example, the Aachen cathedral pilgrimages that took place every seven years. The exposition of the cathedral relic, however, was a far from normal occurrence. The tradition of exhibiting the relic certainly goes back into the early modern period, but the rhythm of pilgrimages seems at first sight to have no inner logic.

Even in the Middle Ages numerous legends had formed concerning the whereabouts of the alleged Holy Coat, legends which increasingly, but by no means exclusively, came to centre on Trier. The first report of an actual, tangible object comes at the end of the twelfth century. The relic was not put on public display, however, until the initiative was taken by the Emperor Maximilian I at the Trier Imperial Diet of 1512. The 'Holy Coat' was exposed for 23 days in May of that year, together with a range of other cathedral relics. On the basis of the great public success of the exposition the Elector of Trier, Archbishop Richard von Greiffenklau, applied for papal recognition of the pilgrimage. As a result Pope Leo X, in his bull of 1514, *Salvator Noster Dominus*, and in executive instructions that followed in 1515, granted plenary indulgence for a pilgrimage that would take place every seven years. Thereafter, beginning in 1517, four expositions took place at this interval until 1538, with one display outside the sequence in 1539 or 1540. Although the circumstances and course of these pilgrimages have not yet been examined in detail, there can be no doubt that this organised series belongs in the context of the sixteenth-century crisis in the church. In this instance, as in others, the attempt was made to exploit the proliferation of pilgrimages and other late-fifteenth-century popular religious customs in order to strengthen, both ideologically and materially, the institutionalised Catholic Church. Significantly, the Trier pilgrimage was a particular thorn in the flesh of the Reformers. Luther, in his appeal 'To the Christian Nobility of the German Nation' of 1520, reckoned it among the newly established pilgrimages that should be abolished again. In 1531 he asked, in his familiar, earthy fashion: 'What in the World is this new Pox of a Fraud in Trier, this Coat of Christ? What Manner of Annual Fair hath the Devil held here, and what thousands of false Miracles hath he sold?' The victory of the Reformation in Germany seems, in turn, finally to have disrupted the pattern of pilgrimages in Trier. Only in 1585 was there another brief exposition of the Coat. Its immediate occasion was the restoration of Catholicism in the Trier Electorate. It was the first time the pilgrimage was used for the only purpose for which it continued to be staged, at irregular intervals, in the following centuries: to summon the faithful and to demonstrate regained strength during or after fundamental crises in the church's existence.

The only exposition in the seventeenth century, in 1655, marked the church's revival after the convulsions of the Thirty Years' War. To all appearances it was also connected with the formation of the Rhenish Alliance of Catholic territorial states (Electoral Cologne, Electoral Trier, Münster, Palatine Neuburg and Electoral Mainz). The next occasion, in September 1810, was intended to demonstrate the reconstruction of church organisation after the old nobility church had crumbled under the blows of revolution and secularisation. Napoleon himself backed the efforts of the French bishop, Mannay, to retrieve the relic from Augsburg, where it had been transported. The 1844 pilgrimage fell between this one and that of

1891. The latter is clearly connected with the end of the *Kulturkampf*[3] and the repeal of the anti-socialist law. The Bishop of Trier, Korum, depicted it unambiguously as an instrument of aggressive Catholic social policy aimed against the labour movement. It is not surprising that, on 30 August 1891, socialist workers distributed political propaganda to a pilgrimage procession of Saar miners. The next exposition, in 1933, had been decided on before Hitler's seizure of power. The original spur for it was probably the ending of the Allied occupation of Trier province in 1929. The separation of the Saar from the German Reich also played a part. As the heavy influx of pilgrims from the Saar showed, the pilgrimage strengthened the national cohesiveness of the Mosel Catholics with the Saar Catholics of the Trier diocese. The course of the pilgrimage further demonstrated that it, too, not only had internal religious causes but also contained heavily political implications. All the evidence indicates that it was conducted with the full agreement of the new National Socialist authorities. Mention need be made here, even if individual details require clarification, only of the fact that Storm Trooper personnel in uniform were responsible for security in the cathedral precincts. The circumstances of the latest pilgrimage, in 1959, still await full description. It can be presumed, however, that it refers back to the high point of Christian Democratic political strength in the Federal Republic, in 1957. The visit of Chancellor Adenauer to Trier points clearly to this. All told, a clear line extends over the three hundred years between 1655 and 1959: throughout, admittedly in varying circumstances, the institutionalised Catholic Church is evidently striving to make certain of the visible support of its faithful, during or after times of threat to its existence. This, then, is the wider context in which the 1844 pilgrimage must also be seen.

It is true that in 1844 the only link, for contemporaries, was to the pilgrimage of 1810. The link arose, in particular, from the way the earlier pilgrimage had been staged. The French bishop Mannay showed in 1810 how masses of people could be set into motion on the church's behalf without jeopardy to the sovereign authority of the state. The same happened in 1844, and the recourse to Mannay's Pilgrimage Statute on that occasion was not fortuitous. It was pilgrimage from above that was here being freshly developed at the start of the nineteenth century. This opened up the possibility for the Roman Catholic Church of influencing and directing the masses towards a definite purpose.

The last, eighteenth-century Trier Electors had not perceived the opportunities for advancing church policy that were provided by the manipulation of pilgrimages. It was not merely owing to external causes such as wars that no Holy Coat pilgrimage took place in Trier throughout the eighteenth century. The enlightened church hierarchy of the time was opposed to pilgrimages on theological grounds. As I see it, however, the suspicion of pilgrimages on the part of the ruling landed Trier archbishops is more to be explained in terms of the way pilgrimages were organised. Since the late Middle Ages, or at least since the Reformation, they had been run first and foremost by religious brotherhoods, i.e. corporations of lay Christians, and not by the church and priesthood proper. Originally the church assumed close control over the corporation pilgrimages. The brotherhoods, however, had always tended to develop a devotional dynamic of their own. In the eighteenth century, pilgrimages in the Rhineland had reached such a pitch that, in the Trier district at Whitsun, for example, 'the whole diocese' was said to have been 'on the move'. The last Elector of Trier, Bishop Clemens Wenzeslaus, tried in the 1770s to curb this proliferating growth by means of strict prohibitions. Thus the episcopal Vicariate-General proceeded, for example, against the so-called 'apostles' who accompanied all processions in Limburg. They were enjoined to remove their misshapen headgear, to desist from 'bellowing' while praying and to 'abstain in future from all clapping of the hands, waving of the fingers, and kissing' during the solemn arrival of the Good Friday procession. These measures sprang not merely from the revulsion of enlightened theologians at the carnival atmosphere of most pilgrimages and places of pilgrimage but from freely avowed, if ill-defined, political anxiety at uncontrolled popular activity: unease at the sight of the pilgrims 'idling and swarming around', concern at the 'enthusiasm of the common people'. The prince's measures were so wide-ranging that large pilgrimage centres suffered severe economic setbacks. This was particularly true of the city of Trier, which had in any case been pushed into a marginal economic position since the seventeenth century. Significantly, the revolutionary disturbances in Trier in 1789 can also be attributed to the Electoral prohibitions on processions. In 1790 the City Magistrate of Trier, impressed by these disturbances, prevailed upon Clemens Wenzeslaus to have the 'Holy Coat' returned to Trier from the fortress of Ehrenbreitstein, where it had been evacuated. Owing to further revolutionary events, however, there was no public exposition.

Although the Bishop of Trier, Mannay, organised a pilgrimage to the 'Holy Coat' in 1810, with Napoleon's support, this was not the signal for a free resumption of pilgrimages. The French also tried to restrict processions in the areas of the old Reich that they had occupied. The religious corporations in the Rhenish departments were dissolved by consular decree on 9 June 1802. All processions, regarded as 'arlequinades sacerdotales et rassemblements fanatiques', were met with hostility. It was only during the transition period between French and Prussian rule that the wild pilgrimage spirit flared up again in the areas on the left bank of the Rhine in the former religious Electorates of Cologne and Trier. The suppressed brotherhoods re-formed. It would be jumping to conclusions, though, to connect the organised Holy Coat pilgrimage of 1844 with the general upsurge of pilgrimages in the second and third decades of the century. This upsurge was, in fact, a passing phase. The Restoration Prussian state insisted, as is known, on the late-absolutist conception of an established state church. The Catholic Church in Prussia, its economic and social base critically affected during the French revolutionary period by the secularisation measures, was at first hardly in a position to keep free of the leading-strings of an authoritarian state. Rebuilding church organisation, and procuring and providing long-term security for church finances, were the main priorities. In addition, the Archbishop of Cologne, Count August Spiegel, and his Trier colleague, Joseph von Hommer — both latter-day representatives of the old aristocratic imperial church — were favourably disposed towards the Prussian practice of a restored established state church. It is not surprising, therefore, that the actions of the Rhenish church leaders and of the Prussian state government during the 1820s and early 1830s coincided to hold down the pilgrimage movement in Rhine Province.

On the state side this policy was pursued systematically, after it had become clear in the early 1820s that the first Prussian pilgrimage regulations of 1816-17 had remained largely ineffective. In August 1825 the Prussian Minister of Public Worship and Education, von Altenstein, ordered a detailed survey of all pilgrimages in Rhine Province. All district presidents in the province were asked to provide 'as exact a list as possible of public pilgrimages occurring in their district, with accounts of distances travelled, approximate numbers of participants, the time customarily spent on pilgrimages and the time of year in which such pilgrimages are held'. From the research of the district presidents — which was painstaking, though mainly a matter of estimates — it emerged that in Rhine Province in the mid-1820s about 150,000 people per year made journeys of pilgrimage, out of a total population (in 1828) of 2,203,000. The correspondence of the authorities shows that the government regarded pilgrimages less from the viewpoint of church policy than from those of state security and the economy. It was laboriously calculated that subjects going on pilgrimage spent 75,000 thalers a year, leaving out of account losses caused by the 'suspension of commercial activity'. It was feared above all, however, that the uncontrolled activity of the 'lower classes' might endanger the security of the state. The interest of an 'intelligent state officialdom' (Altenstein) lay, ultimately, in defeating pilgrimages by indirect means. An ordinance of Altenstein's to the Düsseldorf government on 7 February 1839 says explicitly:

Inasmuch as pilgrimages are indeed an evil, they must be combatted from within, by the promotion of newer thinking. Outward hostility may easily make the evil worse, and there would be a danger of provoking the fanaticism of the lowest classes against the state government by a direct assault on its religious interests, a result which is now, particularly, to be avoided.

Only the Catholic clergy was capable of carrying out the task of enlightening the potential masses of pilgrims in the way that Altenstein wished. In point of fact, Spiegel and Hommer had always been ready to fulfil the task the state required of them. In a pastoral letter of May 1826, Spiegel had already attempted to dissuade members of his diocese from taking part in pilgrimages, using the enlightenment theological argument that 'God and His Saints' were not bound to any single place. Fully in accord with the government, he warned as much against 'neglect of the obligations of occupation and rank' as against 'coarsest excesses'. In similar fashion, if more restrainedly, Hommer sought in 1827 to deter his flock from pilgrimages on the ground that they opened the door 'immodestis et excessibus scandalosis'. He attempted to get a picture, by means of questionnaires sent out to his priests, of the existence and activities of brotherhoods and of the prevalence of processions, in order to have criteria for assessing pilgrimages and placing them under stricter surveillance. In a letter Spiegel summarised the goal of the joint efforts of the Prussian government and the Catholic hierarchy in the Rhineland: 'Devotion and piety are nourished, order, diligence and work in the domestic realm are not interrupted, expense is spared, and there is less cause for moral transgression.'

IV

The united hostility of the Prussian government and the Rhenish church hierarchy towards the phenomenon of mass pilgrimages prevailed until 1836, the year of the deaths of both Spiegel and Hommer. Eight years later, the mass pilgrimage to Trier took place, at the church's instigation and with state approval. At first sight, then, a totally new situation in church policy seems to have emerged. Nevertheless, a striking degree of continuity with regard to pilgrimages can also be perceived during the years 1836-42.

It is well known that the Catholic Church in the Rhineland and the Prussian police and bureaucratic state came into conflict over fundamentals of church policy during these years and that the church seemed to be being driven into the camp of the state's enemies. The so-called 'Cologne Disturbances' stand out in this conflict: in the course of them, the Archbishop of Cologne, Droste-Vischering, was imprisoned by the Prussian authorities. It is less well known that during exactly the same period there occurred what contemporaries themselves called the 'Trier Disturbances'. In Trier, it took six years for a new bishop to be selected and approved after the death of Hommer; in Cologne, the question of so-called 'mixed marriages' took equally long; and in both cases what was at stake was the state's right to intervene in official church business — i.e. in matters which the Rhenish Catholic Church leadership claimed to be internal questions.

This collision of claims to authority between church and state did not come from out of the blue. It must, it is agreed, be seen in the context of the controversy within the church between a traditionalist, strict-ecclesiastical tendency and a late-absolutist, state-church trend — in hierarchical terms, between 'ultramontanism' (i.e. centralist loyalty to Rome) and 'state episcopalism'. With the ultramontanists' victory within the Rhenish church leadership, the Catholic Church acquired a spirit of independence *vis-à-vis* the Prussian government which the Prussian bureaucracy, accustomed to the subordination of a state church, at first misconstrued as provocative and threatening. Some elements in the Rhenish middle class felt the time was at hand when an alliance between liberalism and the church might be formed in Germany, following the French and, especially, the Belgian precedents. In reality, neither option was available to the Catholic Church. Rather, the Catholic leadership and the Prussian state government continued to be allied on a conservative basis against the forces of revolution that threatened them. The Cologne and Trier conflicts merely altered the modalities of their collaboration. Henceforward it was a question, not of the subordination of church to state, but of their equality and co-operation. Here was the origin of the theory of the alliance between throne and altar. Certainly, the vehemence of the conflict at first concealed from contemporaries the fact that its most important product was precisely the continuation, through change, of the relationship between state and Catholic Church. Nevertheless, the Trier pilgrimage of 1844 was already a first indication of the new disposition of forces in the field of revolution and conservative tenacity.

The pilgrimage to the cathedral relic in Trier was launched in 1844 by Bishop Wilhelm Arnoldi. Hagiographical church histories have painted a stylised picture of Arnoldi as a non-political *anima candida*. He was no such thing, however. The care with which he prepared and publicised the pilgrimage venture contradicts this in the first place. Pamphlets, tracts, newspaper articles and, especially, sermons boosted the pilgrimage, inside and outside the Trier diocese, from the spring of 1844 onwards. Arnoldi devoted special efforts to influencing the press. He put pressure on the middle-class, radical *Triersche Zeitung*, of the critical attitude of which towards the church's pilgrimage policy he was well aware, by inducing the clergy and Catholic dignitaries in the city of Trier to impose a boycott. The threatened loss of Catholic subscribers caused the newspaper so to restrain itself during the pilgrimage affair that it was rebuked by the fellow-radical *Sächsische Vaterlandsblätter* for glossing over the issue and approving of the pilgrimage, as well as for using 'hypocritical and ambiguous language'. Earlier, in 1843, the Koblenz *Rhein- und Moselzeitung* had been forced by a similar boycott to accede to the influence of the strict-ecclesiastical circle of Koblenz intellectuals centred round Joseph Dietz. Significantly, however, the decisive shift in this paper's editorial policy took place only in June 1844. The new ultramontane line therefore first came fully into view during the Trier pilgrimage. It is as good as certain that this publicity backing was synchronised with Arnoldi's project, although the relationship between the Koblenz activists and their bishop was not without its tensions. The Bishop of Trier clearly also had a hand in the petition of Trier citizens of late 1844 which demanded (to no avail) the lifting of the ban on the *Historisch-Politische Blätter* that was in force in Prussia. There are a striking number of clerics among the signatories, with the canon, Müller, at their head.

Arnoldi's most important publicity manoeuvre, however, was in Luxemburg. Here, from 1 July 1844, at his initiative and at that of the Luxemburg Vicar Apostolic, Johann Theodor Laurent, the *Luxemburger Zeitung* began publication. Arnoldi seems not only to have had a financial role in this undertaking, but also to have recruited August Reichensperger, who had been transferred from Cologne to Trier as recently as February 1844, as a contributor to the new paper. Further, he no doubt hoped, by founding this newspaper, to bypass the restrictive Prussian press laws. At any rate, an application to move the editorial offices of the *Luxemburger Zeitung* to Trier was rejected in November 1844 by the Prussian Minister of the Interior, Count von Arnim. Apostrophised by the *Triersche Zeitung* as the most 'splendid oddity of the nineteenth century', the *Luxemburger Zeitung* was none the less the most important publicity organ of the Trier church leadership during the Holy Coat pilgrimage.

Arnoldi's political temper was revealed – more clearly than in his press policies, where he mainly stayed in the background – in his sermons and pastoral letters. He possessed pronounced gifts as an agitator: it was said in 1842 that he had preached his way to the bishopric. His sermons were in no way confined to pious edification; he took decisive stands on political questions. His Lent sermons of 1839, in particular, reveal a clear anti-revolutionary, conservative, traditionalist standpoint. In them he broadcast polemics against the 'abominable spectre of revolution', attacked the 'enemies of religion' with their 'hollow phrases of popular happiness and freedom' and condemned the 'fanatical, irreligious or tyrannical adherents of party'. In his pastoral letter of 6 January 1845 critics of the pilgrimage, especially Ronge's German Catholic counter-movement, were sent packing as 'abetters of unbelief and revolution'. From this counter-revolutionary position, he was able to commend the church as the guarantor of the monarchic state:

> The sacred authority of the church is the greatest bulwark of the sovereign's throne; and as long as the Catholic shall be a faithful child of his church, so long shall he also be a faithful subject. For our Mother Church warns ceaselessly against the irreligious and seditious principles that, sometimes covertly, sometimes openly, penetrate society in manifold forms and throw it into ferment.

It must remain an open question whether or not Arnoldi acted on his own initiative when he switched from being a propagandist to being an activist on behalf of counter-revolutionary church politics. He told his own cathedral chapter, the members of the diocese and the Prussian government authorities in 1844 that 'pious requests' for a pilgrimage had repeatedly been conveyed to him. There is no doubt, certainly, that memories of the 1810 pilgrimage remained vivid in the Trier region during the Prussian period. Bishop von Hommer seems to have aired earlier the question of a new staging of the pilgrimage – at any rate, he was deeply enough taken up with the matter of the 'Holy Coat' for a brief written account to have been produced. In it, he posed the question whether 'the thing is indeed genuine'. His answer was: 'Complete certainty as regards the genuineness of the Holy Coat cannot, therefore, be demanded.' This carefully neutral verdict chimes exactly with his attitude towards the idea of pilgrimages altogether. It seems likely, then, that he would consistently have refused to organise a new exposition of the Coat in Trier.

Hommer's recognition, however, that pilgrimages were 'never entirely to be done away with' was also borne out in the case of the Trier Coat. After his death, discussions about a new cathedral pilgrimage began afresh. They can, at any rate, be traced back to 1841, the period of interregnum between bishops. In July of that year, the *Triersche Zeitung* got going a vigorous controversy over the religious meaning of pilgrimages. Peter Alois Licht, a priest from the little Mosel village of Leiwen, north of Trier, who had already come to the fore in 1831 as one of the so-called Trier 'reform' priests, criticised pilgrimages as 'religious nonsense' and as 'a mockery of thoughtful Catholicism'. A terse rejoinder was followed by several contributions, mainly polemical, from opponents of pilgrimages. By contrast, the newspaper declined to print an extended reply by Jakob Marx, the Trier professor of ecclesiastical history and an adept propagandist, in which a pro-pilgrimage position was adopted. Marx was obliged to publish the rejected article as a pamphlet. His argument was certainly tactically appropriate, while still unambiguously spelling out the basic position: it did not amount to an unconditional defence of the Catholic cult of pilgrimages. He ranked pilgrimages lower than parish services, and described them as 'not essential for spiritual welfare'. Provided, however, that they were overseen by priests and protected from abuses, he had no objection to them. Indeed, he regarded them, if conducted well, as beneficial. Neither in Marx nor in his adversary Licht is there any overt reference to the 'Holy Coat' as an object of pilgrimage. It is striking, however, that they had already adopted, in 1841, the rival ideological postures that defined the internal church discussion of the Trier pilgrimage in 1844: in Licht's case, the hostility of a theologically and philosophically trained priestly caste towards the devotional practices of the broad lay masses; in Marx's, the notion of control and exploitation of these lay customs for purposes of church policy. Strikingly, too, both men at once proceeded to immerse themselves more deeply in the subject of pilgrimages. In 1842 each produced a further pamphlet. In the same year, too, Licht reacted to a public call by the *Triersche Zeitung* for a new Holy Coat pilgrimage, in which a 'speedier circulation of money' and 'material advantages' for the city were invoked: this time, however, his contribution seems not to have been accepted. In 1842 the Piesport priest Philipp Lichter also came out in print against Licht for the first time; in 1844 he was one of the more banal defenders of the Holy Coat pilgrimage. Licht's 1845 pamphlet, finally, 'Katholische Stimmen gegen die Triersche Ausstellung im Jahre 1844' ['Catholic Voices against the Trier Exposition of 1844'], contains the only regional reaction of any weight against the Trier pilgrimage. Marx's book of 1844 [*Geschichte des heil. Rockes in der Domkirche zu Trier*] constituted the most important piece of advance political publicity for the pilgrimage, and his 1845 work [*Die Ausstellung des h. Rockes in der Domkirche zu Trier im Herbste des Jahres 1844*] was its semi-official summary and evaluation.

On the basis of this propagandist activity, Marx should be seen as the source of ideological inspiration, and the true strategist, of the pilgrimage of 1844. Various factors indicate that he, more than anyone else, influenced Bishop Arnoldi over the pilgrimage question, or at least enjoyed his special confidence. Supporting this assumption is the fact that Marx was a chaplain in Wittlich during the same period (1831-4) that Arnoldi was town parish priest there. Arnoldi had read Marx's pilgrimage pamphlet of 1842, as his extant personal copy shows. It is only through Marx, too, that we know that Arnoldi, shortly before his consecration as bishop, had conferred with Metternich in Koblenz in 1842 about activating the cult of the Trier relic. Indeed, the fact that it was precisely he who knew of this otherwise unknown conversation (and of its content) implies that he took part in it — as it also again proves, incidentally, Arnoldi's systematic political preparations for the pilgrimage. Finally, Marx claims to have written the document of consent to the 1844 pilgrimage 'at the request of His Lordship the Bishop of Trier', a claim which none of the other numerous pilgrimage publicists was able to make.

Marx declared quite openly that the Trier pilgrimage was a 'festival of the Church militant, yet also of the Church victorious and triumphant'. He extolled it without concealment as a festivity in which the 'attractive force of the Christian faith' had been revealed. At the same time, however, he rejected the accusation that the Trier events were conceivably therefore a 'demonstration' directed against public order. The pilgrimage's intention was not to 'intimidate, or deflect from its path, one party by proclaiming the opinions, the strength and the influence of another'. It had been 'aimed against no-one' and its 'motive and purpose' had lain 'within itself'. Here Marx attacked the attempt by the opponents of the pilgrimage to cast the church in the role of an enemy of the state: in the language of the ideology of the authoritarian Restoration state, it would thus have become a political 'party', contributing, by its propagation of certain 'opinions' or 'tendencies', to the break-up of the monarchic order. In Marx's view, however, this was quite impossible, 'for the Church is not a party, any more than the State is a party in regard to a tiny band of revolutionary subjects who would seek to overturn its Constitution and even to seize the governing power for themselves'. This was not mere rhetoric. Marx had already demonstrated his loyalty to the Restoration Prussian monarchy at the height of the church crisis in Cologne and Trier. Indeed, in 1838 he took an active part in the events surrounding the selection of the bishop of Trier, as an observer for the Rhenish Chief *Land* (Provincial) Administrator von Bodelschwingh. There can be no doubt, therefore, that the political stance of the church instigators of the relic exposition in Trier in 1844 was basically conservative. The point, for them, was not independence from the state, in the sense of 'church freedom' — a phrase often quoted, and often misinterpreted in a liberal sense — let alone the separation of church and state; it was, first and foremost, the demonstration of the powerful contribution the Catholic Church made towards sustaining the authority of the state in *Vormärz* society.

If this basic point is recognised, it is easier to see why the Prussian governmental authorities viewed the Trier pilgrimage with benevolent neutrality; indeed, with partial sympathy. Contemporary critics could not grasp how 'so enormous a concession on the part of the state' could be made to a church leadership which shortly beforehand had been suspected of rebellion and high subversion. The Trier pilgrimage, however, displayed to the Prussian state a church that represented the continuation of traditional co-operation over the control of pilgrimages, even if the methods were new. Indeed, no suspicion that the Trier pilgrimage might be an organised mass movement, with the church seeking an extension of its authority at the expense of that of the state, occurred to the government.

Arnoldi, in his communication with the Chief *Land* Administrator of the Prussian Rhine Province, von Schaper, on 19 April 1844, disclosing his plans for the pilgrimage, had immediately found the right words. His decision to stage a new pilgrimage, in accordance with the 'ancient tradition' of Trier, was in no way based on ecclesiastical and religious arguments. Instead, he made it his business to highlight the effect of the pilgrimage in sustaining state authority: 'The religious sentiment which prevails in pilgrimages', he wrote, 'is the best surety against all disorder.' To lend weight to this claim, he pointed out that there had 'not been the least disorder either' at the Trier pilgrimage of 1810 and that the septennial Aachen pilgrimage always took place 'without the slightest disturbance of public peace and safety'. He asked the Chief *Land* Administrator, in conclusion, for 'his kind co-operation' in neglecting no measures that 'might in any way serve to prevent disorder'. He made no fewer than four references to the point that the pilgrimage would pass off in 'peace' and 'order' or would contribute to their maintenance. 'Peace and Order' [*Ruhe und Ordnung*] was, indeed, the key political expression, cropping up in stereotypical fashion, of both church and state pronouncements on the Trier pilgrimage. This shared usage indicates a harmonising of political thinking, even though Prussian civil servants and Trier church leaders did not come to any explicit understanding. The formula 'Peace and Order' must, in fact, rank as one of the standard formulae of Restoration ruling-class ideology in the nineteenth century; indeed, it can be called the direct counter-formula of the revolutionary triad 'Liberty, Equality, Fraternity'. It was thus a matter of far-reaching significance when the Rhenish Chief *Land* Administrator, in his answer to Arnoldi, declared that he did not doubt that the 'celebration [would] take place without any disturbance of peace and order'. Although he by no means explicitly saluted Arnoldi's pilgrimage project, these words signalled to the bishop that he spoke the same political language. His attitude was matched by that of the subordinate Trier governmental officials whom the Chief *Land* Administrator had previously consulted. The Lord Mayor and Chief Administrator of Trier, Görtz, referring back to the 1810 pilgrimage, believed that 'peace and order' would be fully guaranteed if, once again, the pilgrims did not come individually but were brought to Trier in organised groups (processions). This message was passed on in turn by the District President. Certain reservations concerning Arnoldi's plan for the pilgrimage were, it is true, registered internally, by the Minister of Public Worship and Education, Eichhorn, and the Minister of the Interior, Adolf Heinrich Count von Arnim. They felt that the revival of 'ecclesiastical ceremonies' in Trier, 'in view of the conspicuous shortcomings that the identity of the said relic displays from the point of view of historical criticism, would, in the interests of the Catholic Church, have perhaps been best left undone'. Nevertheless, they authorised the Rhenish Chief *Land* Administrator to permit the pilgrimage, since 'doubts concerning general affairs of state' did not arise. This authorisation was granted on condition that there would be 'prompt communication with His Lordship the Bishop' in order to ensure 'appropriate dispersion of the processions and the maintenance of order by the police'. Despite acknowledging modern scientific and historical criticism, then, they were prepared to grant the Bishop of Trier one mass mobilisation in the Rhineland, provided that 'order' was not disrupted. The fact that order, in the ministers' statement, features as order maintained 'by the police' should not be interpreted to mean that they saw the pilgrimage as basically a mere police problem. The Restoration Prussian state was the 'state as order' (E.R. Huber): 'order' was thus, quite simply, the highest principle of state and the police the means of realising it. Reliance on police regulation was entailed in this general concept of the state.

The state government authorities could be certain that the Trier church leaders wished, by means of the pilgrimage, to support the principle of order in the Prussian monarchy, and not at all to call it in question. Not only was the same political language spoken on both sides, but actions followed suit. The church leadership and the government agreed from the start that the pilgrims should not be simply left to their own devices and that their processions should be closely planned beforehand. At the government's suggestion, the Trier church leaders worked out a detailed procession scheme on the lines of Bishop Mannay's pilgrimage regulation of 1810. The processions of pilgrims from the Trier diocese were thus worked out in advance, general-staff fashion. The parochial congregations of each deanery were allocated two 'suitably separated days' for the pilgrimage to Trier. Half of the parish members were to set out on each of the two dates. The first two days of September and the second half of the month (from 15 September onwards) were reserved for external processions. This division was meant to produce a relatively even flow of pilgrims to Trier, and the aim was achieved, if the opening days are left out of account. The individual processions were each assigned precise points of assembly in Trier. Routes through the city to the cathedral, inside the cathedral and out of the city again were all exactly laid down, with bureaucratic reporting procedures to ensure their observance. But the critical and fundamental point is that the organisation of the processions was not left to religious brotherhoods, say, or even to chance, but was strictly placed in the hands of the parish priests. Pilgrims from every three parishes had to unite into one procession, each of which was led by at least one priest. Before arriving in Trier, the processions from the sub-districts ('definitions') of each deanery had likewise to merge into single processions, again headed by a priest as 'principal leader'. Parish priests were required to ask for 'the fullest acquiescence in the relevant regulations' on the part of the participants, with the result that the clergy was assured of a role of leadership and authority in the pilgrimage. A contemporary opponent of the pilgrimage noted:

> It was not a voluntary, organic popular movement, taking its own shape: it was fabricated, stirred up from outside with all available means — a plain matter of agitation. The cathedral chapters put themselves at the head, they issued instructions to the deans, the deans commissioned the parish priests with making appeals and arousing enthusiasm, the priests worked upon the people. Meeting-points were determined; days were set when the solemn processions would depart, with flags flying, drums beating and cannons firing; stops for refreshment were arranged: in short, a complicated strategic plan was drawn up, in which everything was already disposed and decided upon before the people, whose part was to play the puppet in the hands of the puppet-master, had heard a single word about it.

The Trier pilgrimage was thus fundamentally different from the numerous processions of pilgrims in the Rhineland that had been jointly opposed by the Rhenish bishops and the Prussian government in the 1820s and 1830s. The question, in the Trier case, was not whether the diffuse pilgrimage activity of the lower social strata might pose a revolutionary threat to the Restoration state system; rather, it should be seen as a successful attempt by the Rhenish clergy to secure, from above, pro-state influence over broad masses of people in an ecclesiastical sense. Jakob Marx's subsequent assessment was not unfounded: by means of the pilgrimage, 'the peace, order and edifying spirit of a temple — of a House of God — had come to pass everywhere'. For him, the revitalisation of the church, and its firm anchorage in the people, also had a pro-state significance. Prussian officials, too, saw in the pilgrimage a 'gratifying sign of the growing influence of the priesthood and of the obedience of the faithful towards their spiritual pastors'. On both sides, then, independently of their differing religious standpoints, the planning, direction and assessment of the Trier pilgrimage indicated an anti-revolutionary concern for security that was to form the basis in the future for a long-lasting conservative *rapprochement* between the Catholic Church and the Prusso-German state.

This interpretation is abundantly confirmed by the behaviour of Arnoldi and Jakob Marx in the 1848 revolution. In Trier on 14 April both men, along with other dignitaries, signed the election manifesto of the advocate Friedrich Zell, which came out against violent subversion and the republic, called for a constitutional monarchy on a pan-German, federalist basis and appealed, in the hackneyed phrase, for 'Peace and Order'. In the crisis of 1848, then, the leaders of the Trier pilgrimage of 1844 redeemed their anti-revolutionary pledges. It is no surprise that the Trier democrats, with Ludwig Simon, Karl Grün and Victor Schily at their head, publicly burned Zell's election manifesto.

V

Now that the intentions of the organisers of the pilgrimage have been made clear, we must still discuss whether and to what extent their political calculations worked out. We must ask how the mass of pilgrims drawn by the spectacle in Trier were induced to embark and what sort of consciousness they developed during the pilgrimage. This takes us into the difficult methodological territory of the social history of ideas and the problem of inquiring into the mentality of predominantly illiterate people. Because of the rigid pilgrimage regulation, the Trier pilgrims did not in general feature as individuals: they set out in groups, and were likewise led in groups past the supposed Holy Coat. The horizon of their experience was the procession of hundreds, sometimes thousands, of participants. They were thus held, from the outset, to a form of ritualised group behaviour that took its cue from the familiar range of experiences connected with normal church ritual (parish processions on Good Friday, Whitsun or Corpus Christi). Individual pilgrims made their pilgrimage collectively, not after deep and careful reflection. To that extent we can assume that the pilgrims' consciousness bore the uniform stamp of a group-specific mentality. There was, let us say, the mentality of a pilgrims' collective.

Only the inhabitants of the city of Trier were something of an exception in this respect. Supporters of the pilgrimage described their behaviour as an effusion of collective religious emotion. The statistician Delahaye, for example, gave the following account:

The prevalent mood in Trier was therefore, necessarily, the best and most gratifying, and it was as though the exposition of the Holy Coat had caused a new spirit to enter among us: the spirit of piety, friendship and love. Never before had greater charity and fellow-feeling been seen. Indeed, each citizen of Trier, in accordance with the teachings of our religion, regarded other men as his brothers, and it seemed as though all in Trier were members of one family.

Edifying idylls of this sort, however, were disputed by militant opponents of the pilgrimage. Their most powerful charge was that the people of Trier were only interested in money. The 'monetary speculation of the tradesmen and innkeepers of Trier, and the covetousness of the cathedral clergy' were particularly pilloried. In fact, according to the carefully kept accounts of the cathedral bursar, the cathedral's receipts from donations were quite considerable. They amounted to 16,952 thalers, 14 silver groschen, 4 pfennigs, as against merely 2,273 thalers, 4 silver groschen, 8 pfennigs in expenditure. Arnoldi passed on half (7,327 thalers) of the net receipts to the president of the church committee that was responsible for the rebuilding of the episcopal seminary. The Cologne cathedral building fund received 211 thalers, 5 silver groschen, 9 pfennigs, expressly collected for this purpose. The outcome of the pilgrimage, however, was a source of satisfaction to the higher Trier clergy not so much because of the filling of the collection boxes as because of the opportunity they had gained for influencing unexpectedly large masses of pilgrims. Arnoldi, on his own admission, was in a state of 'continuous joyful excitement' owing to the daily influxes of tens of thousands of pilgrims.

The case of the Trier citizenry was rather different. There can be no doubt that a large number of people in Trier welcomed the influx of pilgrims mainly because it promised extra profits. In addition to the regular commercial supply of places of accommodation, beds for 1,787 people and straw mattresses for 10,396 were made available in private houses. At least 197 people obtained restaurant and liquor concessions from the City Magistrate for the duration of the display. Specially large market booths and stalls were set up in two central squares in the inner city. Resident traders and shopkeepers were at pains to ensure that outsiders did not obtain sales concessions for these stalls from the city authorities. None the less, business did not at first go as well as had been expected. Petitions to the Lord Mayor and to the District President were the result. In the end, however, at least the traders in devotional articles seem to have recovered their costs. In particular, pictures and medallions of the 'Holy Coat', and rosaries made out of all conceivable manner of materials, were disposed of in 'incredible quantities'. An impartial witness reported that a single woman trader, even in the week before the relic went on display, was selling for 400 thalers apiece 'little Coats of the Lord' which she had made out of old remnants of ribbon. Two other traders are reported to have sold, respectively, 80,000 and 52,000 medallions of the Virgin Mary in three weeks.

Trier's interest in the pilgrimage, then, certainly had a lot to do with the profits of small traders, landlords and craftsmen. But even they were not motivated only by business considerations during the pilgrimage. Significantly, in fact, the Trier lower middle class rushed to join the so-called 'Guard of Honour' that organised security in the cathedral during the pilgrimage. Nine guild 'unions' combined to set up this Guard of Honour (building artisans, tailors, firebrigadesmen, Trier master boatmen, Barbeln master boatmen, butchers, coopers, joiners and bakers). They mobilised no fewer than 1,062 citizens of Trier, very largely from within their own ranks, to perform guard duty in the cathedral over the 50 days of the exposition. Even if the profit motive at first took precedence in many cases, the lower middle class in Trier was thus gradually sucked into the pilgrimage collective — this quite apart from the fact, indeed, that at the outset of the pilgrimage (on 18 and 19 August) the Trier parishes processed to the cathedral in serried ranks. What was taking place here was a process which may, in the terminology of modern sociology, be called one of 'socialisation'. Individuals within the pilgrimage milieu developed expectations of integration and subordination that compelled conformity of behaviour. The extent to which this process of socialisation went is shown particularly strikingly in the behaviour of Jenny von Westphalen, the Protestant official's daughter who had been married to Karl Marx since June 1843. Only a temporary visitor in Trier, she was an outsider in the pilgrimage city in more than a denominational sense. None the less, her mother made a room available for visiting pilgrims, and Jenny herself acquired 'a little medallion' for her child and 'a little rosary'. Even though the growing hubbub over the pilgrimage seemed to her to be going 'to extremes', hers was clearly a case of the conformation of someone on the social margin to the behaviour-pattern of the Trier pilgrimage collective. We may exclude the possibility, incidentally, that Jenny Marx, specifically, was a unique instance. We simply know more about her than we do about other, anonymous, individuals. In any event, Protestants occasionally came out publicly in favour of the pilgrimage. It is probable, even, that individual Protestants came to Trier as pilgrims, especially from the Saar, at that time half-Protestant.

If we try to characterise more precisely the mentality-structure of the Trier pilgrimage collective, the question at once arises how it was actually transmitted. We can certainly at once rule out the idea that simple pilgrims got hold of the polemical scholarly publications that went into the historical traditions and archaeological authenticity of the Trier relic. The great mass of pilgrims would never have seen anything, either, of the flood of less scholarly pamphlets generated by the pilgrimage. It is probably true that only a minority of pilgrims were completely illiterate. None the less, few of them had much to do with books. Rudolf Schenda has shown convincingly that the reading-matter of the literate members of all social classes in Germany in the early nineteenth century was confined, basically, to primers, the Catechism and the Bible. At most, devotional books were also bought. This thesis is confirmed by the Trier pilgrimage. Within the Trier diocese, no fewer than twelve cheap, small devotional books were put onto the market for the simple pilgrims, with episcopal approval, perhaps even at episcopal instigation. These booklets are all very alike in format and intellectual level. We can assume that they all performed the same function, even if each individual pilgrim bought only one of them for himself. The popular devotional books thus undoubtedly formed the intellectual reservoir from which the mentality of the pilgrimage collective was supplied. For when 'speech' proved inadequate, the pilgrims 'gave vent to their feelings in song'.

For the most part, these devotional booklets contain religious songs, liturgical directions and popular accounts of the tradition of the 'Holy Coat'. What is interesting about them is not the material stemming from the traditional stock of Roman Catholic liturgy (the Mass, particularly): the important things are the texts that were produced expressly for the pilgrimage. Three points seem to me to arise from consideration of them.

In the first place, the suggestion is implanted that the Trier Holy Coat relic is genuine. It is said, flatly, that the 'unbroken tradition of the church in Trier, acknowledged by the church's highest leaders', testifies to the relic's authenticity. If the books do not simply suppress the fact that the tradition is not securely established further back than the twelfth century, they try to account for this gap with the argument that the church had to keep the existence of the precious relic a secret during periods of war. Finally, there is a particularly noteworthy juxtaposition of the 'Holy Coat' story with a sort of supplementary legend:

> The seamless Holy Coat of Christ was, according to the evidence adduced here, skilfully woven for Her Son Jesus Christ by the Blessed Virgin Mary. For womenfolk in the East were wont to manufacture their own clothes, as we learn from the Holy Bible.

Quite evidently, this manipulation of legends was meant to link the veneration of the Trier relic to the well-tried cult of the Virgin. The familiar figure of Mary gave the 'Holy Coat' the final seal of approval, on top of the backing it received from the Trier pilgrimage collective in any case by way of the materials in the devotional books. The pilgrims undoubtedly believed, without reservation, that the fabric on display was the last item of clothing worn by the historical figure of Jesus. The dogmatic ruling of the Roman Catholic Church that had prevailed since the Council of Trent, that relics were to be exposed for veneration and not for worship, was virtually power-less in the face of this conviction, even though many propagandists for the pilgrimage emphasised the distinction. It is quite probable, therefore, that many people were heard to pray, 'O Holy Coat, intercede for us', and that the addition to the *Ave Maria*, 'Thou Who didst wear the Holy Coat for us', was 'so widespread among the processions' that it was 'as though the Bishop had prescribed it'.

The second mentality-component arises directly from the first: the devotional booklets fed the pilgrims' naïve faith in miracles. There was, for example, a 'Litany of the Holy Coat', which in fact amounted to a litany of the miracles Jesus of Nazareth was supposed to have performed 'in his Holy Coat'. Numerous songs celebrated 'the Coat in which Our Saviour/His miracles performed'. And in the pilgrimage catechism the implied physical survival of the Holy Coat throughout the life of Jesus was also, quite super-erogatorily, characterised as a miracle. One miracle is thus 'explained' in terms of another. It is hardly surprising, therefore, that the Trier pilgrimage collective was almost limitlessly predisposed towards the finding of miracles. Reports of supposed miracle cures accumulated and were assiduously cir-culated by the church. The case of the Westphalian Countess Johanna von Droste-Vischering caused a particular stir. After a week, the bishop was forced to accede to what were called the pilgrims' 'urgent requests' and permit general touching of the relic. This ritual touching also drew in the numerous devotional objects which the pilgrims acquired in Trier. The mentality of the pilgrims' collective thus revealed pronounced symptoms of magical religion.

The effects can be memorably exemplified from the diary of a woman pilgrim from Koblenz that has fortunately been preserved. The painstaking reports of this simple woman show that the pilgrims were exposed to con-siderable physical deprivation on their journeys. Marching for days on end, the woman was able to pay only for damp straw bedding, weak coffee and a little food. Nevertheless, she walked from one place to the next, and one church service to the next, in a state of positively chiliastic expectancy, before finally arriving at Trier Cathedral in her procession. Here she wit-nessed how 'everyone wept' when a lame priest was carried into the cathedral for the procuring of a miracle. She herself pinned all her hopes on getting into the cathedral a second time, after her initial attendance in the procession, so that she could 'get touched' 'several religious things' that she had bought in the interval. And she did indeed have 'the good fortune to be able to kneel down before the Holy Coat for a moment'. When she returned home, she recorded relief from chills as her own private Holy Coat miracle.

A third element, finally, in the mentality-structure of the pilgrimage was that of compensation. The pilgrims sang a song about 'The Coat of Poverty', part of which runs:

> He too was always poor and needy
> When He dwelt with us here on earth.
> Do not complain, then, humble people,
> If life is hard and full of woe:
> For Jesus bore far greater sorrows
> Because He loved His children so.

The pauperised pilgrims thus found consolation even in their sorry social condition. They accepted, in place of a present-day solution of social problems, the promise of redemption in an imagined hereafter.

This was the very point on which the critics of the pilgrimage fastened. An anonymous writer from Wesel was particularly reproachful:

> Our time is a hard one: it weighs upon our German land like an oppressive nightmare. Public penury is in a condition of dreadful increase; distress mounts; hunger cries out for a scrap of dry bread; despair has awakened and cast aside the terrors of authority; crime bestirs itself and stalks abroad; the bells of insurrection have sounded in this Germany of peace and toleration, and the red torch of strife glowed in the hands of once calm and industrious men. These are the signs of hard times in our country, who will gainsay them? And while the public weal thus languishes, while nagging cares and sorrows cause alarm, and misery cries woe and weeps — now is it that the false, provoked religious sentiment of our time applies its salvations to the human heart.

Here, the Trier pilgrimage is being unambiguously linked to the Silesian weavers' rising of the same year: alarm at the sensational hunger rising leads to criticism of a church that seeks to compensate for the 'languishing public weal' by appeal to salvation in the next world.

Significantly, a whole string of ultramontanist writers did not dispute the diversionary character of the religious events in Trier. It was admitted that the Trier pilgrims were predominantly poor and intellectually and politically immature. Thus, the pilgrimage was a time of 'happy relaxation' for these people, enabling them to overcome for a while the 'monotony of daily circumstances', to forget 'for a short time all distinctions in life's fortunes'. An anonymous writer asked:

> Shall the poor man, then, merely because he is poor, never look out beyond the confines of his lowly estate? Shall he always remain immured in his pitiful cottage, beneath his needy thatch? False friends of the people, who sit before your groaning boards and sparkling wines, and offer your counsel on the means of preventing the misery of the poor — continue, then, continue to imprison the poor, imprison them day and night in factories, imprison them on Sundays and holidays in their home!

It is noteworthy that this writer, too, connects the Trier pilgrimage with the Silesian weavers' rising (he describes it as the 'disturbances among the Silesian workers'). His conclusions, however, were derived from traditional Christian sentiments of devotion and charity: religion was, for him, 'quite peculiarly consolatory for the poor here on earth'. Most of the poor who had been to Trier, he said, had 'henceforth borne their misery and hardship more patiently and more joyfully'.

Other apologists for the pilgrimage put it even more clearly:

> The Gospels, however, convey to all men without distinction the consolatory teaching of God's love, by pointing, from amidst the inequality of wealth on earth, towards the Kingdom of Heaven. The man who keeps this teaching in his heart is contented with his portion in the present unequal division of wealth, even if he must earn his bread by the sweat of his brow.

And:

> Those, however, who seek to introduce Communism by stealth, and, moreover, in the manner displayed by the *Breslauer Zeitung* and Ronge's letter — they are greatly in error: they arouse the dissatisfaction of the proletarians with God and the world; they make them covet the property of others, and they prepare the way for such disturbances as we have seen in our mountains; they cause the innocent and guilty alike to become victims of the mob.

Here, the Christian doctrine activated by the Trier pilgrimage is being propagated as an immunisation device against the spread of communism.

Another pro-pilgrimage writer, arguing similarly, showed realism and foresight: 'I say to you that, until you find means of satisfying, more effectively than the church does, the needs which the church is so well able to satisfy, all your efforts will be in vain.' He concluded with an appeal 'to work for an improvement of actual conditions'. For the time being, the church was far superior in influence 'among the common people upon whom we presume to make an impression'.

Without a doubt, this perception showed a thorough recognition of the results of the Trier pilgrimage. Even during the pilgrimage, many observers were struck by the astonishing submissiveness of the pilgrims towards the priests who accompanied them. In his unofficial summing-up Jakob Marx asserted with satisfaction that, thanks to the pilgrimage, the links between parishioners and priests, and between parishes and the bishop, had been significantly improved. The radical Mainz ultramontanist Caspar Riffel wrote in similar vein: 'And, with the people in procession trustfully following the leadership of their priests, an even firmer and more lasting bond was forged between them.' Even Prussian civil servants regarded the pilgrims' submissiveness towards the priesthood's authoritarian leadership as a gratifying result of the Trier pilgrimage.

The fact that the Catholic Church leadership was able, by means of an enterprise like the Trier pilgrimage, to secure its conservative influence over the masses was a pointer to the braking role it was to play in the middle-class revolution of 1848-9. The Catholic Church was successful at the first attempt where the middle-class movement of 1848 foundered and where the labour movement was still unprepared – namely, in securing a long-term, broad, mass foundation. Having thus tested in advance its understanding with Restoration state power, the church hierarchy was able, after 1849, to act as an element in the reactionary stabilisation of the system, despite all the later attempts by a Catholic emancipation movement to urge the clerical leadership into an alliance with middle-class (and, indeed, reluctant) liberalism. By 1852, a Catholic professor of theology had already summed up his church's policy in the revolution:

Every aspect of supreme state authority tottered this way and that, in the upheaval; only the church's organic framework stood firm, just as it did during the decline of Roman authority in the West – and, as then, so now the church again proved to be the most conservative force in society, and one which, as events showed, is more indispensable to it than ever.

Notes

[1. *Vormärz*: literally, 'pre-March'. The period of German and Austrian history between the Congress of Vienna in 1815 and the March revolution of 1848.

2. Joseph Görres (1776-1848), writer and journalist, one of the German Romantics. After 1827 he was the leader of a Catholic academic circle in Munich and perhaps the most important intellectual influence on Catholic thought in Germany.

3. *Kulturkampf*: the conflict between the state and the Catholic Church in Bismarck's Imperial Germany (especially Prussia) after 1871.]

4 CRIME AND NINETEENTH-CENTURY SOCIETY

A. CRIME AND INDUSTRIAL SOCIETY IN THE NINETEENTH CENTURY (extract)

J.J. Tobias

Source: *Crime and Industrial Society in the Nineteenth Century* (Batsford, 1967).

It will perhaps seem natural to a twentieth-century reader that a discussion of the effect of economic and social conditions on crime in the nineteenth century should commence with poverty. However, the first point to note is that in fact poverty, in the sense of the immediate pressure of want, was not throughout the century regarded as a prime cause of crime. It may be said in general terms that it was only in the years immediately after Waterloo that such a view was held.

However, the Royal Commission on a Constabulary Force which reported in 1839 took a different view. Crime, it said, was not caused by want but by the superior attractions of a criminal life.

We have investigated the origin of the great mass of crime committed for the sake of property, and we find the whole ascribable to one common cause, namely, the temptations of the profit of a career of depredation, as compared with the profits of honest and even well-paid industry. . . . The notion that any considerable proportion of the crimes against property are caused by blameless poverty or destitution we find disproved at every step.

The Commission's Report was written virtually single-handed by Edwin Chadwick, and Professor S.E. Finer says that he used a 'smoke-screen of "evidence"' as a means of re-presenting in 1839 his proposals for police reform made in 1829. Whatever use Chadwick made of it, the evidence was there. Enough of it survives to testify to the thoroughness of his investigations and to show that, on this issue as on many others, the view put forward in the Report is a fair reflection of the opinions of the witnesses. The Report either transformed the views of the general public about the effect of want on crime (which is by no means impossible, for it had a profound influence on thought on criminal matters) or is the expression of a new attitude just making itself felt; from 1839 we hear much less about the effect of want. From this time contemporary opinion plays down the effect of poverty in the direct sense.

Cyclical fluctuations in trade were none the less still thought to have an effect on crime. At mid century there were those who argued that committals to prison were correlated with the state of trade and with wheat prices. This was by no means a unanimous view, however. Then and later there was a well-informed body of opinion which felt that any connection between trade fluctuations and crime worked the other way. Crime was thought to be higher in good times, because of the greater quantities of drink consumed. Matthew Davenport Hill, the Recorder of Birmingham, in 1857 wrote: 'In the manufacturing districts a flush of prosperity, which suddenly enhances the rate of wages, overwhelms the working classes with temptations to indulge in liquor — a cause of crime which is more potent for its increase than the diffusion of plenty is for its diminution.' The Rev. J.W. Horsley, a prison chaplain, found the same thing in London in the 1880s: 'Our prison population rises with prosperity and the consequent power of getting drink. Bad times and the slackness of work in winter produces less crime, and not more.'

The view that crime was not as a rule the result of want appears to have been generally correct. However, an analysis of the connection between the two must begin by making a distinction between the commission of crimes by those who were already members of the criminal class and the commission of crimes by those hitherto honest.

For members of the criminal class crime was a bread-and-butter matter. When funds were low they went out to raise more, in the spirit of the frontiersman taking down his gun when the time came to fill the pot. They stood little chance of meeting their needs in any other way, for there is ample evidence that even those who wished to 'go straight' would have found it virtually impossible to do so. In some cases people in this class would take honest work for a brief while, if opportunity presented itself, and therefore they stole less in busy times, when employers were less particular. Apart from this, however, and from the opposite effect that opportunities for theft may have been greater in times of prosperity, these people were more or less detached from the economy on which they preyed and immune from its fluctuations.

Discussion of the effect of want on the entry into crime of the honest poor must again be divided, this time on the basis of age. So far as the adult poor is concerned, there is ample descriptive testimony to back up the view that want played little part in causing crime. People of honest habits would suffer the most extreme hardships before descending to crime — if a man is honest to twenty he is honest all his life, it was said in 1839. This generalization suffers the weaknesses of all generalizations, no doubt. There were surely many who stole a little here or there without being detected; there were those, honest whilst in work, who soon succumbed to temptation when times were bad; there were those who turned to crime part way through life. But the impression gained from studying the evidence is that stated — on the whole honest people remained honest despite appalling suffering and often great temptation. To misquote Clive, one is astonished at their moderation.

If we thus accept as correct the view held after 1839, what of the contrary view common before that date? We cannot dismiss the possibility of a reduction in the effect of want on crime having taken place in or by the 1830s. Such a reduction could have occurred if the connection between the two had in some way been associated with the long wars which had just ended. Perhaps men discharged from the services stole when forced to do so by distress, reverting to their former practice of 'living off the country', while later generations were less likely to switch from an honest life to crime and (if possible) back again. Or perhaps there is truth in the notion that long wars have an unsettling effect on society, an effect which would lead men to steal more readily and which twenty-five years after the end of the war had worked itself out. A decline in the effect of want on crime could also have been caused by a decline in employment opportunities, but in this case it would have affected the young rather than the adult poor. We do not, of course, have to believe any of these explanations. It is quite easy to accept that the simple and naïve view that crime and poverty were directly correlated was widely held among the general public until it was denied by the Royal Commission on a Constabulary Force in 1839. The Commission's Report, on this view, would be the means of bringing the ideas of the informed before the uninformed.

On the whole, therefore, there is little ground to think that the immediate pressure of want was a major cause of adult crime, or that cyclical changes in this pressure altered its level.

B. CRIMINAL STATISTICS AND THEIR INTERPRETATION (extract)

V.A.C. Gattrell and T.B. Hadden

Source: E.A. Wrigley (ed.), *Nineteenth-Century Society: Essays in the Use of Quantitive Methods for the Study of Social Data* (Cambridge University Press, 1972), pp.364-5 and 368-71.

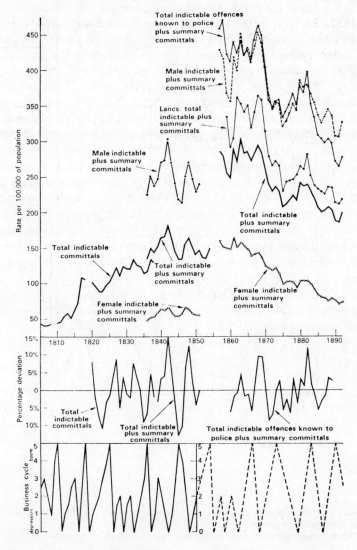

Figure 4.1: Offences against property: England and Wales, 1805-92; Lancashire (total only). 1858-92

Figure 4.2: Assaults and drunkenness, England and Wales and Lancashire, 1857-92

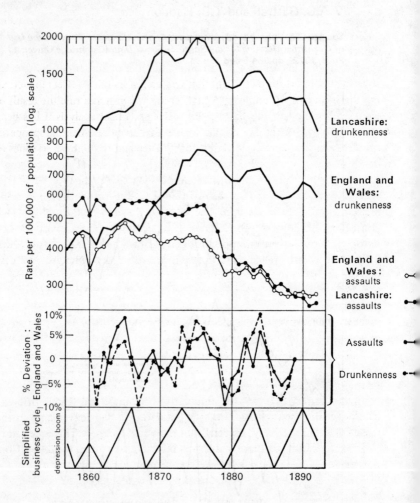

Assaults = Offences against the person tried summarily plus indictable offences against the person known to police.
Drunkenness = Offences of drunkenness and disorderliness tried summarily.

The particular significance of these graphs (Figures 4.1 and 4.2) resides in the light they throw on two theories of criminal behaviour. First, it was assumed by one school of nineteenth-century criminologists that the incidence of criminal activity was unconnected with economic hardship and could be better explained in terms of the irremediable depravity of the habitually drunk or of the so-called criminal class. This view has been restated by Tobias, who quotes an ample number of contemporary literary sources to support his own claim that depression had little effect in increasing the incidence of 'crime' and that 'crime was not as a rule the result of want'. Secondly, on the basis of extensive statistical analysis it has been established by present-day criminologists that twentieth-century property offences tend to increase in times of affluence and to diminish in times of depression — a conclusion which would seem if anything to corroborate the theories of nineteenth-century observers. Our examination of the nineteenth-century statistics disproves the earlier theories and in some measure qualifies the modern. The rates for property offences — which constituted the vast preponderance of all serious crimes committed — entirely contradict the interpretation put forward by the sources on which Tobias has chiefly relied. And they imply further that whatever the case may be in this century, it was quite different in the past: far from being of universal application, the sociological explanation for the incidence of property offences must change with time. Figure 4.1 shows that fairly consistently, in nearly every decade of the nineteenth century, the year-to-year movements in the incidence of property offences were inversely correlated with the fluctuations of the trade cycle. They increased in times of depression and diminished in times of prosperity: more people stole in hard times than in good. [. . .]

In the period 1819-36, the fluctuations for male and female offences combined are not dramatic, but they still reflect the movements in the trade cycle fairly closely, especially in the years 1826-36. This is certainly clear in the graph for those years showing their percentage deviation from the secular trend. Very much more conspicuous are the fluctuations in the incidence of property offences committed by males in the periods 1836-51 and 1857-80. Here six major peaks (1837, 1842, 1848, 1863, 1868, 1880) correspond with troughs in the trade cycle (1837, 1842, 1848, 1862, 1869, 1879). Conversely the major troughs in the graph for male offences (1845-6, 1860, 1866, 1872-3) all correspond with peak years of prosperity or with years of rising prosperity. Similar correlations are less marked in the case of the female index, since the actual number of offences committed by women was always rather low in comparison with those committed by men: but they are detectable nonetheless. If female offences were presented in terms of their deviation from their secular trend, the correspondence between their movement and that of male offences would be evident at once. No less than men, women stole more frequently in times of depression than they did in times of prosperity. [. . .]

The *long-term* trends in assaults and in drunkenness in the nation at large and in Lancashire specifically are best clarified in their 'direct' graphical representation (Figure 4.2). The county rates closely followed the pattern of the national, though it is noticeable that for most of the period the Lancashire drunkenness rates were almost double those of England and Wales as a whole. From 1858 to 1876 the incidence of drunkenness in both cases more than doubled, and they rose with particular rapidity after 1867 − a rise which provoked the licensing statutes of 1869 and 1872 but whose continuity was not apparently affected by them. One historian has referred to the 'frightening burst of debauchery' which was caused by the boom of the 1870s. The propriety of the phrase is amply borne out by the official rates. The passage of the 1856 Police Act notwithstanding, this overall increase is too marked to be explicable solely or even chiefly in terms of developments in police efficiency. On the other hand, the decline in drunkenness from 1876 onwards must represent a real decline, since, if other things were equal, the tendency of police developments would be to inflate the rates from year to year. The same argument holds true, of course, for the decline in the incidence of assaults which is detectable from the mid 1860s onwards. There will be room for debate in interpreting these trends in detail, but the long-term movements in drunkenness can probably best be explained in terms of cyclical advances and recessions in the standard of living of the population at large, and possibly also, in the latter decades, in terms of the development of new standards of respectability and temperance. The decline in criminal violence was probably more directly an achievement of the deterrent effects of police control.

The *short-term* fluctuations in these offences are of particular interest, and they are best brought out in the diagram representing their annual percentage deviations from the secular trends. Here two kinds of correlation are immediately visible: the first between the rate of assaults and of drunkenness, and the second between the troughs and peaks in both kinds of behaviour and the troughs and peaks in the trade cycle. It is true that in the latter case there is a certain disjunction between the correlations, although this is probably because the economic index is too crude to reflect the precise timing of the qualitative and quantitative changes in economic conditions which might have affected the criminal rates. It would require a much more sensitive analysis than is possible here, for example, to explain why the troughs and peaks in the rates preceded the trade cycle turning points of 1862, 1866, and 1868 by a year, and why they lagged behind by a year or more in 1873, 1879, 1883, and 1886. But the overall pattern is clear enough. In times of depression the incidence of assaults and drunkenness declined, and in times of prosperity they increased. The likely implications of this pattern need not be laboured: high wages and high employment led to a higher consumption of liquor, and this in turn contributed to a higher incidence in violent crime in the year in question. [. . .]

C.   CRIME AND THE DEVELOPMENT OF MODERN SOCIETY (extract)

Howard Zehr

Source: *Crime and the Development of Modern Society* (Croom Helm, 1976), pp.79-83 and 133-7.

Patterns of Property Crime

[. . .] Cycles of theft do appear to have been related to fluctuations in material conditions, and levels of as well as trends in theft were related to community size and growth. But there is little to suggest a strong relationship between theft rates and the process of urbanisation itself, and this lack of evidence is important. Many commentators on the nineteenth-century city have viewed urbanism with some alarm, seeing cities as chaotic jungles seething with crime, disorder and vice. Urban growth bred social disorganisation and anomie; social disorganisation and anomie bred prostitution, crime and popular disorder. [. . .] The lack of evidence for a connection between theft and urbanisation is another. If it were social disorder and 'uprootedness' which breeds crime, one would expect crime rates to be higher in new and growing cities than in older, more static cities, and that theft rates in new and rapidly growing cities would rise at first, then begin to drop as the city came of age. Moreover, since most critics of the city — which, at least until very recently, has included most commentators on the city — would agree that property values were especially protected by the rural social order in the somewhat more idyllic age before massive urbanisation, it is precisely property crimes such as theft where the effects of social disorganisation should be most obvious. Yet no such pattern is apparent. There are a few hints that the process of change may have made some difference, most notably in some of the German data, but this factor is completely overshadowed by community size; urbanisation was accompanied by rising theft rates, but primarily because large communities tended to have higher theft rates than small, not because the process of change itself drove rates up. The primary causes of urban theft rates, then, will have to be sought elsewhere – in the increased opportunities for crime in the city, the greater difficulty of crime solution in a large community, or perhaps in the replacement of old 'rural' value systems by new, modern values, rather than in 'normlessness' and social disorganisation.

Likewise, the theory that theft is motivated by actual need, although less widely held than the disorganisation theory of the city, requires some qualification. There is, to be sure, some justification for explaining theft rates during the first half of the nineteenth century in this way; witness, for example, the concordance of a subsistence crisis and very high theft rates in the 1840s. But as a general explanation, the need argument has obvious inadequacies. The upward trend in theft rates itself belies this. In spite of the fact that all indexes indicate some lessening of the cost of subsistence and a general improvement in standards of living for many segments of the population seems clear by the end of the century – certainly no subsistence crisis equal to that of the hungry 'forties occurred after 1850 – theft rates moved steadily upward, finally reaching a peak, at least in France, which was higher than any previous level. Moreover, most students would now admit that rural poverty was at least as intense as urban by the end of the century; yet urban theft rates were usually higher than rural. Cross-sectional correlations between theft rates and the few economic indexes available were not high. And finally, the relationship between cycles of crime and indexes of the most basic subsistence costs loosened after about 1860. Almost no one would deny that material hardship was responsible for many thefts, but clearly this explanation alone is inadequate to explain the behaviour of nineteenth-century theft rates.

Many nineteenth-century commentators, and the middle classes in general, would have argued then that they were right all along – that it was 'cupidity' which motivated theft. And, while such a moralistic explanation is too simplistic, they at least may have been correct in pointing to the human psyche. For the apparent change in the economic determinants of theft in both Germany and France during the latter half of the nineteenth century suggests that, as in the Merton-Gurr argument [. . .], the sense of deprivation is relative rather than absolute. Men may steal because they are in need, but the assessment of need depends upon what they have been led to expect or desire. The incidence of theft is dependent in part upon the relationship between what is expected and what is actually attained, not simply upon outright hardship.

Which variable is the best predictor of theft rates will depend upon levels of expectations. During the first half of the nineteenth century, expectations generally were low; prior to and during the early stages of massive industrial-isation incomes were low and variable, basic living costs were high and subsistence crises frequent. That prices of basic staples should have had an effect upon theft rates is logical. But the 1840s mark the end of large-scale subsistence crises in the Western world. Industrialisation, although it brought hardship, eventually also meant improvement for large segments of the population, especially after its early stages. Incomes rose. The price of basic staples fluctuated somewhat less from year to year than before and in the long run either remained steady or rose more slowly than wages. New industrial products became available to those who could not previously afford them. Democratic ideals spread. While this improvement in standards of living should not be overemphasised − certainly substantial segments of the populations in Germany and France still lived in poverty − standards of living and thus expectations were quite clearly higher by the beginning of the First World War than they had been seventy years before. This is why prices of very basic staples such as bread were replaced as determinants of crime by more general economic indexes and since standards of living were higher and industrialisation began earlier in France, the change naturally occurred earlier there than in Germany. The changes in mentality, divorc-ing expectations from outright subsistence needs, followed the same pattern.

And the same general argument might be applied to the connection between theft rates and urbanism, a connection which increased as the older economic determinants of crime loosened their hold. Constraints are fewer, to be sure, in the city than in the countryside; there are more op-portunities to steal in the city, less chance of being apprehended, and in general informal sanctions are replaced by less effective formal controls. Given the same tendency toward delinquent behaviour, then, an urban dweller was more likely to commit such a property crime than a rural dweller. At the same time, though, urbanisation has usually meant increased expectations; social classes tend to be more fluid in the city than in the countryside, contact between the rich and poor frequent, and the hope of advancement greater. The motivation to steal, therefore, was greater in the city because expectations were higher, and this became increasingly true as the industrialisation process matured.

If this interpretation is correct, what we have in fact witnessed during the nineteenth century, first in France, then in Germany, is nothing less than the transition from pre-modern or pre-urban to modern or urban criminal patterns. During the early part of the century, expectations in general were low and property was protected by village traditions and by informal controls upon behaviour; thus, at least outside large cities, theft rates were relatively low and fluctuations were closely related to actual subsistence crises. At the same time, the magnitude of these crises, in a situation of general demographic pressure, caused a rapid, general increase in rates. The transition from a pre-industrial to an urban, industrial society in these countries, although still incomplete by 1914, meant a new value system and a new social organisation as well as new and higher standards of living. A modern society implies — and, in fact, requires — rising expectations, a desire to acquire material goods, which was not characteristic of the pre-industrial mind. Modern industry, for example, would be unthinkable without growing markets and a work force motivated by the desire to improve itself, one of the first tasks of early industry was to teach workers to continue working beyond what was required simply to maintain previous standards of living. At the same time, modernity and urban life have usually implied fewer informal constraints upon the individual and, relatedly, a declining respect for the sanctity of property. Modernisation, in other words, meant rising expectations — expectations that society often was unable to fulfil — along with a reduction in constraints upon the individual. Beginning in the cities, these values and conditions gradually spread to the countryside. That new patterns of criminal behaviour accompanied these changes is hardly surprising. In urban areas, theft rates rose as cities grew; but such crimes also increased, although more gradually, in many rural areas as modern, urban values spread. The economic determinants of theft also shifted, reflecting higher standards of living and new values which were in part the result of the interrelated processes of industrialisation and urbanisation. New definitions of well-being thus sustained the increase in theft which earlier subsistence crises had first produced, though now at a more moderate rate. Thus the two main analytical problems of this chapter — the effects of economic conditions and of urbanism upon theft rates — are not so unrelated as they at first seemed.

Rising theft rates usually have been treated as a growing malaise, a sign of increasing rejection of society's values and a symptom of an illness in society. In fact, however, the new patterns of crime should not be seen as pathological but as symptoms of modernity. For not only do they grow out of and reflect basic characteristics of modern life, but they imply an acceptance of modern society's values — if not of society's norms governing methods of attaining them — on the part of offenders. Nineteenth-century theft rates reflect, in Merton's term, a state of anomie — an acceptance of prevailing social goals, but a willingness to use means which society considers illegitimate in order to attain those goals. They thus also reflect both the successes and failures of nineteenth-century society: they signify the spread of modern values and expectations but also the failure of nineteenth-century society to meet these expectations. High theft rates are not necessarily a permanent characteristic of modern society, but nineteenth-century patterns of theft are a sign that society was coming of age. [. . .]

Patterns of Violent Crime

[. . .] Some conclusions of a general nature are possible, the most interesting of which are as follows:

1. In general, violence became more frequent but less serious during the course of the nineteenth century. However, a major element of this pattern began to change at the end of the period as rates of violence began to move downward.

2. Contrary to usual assumptions, interpersonal violence was not higher in cities than in the countryside although the initial or most disruptive stages of urban and industrial growth may have caused it to increase.

3. In the long run, tradition remained one of the most important determinants of patterns of violence at the end of the century.

4. Modern and pre-modern patterns in the overall composition of crime seem to have obtained. Violence was low in relation to theft in old, established urban-industrial centres but quite high in relation to theft in rural areas. New urban-industrial areas experienced patterns more similar to rural than to established urban-industrial centres; theft rates rose in these situations, but so did violence.

5. Total violence was negatively related to theft and positively related to the business cycle during the first half of the period. After about 1870 or 1880, however, the relationship may have loosened.

6. Alcohol consumption was positively associated with violence both longitudinally and horizontally, but alcohol consumption was not sufficient to explain the connection between violence and the business cycle.

7. During the first half of the period, homicide rose relative to suicide in times of prosperity and high alcohol consumption but dropped relatively in times of crisis.

Common assumptions about the nature of urban life, these conclusions emphasise once again, are simply wrong; violence is not necessarily peculiarly associated with the city. Nevertheless, the possibility does remain that urban and industrial growth – or at least the most novel and/or disruptive stages of that process – led to violence. But this does not vindicate the social disorganisation hypothesis. Urban growth, it must be stressed once more, does not lead to social disorganisation. But even if it did, such disorganisation would not necessarily lead to violence. In fact, it will be argued here that increases in violence during urban growth represent the retention of traditional patterns of behaviour in the new setting.

In recent years the traditional idyllic picture of rural society has been seriously shaken; it is now widely recognised that social tensions are much higher in rural societies than previously assumed. High rates of violence in the countryside during the nineteenth century indicate that violence – in the form of tavern brawls, family squabbles, even homicidal feuds – was a traditional means of dealing with these tensions. Interpersonal violence, in other words, was a traditional outlet for frustration, an expression of social conflict. In fact, interpersonal violence was often recognised and tolerated as such by villagers and authorities, causing many crimes of violence to be overlooked and thus omitted from crime records in rural areas.

While the view that urbanisation brings social disorganisation must be rejected, urbanisation and industrialisation do create conflicts and frustrations. In such a situation, violence again was a means of dealing with these tensions, especially since other avenues such as collective action were impractical. Thus violence rose as a traditional response to new conflicts and pressures, implying the retention of customary modes of behaviour in the new setting, not complete disorientation and disorganisation. Furthermore, a high percentage of violence has been found to occur between relatives or acquaintances; in the words of Andrew Henry and James Short, homicide – and, implicitly, interpersonal violence in general – is positively correlated with the strength of the relationship system. In the present day, at least, violence is to a large extent predicated upon primary relationships. While this can only tentatively be applied to the nineteenth century, it can be suggested that high rates of violence in urbanising areas attest to the lack of social disorganisation and impersonality in such areas.

All available evidence points to a decline in violence, particularly serious violence, after adjustments to urban and industrial growth. Several alternate explanations for this pattern may be suggested. Violence is intolerable in an urban situation and thus is strongly reproved and repressed. Thus other methods of dealing with conflict and frustration must be worked out; these ways include theft (and possibly suicide) but also some other avenues such as collective action which have not been practical previously but now become conceivable. The decline in violence, in other words, may reflect an acclimatisation to city life, a victory for urban values and social organisation. On the other hand, however, violence may begin to fall off because tensions and conflicts are reduced as adjustments to urbanism and urban growth are made or family relations are improved due to higher standards of living.

This explanation for urban-rural differentials in violence suggests that frustration may be a factor in violence. But at first glance the behaviour of violence through time does not augur well for the relative deprivation/ frustration-aggression theory [. . .]. According to this view, relative deprivation leads to frustration, and frustration often results in aggression. But how can relative deprivation and frustration, a form of which has already been used to explain the behaviour of theft, also be used to explain both interpersonal and collective violence, given the differences in the timing of cycles? Moreover, how does one explain the negative relationship between criminal violence and the business cycles during the first half of the century? Why would prosperity increase frustration?

A study of homicide and suicide by Andrew F. Henry and James F. Short, Jr provides an explanation for these patterns built upon the frustration-aggression concept but making it more specific by employing reference-group theory. Analysing data from the United States, they found patterns very similar to those discovered here. In simplified form, their tentative conclusions were as follows:

1. Much, if not all, aggression is in fact rooted in frustration.

2. But for interpersonal violence, the relevant category of frustration is status frustration, i.e. frustration is defined 'in terms of loss of status position relative to others in the same status reference system'.

3. Homicide was negatively related and suicide positively related to status, i.e. homicide (and, implicitly, assault and battery) is basically a low-status offence while suicide is a high-status offence.

4. Social classes or categories of low status lose status relative to high-status categories or classes during business expansion while high-status categories lose out relative to low status during business contractions. Thus status frustration is greatest for low-status, homicide-prone groups during business expansion and homicide or interpersonal violence should be positively related to the business cycle. Conversely, suicide should be negatively related to the business cycle.

In other words, a perceived decline in one's position in relationship to the status of those he compares himself to results in acute frustration, which may lead to violence. During business contraction, it is the upper classes which are hurt most obviously and which lose most in relation to lower-status groups. Thus suicide, which is predominantly a higher-status form of aggression, rises. During periods of prosperity, however, the condition of lower-status groups does not improve as rapidly as that of higher-status groups, lower-status groups, in other words, lose ground relatively (or, in the terminology of relative deprivation theory, status expectations are unfulfilled). A sense of frustration results and interpersonal violence rises as a consequence.

The positive relationship between violence and the business cycle during the first half of the century — a pattern which has been confirmed by a number of studies from other times and places — is thus explainable after all. Why this pattern appears to have dissolved later is unclear, however. One possibility is that new modes of behaviour were adopted; in modern society, perhaps, violence is seen as a less appropriate outlet for frustration, even though the frustrations persist. Perhaps the availability of other outlets such as collective action plus greater prosperity and smoother family relationships reduced the need for interpersonal violence despite frustration. But it is also possible, as was suggested in the discussion of theft, that the indexes of crisis and prosperity used here became less appropriate as expectations and standards of living rose; perhaps, once again, the relationship would be seen to continue if better indicators of business cycles and of status frustration were used.

This interpretation raises several interesting possibilities. Alcohol consumption, it has been maintained, was insufficient to explain the connection between prices and prosperity. The concept of status frustration suggests, rather, that both violence and alcohol consumption were symptoms of the same phenomenon, i.e. of frustrations due to loss of status. Secondly, this interpretation suggests an interesting explanation for the positive correlation between violence and urban growth. Henry and Short found a similar correlation, but concluded that it was an anomaly caused by such factors as the operation of organised crime in disorganised areas. The status frustration theory, however, may be particularly applicable among low-status groups during the early stages of urban and industrial growth. Evidence for this possibility is mixed. For many groups, certainly, urban life and new industrial jobs meant an increase in status. But many were disappointed; the conditions of urban living (e.g. housing) were demeaning, jobs were hard and often did not live up to expectations. The ownership of tangible property, considered so important in rural life, was given up in the city or prior to the move. Low-status groups therefore felt themselves to be losing status during the early years of urban-industrial growth and, once again, the resultant frustrations were expressed through violence. Later, as values and conditions changed, frustrations dropped. Along with the other factors in maturing cities, this made violence no longer so necessary or appropriate as earlier.

These interpretations are inherently quite speculative. Macro-analysis, though in many ways a precondition for any closer study, is not adequate to deal with such issues with any degree of precision. Distinctions need to be made between the criminal behaviour of various social classes, age and marital groups, and different sectors of cities, to cite just a few cases. Nevertheless, these interpretations do generally fit the patterns of violence observed in Germany and France during the nineteenth century and they do provide reasonable explanations for patterns that are otherwise quite surprising.

5 IMPERIALISM

A. INTRODUCTION TO *IMPERIALISM*

Hans-Ulrich Wehler

TRANSLATED BY CHRIS BAGGS

Source: *Imperialismus* (Kiepenheuer und Witsch, Cologne, 1970).

It is undoubtedly true to say that the concept of imperialism raises first and foremost a problem of definition. Indeed, it would seem imperative to state clearly what is meant by this word which has, over the past few decades, become such a worn-out term in political polemics, eventually even becoming a propaganda stereotype in the East-West conflict and in the struggle of anti-colonial freedom movements. Therefore this introduction outlines (I) quite briefly the theory of imperialism which seems to offer the most possibilities today for further sociological research and (II) some other theories which are still under discussion today or have been revived, and then (III), using the perspectives gained in (I) above, considers more closely a few problems concerning the nature of imperialism.

I

It is above all the overseas expansion of Western countries, beginning in the last third of the nineteenth century, which forms the point of departure for this discussion, although continental expansion is also included. This expansion was termed 'imperialism' by contemporaries during the 1870s and 1880s, as domination and rule, which are necessarily linked to the concept of imperialism, were the result no matter what different forms they took. For this reason imperialism should be understood to mean (a) not only direct, formal, colonial rule over foreign territories, but also the indirect, informal domination of developed industrialised nations over less developed areas of the world. Under no circumstances does imperialism just mean the form of domination first mentioned, namely colonialism in the narrow sense. This imperialism had its origins in (b) specific socio-economic and political processes in the industrialised nations, and these processes (the causes and impetus of this extraordinarily far-reaching and fundamentally important phenomenon in world history) have, ever since, represented the central points at issue in political and academic discussions, as well as raising very important questions for the fields of social science and history. Thus imperialism cannot be seen exclusively or even predominantly as a question of foreign or colonial politics, as it has so often been, but should be understood much more as one result of the development of industrial economic societies — societies, moreover, which are involved in oligopolistic competition with each other. It must be added straight away that it would therefore not be enough, to contradict this theory, merely to contend that imperialism can be defined differently (i.e. simply as the foundation of a colonial empire continuing a tradition of power politics, or as an exaggerated form of nationalism). It would have to be shown that these processes (which are still to be discussed) in Western societies and their interrelationships — one result of which is here considered to be imperialism — either never took place, or have been incorrectly described, or, if they are acknowledged, were none the less not the cause of imperialism.

On the other hand, the theory of imperialism favoured in the present work must of course satisfy the demands made of any sociological theory. It must combine a maximum of empirically obtained and verifiable information with as much explanatory power as possible. Moreover, when compared with other theories it must stand the test in various social and cultural fields of examination and must also be in a position to open the door to new and fruitful lines of enquiry. Still to be enquired into are the content of this theory, and the further problem: why there must be a critical historical theory of imperialism.

II

In the debate over the neo-Marxist theory of imperialism (see III) there are essentially six general theoretical positions that have recently been repeatedly advocated. Yet they all seem to be either of too general a nature to provide, without further addition, satisfactory theories for the problems concerning imperialism in the nineteenth and twentieth centuries; or else, rather than solve old difficulties, they simply raise new ones.

1. The following interpretation may be tempting above all to the historian: namely, to see imperialism as embedded in the general history of colonialisation over the last few thousand years, or even the last five centuries, and to regard the continuity of this development as the only essential feature. Certainly in this way imperialism is seen more relatively, as a new wave in an ancient movement, and the argument that it brought forth fundamental qualitative changes in the modern world after the revolutions at the end of the eighteenth century is thereby either basically denied or at the very least much weakened. Continuity, especially in recent European expansion, cannot be denied, and to be reminded of this fact now and again is a good safeguard against over-congested thinking. But a rather imprecise derivation

in terms of continuity is simply not enough for analysing and explaining modern imperialism adequately. On the contrary, a special theory for one subset of this concept of colonialisation is then needed, which otherwise deals with centuries or even the whole of human history. The proponents of such a theory are thus left once more facing the problem they originally set out to answer.

2. There are also major weaknesses to be found in the concept which interprets imperialism as one of the numerous consequences of the 'eternal' disparity in power potentials and, clutching this universal key, rests content with a general conflict theory from Neanderthal man to General LeMay. Moreover, in this case there is the additional danger whether conflicts can be reduced to so-called metaphysical invariables such as lust for power, ambition, hankering after prestige and combativeness on the part of the powerful. This static anthropology and psychology can, however, hardly help the historian to progress, as his concern is precisely the social context in which power is achieved and asserted, the objectives it strives for within this context, the methods it can make use of at any given time and the social consequences it produces. A category such as lust for power, which is, supposedly, doctrinally neutral, is much too weak in explanatory power and too unspecific to be used without further ado. Admittedly it is an advantage when a sociological theory can achieve as high a general level of validity as possible, but this vague, almost banal generalised formula about disparity in power is quite incapable of furthering concrete investigation into Western imperialism. Were one to develop, at the behest of all the research questions which still need to be answered, a subsystem of this theory that could fully come to terms with all the consequences of the socio-economic, technological and military superiority of the industrialised nations, then one would immediately be directed back to questions about unequal growth (and its causes), the direct and indirect results of which are undoubtedly differences in the effective use of power.

3. Similarly unsatisfactory is the related thesis that imperialism was, as it were, a natural consequence of the technological superiority of the Europeans and Americans. This superiority was without doubt vitally important in the actual conquest of colonies, the gaining and maintenance of influence and the execution of effective control. It made it possible to carry out, with great effectiveness, decisions of an economic or political nature. But, to begin with, the position of Western technology around 1840, for instance, was already sufficient to help bring about the occupation of large overseas territories, as a glance at India shows. Using this reason, therefore, it is not

possible to explain post-1880 imperialism convincingly. Even if it was easier to subdue the Sudan in 1898 than Abyssinia in 1868, Napier nevertheless managed the latter as Kitchener the former. What was of fundamental importance were the decisions in favour of conquest, not the methods used to carry it out. Secondly, technological advance, the continued march of which undoubtedly constitutes a fundamental process in modern economic growth, has in fact had more of an indirect effect on the economy (through growth in production, problems over markets and investment) and on society (through difficulties over supply, income distribution and consumer habits). In short, technological superiority as such did not directly, let alone automatically, unleash imperialist expansion, but rather contributed as an impetus to other areas. In certain respects imperialism was a result of social and political inability to cope with the economic consequences of permanent technological innovation and its social effects within one nation.

4. One theory, current for quite some time, maintains that imperialism is a failed branch of nationalism. The original bourgeois nationalism, at the beginning wholly directed towards the unity of the nation state, self-determination and also ethnic homogeneity, was driven beyond its own limits, after fulfilling its most immediate short-term objectives, and ended in imperialism, betraying the original principles by readily exchanging them for colonial rule over an empire of many nations with oppressed 'foreign races'. Consequently, imperialism is seen as a boundless, extreme form of nationalism, the emancipatory elements of which had been perverted by lust for power, a need for increased prestige and an ideal of 'oligarchic rule', all of which took the place of the former 'democratic ideal of equality'. Now it cannot be denied that imperialism manifested itself in the shape of nation-state rivalry. To some extent it did indeed stubbornly try to put the principle of the nation state above the urge for supranational expansionist politics. But it is impossible to stifle several objections to defining imperialism as an extreme form of nationalism. Between, on the one hand, the early liberal wish for peaceful co-existence between nations with equal rights and, on the other hand, imperialism, involving control over peoples deliberately kept dependent and permanent international conflict, there is a gap which can be concealed only artificially. To all attempts in imperialist Germany (i.e. by Wilhelm Hübbe-Schleiden, Timotheus Fabri, Max Weber, Friedrich Naumann, Karl Lamprecht and many others) to present imperialism as a natural projection of nationalism into the arena of world politics, there clung an element of an unnatural structure, from which the effect on the masses of such an exonerating ideology was not necessarily ruled out. Naumann's description of nationalism as 'a desire by the German people to

extend their influence over the globe' typically disguised a claim as if it were essentially a determining factor.

In the first instance, extreme nationalism characterises a social-psychological phenomenon, which is accorded great potency. What is often overlooked in this phenomenon is that at its root lie social changes in the broad sense, and the socio-cultural persona of the individual and the psychological frame of mind of large groups in society are to a large extent determined by these changes. These deeper causes should therefore not be disregarded; on the contrary, they should be the first to be analysed. If, for instance, imperialism as extreme nationalism does serve to satisfy a collective and pent-up desire for self-assertion, then one should be able to explain why this desire varies, being at times latent and then again virulent. Without recourse to an analysis of the socio-economic structure, this can scarcely be done in any plausible fashion, assuming one does not want to describe this nationalism in concrete terms. Whoever talks of imperialist 'fever' needs a metaphor for collective reactions, a metaphor which assumes a diagnosis of the illnesses in the 'body' social and politic, as fever is only in fact a symptom of internal pathological processes.

But it is above all questionable whether the decision-making processes from which the politics of imperialism follow can really be understood, using this abbreviating notion that extreme nationalism can, by direct transmission so to speak, determine what the centres of power do in the sense of directing them towards its own goals. Such direct influences are often extremely difficult to prove empirically, if at all; as, for example, in the so-called classic instance of the influence on Washington of the chauvinist American gutter press before the outbreak of the Spanish-American War of 1898. Only too often there is an underlying over-simplified model of how decisions are shaped, whilst any examination of the calculation of interests shown by the parties concerned is neglected. Clearly this calculation can be broad-based and, besides political, social and economic interests, can take into account social-psychological phenomena or can include an impression of them; to that extent these phenomena become an originating factor. But in reply to the really critical question, what provable or probably exerted influence did extreme nationalism actually have on the decisions of the political power centre, all too often one is able to claim only that in ministerial council-chambers and country seats it had at the most an indirect effect. Any conclusive proof that the politicians of imperialism such as Bismarck, Hohenlohe, Salisbury, Rosebery, Seward, McKinley, Taft and Wilson, Witte, Ferry and Crispi, were suffering from this 'fever' of extreme nationalism has, as far as can be seen, yet to be produced. It must also always be considered how far extreme nationalism was fomented by the ruling classes for non-nationalistic reasons and then manipulated by them, and how far it represents some form of compensation for economic changes and shifts in social status, a compensation which, because of its tremendous mass impact, can develop a political dimension in the sense of seeming to divert attention outwards, away from internal problems. Admittedly, in this case an analysis of the socio-economic structure becomes once again a prime concern. Even the thesis that sees imperialism as a nationalistic mass movement and an early form of fascism (there is much to be said for this view and it will be discussed later) is confronted by exactly the same problems. In short: even if, in sociological jargon, there is no lack of short-hand descriptions such as 'extreme nationalism', the concept of extreme nationalism must nevertheless be explained first, before one is in a position to explain imperialism in terms of it. Otherwise one complex variable is merely replacing another. An ingenuous equating of the two, however, scarcely brings one any further forward in producing a theory of imperialism that is convincing and elucidating.

5. J.A. Schumpeter's original theory of imperialism, to which to this day people repeatedly return, directed its attention to the mode of thinking of certain specified groups, and to the fossil-like social structure, as the real motivating forces behind imperialism. Schumpeter saw imperialism neither as a necessary consequence of the capitalist system, nor as having primarily economic origins. Rather, he considered it an atavism, a hangover from an earlier period, which was still effective in determining how events occurred in the present. This atavism was an heirloom of feudalist military circles and the absolutist princely states. It originated in the mentality of the traditional ruling classes, whose ethos under feudalism had been continual fighting and expansion. This pattern of behaviour and response is supposed to have survived the rapid social changes of the last few centuries. Like Thorstein Veblen before him, Schumpeter believed that 'modes of thought and social structures acquired in the distant past, once in being and firmly established, survive for a long time and continue to be effective even after they have lost their meaning and their function in preserving life'. At the same time 'the war machine', created in former times, demanded action: 'created by wars which needed it, the machine created the wars which it needed'. Just as warfare occupied the lives of the old military nobility, so imperialist expansion was undertaken simply for the sake of expanding. For this reason Schumpeter defined imperialism 'as the objective disposition of a state to expand through the use of force, and without any specified limits'. Not only was any form of economic imperialism or imperialism with limited aims thereby excluded, but Schumpeter even denied that so-called classic

English imperialism was really imperialism. In a similar arbitrary way he defined capitalism as, by its very nature, a peace-loving system which was against 'expansion through force' as a matter of principle — though, as E. Heimann has objected, it would be far easier to demonstrate the intrinsic expansionist drive in capitalism than to prove Schumpeter's expansionist drive within feudalism. As capitalism absorbed all the energy which previously flowed into expansionist efforts, 'a purely capitalist world could therefore not be fertile soil for imperialist drives'. If, nevertheless, imperialism emanated from industrial states, then essentially it described a series of industrial accidents brought on with monotonous regularity through the fault and harmful influence of old elites. Schumpeter's ideal of an international division of labour within the framework of a world-wide system of free trade that guaranteed peace took no account of the reality of the situation, namely the fundamental problem of unequal growth between the various areas of the world, which caused differences to continue to be maintained and tension to be aroused. His theory (which, moreover, tended towards turning the 'super-structure' into an absolute) could explain neither English imperialism, nor American, French, Italian, German or Japanese, though it no doubt recommended itself as a sort of counter to neo-Marxist theories, as, in it, imperialism was debited to the account of pre-industrial elites and not to the system of industrial capitalism itself. It is true that Schumpeter's essay 'On the sociology of imperialism' contains a wealth of superbly well-formulated insights, but the unhistorical, arbitrary nature of his definitions has undermined the empirical verification of his theory. Schumpeter did not understand that imperialism, in the sense of social imperialism (see below), could and had, in reverse, become an attractive proposition for the traditional ruling groups, who exercised considerable influence on this form of the idea through their interests in society and the way they thought. Consequently, Schumpeter did not even analyse the most important imperialist drives of those groups who, as he saw it, were to the fore in society.

6. Of late, Anglo-Saxon historians have been stressing, just as earlier German historiography did, the primacy for imperialism of politics *per se*, with 'politics' usually understood in the Weberian sense as a struggle to gain, maintain and extend power, above all in the areas of foreign policy, diplomacy and military strategy. In a typically blunt statement of this theory, D.K. Fieldhouse has actually seen 'the main characteristic of the new situation' after 1870 thus: 'that once again economic factors were subordinated to political ones'. Imperialism is seen as a result of the relations between the international powers. Quite apart from the fact that this laconic

statement must first of all be proved by comparative studies (and in the opinion of the author of the present book these would not show it to be globally true), this watertight division into politics and economics is based on an illusory and completely erroneous theoretical conception – wrong at any time, but especially so for the age of industrialisation. Not only does American imperialism, which definitely did not advance into Latin America and the Far East out of ostensibly purely political reasons, offer countless counter-examples, but so too does English imperialism in the late Victorian period. This latter case will therefore be specially picked out and cited here. Even at that time India occupied a key economic position in the British Empire, a position taken to be clearly self-evident by the decision makers in London. To refer, then, to the occupations of Egypt, the Sudan, Wadelai and Uganda as 'purely politically' motivated, when these seemed to be required by the needs of British Indian politics and not by any direct economic interest in the regions, seems a highly dubious case of short-sightedness and of simple failure to be aware of the economic (and the attendant social and internal political) constraints put on the system by the politics of Empire; the system is seen, without any further consideration, as some form of natural economic strategy. The same holds true for the 'political' reaction in London to Russian advances into Asia, i.e. towards India. The second important argument of this school, namely that after 1870 there were no special economic grounds to justify talking about a preponderance of economic or at least 'non-political' motives, is based on an ignorance of economic history. The industrial revolutions, which had taken place by then in various countries (USA, Belgium, Germany and France), and the consequent beginnings of the collapse of the long-standing British monopoly position in world markets and the concurrent massive industrial, economic and social growth problems experienced by the younger industrial nations, all produced on the contrary, a fundamental change in the economic situation, which had far-reaching political consequences. For this very reason David S. Landes has pointedly seen the 'shift from monopoly to competition [as] probably the most important single factor' for imperialism as well. In the end this theory suffers from the narrowing down of 'politics' to mean 'foreign policy'. For this reason it fails to see the immense importance of imperialism for internal affairs and the domestic politics which motivated it. But it is precisely on these factors that everything depends, as they represent the forces that organise and determine foreign policy in imperialist nations; foreign policy is so often subordinate to the primacy of domestic politics.

III

Either implicitly or very explicitly, these ideas about imperialism represent attempts to modify or refute a critique of imperialism which has been developed, chiefly since the turn of the century, by the Englishman John A. Hobson, by German and Austrian neo-Marxists and by Lenin and Bukharin, and which has been expanded to form an effective theory. Common to the advocates of this critique was the fact that, to a greater or lesser degree, they were all in the position of outsiders within their particular society and, from the fringes, were therefore able to observe society with keener eyes than either the Liberals or Conservatives. It is for the same reason that left-wing criticisms of imperialism have abated, with the increasing integration of the organised labour movement into the bourgeois state, whilst such criticisms within the Soviet sphere of influence have — and this is social sciences' loss — become frozen at a particular standpoint and become mere dogma.

The 'radical' left-wing liberal Hobson elaborated his influential theories whilst under the sway of the strained imperialism of the 1890s and the Boer War in particular. In 1902 his ideas were brought together for the first time in his book *Imperialism* and to this day have remained the most well-known non-Marxist theories. Hobson took as his starting-point the development of the industrialised economy, its tendency towards over-production and the pressure to find new outlets and investment markets for capital export; in all this he saw powerful expansionist forces at work. At the same time he revived the theory of under-consumption, long since considered dead and buried in academic economics, and he developed his criticisms of income distribution and, by extension, of the power structures in society, which he considered a decisive cause of imperialism. Hobson believed that these problems of production, distribution and income would be solved through democratic parliamentary social reforms, without the need for any revolutionary changes in the total system, and that these reforms would destroy the roots of imperialism. From the earlier English critics of colonial politics, from whom Hobson took almost all his theme, he took over the indictments made against those parasitical groups of interested people who, without regard for the common weal, attempted to influence national politics in the direction they wanted and, often enough, were successful — such as the interests of capital in a period of over-saving. From this arsenal of earlier criticisms also came the idea of the disastrous repercussions of colonial politics and administration on political and social relations between metropolitan states. This argument, merely hinted at earlier, is generally linked with the name of Hobson, and it has been borne out historically. At the same time, however, Hobson saw very clearly – and this has often been overlooked – that there were specific socio-psychological needs within the mother country that were met by imperialism, and he also detected the advance of militarism and the creeping erosion of democratic institutions that imperialism caused. Furthermore, Hobson put forward the idea of an aristocracy of workers who benefitted from imperialism, and above all he recognised the internal political function of expansionist politics, which, in the form of social imperialism, diverted attention away from domestic problems and towards overseas affairs, thereby helping to maintain a politically conservative socio-economic *status quo*: all points which have always proved themselves fruitful, if not essential – even more so over the last few years – for an understanding of the complex phenomenon of imperialism.

Even before Lenin adopted large amounts of Hobson's argument (Hobson's influence, on the other hand, on other socialist critics in Europe has been greatly over-estimated and is not traceable to any concrete degree), a number of factors had been elaborated during the discussions on imperialism which had taken place in German and Austrian social democratic circles from the early 1880s onwards, and, from an early stage, these discussions had concentrated on what were subsequently to prove the central features. To some extent the earlier liberal criticisms of colonial politics were simply taken over in this process; to some extent, also, this socialist criticism of imperialism before 1914 grew from a need to produce a conclusive analysis of the contemporary scene and, by so doing, to supplement and extend Marx's theories, which were often found to be inadequate in this respect. Thus, for instance, for Rosa Luxemburg, who in 1912 could claim that imperialism was 'the central axis of political life', it was Marx's concept of surplus value that raised the real problems, and the question of how to realise surplus value formed the central point of her work *The Accumulation of Capital*. Rudolf Hilferding further developed Marx's theories on economic centralisation and concentration in his work *Finance Capital*, in order to come to terms with key socio-economic phenomena of the outgoing nineteenth and the early twentieth centuries.

With varying degrees of emphasis, it was particularly the 'endogenous' economic, social and political problems of the capitalist industrial economy that were held responsible for imperialism by the socialist theorists, who by no means merely wrote empty theory but (e.g. Hilferding, Bauer and Luxemburg) had at their disposal important and, at that time, very impressive empirical evidence. As their starting-point they used the fact that the English monopoly position had been broken by industrial revolutions in several other countries, whereupon in place of free trade a system of protectionist national economies had developed, each competing bitterly with one another. Within each capitalist state during the phase of high industrialisation decisive changes took place. The abandoning of liberalism in economic and social policy was matched by the rise of powerful, politically influential pressure groups, a frantic move towards concentration in industry and banking, the exploitation of the home market behind growing protectionist barriers, and policies of confrontation and even repression towards the organised labour movement, policies supported by the bourgeoisie. Throughout, economic development still continued to be subject to massive fluctuations. Thanks to the tendency (inherent in the system) to develop over-capacities, the urgent need to find new markets overseas was felt to be imperative, but it was essentially only exporting that appeared to offer any remedy to the problem of recurring economic depressions, with their effects on both society and politics. As, at the same time, the search for investment opportunities and the drop in profit rates pointed powerful financial interests in the direction of foreign markets, there developed, under pressure from the export of both goods and capital, but also under pressure to maintain traditional social power structures and income relativities, an unnatural competition for spheres of influence and protected colonial markets, which were increasingly supported by the individual nations' armed strength.This division of the so-called 'ownerless' areas of the world amongst the imperialist nations heightened international tension, bringing them to the edge of war. Occasionally such reflections by the socialist theorists became stylised into alleged 'laws' governing all future developments: the chase for realising surplus value, for example, would with 'objective' inevitability lead to capitalism's penetrating the entire world and then, when there was no more room to escape into, this would finally lead, according to the theory of total collapse, to a world-wide crisis of capitalism. Or, alternatively, the continuing fall of the profit rate, or else the state of general stagnation revealed by the various crises and depressions caused by the lack of opportunities for expansion within one country, would inescapably cause a drift into imperialism and from there, similarly via a straight progression, into a world war. As with so many other areas within the Marxist-influenced labour movement, the call to action which could still transform society in good time before the approaching debacle clashed with fatalistic evolutionary thinking which was simply waiting for the favourable outcome of predetermined courses of events.

Lenin took up various elements of this radical and socialist criticism of imperialism — explicitly acknowledging Hobson's and Hilferding's preliminary work — and, conscious of their possible mass effects, and not without sharpening them up ideologically, he turned them into an instrument of struggle within his revolutionary programme. Apart from various contentions which cannot be verified empirically, Lenin's work has essentially two general disadvantages from the point of view of academic research, which should be pointed out here: first, the rigid system of dividing everything into periods, a system which proved long ago to be inadequate, as it does not do justice to the historical course of events; and secondly, the contention that capitalism was stagnating or decaying. The undeniable contradictions and crises within the development of industrialism were considered to be the only road, or at least the only major one, open to a system which, since the mid-1890s especially, has in fact advanced in ever new waves of high industrialisation, based on the scientific use of technology.

On the other hand Lenin's theory has two great advantages, which can be seen quite clearly: first, that he focused attention on the problem of unequal development and its very varied effects; and secondly, the determination with which, in contrast to the partial criticisms of particular elements within industrial capitalism, he persisted in his criticism of the whole system and kept fixed in his sights an image of the totality of economic, social and political, even social-psychological interrelationships.

Today it is easy to criticise from a historical perspective several ideas within the neo-Marxist critique of imperialism, as has been hinted at in relation to Lenin. Imperialism cannot simply be equated with the export of capital. The latter was important for a while, but its main direction, which was not towards the colonial areas in the tropics, has often been mistaken. Imperialist control and domination can often be combined with capital imports from the dependent territories into the metropolitan countries; for a long time it has, conversely, been caution over the export of capital to underdeveloped regions that has been a characteristic feature. Deriving the reasons for the First World War from one field, namely purely from economic motives, has been abandoned. The objective, functional significance which the former colonies and spheres of influence in Asia and Africa are supposed to have held for the West has without doubt been overvalued (which does not, of course, invalidate their significance in the minds of the people involved at the time). Conversely, imperialism has, for all that, been of fundamental importance in forcibly bringing these areas into the modern world. The realisation of surplus value has been too closely linked to the acquisition of overseas markets, whilst the revolutionising of the static home market through a dynamic wages policy, etc. has in general been undervalued. In comparison with Hobson, the German and Austrian neo-Marxists perhaps tended to emphasise the problems of production, rather than income or distribution problems. Admittedly, it was not until the decade after World War I that it became clear that, in comparison with the previous century, the industrialised nations were experiencing a relative (!) decline in foreign trade and yet a massive expansion of the home market. The idea of finance capital has all too often been plucked from the German context and applied to other countries, where industrial capital was the most important element. Similarly, other loaded and careless generalisations could also be criticised.

But in spite of these obvious failings – and what historical theory, let alone what general social theory, does not contain them? How often, for instance, have German neo-Rankean historians before and after 1914 wrongly interpreted their own period? – it is nevertheless true that these early critical theories of imperialism brought out three general points which are still of fundamental importance for any modern theories: (1) the idea of unequal economic growth and the 'endogenous' problems of a permanently expanding industrial economy; (2) the social and political consequences and side-effects of this process of modernisation, above all the causal significance of social changes for expansionist politics; and (3) the special function of imperialism as a conservative policy of diversion and control, which, to the benefit of the traditional social and power structures, attempted to divert abroad those emancipatory strivings which otherwise endangered the system.

As stated earlier, these theories also offer most points of departure for sociological research into imperialism today, as economic, social, political and ideological factors can, within the framework of an analysis encompassing the whole of society, be combined with these focal points. Problems of industrial economics and social change, of political power and influential ideologies thus do not stand on a par, unrelated to one another, and will not be each overvalued in turn as the one and only motivating factor; rather, with the help of a refined explanatory model, they can all be tested for their individual importance within the decision-making process. An answer can then be attempted to the decisive questions concerning the driving forces, projected aims and effects of imperialism within the metropolitan nations. Investigations of the progressive forms of imperialist expansion and the practicalities of how control within the dependent regions was carried out (by means of particular legal measures, a military presence, limited autonomy, direct territorial rule by the government) generally raise fewer complex theoretical problems, but make rather more practical demands, such as those of establishing empirically watertight evidence wherever possible and interpreting the function of the various relationships, whether of a legal, superordinate or subordinate nature.

In any case all these questions can no longer be approached simply by means of the basic principles of the traditional theories of understanding usually found in historical studies. It is true that these can help to squeeze out those factors which, within the range of experience of a given period, were considered important by the people involved and which presumably determined their actions. But precisely this question is a central research problem for the historian, and to take a step behind the traditional theory of historical understanding is therefore impossible for this reason as well. But it is just as unsatisfactory merely to uncover the thoughts which guided the actions of the individual participant. What is needed much more is to be able to find out the significance which specific actions can acquire when looked at from today's various theoretical points of view. Nowadays that generally involves combining economic theories with sociological and political ones. Only with their help can one clarify (as far as this is possible using research methods) the 'objective' bases which form the preconditions and restrictions, even to the point of obligations, within the system and within which 'subjective' decisions and wilful impulses occur.

No doubt forms of exploitation and domination of overseas territories could be found in earlier Dutch, Spanish and Portuguese colonial policies which anticipate various features of imperialism. But, in line with the earlier discussion of terminology, one should not talk of imperialism until the point when the first industrialised nation, Great Britain, began to extend its formal and informal dominion over vast areas of the globe. The industrial revolution represented, in three ways, a turning-point in the traditional expansionist movement, especially when several other Western countries had passed through the stage of their industrial revolution.

1. Industrialisation created a novel, qualitatively altered, sharp difference, unparalleled in history, between the industrial nations and the under-developed regions, which in a relatively short space of time found themselves subjected to direct or indirect control by efficiently organised, socio-economically and technologically 'developed' nations.

2. The spread of industrialisation led to a network of competing industrial nations, and out of this competition there gradually grew a world economy and, potentially, an international political structure which regarded the whole globe as its sphere of activity. Moreover, imperialism laid down the preconditions by which the less developed regions could gain entrance to this world-wide, economically and politically interlocking system.

3. Today, many aspects of imperialism still live on in the economic markets of the modern world and in the relations which exist between industrialised and developing countries, especially in regard to the latter's domestic

problems – this even if it is for the most part a variant of imperialism: colonialism itself lost its meaning with the collapse of the colonial empires after 1918.

If one begins by examining the country which experienced the industrial revolution first, it is extremely instructive to note that, at an early stage and contrary to a widely held belief, the causes of British expansion can be attributed to problems within an industrialised economy: that is, the demands for expansion were derived from the needs of the particular economic and social system. These causes and demands did not, therefore, suddenly appear for the first time during the imperialism debates in the 1880s, let alone only after 1898-1900. As early as the beginning of the nineteenth century Lord Brougham, Simonde de Sismondi and Hegel declared on several occasions that, in view of the limited absorption capacity of the domestic market and the vigorous and powerful growth of industrialism, there was an inescapable necessity to acquire overseas markets, both for the exporting of goods and capital and for providing colonial settlements for emigrants. In particular, according to Sismondi, who at an early stage recognised the importance of supply and income distribution as well as purely production difficulties, excessively slow changes in domestic income patterns were matched by pressure to push forward overseas. The neo-Marxist theory of imperialism could even have latched directly onto Hegel's Philosophy of Right! The problems of unequal growth and the power relationships between developed and underdeveloped countries were openly discussed even earlier by Hume and Tucker. In this instance, Lenin was returning to a topic very familiar to the English and Scottish economic theorists of incipient industrialisation.

A group of Jeremy Bentham's pupils, the so-called 'colonial reformers' around Wakefield, Durham, Roebuck, Buller, Molesworth and others, continued this discussion in a germane fashion during the 1830s and 1840s. In their case the centre of interest had clearly shifted from analysis to programmatic demands, which were formulated in the light of contemporary social tensions, due to come to a head in the Chartist movement. At the very same time, in Carlyle and a little later in John Stuart Mill and his follower Cairnes, colonial and informal free-trade imperialism to a certain extent became a safety valve for vastly overproductive industry and also provided an ideology with which to distract bourgeois society, which had been shaken to its very core. The vehemence with which Great Britain, clearly following the bidding of the problems raised by industrial growth, forged ahead not only in Latin America but also in the Far East, where at the start of the 1840s the Chinese Empire had been forcibly opened up to British trade, seemed to confirm both the diagnoses and the demands. (Even today it must seem an impossible task to a champion of the primacy of foreign policy to prove his case in relation to English policies towards China, certainly up to the peace of Nanking!) In France Louis Blanc to some extent took up this thread of continuity, especially after the crisis of 1840, soon to be followed by Moses Hess and, after the first world economic crisis of 1857, by Karl Rodbertus-Jagetzow with the first fully fledged socialist theory of imperialism. It is not possible to prove the existence of a directly comparable theory of imperialism in Marx, although his theories of economic development and social conflict contain elements onto which a critique of imperialism could and can fasten.

1. Marx took over from the English specialist literature the concept of the 'agrarian revolution', which, in a narrow sense, preceded the industrial revolution and helped make it possible. Applied to developments in Germany, the whole question of the 'emancipation of the peasants' during the first half of the nineteenth century can be seen as the German agrarian revolution. This is not the place to investigate its economic connections with German industrialisation, but its social-historical and political results have been at least as important. The economic upturn in agriculture during the period of the industrial revolution in Germany maintained, or even produced, the foundations of economic prosperity for a pre-industrial ruling élite, namely the aristocratic class of big landowners — thereby, however, strengthening their power position within society and their political influence at precisely the same time as the industrial upper-middle classes were growing up and attempting, in vain, to carry through their own political demands. When in the mid-1870s the European agriculture market collapsed under the pressure of overseas competition, a decade began in which large-scale agriculturalists fought a constant bitter fight in defence of their economic, social and political position. Without this reference, on the one hand, to the agrarian revolution and the structural crisis in agriculture after 1876, with its effects on society, and on the other hand to the rise of the organised labour movement, which acted as a warning sign to the industrial world, it would be difficult either to give a satisfactory explanation of the support given to German imperialism by decisive groups of conservatives, or to shed adequate light on the reasons behind their move towards the policies of the reactionary 'conservative alliance' and their sanction of the 'terrible fleet' as the instrument of imperialist politics. In general, and adopting the approach taken by Barrington Moore, Hans Rosenberg and H.-J. Puhle, a more thorough investigation of the influence of German agrarians on politics during the industrial period (up to and including the 1930s) would be well worth while.

2. In a way that only few people before him had done, Marx recognised with the utmost acuteness that, with the breakthrough of the industrial revolution, a fundamental turning-point in world history had been reached. Admittedly, this new industrial economic growth – the *Communist Manifesto* is after all in part a hymn in praise of the industrial bourgeoisie's achievements – did suffer from massive fluctuations in the economic climate and from disturbances to growth, which developed into depressions lasting several years. It is less important to note that for a long time Marx and Engels believed in a growth pattern based on a cycle of approximately ten years – a pattern which Juglar had at the same time similarly observed, but which as a general economic cycle for industrial economies does not stand up to empirical examination – than that they understood, as it were, the basically fluctuating nature of the process of growth and the unevenness of economic development. A permanent tension grew up between the uncontrolled forces of production and the limited ability to consume, a tension which sought to resolve itself in ever new crises. Marx and Engels placed great value on the social and political disturbances caused by this unstable growth, and the periods of economic crises especially, using them as the basis for predictions which did not come true. Later conclusions from the imperialism debate, for instance that 'the strongest root of capitalist expansion undoubtedly lies in the lack of stability of the economic process' and that imperialism 'offered an alternative to the stagnation of the whole of economic life which called all classes into action', were all implicitly anticipated by Marx and Engels.

3. At an early stage Marx saw the process of concentration taking place in industry, the growth of oligopolies among large-scale enterprises, the squeezing out of middle- and small-size businesses, restraints on competition and the growing importance of fixed capital, which favoured the process of concentration. From his diagnosis and prognosis (as Hilferding was the first neo-Marxist to bring home), a modern theory of economic concentration could be developed and was produced under another name, by bourgeois academics such as Max Weber, as the theory of large-scale enterprise. Under the pressure of this process towards concentration, there arose, after a genuine structural change, the system of oligopolistic organised capitalism, which switched part of its internal market rivalry overseas into general competition between government-promoted economic interests.

One of the most important representatives of modern macroeconomic analysis, W. Leontief, has rightly acknowledged, fifty years after Marx's death, that Marx, on the basis of his 'brilliant investigation of the long-term tendencies of the capitalist system', produced 'an unsurpassed set of prognoses that were to come true later'. Even if both Marx and Engels, as mentioned above, did not develop any explicit theory of imperialism as such, and if their relations with earlier colonial politics remained characterised by a deep sense of ambivalence — on the one hand acknowledging the advance of progress and on the other criticising the brutal exploitation that went with it — their economic theory did offer, in conjunction with their theory of social conflict, numerous points of reference, not only for the neo-Marxists, but also for the social sciences in general.

1. From an economic point of view the constant instability of growth, in the face of a relatively static domestic market and a distribution of income which did not match the dynamics of the economy, led to expansion beyond national borders and to the exporting of goods and capital. At the same time it was through this enlarging of sales and investment markets that the development of the nation's economy was to be stabilised — retaining walls were built out into foreign parts to hold up the continually overflowing growth at home. Above all, during crises and depressions, when unrestrained production, the oscillations of the economic process and the pressure of competition produced their most violent results, overseas trade appeared to offer the only quickly effective relief mechanism. Therefore a strongly expansionist impulse was a consequence of precisely these disturbances to growth — or rather of the short-term stoppages which contemporaries felt to be such. At the same time the move towards concentration and, very soon afterwards, the dependence of strategic industries on foreign raw materials intensified the trend towards extension of industrial domains. As this concentration process in large-scale enterprises, cartels and national transport industry was to some extent being extended overseas, foreign markets which could be monopolised appeared to be the optimal goal. In place of the free-trade 'informal empire' there thus emerged formal colonial rule, or at least the total penetration of well-defined spheres of interest protected by the individual nations.

2. From social and political points of view the process of industrialisation is bound up with the disintegration, at times rapid and at times slow, of the traditional social and power frameworks — especially, of course, after the 'great leap forward' of the industrial revolution. New groups thrust themselves and their demands forward with greater or lesser vigour. Throughout, the direct consideration shown to the interests of capitalist expansion by government policies can be seen repeatedly. When Schumpeter claimed that it could never really be said that 'the state does this or that. It is always a

matter of recognising who or which interest group it is that gets the machinery of state working and then speaks through it', it is often possible to detect, within the meaning of Schumpeter's statement that 'the government at any given time reflects the power relationships within that society', the influence exerted by powerful economic interests on the politics of imperialism. It is here that the frontal attacks made by the liberal criticism of colonialism and by Hobson and his successors on the parasitical groups which did lucrative business at the national exchequer's expense come face to face with their very substantial opponents. (One need only think of the Hamburg shipping magnate Woermann and the German colonial societies, of the companies in Latin America favoured by Washington, or an English charter company.) But undoubtedly it is a rather misleading and simplistic model which would hope to find an explanation of imperialism exclusively in such a straightforward pursuit of primarily economic objectives. Imperialism offered much more, both to politicians who acted responsibly and to socially conservative groups, which to a large extent still determined the decision-making processes in their traditional manner but which were also exercising considerable influence in those countries already exposed to the changes brought about by industrial society. It offered them the chance to divert into overseas expansion those forces which threatened the system, and, by so doing, it prolonged the life of the *status quo*. In this process two kinds of social imperialism (often linked in historical reality) can be distinguished: first, a rather spontaneous variety, which believed, with an almost naïve conviction, that successful expansion would prove an economic remedy and would help society recover its equilibrium; and secondly, a coolly calculating and manipulating variety, which employed social imperialism as an instrument for practising power. This type of social imperialism, designed above all to provide a substitute form of satisfaction, pressed for an enlargement of markets, a restoration of the economy and a guarantee of its growth, hoping thereby to remove a constant trial of the strength of society's constitution and also to stabilise internal power relationships. The dynamic engendered by an industrial economy and by the forces of social and political emancipation was to be diverted into foreign expansion, forming a distraction from the internal deficiencies of the socio-economic and political system and making up for them by means of real successes, or at least by means of an increase in the ideological prestige of the nation. With the help of a diversionary strategy prefigured by Machiavelli, now indeed employing totally modern methods, the conservative utopia of a traditionalist social and power hierarchy was to be realised in the industrialised world.

Following this line, it should be possible to discover the most important motivating strand of German imperialism after the end of the 1870s. If there is a continuity in German imperialism, then it is to be found not so much in purely economic interests, but in the pre-eminence of social imperialism from Bismarck to Hitler. In Bismarck's expansionist politics this element of social imperialism was obvious from the very beginning; indeed, it was the dominant element. It formed the inner motor for Wilhelm's world politics, which attempted to overcome the tensions within German class society through policies that were both prestigious and risky. It formed a core element in Tirpitz's aggressive policies (Tirpitz is really the key figure in the politics of the Reich from 1898 to 1914) and, after 1914, in the war aims policies. And it surfaced once again in National Socialist imperialism, both on the continent of Europe and as planned for overseas. There are numerous problems here which stand in need of further research, and it is high time that this problem of continuity was investigated. If it is possible to talk of an 'age of imperialism', then it ought to extend to 1945, on account of the final, extremely exaggerated forms of German, Italian and Japanese imperialism.

As mentioned above in connection with this matter, the question arises whether early examples of fascism can be found in the imperialist movement. In the light of the almost contemporary emergence of political anti-semitism in Germany after the second world economic crisis of 1873, this question would seem to be answerable in the affirmative. If fascism is defined as, amongst other things, a flight from the industrial world into the social romanticism of an apparently integrated quasi-corporate society, as the search for scapegoats who are held responsible for collective and individual bad luck, as a right-wing radical protest by lower-middle-class groups which, as the politically under-age *déclassés* of industrialisation, rear up in anger at their loss of social status and economic position and which see in an authoritarian regime a guarantee for their ideas about law and order, etc. – then, indeed, organised anti-semitism is a form of early fascism. However, until Tirpitz's Vaterland party of 1917 one thing was lacking – a mass basis.

If we look at the social composition of the so-called colonial movement from the early 1880s, then, as far as it is possible to come to grips with the membership of the Colonial Clubs or the response shown to expansionist slogans, we are dealing with middle-class groups. Even the 'enthusiasm for colonies' shown in the German Reich can, like anti-semitism, be understood as a crisis ideology that afforded a safety valve for common frustrations. The self-confidence of numerous individuals whose economic and social status had been destroyed, or at least severely diminished, by industrial-isation and its interruptions to growth and its social upheavals, and the collective need for recognition on the part of large sections of the middle classes who had been as sorely affected as the lower-middle-class craftsman and small trader – the farmer and the lower- and middle-ranking civil servant – had been hit very badly for some years. The process of socio-economic development was difficult to understand, and it encouraged emotions which hankered after some form of aggressive discharge (via anti-semitism or Anglophobia) or which had to be rendered harmless through appropriate compensation. At this point imperialism, as paraphrased by vulgar nationalism, offered a diversion from the miseries at home; it promised economic benefits, job opportunities and an increase in national prestige, which made part-amends for the degradation felt in their daily lives by the various classes who wished to equate the ideals of their specific group with the norms of the whole society and who therefore identified to a very large degree with national (pseudo-) successes. Not only was there the loudest possible demand for a strong state in which, thanks to foreign successes, the internal lack of freedom was tolerated, but racism also gained a point of entry to the arena of international politics, replacing liberal ideals of equality with the concept of the oligopoly of a few, racially superior, nations.

If one looks at the ideology and practice of National Socialism, then unquestionably one can find in imperialism several early fascistic elements – its mass-movement appeal, its social resources and its racist and state-authoritarian crisis ideology. Once again it is a question of the problem of continuity in modern German history. And if the warmongering theories of German fascism demanded 'total war' from an early stage, it is possible to trace this line back to colonial wars during the Wilhelmine Empire. During the suppression of the Herero uprising in German South West Africa between 1904 and 1907, an early form of total war had been waged. The German military machine crushed the rebellion by ruthlessly employing everything at its disposal. The military command referred to its war aims not as 'victory' but as 'destruction'. They consciously waged 'a war which did not allow for a peaceful solution', a war which ended with the slaughter of half the Herero tribe and the deportation of a further quarter to prison camps, where there was a planned policy of extermination. In fact, the way in which colonial uprisings were put down has always been regarded by critics of imperialism as an ominous degeneration in the art of warfare.

If the theory favoured in this book allows for a fairly precise definition of when imperialism began, then questions about how long it lasted or when it ended raise various problems. This particular work restricts itself to the period up to 1917-18, as (a) the Russian revolution forms a significant turning-point in world history as well as in the history of Western imperialism, especially when the long-term effects are considered; (b) the collapse of formal colonial empires after 1918 introduced a fresh change in the relationships between industrial countries and underdeveloped areas; and (c) – a pragmatic reason – up to now the period to the end of the First World War has been most thoroughly investigated by modern research into imperialism.

Despite the first two points and despite the ending of an era in 1945, when the age of imperialism as understood in this study came to a close, domination, the genesis of which reaches back to the early phases of imperialism in the nineteenth century, continues to exist in the relations between the industrial nations and the Third World. In spite of the formal sovereignty of the new nations, imperialism has fixed the long-term conditions under which the old industrial nations and the developing countries come together in world markets and in international politics. Disparities of growth cannot be made good that quickly: only some form of universal social welfare policy on the part of the industrial nations is capable of bringing fundamental changes any sooner.

Clearly, most forms of rule and dependence have altered; Portugal's colonial policies today can be seen as a special case. To some extent there exists, in the era of 'decolonisation', a return to, or a preference for, the 'informal empire' where that is possible – such as the USA, for example, continues to practise in Latin America. Quite apart from the difficult research problems that there have always been, and that especially apply today, in analysing camouflaged and indirect domination, and quite apart from the stigma now irreversibly and universally attached to the idea of imperialist rule (and no longer just by a few critics), a developing trend has nevertheless in the meantime become clearly recognisable. The dependence of industrial nations, for their economic activity as well as their social policies, on their overseas markets in underdeveloped areas – a dependence which was considered by numerous contemporaries in the nineteenth and twentieth centuries to be an 'objective' necessity – no longer exists today, however much the reverse continues to be true. Armaments, space exploration and social investments (until now always the last to be considered) give the modern interventionist and 'tax' state, along with foreign trade with other industrial countries, the opportunity to regulate its affairs in such a way that it can deal, after a fashion, with the problems of economic and social dynamics. Certainly, this cannot for the most part be characterised as rational control over the forces of production and their utilisation, in the sense of the ideals of social equality; nevertheless, the function of the Third World for these countries has changed in principle. An analysis of the present-day remnants of imperialist rule ought, therefore, to attempt primarily to find out the impact of unequal growth on the developing countries and on the forms of dependence which still exist for them. The inequalities and the gap between industrial and developing countries have in fact increased since 1945, but they can no longer be convincingly explained in terms of the theory of imperialism expounded here.

Still, there is no dispute that these differences represent one of today's major problems. If the social sciences are to make processes in society understandable, then that aim should also apply to the part of historical studies which is trying to analyse and explain the history and development of relations between the industrial nations and the less developed regions. If such history wants to fulfil thereby [in Mommsen's words] its 'duty to educate politically', so helping to avoid new erroneous developments, then it needs in addition a critical theory which will not yield to the power of 'events which have taken place in history' and will not, under the sway of historicism, consider these events to have been unavoidable. It must also undergo [what Horkheimer calls] that 'theoretical strain' which 'casts a critical light' on past and present society because of its 'interest in a future rationally organised society'; otherwise, without 'some concrete utopia', the 'basis of hope in any fundamental improvement in human existence would be removed'. Not until there is such a critical theory can research into the history of imperialism meet the political needs of the present day and help sharpen a critical consciousness towards the problems of the Third World.

B.   ECONOMIC FACTORS IN BRITISH POLICY DURING THE 'NEW IMPERIALISM'

D.C.M. Platt

Source: *Past and Present*, no. 39, April 1968, pp. 120-38.

No consensus can be expected on a subject as complex and as politically explosive as the causes of imperialism. But over the last few years explanations of the 'New Imperialism' — the violent phase of European imperial expansion in and after the 1880s — have fallen very much within the same general pattern. Recent work by the Oxford historian, D.K. Fieldhouse, synthesizes a fashionable trend by which British participation in the 'New Imperialism' has come to be explained primarily as a *political* phenomenon. Bismarck's interest in Africa in 1884-5 'really began the new phase of political imperialism'; the factor which accounted for the suddenness and speed of territorial partitions among the Powers after 1882 was the formation of 'new diplomatic patterns within Europe'; 'colonization was more the product of political ambitions, international rivalries, and complex situations in the non-European world than of simple and universal economic forces'. Economic factors, indeed, had little part in the 'New Imperialism' since

> the rapid expansion of European commercial and financial influence throughout the world − the true 'economic imperialism' − did not change its character after 1870; and was no more likely then than before to have resulted in significant acquisitions of land.

The contrast in emphasis with the 'classical' explanation of the 'New Imperialism' − an explanation dating effectively from the publication of J.A. Hobson's *Imperialism. A Study* in 1902 − is certainly striking. [. . .] Fieldhouse felt that 'one major weakness of the Theory [of Capitalist Imperialism] was that capital exported on a large scale and tropical colonies annexed only rarely coincide'. He had argued earlier that British investment in tropical, colonial areas was 'quite marginal to the total overseas investment'; it would be unrealistic, therefore, to maintain that the reason for the annexation of these areas was Britain's urgent need for a market for surplus capital, and 'with the rejection of this hypothesis, so ingeniously conjured up by Hobson, the whole basis of his theory that "imperialism" was the product of economic necessity collapses'.

But does it? It would certainly be difficult to sustain Hobson's argument that the need to find outlets for surplus capital was the 'economic necessity' behind British imperial expansion in and after the 1880s. But the pressure he described of increased foreign competition and of the closure of overseas markets (home and colonial) by revived Protectionism was real enough, and though he may have gone too far in basing his argument on surplus capital and what Fieldhouse called 'the "faceless men" gambit', the argument for the economic basis of British imperialism begins to look much stronger if it is confined to the need to protect the existing outlets and volume of British trade and investment overseas against unprecedented assault from foreign tariffs and competition in the quarter century before 1914. This, in fact, was the broad 'economic necessity' behind certain aspects of British imperialism, rather than the narrower needs of individual British capitalists to find profitable outlets for their surplus capital overseas; and it was directly reflected in British imperial expansion through the responsibility traditionally recognized by H.M. Government to preserve a 'fair field and no favour' for British commercial interests overseas.

For the first three quarters of the nineteenth century this responsibility imposed no very serious burdens on imperial policy. Britain's position as the world's principal exporter of manufactured goods and of capital was virtually unchallenged. It was up to the Government to open areas of the world to trade – and this was done in Latin America, in the Levant, and in the Far East. Where monopolies or artificial inequalities were seen to favour foreign competitors, the Foreign Office felt itself bound to protest, as it was bound to maintain the rights secured to British interests by the most-favoured-nation clause written into the standard Victorian commercial treaty. But once the treaties had been signed, the positive promotional function of H.M. Government was over, and British traders and investors were expected to make their own way in equal competition with the traders and investors of other nations.

By the mid-70s it was obvious that foreign competition would threaten the whole existing pattern of overseas trade; and the international commercial depression of the 1870s and 1880s drove home the lesson of the need to maintain as much as possible of Britain's share in the diminished markets of the world. The Royal Commission on the Depression of Trade and Industry quoted evidence in its final report of December 1886 to show that Britain had lost her advantage in production, and that the superior adaptability of the Germans was putting them ahead; in neutral markets, especially in the East, we were 'beginning to feel the effects of competition in quarters where our trade formerly enjoyed a practical monopoly'.

The mere fact of increased foreign competition would not in itself have persuaded H.M. Government to alter its *laissez-faire* attitude towards overseas trade. *Laissez-faire* was a tradition which, even if diluted by pressure for social reform at home, still continued to govern the relationship between officials and traders overseas. The remedy for increased foreign competition – as officials never tired of reminding British traders – was not increased government intervention but greater zeal and efficiency among the manufacturers and traders themselves. But this remedy could not be expected to apply to situations in which British trade and finance were meeting with government-aided, foreign competition overseas. In and after the 1880s a 'fair field and no favour' was threatened from two directions: 'unfair' pressure by foreign diplomatists at Oriental courts on behalf of their nationals, and the closure of international markets by revived Protectionism.

It was not easy to see where the answer lay. In 1885 Lord Salisbury had authorized British diplomatists in the Far East to support British commercial interests where foreign diplomatic representatives were interfering to their detriment, and in 1886, after an exhaustive examination of British official policy towards the promotion of overseas trade, James Bryce (Rosebery's

Under-Secretary of State) recognized the need for 'action (firm but cautious) by Diplomatists in remote countries in counteracting the pressure used by the Representatives of other States to push the mercantile interests of their countrymen'. So far as British diplomatists were able to rid themselves of the *laissez-faire* tradition — as Sir Claude MacDonald did so successfully during the 'Battle of Concessions' in China in 1898 — they were able to neutralize foreign diplomatic pressure by exercising their own influence on behalf of British commercial and financial interests. But competitive pressure at an Oriental court was likely to lead to dangerous political rivalries between the Powers, and the only satisfactory solution was a mutual agreement defining spheres of interest and activity. It was by this path that commercial and financial competition developed into imperialism.

But even more influential both in the earlier phase of the 'New Imperialism' (when there was still territory to annex) and in the later (when annexation was replaced by the allocation of spheres of interest among the Powers) was the fear that the formation of new European colonies would be followed by the closure of their markets to all but the colonizing Power. The revival of Protection in the 1870s had dashed British hopes for universal Free Trade, and British exporters saw themselves excluded not only from their traditional European markets but also increasingly so from the world markets in which they had hoped to compensate themselves. It is perfectly true that the new colonial markets offered little in relation to world trade as a whole, that it was many years before they gave any return on investment, that the history of the next quarter century indicated that, so long as good times lasted, there was room enough for all. And it is the poverty of the actual commercial and financial return on the 'New Imperialism' which has raised doubt among historians as to the economic motive for annexation in the first place. But hopes were high at the time, and it was difficult to be rational about the relative importance of markets when, in the world depression of the 1870s and 1880s, exporters in general were feeling the draught. Quite apart from the emotional exaggeration common to imperialists, the range of available information and experience for the newest areas, above all for Africa, was simply insufficient; nobody in the early 1880s could have made any reliable predictions for trade and investment prospects in the area. But even in the Far East, where a great deal was already known about the state of the market, there was no certainty as to ultimate commercial opportunities, more particularly during these decades of heavy overseas investment and rapid technological change when the opening of a railway, the development of new industrial or mining techniques, or even a political upheaval, might alter prospects almost overnight. On the whole, traders tended to be optimistic, officials pessimistic, yet Lord Salisbury, disinclined as he was to hyperbole and in face of general pessimism among his own officials, felt able to assure Sir William White in September 1885 that 'the Power that can establish the best footing in China will have the best part of the trade of the world'.

The precise value of the new markets was unknown, though even at the time some commentators had a pretty shrewd idea. But whatever their value, it was clear by the early 1880s that tariff barriers were likely to close them off to international trade. Germany never in fact directly excluded British trade and investment from such colonies as she had, but there could be no certainty that German colonial tariffs might not be imposed at any time, any more than there was certainty, for Continentals, that Britain herself would remain loyal to Free Trade. In practice, German government transport subsidies, 'tied' loans, and negotiated preferences for German financiers, contractors and investors, had much the same effect as a tariff wall in excluding British competitors from Asiatic Turkey and Shantung. As for France, there was never any doubt about her intentions. 'We do indeed believe, and assert emphatically', said Etienne, the Under-Secretary of State for the Colonies, in 1891, 'that since France must incur the obligations involved in a colonial domain, it is just and proper that this domain should be reserved as a market for French products'. [. . .]

[British] policy was developed in the light of what politicians, officials, and businessmen believed (however incorrectly) to be the case at the time, and at the time, except to the ever-optimistic Board of Trade, the prospects for British overseas trade looked decidedly bleak. The irony is that if Britain had not felt bound by her Free Trade principles to reject tariff retaliation, the pressure for imperial expansion to safeguard British trade and finance might never have existed. But the fact of the matter was that unless Britain was prepared to manipulate her tariffs as a bargaining-counter in obtaining fair terms for British trade in the new, protected colonial markets, the alternatives (in the 1880s and 1890s) seemed limited to taking a share in the colonial scramble or losing the markets of the underdeveloped world altogether. [. . .]

The argument on the nature of British imperialism tends to focus on British expansion in Africa. But while the Partition of Africa was certainly the most dramatic phase of the 'New Imperialism', no analysis of imperial expansion in the decades before the First World War can be accepted as complete which confines itself simply, as in Africa, to actual territorial annexations. Recent historians of British imperialism have found it difficult, if not impossible, to separate a discussion of 'formal' from 'informal' empire.

[. . .] During the later stages of the 'New Imperialism', the partition of the more developed civilizations of the Levant and the Far East into spheres of interest or influence was annexation masquerading under a different name. Irreconcilable international rivalries meant that such 'informal' divisions merely replaced colonial frontiers as the favourite instrument by which the division of the world among the Powers might be completed.

But if the Scramble for Africa must, as always, begin the discussion, it might be asked at once to what extent the interests of British trade were responsible for H.M. Government's decision to take its share. Robinson and Gallagher have argued that trade bore very little responsibility. [. . .] British official policy, for Robinson and Gallagher, was determined by political objectives in the Mediterranean and the East, and the decisive factor in British territorial annexations in Africa (north of Rhodesia) was the need to maintain the security of the routes to the East.

This explanation is satisfying so long as it is limited to the North East; it is much less so when it is extended to West and even Central Africa. Fear of a French monopoly of Congolese markets was certainly the Foreign Office motive for concluding the Anglo-Portuguese Treaty of 26 February 1884. And the anxiety to preserve an Open Door for international trade in the Congo region formed the basis of British policy during 1884 and at the Berlin Conference of 1884-5. In the general partition of Africa which followed, British statesmen were perfectly open about their commercial motives, and, indeed, they had no reason to disguise them. In 1884 Lord Salisbury, under whom the partition was largely to take place, criticized Gladstone's opposition to territorial annexations on the grounds that its effect had been to permit France and other Powers who practised a discriminatory tariff policy to monopolize the new markets in the under-developed areas. He warned his audience that as the markets of the civilized world were closed by tariffs, those of the uncivilized world were threatening to become the only fields in which British traders and manufacturers might do profitable business, Gladstone's refusal to annex had lost these markets time and again to British trade. Four years later Harry Johnston, one of the most active of the agents of British expansion in Africa, was invited to a week-end at Hatfield in the course of which Salisbury discussed British policy in Africa and suggested, indirectly, that Johnston might care to write something which would explain official policy to the nation. Johnston subsequently published an important article on 'Great Britain's Policy in Africa' in which he summarized the main points raised at Hatfield. Observing that the total trade of Africa, imports and exports, had reached about £31 million in 1887, he argued that British policy must now assume a more positive rôle:

If free trade were a universal principle, it would matter relatively little to our merchants what particular nation ruled the new markets for our commerce, but inasmuch as protectionist Powers may, and do, possess themselves of new tracts of Africa and then proceed to stifle or cramp our trade with differential duties and irritating restrictions – witness the Portuguese everywhere in Africa, and the French in Senegambia and Gaboon – then it becomes a necessity for us to protect ourselves and forestall other European nations in localities we desire to honestly exploit.

Johnston concluded that all Britain wanted was a 'fair field and no favour', and that 'it is to secure this for our commerce and our civilization that we are forced to extend our direct political influence over a large part of Africa'.

By 1896 the Partition of Africa was well on its way to completion. Now, if ever, British statesmen might have been expected to confess to the underlying strategic motives for annexation. But when Chamberlain addressed the Birmingham Chamber of Commerce, he was merely reflecting a common belief (however mistaken) in claiming that if Britain had stood aside in the Partition of Africa, 'the greater part of Africa would have been occupied by our commercial rivals, who would have proceeded to close this great commercial market to the British Empire'.

It is difficult, no doubt, to delimit the part played by trade in British imperial expansion in Africa. In some parts of Africa it was considerable, in others negligible. The 'partition' of China is far less complex. H.M. Government's motives for participating, when considered for the entire period 1880-1914, were almost exclusively in defence of existing British trading interests, in defence of a 'fair field and no favour' for British trade and finance in one of Britain's more important overseas markets.

[. . .] For much of the nineteenth century, H.M. Government had little trouble in achieving and maintaining [the 'Open Door']. Under pressure, China was gradually opened to world trade on equal terms to all comers; but British trade enjoyed an overwhelmingly superior competitive position, and no government intervention was necessary to guarantee fair treatment in relation to the trade of other nations.

The problem which the British Government faced in China in the last decade of the century was the extent to which its perfectly genuine wish for a continued 'Open Door' in Chinese trade and finance could be reconciled with the new determination of Russia, France, and Germany to carve out areas of exclusive interest. It saw a 'fair field and no favour' for British trade and finance threatened not only by foreign diplomatic pressure at

Peking, but also by French claims to exclusive concessionary rights in Kuangtung, Kuangsi, and Yunnan, by German claims for preferential treatment in Shantung, and by Russian claims in Manchuria and the North. [. . .]

At the very beginning of January [1898], Salisbury's immediate reaction to Russian exclusive claims in the North had been to consider jettisoning altogether Britain's traditional policy of an Open Door in Chinese finance and claiming a first refusal on concessions in the Yang-tsze valley. [He was] advised against it at the time, but by the early summer H.M. Government had cut out its own sphere in the wealthiest and most populous region of China. [. . .]

What happened in China during the decades following the Sino-Japanese War was a reflection of many elements in the 'New Imperialism': German ambitions for a coaling station on the Pacific and for markets for trade and investment; Japanese claustrophobia; the continued expansion of Russia towards defensible frontiers and a warm-water outlet; the rounding-off of French claims in South East Asia; a growing interest in the United States in the new problem of the disposal of surplus manufactures; and the British reaction to all these pressures in defence of our traditional trading ascendancy on the China coast. Whatever the motives of the other Powers – and for Germany and the United States alone were economic factors really important – Britain's own motive was almost exclusively economic – to maintain as far as possible a 'fair field and no favour' for British trade and finance. It was for this reason above all others that she participated in, and even promoted, the economic partition of China.

One of the problems in defining, or explaining away, the 'New Imperialism' has been the need most historians have felt to isolate the factor which started off the whole process. It may have been emergent nationalism in Egypt, or the European ambitions of Bismarck, or Russia's need for defined or defensible frontiers. It was less likely, in the late 1870s or early 1880s, to have been the pressure of capital for foreign outlets, or the urge to find markets for surplus manufactures, if only because real competition was still in its infancy and imperial policy was formed by statesmen whose interests and responsibilities extended beyond the profits of individual business enterprises.

But does it matter which started which? The argument in any case is by no means over, nor will it ever be possible to be sure that the expansive pressure of German and United States trade and investment would not have ended in a partition of the remainder of the world whatever had, or had not, happened in Egypt in 1882. The timing of the economic partition of

China, while clearly a part of Russian expansionist strategy, was equally the culmination of bitter economic rivalries dating back as far as the early 1880s. [. . .]

Even if for much of the imperial expansion after 1880 it can be accepted that a political incident such as the French protectorate over Tunisia or the English occupation of Egypt actually served as the ignition, the accelerator in and after the 1880s was often the pressure of economic rivalries. The 'New Imperialism' would not have moved off at all in many parts of the world if it had not been for the inescapable fact that the last decades of the century were years of profound economic as well as political change. 'In the furious commercial competition that now rages like a hurricane throughout the world', Curzon concluded from his study of Anglo-Persian trade, 'the loss of a market is a retrograde step that cannot be recovered; the gain of a market is a positive addition to the national strength. Indifference to Persia might mean the sacrifice of a trade that already feeds hundreds of thousands of our citizens in this country and in India. A friendly attention to Persia will mean so much more employment for British ships, for British labour, and for British spindles.'

There are, therefore, not one but two principal explanations of British imperial expansion during the 'New Imperialism'. The fashionable theory that British expansion was designed simply to maintain the security of the existing Empire against a new threat from the Continental Powers can explain a great deal. It describes the principal elements, for example, in the British occupation of Egypt, in the British advance into Upper Burma, the Sudan and Tibet, in British policy towards East and South Africa, in the Anglo-Russian agreement over spheres of influence in Persia. It accounts very largely for the political rivalry in Central Asia.

But the new threat which Britain faced in and after the 1880s was not confined to imperial frontiers and communications; it extended also to the security of British trade and finance. Increased foreign financial and commercial competition posed its own private problems for British overseas interests. But the responsibility of the government was engaged when foreign diplomatists were using their influence to damage competing British interests, and when it became obvious that, unless Britain took a share in the colonization and partition of the remainder of the underdeveloped world, she might find herself excluded altogether from the outlets on which, she believed, the future prosperity of her trade and finance might well depend. Before 1880 British statesmen had not been especially worried by foreign colonial expansion. Nor were they worried by expansion *after* that date provided that the markets remained open to British trade and investment and that no strategic interests were damaged. [. . .] H.M. Government's part in the 'New Imperialism' might have been restricted entirely to areas of strategic interest if it had not been for the revival of European Protectionism and the threat to the fair and equal treatment of British trade and finance. But it was this threat which led Britain to the conference table over the Congo, which persuaded the British Government to accept official responsibility for the government of West Africa, which drove Salisbury to consent to the economic partition of China, which served as the background to political rivalry in the Levant, and which was at least partially responsible, in common with the political security of Australasia, for reluctant annexations in the South Pacific.

The economic analysis of imperialism is not at fault in its basic assumption that a link of some kind or another existed between imperial expansion on the one hand, and increased foreign competition, diplomatic intervention, and the erection of tariff barriers on the other. The fault lies rather in the isolation of surplus capital as the major impetus towards expansion, and in the failure to provide any really convincing explanation of the means by which the aspirations of individual traders and investors were converted into imperial policy. [. . .] Critics of the whole concept of economic imperialism have had no real difficulty in destroying the extensions of Hobson's argument, particularly in relation to the responsibility of surplus capital. But in their enthusiasm at demolishing some of the more obvious absurdities of the 'capitalist conspiracy', recent writers on British imperialism have tended to reject the economic argument as a whole and to replace it by political or sociological arguments of their own.

Fieldhouse, it will be remembered, has declared that 'the rapid expansion of European commercial and financial influence throughout the world — the true "economic imperialism" — did not change its character after 1870; and was no more likely then than before to have resulted in significant acquisitions of land'. But the point is that the character of this expansion *had* changed. It is obviously true that economic factors carried more weight in some parts of the world than they did in others; that they were more influential in determining the policy of one Power than of another. No one would seriously argue that Russia's imperialism was more than marginally economic; Russian textile manufacturers looked for supplies of raw cotton and outlets for finished products, but their connexion with the Russian Government's final decision to advance into Turkestan, Persia and China was tenuous indeed. Nor, after [the work of] Brunschwig, can it be maintained that economic pressures were all-important in France. Even for Germany and the United States, where the economic motive is much less obscure, it is at least arguable that German expansion, in Ludwig Dehio's phrase, was a direct reflection of 'the elemental urge to achieve power', and that U.S. 'dollar diplomacy' was based on strategic rather than economic calculations. But the fact remains that Germany and the United States, in and after the 1870s, were fighting their way into international markets, and Britain, after decades of monopoly, was battling for survival. In 1870, the United Kingdom contained 31.8 per cent of the world's manufacturing capacity, as compared with 13.2 per cent in Germany and 23.3 per cent in the United States. By 1906-10, Britain's relative share had dropped to 14.7 per cent, while Germany now held 15.9 per cent and the United States 35.3 per cent. For Germany these figures, translated into 'imperialism', meant pressure for colonies in Africa and in the Pacific, economic intervention and partition in the Levant, an aggressive financial diplomacy at Peking, and the claim for preferential treatment in Shantung. For the United States, they meant a new interest in the Pacific, and – particularly during the Taft administration – the search for economic advantage in the Caribbean and equal shares in the economic partition of China. For Britain, they meant a desperate struggle to maintain at least the volume, if not the relative position, of British trade and investment overseas.

Quite apart from the competition of the emergent industrial nations, revived Protectionism was a new and dangerous element which threatened the exclusion of British trade from existing and prospective markets. This, and the transformation in the character of Continental financial diplomacy, could often find no satisfactory answer other than 'significant acquisitions of land'. It was in the name of equal favour and open competition that H.M. Government was compelled on occasion simply to apply diplomatic pressure, at others to colonize, and at others still to reach an international compromise whereby underdeveloped nations were divided into spheres of interest or influence. It was this which, in turn, lay behind British official support of mercantile interests in West Africa; behind the promotion by the British legation at Peking of the claims of the Hong Kong and Shanghai Bank group and the Peking Syndicate; behind the creation, under British official auspices, of the National Bank of Turkey; behind support of the Smyrna-Aidin Railway, the Euphrates Steam Navigation Company, and, in some respects, the Imperial Bank of Persia.

There is much in late-Victorian imperial expansion which cannot be explained by economic factors. But there is much which can. Any government is bound to obtain fair treatment and security for its subjects and their interests; it exists precisely for this purpose. In the late nineteenth century, British trading and financial interests overseas were threatened by diplomatic pressure and the erection of tariff barriers; the struggle to guarantee 'fair' treatment might often be limited to counter-pressure by British diplomatists, but it could also mean pre-emptive imperial expansion. Sinister pressures by individual City financiers had no more effect on late-Victorian and Edwardian officials than they had had on Palmerston's Foreign Office and the Cobdenite Board of Trade: why should they? But no British Government could stand aside indefinitely when the whole future of British trade and investment overseas seemed in jeopardy. Cries of alarm from the City, when directed not merely at increased competition but at discrimination and Protection, found a sympathetic audience in an otherwise *laissez-faire* Whitehall. Commercial and official opinion of government responsibility, and of the measures necessary for the defence and promotion of British trade and finance, for once coincided. Imperial expansion was only the most spectacular, and in Whitehall the least popular, of the remedies supplied. It was as simple as that.

6 THE GERMAN SOCIAL DEMOCRATIC PARTY 1890-1914 AS A POLITICAL MODEL

J.P. Nettl

Source: *Past and Present*, no.30, April 1965, pp.65-95.

In Imperial Germany before the First World War, political parties played a limited and somewhat unusual rôle. It is normally held that what defines a political party — and makes it different from other interest or pressure groups — is its willingness or constitutional ability to take power; to achieve its desired ends through the given structure of political power in society. This applied to all constitutional societies prior to 1914 with the exception of Germany. Here political parties as such had no opportunity for wielding power. The Imperial Government was carried on independently of them. The formation and composition of Government was not related to the power and strength of political parties as expressed at elections, and did not in any way represent the political groupings in the legislature, the *Reichstag*. The parties were of course able to influence Government in a negative way, by obstructing legislation, and by interrogating the Government about its administrative actions. Consequently the Imperial Chancellor found it necessary in matters of legislation to work with the support of a majority in the *Reichstag*, and often conducted complicated manoeuvres to obtain one. The parties that made up such a majority at any one time, however, had no expectation of sharing power; the most they could hope to obtain, by co-operating with the Government, was legislation favouring their particular interests. In consequence the political parties in Germany before 1914 can better be described as politically organized interest groups, attempting to exert pressure on the Government in order to gain sectional advantages. The normal function of parties, to aggregate demands into a platform on which to be voted into power, could not be fulfilled, and so aggregation of interests remained limited. Constitutionally speaking, political parties did not exist at all; since, however, the political wishes of the electorate were expressed through organized parties, the Government had to form its majorities in the *Reichstag* by negotiation with party leaders instead of creating majorities out of undisciplined individuals, as the constitution suggested. The parties in turn 'were dominated [in the imperial period] by the alternative of supporting or opposing an [anyhow] existing Government'. In fact the idea of a Reich party, pledged simply to support the Government, recurred in the constitutional thinking of the time, and the

Government's emotional manipulation of the 1907 *Reichstag* elections strongly suggested the emergence of such a 'national' platform.

Only two parties in Germany represented an exception to this general rule; the Catholic Centre Party and the Social Democratic Party (the SPD). Both began by representing socially defensive organizations rather than positive interest groups. Both considered themselves largely outside the course of political life in Imperial Germany. This applied far more to the SPD than to the Centre, for Socialist opposition was total and not merely limited; unlike the Centre it could envisage no possibility whatever of coming to terms with political society. With a philosophy that postulated not amendment but total collapse of the existing order, and made the party base its policies on that assumption, the SPD occupied from the moment of its foundation a pariah position. For twelve years, from 1878 to 1890, it was illegal; after Bismarck departed and the special anti-socialist legislation was repealed, the SPD never lost the conscious feeling of being an outcast, and adopted attitudes accordingly. Memories of the illegal period dominated the party's ideology much as the great depression dominates the ideology of the English Trade Unions today; in both cases a memory of being rejected by an existing order, whether political or economic.

This made the SPD a very unusual phenomenon in political life. There have always been political groups committed to the total destruction and overthrow of existing government, but these have generally been conspiracies or sects, whose very existence has depended on tight organization and secrecy. With a platform of irreconcilable opposition the SPD, on the other hand, soon grew into a legal mass movement, whose official philosophy was based on the probably violent collapse of society, and whose policy attempted to hasten this event as much as possible. Right from the start it kept itself apart from society, first by emphasizing philosophical and moral differences, later completing the social containment of its members by organizational means. Thus the whole ideology of separation had strong moral overtones, which equated participation in society with corruption, and claimed to provide within itself a superior alternative to a corrupt capitalism. In fact the noisy official self-differentiation by Socialists was carried to such lengths that to discover substantial capacities in them for normal human behaviour – faults as well as virtues – was a major sociological triumph, achieved by no less a practitioner than Max Weber. And this rather obvious discovery still continues to illuminate unlikely areas of sociological inquiry today. In fact, though great emphasis was always placed on this moral aspect as part and parcel of the doctrine of developing class-consciousness in Marxist philosophy, it was never considered sufficient, and the SPD increasingly developed organizational forms through which the activities and aspirations of its members could be expressed. But the two were not compatible; as organization grew moral fervour declined, and the one even became a sophisticated substitute for the other.

This non-participating opposition must be distinguished both from revolutionary conspiracies and political parties acting through and within the system. The SPD is not, of course, a unique example of such non-participating opposition. Circumstances of extreme dissatisfaction in various societies have produced similar phenomena from time to time. The RPF in France was founded in 1947 as a protest against the revival of a totally unacceptable *système politique* in the Fourth Republic. It refused to participate and, much like the SPD, used its presence in the political organs of society — legislature and civil administration — to provide a continuous and vociferous indictment of that society. Similarly, such parties arise in emerging colonial nations where a tradition of political organization exists: the Indian Congress, the Convention Peoples' Party in Ghana, the RDA in French West Africa. As these protest parties develop, they increasingly prohibit participation in colonial government, except as a clearly defined prelude to the departure of the colonial power. In all these cases, there is a strong element of inheritance expectation, whether by voluntary handling over of power or as a result of a cataclysm. In fact this expectation of inheritance is the moral force which makes non-participating opposition possible, yet prevents violence except as a last resort. Such parties, including the SPD, might well be called 'inheritor parties'.

Like all political parties, the SPD was mostly concerned with day to day problems of policy. The leadership particularly tended to be preoccupied with empirical problems, to which it tried to find a solution in accordance with its philosophy. The maintenance of that philosophy and its development as a means of dealing with problems in their widest context was the task of the intellectuals. The SPD was, right from the start, well supplied with these. As a result of its pre-eminent position in the Second International, it attracted some of the best Marxist brains from other countries, particularly those where government policy kept Socialism confined to illegal conspiracies. Nonetheless, the continuing debate on policy within the party occasionally produced differences large enough to bring into question the SPD's entire *raison d'être*. Perhaps the most important of these self-examinations was the revisionist controversy, which began in 1898 and lasted — as a debate over fundamentals — until 1903. [...] In the course of it the problem of the SPD's relationship to society came to be critically examined; to this extent the whole revisionist debate is an important landmark in our analysis of the SPD as an inheritor party.

Instead of concentrating on what they said or how, we will examine those who said it and why, in order to see what forces and ideas they represent. On the revisionist side there were first the theorists, people like Bernstein, who unconsciously paid tribute to the importance of Marxist philosophy by providing a theoretical basis for the sum of their own empirical observations, both of society and of party policy. It is important to recognize that this theoretical analysis was almost inadvertent, and always reluctant. Bernstein's articles began as an armchair exercise in the lofty quiet of the *Neue Zeit*. He was unaware of the savage storm of controversy that he was about to cause, and was astonished when it broke. Revisionism was not an intellectual attack on Marxist teleology, but a groping attempt to formulate coherently a mass of disturbing but strictly empirical data.

Bernstein's main supporters were the practical men of the party, the Trade Union leaders, practising members of various professions who happened also to be Socialists, and above all the representatives of Social Democracy from South Germany. All these people had in some way broken through the isolation from society in which most Social Democrats found themselves. Thus it is interesting to note that among the lawyers in the SPD, those that were actually practising were revisionist, while those who had been disbarred, or whose practice had suffered because they were Socialists, supported the leadership. The exception to this was a group consisting among others of Liebknecht, Rosenfeld and Haase, whose legal work was wholly confined to the defence of Socialist interests and members in the courts; these too supported the leadership, since their practices were almost a Socialist vested interest. Similarly journalists like Schippel and David, who had established a national reputation in their particular subjects, supported the revisionists, while those who wrote exclusively for the party press — especially in the provinces — were among the most vociferous supporters of orthodoxy.

The South Germans, who provided the revisionist shock troops at party congresses, and in between continued to co-operate with 'society' at home, strenuously made the excuse of special conditions, a different political climate. [. . .] From our point of view it should be noted that it was only in the provinces of South Germany that the SPD could take part in communal affairs, and occupied its share of local government posts in accordance with electoral strength. Similarly, the different laws and their interpretation in North and South Germany had repeatedly proved useful to the SPD, whose members often found refuge in another province from impending deportations or prosecutions in Prussia. Undoubtedly the insulation between society and the SPD was thinner and more porous in the South.

The line-up in the revisionist controversy therefore was closely connected with the experience of collaborating with existing society. The continuing debate about policy was concerned with the same problem. By postulating that capitalism had softened sufficiently to make it possible for Social Democracy not only to come to terms with it, but actually influence it in the desired direction — which meant the acceptance of a status similar to other political parties — Bernstein and his supporters were altering not so much Marxist theoretical analysis as the party's established practice of political isolation. The alienation of being permanently and irrevocably dissociated would thus be broken; not only policy would change, but the moral and organizational structure of isolation was threatened.

Significantly this effort to throw a bridge across the gap from the Socialist camp was matched by a similar attempt on the part of society. Sombart, Schmoller and other academic social scientists recognized that it was not desirable to perpetuate the gap between the Socialist camp and society, and attempted to persuade society, particularly the Government in its administration and legislation, to meet the working classes half way. Sombart himself coasted close to Marxist shores for many years; he perceived that what really kept Social Democracy isolated from society was not policy — which could be altered — but an ideology and a philosophy of separation which could only be destroyed by contact. In return the SPD intellectuals, Mehring and Luxemburg, recognized how close he was to the truth and reserved a specially vitriolic hatred for the *Kathedersozialisten* [armchair socialists], though in private they acknowledged the validity of some of Sombart's comments. Paradoxically however, while the revisionist impetus from within the Socialist camp came from professional men, Trade Union leaders and Southern politicians, it was only from a few academic intellectuals like Sombart that a corresponding effort was made to persuade a disinterested and reluctant public on the other side.

Opposed to the revisionists in the SPD were two main groups, those who believed that the gap between society and Socialism was natural and desirable — the Marxists — and those who believed that society had irrevocably cast them out and that Socialist isolation was mainly the product of Government policies and attitudes. At that time there was no visible difference between these two points of view. The SPD Executive and the substantial force who supported it came down belatedly but firmly against the revisionists and between 1901 and 1903 rebuilt the broken defences against society on all fronts. Chronologically the defeat of the revisionists at the 1903 party congress was followed shortly by the opening of a revolutionary period in Germany during which a series of Trade Union strikes coincided with mounting political agitation for suffrage reform in Prussia. Then in January 1905 came the outbreak of the Russian revolution with its considerable impact on the SPD. To all appearances, the defeat of the revisionists was therefore followed by a sharper confrontation between Social Democracy and society; in an atmosphere of general satisfaction there was no point in any further self-examination in the victors' camp. Nonetheless the mobilization of support for the 'old and tried tactics' against the revisionists created what was in fact an alliance of two different groups. During the period of political deflation after 1906, and particularly after the defeat of Social Democracy in the 1907 *Reichstag* elections, the orthodox majority of the party gradually broke down into these two different and finally conflicting groups. It was the development of this particular conflict which eventually brought about a division in European Socialism of much greater historical significance than the revisionist controversy. In effect, it was the disintegration of the majority against the revisionists which finally produced the split between Communism and Social Democracy, and the rest of the paper will be concerned with it.

On the surface the split took place over increasingly sharp differences about policy. From 1910 to 1914 alternative policies emerged with regard to almost all problems with which the SPD was faced. Most recent history has analysed these divergencies in terms of policy, though with considerable sophistication; the most recent and thorough history of the SPD traces the emergence of distinct groups by systematically analysing alignments over different problems, and treating these chronologically. At the same time the possibilities offered by previous attempts at a more sociological analysis are deliberately played down. But there are difficulties with this attempt to create systematic groupings and sub-groupings according to policy decisions. For one thing, this method is arbitrary and at the same time overcomplicated. Composition and size of these political 'groups' was in a constant state of flux; they had no real basis of cohesion. As soon as we regard the SPD correctly — as a political society in its own right — the policies of these groups *in vacuo* and even the groups themselves lose much of their meaning, and any history based on them becomes as arbitrary as a history of the French radicals under the Third Republic in terms of their policies and ministerial groupings. The shifting middle position in the pre-war SPD, which during the war crystallized into the Independent Social Democratic Party (USPD), had no real basis for permanent existence, and indeed ceased to be a political factor of any importance in 1920; it can be argued that the USPD was a precipitation of wartime conditions. It seems therefore more meaningful to search for the central division and to treat the momentary voting line-ups as so many *ad hoc* agglomerations of individuals. Naturally there were policy disputes, and people did align themselves differently on each occasion, but underneath there is a consistent divergence based on fundamental differences between left and right, which the USPD only obscured for a time. It is usually argued that this final polarization was due exclusively to the pull of the Soviet Union acting through the Third International; that if there had been no Soviet Union there would have been no Socialist split into two camps. The present author believes, however, that this particular split was already endemic in German Social Democracy before 1914 and would probably have happened anyhow.

Why has this problem been so difficult to identify? To a large extent the reasons are to be found within the SPD itself. The system of frequent meetings, culminating in annual meetings of delegates at provincial party congresses and finally the national congress, allowed for and even encouraged the full and free expression of views. Under such circumstances it is usually supposed that there is no need to look for hidden motives. People can and do tell the truth as they see it, and opponents within the party soon put right any suspected — or even unconscious — intent to deceive. At least until 1912 vote catching was deplored; the German political system made that scale of aggregation pointless. As far as self-expression was concerned the SPD was extremely democratic. The party press debated problems at great length, and opened its pages to the representatives of all divergent opinions. From 1911 onwards this practice began to be progressively curtailed; the far left opposition to the Executive had difficulty in getting the party press to print its views without a certain amount of censorship. But for most of the period before the war almost any view could get a public airing. At the party congresses there were no attempts to restrict the expression of opinions other than those dictated by time. Even in 1913 Rosa Luxemburg and her supporters were able to put forward a strongly worded resolution on the mass strike, and to speak at length on its behalf. Like any legislature, the SPD congress jealously guarded its rights and privileges; there was no guillotine and the chairman's rules of order were lax. Above all the opposition had many opportunities of putting its views to meetings in various localities all over the country. Local party secretaries were more concerned with having interesting and provocative speakers in order to provide a worthwhile evening for their members than with any attempt to impose a party line, though here too provincial executives tried from 1912 to exercise an occasional veto. With so much public and free debate, it appears pointless to search for unsolved mysteries.

So any history based largely on official documents and published articles must give the impression of free interplay of opinions followed by majority resolutions at the congress — all very open and democratic. The rare attempts to deceive the congress or to keep things from it usually failed, and caused a scandal in addition. Yet careful analysis of the congress proceedings and particularly of the private papers of the SPD leaders shows that in the last years there was more and more manoeuvring behind the scenes, and in addition the Executive even began to insist that its proceedings and communications must be privileged and secret like those of any other successfully functioning administration. This bald demand met vociferous resistance; though the Executive's attitude was vindicated by a majority, it learnt its lesson and the expulsion of Radek in 1913 for instance was handled with kid-glove regard for the party congress's susceptibilities. The overpowering form of democracy deceptively hid the lack of content. The Executive always managed to manoeuvre in a variety of ways in order to avoid public defeat on important questions. Like the Imperial Government, it found the manipulation of the legislature simpler than flouting it. But manipulation inevitably means distortion.

But in spite of the flood of discussion on every conceivable subject, there were in fact some universally respected taboos. These add to the difficulty, since they mainly concerned questions that would have illuminated our present problems if they had been discussed. Thus in all the years from 1882 to 1914 there was only one article in *Neue Zeit*, the theoretical organ of Social Democracy, on the subject of post-revolutionary society, and this treated the problem merely in a historical context — as a discussion of past millenarian societies. Even the revolution itself was little discussed; the technique of it not at all. The all-important topic of war was treated as an abstract evil, simply to be denounced. Interest was focused largely on contemporary questions of the day and their importance in the context of present Socialist attitudes, while broader questions affecting the SPD's future tended to be ignored. After the revisionist controversy, most party members took the formally hostile relationship between Social Democracy and society and the final revolutionary catharsis largely for granted. Organizational problems, except in their immediate and technical aspect, were part of this limbo; there was no attempt to relate organization to policy. More than this; such matters were held to be rather unimportant and technical and therefore properly the concern of the leadership. While anyone was free to debate policy, the few critics of the SPD's structure and style of administration were told right from the start that they had no experience and did not know what they were talking about. [. . .] As we shall see, the basis of the radical opposition to the leadership was the demolition of the organizational taboo; underneath the surface criticisms of policy Rosa Luxemburg and the others raised fundamental questions about organization and its rôle in defining the relationship between Social Democracy and society.

Before 1914 the only thorough attempt to relate problems of organization directly to the larger aims of Social Democracy was made by Lenin in

What is to be done? His critics, both Russian and German, challenged the policy of centralized control which he advocated; but what shocked them even more than his actual views was the whole concept of elevating organizational problems to a place of such primary importance. [. . .]

No valid comparison between the organizational ideas of Bolsheviks and the SPD is possible as their circumstances were entirely different. But we can contrast the relative importance each gave to a correct theory of organization. Thus it was not so much that the situation of the SPD required a different organization from that of the Russian party — the one a legal mass movement, the other an illegal and émigré conspiracy — but that the German party saw no relationship between policy and organization, while Lenin held that this was the crux of the problem. Perhaps the difference will be more apparent if we turn the question round. The SPD was always in search of correct policies; its nature and size gave it the right or even the duty to take issue on nearly all the major questions of the day. It shared many of the preoccupations of society, however much it differed in its policies. Organization had to serve these policies, above all the policy of growth. Lenin on the other hand could only influence Russian society sporadically. His universe was one of small competing conspiratorial groups, and internal problems of organization could easily appear pre-eminent in that world. Organization was not synonymous with growth, but with control. Without a correct power structure there could be no control, and hence no party. Whether in German circumstances any preoccupation with organizational structure as a creative rather than a secondary factor was possible at all is another question. We shall see that only the radical opposition in Germany sensed how crucial this problem was, though they dealt with it in terms of a destructive onslaught on the party's organizational self-satisfaction and not by proposing explicit alternatives.

The defeat of revisionism in Germany — at least as a matter of debate — temporarily settled the problem of relations between Social Democracy and society. The SPD went back to its isolation with a vengeance; vindicated at home, the orthodox majority now felt strong enough to use its pre-eminent position in the Second International to impose the same policy of isolation on other parties. At the Amsterdam Congress of the International in 1904 this problem was aired in a violent debate between the Germans and the French. Where the Germans advocated strength through abstinence and the growth of the party in isolation, the French had always insisted that strength could only be measured by political power.

What at present most weighs on Europe and the World, on the guarantee of peace . . . the progress of socialism and of the working-class . . . is the political powerlessness of German Social Democracy.

The political debate was shot through with social overtones. To many of the French the idea of satisfying social and personal aspirations within an isolated socialist movement was meaningless. The whole conception of socialist 'togetherness' was treated with contempt. Briand said after the Congress: 'Genossen, Genossen, j'en ai assez de ces genosseries' (Comrades, Comrades, I am sick of all this camaraderie). Most important of all, Jaurès poured particular scorn on the philosophy of isolation – and on its philosopher, on 'the political formulae with which your good Comrade Kautsky will supply you to the end of his days'. Though the issue was exactly the same at Amsterdam as it had been at all the German party congresses since 1898, the French saw it far more clearly than the German revisionists and expressed their case more lucidly – isolation or participation; not theory, but personal questions affecting every socialist. In return and for good measure the Germans carried the resolution adopted at their party congress in Dresden the year before almost verbatim at the International Congress – and carried it in the teeth of the French.

The victory was turned to good account. From 1904 to 1914 a steady growth of SPD organization and services took place. On the political side the central executive was enlarged, regional organizations strengthened and new ones created, and more officials appointed at all levels. Equally important was the less publicized extension in the social and cultural field. Party education received a fillip with the creation of the party school in 1906 and the extension and improvement of the *Wanderlehrer* system, the ambulant lecturers who moved from place to place with their instruction courses. The party organized closed excursions, singing groups and even paid a squadron of 'workers' poets' who wrote both tunes and lyrics. Special emphasis was placed on organizing services for children and youth; in 1912 there were 125 local children's commissions and 574 youth commissions. The women's movement made rapid headway under the aegis of the devoted Clara Zetkin. Finally, the *Zahlabend* [payment evening] , when members of local organizations gathered in the pub to pay contributions and talk things over, became not only the most important social institution of Social Democracy at the grass roots, but the focus of political opinion and the accepted means by which Executive and opposition could reach the members. The subject deserves a study of its own, especially in comparison with similar activities in France, Austria and England.

Institutions began to serve curious and unexpected purposes. The local party press became a hothouse for talent, for collecting bright young men, and keeping them within the Socialist orbit; a complex system of cross-posting of journalists developed in the last years before the war. And behind the growing party press stood a network of publishing houses with an increasingly large budget. J.H.W. Dietz and the *Vorwärts* bookshop had a turnover fully comparable to that of any commercial publishing venture.

Two particular features of this organizational proliferation deserve special emphasis. The party spread its net into hitherto untouched or resistant areas. Efforts were made to organize the predominantly rural provinces and a successful stint in 'Siberia' became a passport to high party office. In the course of extending activity it also extended control. Thus between 1906 and 1908 it moved in on the youth organizations which had been spontaneous creations under the guidance of devoted individuals, mostly radical except in the South where an otherwise prominent revisionist, Dr Ludwig Frank, had been active in this field. As a result the numbers increased steadily after 1908, but the radical élan was organized out of existence, or at least driven underground until the war.

Secondly, there was an immediate reflection in the organizational structure of the party to cope with new and increased activity. As the press grew, press commissions proliferated in numbers and power. The youth problem brought organizational salvation in the shape of the *Jugendzentrale* [central youth office] under the formidable Friedrich Ebert. Occasionally the organization was even created before the activity it was intended to regulate, as with the educational commission (*Bildungsausschuss*) formed in 1906 to advise on, and set up, the party school. Until the war there was no climate of opposition to the existence of a bureaucracy; if anything both Left and Right supported organizational proliferation as a form of institutionalized support for their particular cause. The English or American notion of limited government, that it might be better to do without certain activities if they involved authoritative regulation or control, was utterly alien.

By 1911 already the SPD had all the appearance of a state within a state, and when Bebel jocularly referred to the Executive as 'your government' no one took exception or expressed surprise at the phrase. This 'government' presided over a formidable apparatus, and a large budget to pay for it. The finances of the SPD were the envy of the Second International; its primacy was openly admitted to be connected with its *largesse*. The preamble to the Executive's report at each party congress resembled nothing so much as the budget of the Reich; consolidated revenue on one side, expenditure on the other. The Executive's report itself, moreover, was increasingly concerned with welfare and social activities, indicators of organizational growth and influence — such as circulation of party papers — and these items took precedence over the platform speeches on important problems of the day.

The three or four days a year when the party congress met were a miniature reflection of a whole *Reichstag* session, but entirely different in form and content from the annual congress of the other German parties. Unlike them, it was no mere forum of opinion, at which the leadership could test the feeling of the constituencies. The party congress had a vital constitutional rôle in the SPD state; however fierce the dissenting protests of conscience, it never failed to rally to the Executive when party cohesion was at stake. Whatever the problems and disagreements, few delegates left the congress without a feeling of communion with the great, of work jointly and well done. As Bebel's private correspondence shows, this atmosphere was not spontaneous but carefully prepared in advance through personal contact and persuasion.

The danger of controversy between the political leadership and the Trade Unions was removed by the secret agreement of February 1906, in which the SPD leadership undertook to avoid and play down policies offensive to the Trade Unions. In return the Trade Union leaders renounced any attempt at establishing a separate political line for themselves, let alone divorcing the Trade Union movement from organized Social Democracy. In Germany political Socialism had preceded organized Trade Unionism and always considered the latter its specialist industrial branch; a client relationship which the rich and growing Trade Unions found increasingly irksome. Now, by admitting the Unions to adult status, friction was reduced and henceforward the Trade Union leadership played an important part in supporting the SPD Executive against the Left. Both the party and the Trade Union leaders were careful to avoid crossing each other's organizational preserves by practising abstention rather than through any attempt to define their respective areas. This mutual self-denying ordinance brought a rich, disciplined membership back into the SPD 'state' − but at the expense of all but the most platitudinous political exploitation. The harmony between Trade Unions and party was unique on the Continent at the time. More than any other single factor it helped to explain the extent to which Social Democracy was able to develop as a 'state', but also why it remained immobile.

All this enormously strengthened the power of the SPD leadership. From the proliferation of services and organizations, there inevitably grew a bureaucracy which thought of itself as 'neutral' in questions of policy, supported the executive at all times and became in turn the structural apparatus of the leadership's control. As an institution the party bureaucracy articulated hidden but powerful interests of its own, which were effectively represented by the Executive. That democracy is not the enemy of oligarchy but perhaps its most fertile soil, was already obvious to de Tocqueville in his examination of the United States as a political phenomenon in the nineteenth century. This prediction was brilliantly documented as an existing fact by Robert Michels. Though his central thesis is the connection between democracy and oligarchy on social and political grounds, the work bristles with incidental insights which he could not always pursue. Thus the development of bureaucracy as both the functional expression of oligarchy and in turn as a further means of increasing its power are briefly discussed, while the notion of a state within a state is only mentioned once. Michels also recognized but did not stress the problem of the relationship between 'party and state', or in our terms between party and society. [. . .]

Last but by no means least, ideology itself performed a new and distinctive function in the new, more strongly structured, inward-looking party. Far from withering away, it provided a suitable umbrella under which to hide the continuing but by definition 'ineffective' or 'useless' political activity. The more the party isolated itself, the less (publicly admissible) point there was in canvassing, campaigning, electing or serving in *Land* and *Reich* legislatures; and the more important the ideological refuge. After 1905, party congresses ceased to be the supreme legislative assembly and became a symbol of ritual celebration of political ideology, 'mere honorifics . . . a festivity', from which participants would disperse refreshed and capable of disseminating ideological refreshment. And their product, the assertion of the good old outward-looking ideology of revolution, became merely a means of ensuring continued loyalty and devotion to the proprietors, the SPD. Even today, in countries as pragmatic as Sweden, ideology is still seen as an *instrument* to mould participants and members into greater loyalty — and sociologists examine it in purely functional terms. The SPD could serve as a basic model for their theories.

Although these influences did not manifest themselves openly, they did produce an identifiable state of mind in the party. The revisionist controversy, and the victory of the forces which wanted to concentrate on internal preoccupations and not on the relationship with society, provided the suitable political culture in which these forces could flourish. But this was not an accidental result of the victory of the Executive in the revisionist controversy. Rather it was the other way about. For beneath the verbal explanations of orthodoxy — the 'Marxists' on the one hand and those who took isolation as the inevitable consequence of society's attitude on the other — there was the very real self-interest of a bureaucracy whose power and indeed existence depended largely on the SPD's continued isolation, to whatever reason this was due. It is very noticeable how after 1901 these forces entered the controversy and threw their weight decisively behind the orthodox. When Kautsky said that revisionism, if triumphant, would destroy the very basis of Social Democracy, he was incidentally articulating the real self-interest of Bebel and his colleagues in maintaining the *status quo*. To a considerable extent the question of *why* Social Democracy should be isolated became a formality, and was lost in the self-interest of powerful factors to keep it so.

What therefore distinguishes the SPD from other 'inheritors' is this powerful factor of immobility, of satisfaction with the *status quo* of isolation. Moreover the growing SPD state did not take any accidental form in accordance with particular needs, but followed the pattern of society in which, isolated or no, it was enveloped. The creation of a separate society within the SPD was a re-creation, a mirror image, of German Imperial society. Ideology is necessarily the reflection of knowledge available at the time, and therefore differs sharply from utopia. Since, as we have seen, detailed discussion of future society − utopia − did not exist, and was frowned upon as romantic, there could be no other image for SPD society to copy than that by which it was surrounded, however antagonistic the two may have been. This held true of attitudes as much as organizational forms. One of the most striking examples of the way in which organized Social Democracy reflected society was in its unconscious national attitudes. Overtly the SPD opposed nationalism, but in private Bebel developed a sound hatred of both English and Russians. What is particularly interesting is that in private Bebel lashed out at foreign socialists with the same home-spun invective which he used on opponents in the SPD − as Socialists they were all *en famille* − while his references to the British government were couched in the diplomatic formalities of one head of state discussing the affairs of another. Often the differences between public and private attitudes were obliterated. Thus the SPD regarded the domestic Polish question in much the same way as the rest of society − with incomprehension; the Poles were as fractious as citizens as they were awkward as Socialists. The only remedy was organizational absorption, which was merely a Socialist version of Germanization.

Groups organizing for pressure on or against other groups tend to copy the structure of their opposite number. As we shall see, there did develop after 1912 a form of contact between the two societies at the top, which hastened this process of precise duplication. 'One can see in the organization of the Social Democratic Executive and its organs an involuntary mirror image of the Imperial Germany of William II and of its system of political leadership.'

Moreover the SPD had the additional benefit of philosophy for its position. This did not apply to its organizational mirror image of society − which went entirely unnoticed − but it did cover very adequately the necessity for isolation. Karl Kautsky in his *Road to Power* provided positive content to this isolation, and raised it from the regrettable by-product of policy to a positive revolutionary factor. [. . .] Briefly Kautsky's view was that the mere growth of isolated Social Democracy would subjectively and objectively cause such havoc in the opposing camp that society would disintegrate and Social Democracy be able to step into its place. This was the theory of inheritance at its most extreme. As an index of internal strength, Kautsky postulated doctrinal purity. As an index of growth, however, he suggested an increase of votes and mandates at the coming (1912) *Reichstag* elections, on which the party was pinning special hopes after its lack of success in 1907. Though not always in full agreement with the Executive, Kautsky had become by this time the particular exponent of its ideology. He was the champion of social isolation, and he was also an intellectual, far removed from the immediate problems of organization and even further from any contact with society. It is therefore not surprising that he reflected faithfully and coherently the implicit ideology of the party leadership, even though he often felt exasperated by the Executive and saw himself as a doughty champion of progress.

Yet Kautsky's analysis carried within it the dialectic of its own destruction. The emphasis on success in elections as a positive factor in the overthrow of society justified as well as explained the party's obsession with the coming elections. When in 1912 Social Democracy not only made up for its defeat in 1907, but registered a great advance, Kautsky's theories appeared well justified, while their author was triumphant. But the interest in *Reichstag* mandates contributed to an inflation of the importance within the party of the Socialist group in the *Reichstag*. Much of this was psychological. It had always been the practice for the most important leaders of the SPD to seek election to the *Reichstag* in constituencies where the SPD had strong chances of success. With the increasing importance of election success in party thinking, the status of members of the *Reichstag* also increased. The Socialist delegation was no longer merely made up of party notables, but provided a special cohesion and status for its members. The difference is important, and has been misunderstood. Surprisingly there is little evidence that this tendency, which must have existed from the beginning of the century, ever gave any offence. By 1912 however the opposition, already aroused by many unsatisfactory aspects of party life, began to campaign against the way that 'the letters MdR (member of the *Reichstag*) go to the head of all these good people'.

Now that the SPD with its 110 seats had become the largest single party in the *Reichstag*, it was increasingly involved, if not directly in the affairs of government, at least in the legislature's standing business. It could no longer simply abstain, and for a short time Scheidemann actually held the office of *Reichstag* Vice-President. The reasons why this attempt was not followed through were orthodox Socialist ones – crises of conscience with regard to wearing frock coats, bowing to the Emperor and leading the 'Hoorays' when ceremonial tradition demanded. The interesting thing, however, is that the acceptance of the post should even have been considered – and still within the policy of general abstention.

This increase in the importance of the SPD's *Reichstag* delegation within the party coincided chronologically with an increase in the importance of the *Reichstag* itself. There was, in the two years before the war, a crisis of nerves in Germany, which the Chancellor of the time in his memoirs described as *Reichsverdrossenheit* (national disillusionment) – promptly matched, as will be seen, by a corresponding *frisson* of discomfort within the party. Within this atmosphere of unease, a number of specific incidents took place, like the affair of Zabern, when the *Reichstag* severely criticized the Government, but offered to lend its assistance in dealing with the apparently uncontrollable proliferations of imperial power, like the military. It was not the first time that the *Reichstag* had attempted to go to the rescue of the Government, but after 1912 it did so increasingly from a position of strength.

Thus coincidentally as the *Reichstag* gained in importance, the SPD delegation increased its authority as a group within the party – yet another unconscious interaction between these two divorced societies. At the top, and particularly through the importance of its membership of the legislature, the isolation of the SPD was becoming imaginary rather than real. Though the slogans of total opposition continued, actual contact and collaboration became more frequent. Examples of this are legion; perhaps the most important and noisy incident was the attempt to exploit the SPD's position of power after the run-off elections of 1912 by forcing the creation of a left block in the *Reichstag*. The leadership and Kautsky went to great lengths to explain this as a temporary tactical phenomenon which could only be of benefit to the SPD; that while the party would influence its allies, these latter could have no effect on the solidly orthodox ideology of the party. What contemporary commentators and later historians failed to realize was that the very nature of a double-ballot system of elections made alliances between parties inevitable for the second poll – and this included the SPD – regardless of whether victory was intended as a mere demonstration of strength or was to be used in order to achieve policy purposes. But officially sanctioned electoral alliances were in any case a far cry from the revisionist debate. By harking back continually to the triumph of isolation after 1903, it had now become possible to carry out many of the revisionist recommendations in practice and still preserve the appearance of orthodoxy. Officially, divorce from society was still total. The more perceptive revisionists laughed.

The peculiar significance of the emergence of the *Reichstag* delegation as a power factor in the SPD went almost completely unnoticed. By 1913 the radical opposition was in full cry along the entire line of the Executive's policy. They condemned the collaboration with bourgeois parties, both during the elections and afterwards in the *Reichstag* — but as a matter of policy; as with so many other structural problems, no one was aware of how much power had shifted to the parliamentary delegation. It was only after the outbreak of war, when the SPD *Reichstag* delegation openly took control of the party and installed itself as custodian of policy for the duration, that the constitutional aspect was aired. It was suddenly realized that there was no provision in party statutes or philosophy for the *Reichstag* delegation to have any special function or rôle at all — just as there was no provision in the Imperial constitution for the existence of parties. Even then, however, it was the *policy* of the leadership and its new power base in the *Reichstag* that gave the most offence. The emerging split in the *Reichstag* delegation over the next three years between independents and majority — leaving aside Liebknecht — was partly due to the unconstitutional behaviour of the leadership, though heavily tinged with disagreement on policy. Haase, a lawyer, particularly took the constitutional view when he resigned from the co-chairmanship of the party.

In the last resort, therefore, the SPD ceased on 4 August 1914 to be an inheritor party, and became a pressure group, similar to all the others — 'a stinking corpse' in radical eyes. Most of its dealings with the Government during the war were concerned with obtaining concessions for the sectional interests it represented, the workers. To this purpose the political orientation of the SPD became increasingly subordinated, and indeed members of the parliamentary delegation declared again and again that if they continued to pursue the old political objectives, they would not be able to represent the interests of their members to the Government.

It may well be concluded that in the long run the position of an inheritor party becomes impossible if the inheritance will not mature. A state of isolation cannot be indefinitely maintained. Either it will lead to violence or success. These alternatives are shared by inheritor parties in colonial countries. The third possibility is disintegration, such as befell the RPF which, five years after its foundation, had ceased to be a factor of importance in French political life (1952) and by 1955 had disappeared altogether. The last possibility, presented by the SPD in conditions in which success or violence were impossible, was gradual acceptance of the rôle of a pressure group like others such; competing for rewards instead of inheriting them. The distance it had created between society and itself, the increasing tendencies towards oligarchy and bureaucracy, helped to keep this alignment

at bay and made the process of change invisible to the participants. Nevertheless the tendency was there already before 1914; often a cataclysm like
war only hurries up inherent tendencies rather than altering basic alignments. And once more Kautsky came to the party's theoretical rescue. By
asserting that there were essential differences between conditions during
war and peace, he again reflected the thinking and attitude of the leadership which believed that only the outbreak of war forced it to make
substantial changes and depart from established tradition, but that it could
return to the *status quo ante* after the war, with an additional bonus in
post-war credits. [. . .]

7 THE OUTBREAK OF WAR IN 1914

A. ORIGINS OF THE FIRST WORLD WAR (extract)

L.C.F. Turner

Source: *Origins of the First World War* (Edward Arnold, 1970), Ch.6, pp.91-110.

Sazonov [the Russian Foreign Minister] heard of the Austrian ultimatum to Serbia at 10 a.m. on 24 July [1914] and at once exclaimed, 'C'est la guerre européenne!' He immediately telephoned the news to the Tsar, who commented characteristically, 'this is disturbing'. After a tense discussion with the Austrian ambassador, Count Szapary, Sazonov sent for General Janushkevich, Chief of the General Staff, and discussed plans for a partial mobilization of the Russian Army. Standard histories of the crisis convey the impression that the conception of partial mobilization originated with the Foreign Minister, and Albertini describes it as 'this bright idea of Sazonov's'. It is obvious, however, that Sazonov, who was pathetically ignorant of military affairs, was merely reviving the scheme for partial mobilization already formulated by Sukhomlinov [the Russian Minister of War] in 1912 when Russia had come perilously close to plunging Europe into a major war.

It is significant that Sazonov was contemplating something like a partial mobilization before the delivery of the Austrian ultimatum. On 18 July he told the British ambassador, Sir George Buchanan, that 'anything in the shape of an Austrian ultimatum at Belgrade could not leave Russia indifferent, and she might be forced to take some precautionary military measures'. It is highly probable that he discussed this question with the military leaders before 24 July, and that Sukhomlinov then submitted in extended form the proposal for partial mobilization which he had already formulated in 1912.

The proposal considered by Sazonov and Janushkevich on the 24th was to mobilize the Military Districts of Kiev, Odessa, Moscow and Kazan, but to refrain from mobilizing the Districts of Warsaw, Vilna and St Petersburg in order to avoid alarming Germany. Sazonov certainly seems to have regarded this as an admirable way of exerting pressure on Austria; he did not understand that a partial mobilization involving thirteen Russian army corps along her northern border would compel Austria to order general mobilization, which in turn would invoke the Austro-German alliance and require general mobilization by Germany. Sazonov's ignorance was shared by Jagow [the State Secretary in the German Foreign Ministry], who told the British ambassador on 27 July that 'if Russia only mobilized in the south, Germany would not mobilize, but if she mobilized in the north, Germany would have to do so'. Jagow repeated the same statement to the French ambassador on the 27th and Albertini rightly describes his behaviour as 'a tremendous blunder', because 'partial mobilization would have led to war no less surely than general mobilization'.

Janushkevich was incapable of giving Sazonov sound advice. He had only been in office for five months and Sir Bernard Pares, who knew him personally, says 'he had nothing to recommend him but the personal favour of the Tsar'. Commenting on a letter written by Janushkevich in the summer of 1915, the Minister of Agriculture, Krivoshein, wrote: 'The extraordinary naïveté or, to be exact, the unforgiveable stupidity of this letter written by the Chief of Staff makes me shudder.' What neither Janushkevich nor Sukhomlinov ever understood was that it was very much to Russia's advantage to delay any mobilization until a substantial part of the Austrian Army was entangled in operations against Serbia. [. . .] The possibility that Russia might do this was a source of great anxiety to Moltke and Conrad [the German and Austro-Hungarian Chiefs of Staff]. Albertini rightly emphasizes that for Russia to bring diplomatic pressure to bear on Austria, it was unnecessary for her to mobilize; all that was required was that she should threaten to do so. He thus describes the Austrian dilemma:

> For Austria to take the field against Serbia it was needful, not only that Russia should not come in but that she should pledge herself *a priori* not to come in. Suppose that she had given no hint of any intention to mobilize and that Conrad after 1 August had sent towards the Save those four army corps that would have been needed in Galicia. Then if after 1 August Russia had gone over from words to deeds, Austria would not have had sufficient forces to meet her and the consequences might have been incalculable.

Someone on the French General Staff understood this very well for the military memorandum submitted to Poincaré [the French Prime Minister] on 2 September 1912 had declared that a large-scale operation by Austria in the Balkans would have the effect of putting Germany and Austria 'at the mercy of the Entente'. But Joffre [the French Chief of Staff], with his obsession about a Russian offensive towards Berlin, was not interested in the implications of the Austrian Plan B[1] while General de Laguiche, the French military attaché in St Petersburg, did nothing to enlighten the Russian General Staff on this matter. As a result Sazonov and the Russian generals failed to grasp the immense diplomatic and military advantages conferred on them by the Austrian dilemma.

The Russian Council of Ministers met at 3 p.m. on 24 July and came to the following decisions:

(1) A request to Austria for an extension of the ultimatum's time limit of forty-eight hours.

(2) Advice to Serbia not to engage in hostilities with Austria but to withdraw her troops. (On 24 July Sazonov sent a personal telegram, strongly tinged with panic, to his Belgrade legation and suggested that Serbia should surrender to Austria without fighting.)

(3) A request to the Tsar to authorize in principle the mobilization of the Military Districts of Kiev, Odessa, Moscow and Kazan and of the Baltic and Black Sea Fleets. (After the Council, the reference to the Baltic Fleet was inserted in the resolutions by the Tsar personally, although it ran directly counter to Sazonov's intention not to alarm Germany. Nothing illustrates more clearly the muddled character of Russian policy.)

(4) The Minister of War was urged to speed up the state of readiness of supplies and military equipment.

(5) Funds in Germany and Austria-Hungary were to be withdrawn.

The Austrian ultimatum shook the nerve of Pasich and the Serbian Government, and Albertini is probably correct in his contention that the Prime Minister's first impulse was to yield to the Austrian demands. Whether this would have deterred Austria from war is highly problematical but, by the afternoon of 25 July, a different spirit was prevailing in Belgrade. Encouraged by a report from his legation in St Petersburg of the proceedings of the Russian Council of Ministers on 24 July and by an official Russian communiqué that Russia could not 'remain indifferent' to the fate of Serbia, Pasich resolved on a bolder policy. At 3 p.m. on 25 July Serbia ordered the mobilization of her Army, and that evening Baron Giesl, the Austrian minister in Belgrade, was handed a reply which an official in Vienna described as 'the most brilliant diplomatic document in my experience'. While very little in the ultimatum was rejected, very little was accepted and it would have required a lawyer of high repute to disentangle the real intentions of the Serbian Government. The article demanding the participation of Austrian officials in investigations on Serbian territory was rejected but the reply was so hedged around with reservations, apparent concessions and specious references to the Hague Tribunal that to Europe in general it gave an impression of abject acceptance. Even the Kaiser thought so when he first read the reply on the morning of 28 July.

Meanwhile Russia was proceeding to implement some very significant military measures, and there is no doubt that she was encouraged in this dangerous course by Maurice de Paléologue [the French Ambassador to Russia]. On 24 July Sazonov and Buchanan lunched with the French ambassador. Sazonov expressed the opinion that 'Russia would at any rate have to mobilize' and Buchanan says in his report: 'The French ambassador gave me to understand that France would not only give Russia strong diplomatic support, but would, if necessary, fulfil the obligations imposed on her by the alliance.' According to Buchanan, Paléologue used strong language and gave the impression of being more decided than Sazonov.

A Russian Imperial Council, presided over by the Tsar and attended by the Grand Duke Nicholas and General Janushkevich, assembled at Krasnoe Selo on the morning of 25 July. The Grand Duke, who assumed command of the Russian Army on the outbreak of war, had given Joffre personal assurances that Russia would invade Germany as rapidly as possible; he was on bad terms with Sukhomlinov but got on well with Janushkevich, who served as his Chief of Staff in 1914-16 and was very much under his influence in the July crisis. The council approved the decisions taken on 24 July and adopted various resolutions. These included the return to winter quarters of troops on manoeuvres, the recall of officers on leave, and the promotion of cadets to be officers. Although the actual order for partial mobilization was still to be suspended, the Council decided to introduce immediately 'The Period Preparatory to War', over the whole of European Russia. This corresponded with the German *Zustand drohender Kriegsgefahr* ('State of Threatening Danger of War'), and involved taking many measures preparatory to mobilization. Janushkevich sent out the relevant orders at 1 a.m. and 3.26 a.m. on 26 July, and thereby set in train a whole succession of military activities along the German and Austrian frontiers.

As a result, all fortresses in Poland and western Russia were placed in 'a state of war', frontier posts were fully manned, censorship and security measures were tightened, harbours were mined, horses and wagons were assembled for army baggage trains, depots were prepared for the reception of reservists and all steps were taken to facilitate the impending mobilization. These orders, already in force throughout European Russia, were extended on 27 July to include the Military Districts of the Caucasus, Turkestan, Omsk and Irkutsk. Fay says: 'These secret "preparatory measures" . . . ordered before dawn of the 26th, enabled Russia, when war came, to surprise the world by the rapidity with which she poured her troops into East Prussia and Galicia.' In the light of Russian actions between 24 and 26 July it seems extraordinary that an historian of Fischer's repute should seriously maintain that Bethmann Hollweg's calculations were upset in July 1914 by Russia's 'unexpected backing down'.

These far-reaching military decisions may well have been influenced by the critical internal situation, and the wave of strikes then threatening to paralyse Russian industry and transport. The German ambassador, Count Pourtalès, reported on 25 July: 'From a trustworthy source I hear that in the Ministerial Council here yesterday [24 July] the question of first consideration discussed was whether the present internal situation of Russia is such that the country could face external complications without trouble.'

On the evening of the 25th, in conversation with the Italian ambassador, Paléologue declared that war was virtually inevitable and expressed his approval of the decision taken that day at the Imperial Council. He added that 'France was ready to fulfil her duty as an ally to the full'. Albertini admits that France was bound to give Russia diplomatic support, but comments very reasonably:

> But she was in a position to have exercised friendly restraint and proffered councils of prudence which might have averted the catastrophe. What the French representative at St Petersburg did was, on the contrary, to fan the flames, and thus expose his own country to the most serious risk . . .

On 25 July Paléologue informed Paris that the Tsar had approved in principle the mobilization of thirteen army corps against Austria, and on the 26th his military attaché, General de Laguiche, reported as follows to the French Ministry of War:

> Yesterday at Krasnoe Selo the War Minister confirmed to me the mobilization of the army corps of the military districts Kiev, Odessa, Kazan and Moscow. The endeavour is to avoid any measure likely to be regarded as directed against Germany, but nevertheless the military districts of Warsaw, Vilna and St Petersburg are secretly making preparations. The cities and governments of St Petersburg and Moscow are declared to be under martial law. . . . The Minister of War has reiterated to us his determination to leave to Germany the eventual initiative of an attack on Russia . . .

Although the order for partial mobilization had yet to be promulgated, this singular document indicates that Sukhomlinov regarded the mobilization proclamation as a mere formality which would follow automatically after the preliminary measures covered in 'The Period Preparatory to War' had been completed. This adds significance to the statement by General Dobrorolski, Chief of the Mobilization Section of the Russian General Staff, who says of the situation in Russia on 26 July: 'The war was already a settled matter, and the whole flood of telegrams between the Governments of Russia and Germany represented merely the stage setting of a historical drama.' He admits that local commanders may well have gone beyond the letter of the regulations and introduced measures of mobilization, and he mentions such cases in the Suwalki area bordering East Prussia.

While the Russian military machine was gathering pace along the road to war, some fateful decisions were being taken in Vienna and Berlin. Baron Giesl had not troubled to read the Serbian reply, but broke off relations and left immediately for Vienna. On the evening of 25 July Austria ordered the mobilization of seven army corps against Serbia while another corps (based on Graz) was mobilized as a precaution against Italy, whom Conrad profoundly distrusted. [. . .]

The gravest indictment against German policy in July 1914 rests on the conduct of Bethmann Hollweg on the 27th. By this time it was becoming apparent that any prospect of localizing an Austro-Serbian conflict was illusory. The recall of all officers from leave in France, the holding together of the British Fleet, and the alarming reports of military activity in Russia indicated that the Triple Entente was preparing for war. It is absurd for the Fischer school to contend that Bethmann thought that Russia was 'backing down', in view of the detailed reports pouring into Berlin about her military preparations. As early as 26 July Sir Edward Grey noted: 'Prince Lichnowsky [the German Ambassador in London] called this afternoon with an urgent telegram from his Government to say that they had received information that Russia was calling in "classes of reserves", which meant mobilization.' At 3.25 p.m. on 26 July, Pourtalès telegraphed to Jagow that Major Eggeling, the German military attaché in St Petersburg, had reported that mobilization had certainly been ordered for the Military Districts of Kiev and Odessa, but it was doubtful whether this had been done for Warsaw and Moscow. On the evening of the 26th Pourtalès interviewed Sazonov and was assured that 'no mobilization order of the sort had been issued' but that certain military measures had been taken.

On the evening of 26 July Sukhomlinov sent for Major Eggeling and gave him his 'word of honour that no mobilization order had yet been issued'. He asserted that only preparatory measures were being taken, but that 'not a horse was being requisitioned, not a reservist called up'. If Austria invaded Serbia the Districts of Kiev, Odessa, Moscow and Kazan would be mobilized, but in no circumstances would this be done at Warsaw, Vilna or St Petersburg as 'peace with Germany was urgently desired'. Eggeling's report continues:

Upon my inquiry as to the object of the mobilization against Austria, he shrugged his shoulders and indicated the diplomats . . . I got the impression of great nervousness and anxiety. I consider the wish for peace genuine, military statements so far correct, that complete mobilization has probably not been ordered, but preparatory measures are very far-reaching. They are evidently striving to gain time for new negotiations and for continuing their armaments. Also the internal situation is unmistakably causing serious anxiety.

Eggeling warned Sukhomlinov that even 'mobilization against Austria alone must be regarded as very dangerous'.

This report was received in Berlin at 2.35 a.m. on 27 July and should have left the Chancellor under no illusions about the probable reaction in St Petersburg to an Austrian declaration of war on Serbia. There is, however, strong reason to believe that Bethmann was now resigning himself to the inevitability of war with France and Russia and was gambling on British neutrality. The great object of his policy was to saddle Russia with the responsibility for aggression — firstly to affect British opinion and secondly to rally the Social Democrats in Germany in support of a war for the defence of the German Fatherland. [. . .]

Although historians have frequently asserted that the Russian General Staff was driven into demanding general mobilization, because of the technical impossibility of carrying out partial mobilization, yet this belief has no validity. From a military point of view it would have been quite possible for Russia to carry out a partial mobilization, but this would still have led to a major war because Austria would have been compelled by the threat to her defenceless northern frontier to respond with general mobilization, thus invoking the Austro-German alliance.

The news of the Austrian declaration of war on Serbia infuriated Sazonov. Encouraged by Paléologue and moved by what Baron Taube [legal adviser of the Russian Foreign Ministry] describes as 'the pathological nervosity of his nature', he despatched the following telegram on the evening of 28 July to Berlin, repeated to Vienna, Paris, London and Rome:

> In consequence of the Austrian declaration of war on Serbia, we shall tomorrow proclaim mobilization in the districts of Odessa, Kiev, Moscow and Kazan. Inform the German Government of this and lay stress on the absence of any intention on the part of Russia to attack Germany.

Presumably this telegram was sent with the permission of the Tsar. However, that night Janushkevich sent a very different telegram to the commanders of all Military Districts: '30 July will be proclaimed the first day of our general mobilization. The proclamation will follow by the regulation telegram.' In a telegram to the Kaiser at 1 a.m. on 29 July, the Tsar appealed for his help to try and avoid a European war and remarked: 'I foresee that very soon I shall be overwhelmed by the pressure brought upon me and be forced to take extreme measures which will lead to war.' Matters were rapidly getting out of control, and the events of 29 July were to compromise hopelessly the slender prospects of maintaining peace.

On 29 July Moltke presented a memorandum to the Chancellor and warned him that Russian military measures directed against Austria would lead to Austrian general mobilization. Moltke said: 'The instant Austria mobilizes her whole Army, the clash between her and Russia will become inevitable. Now that is for Germany the *casus foederis* . . . she must also mobilize.' However, Moltke's language was far from being that of an ardent militarist thirsting for war. On the contrary, he predicted that Austrian and German general mobilization would bring the Franco-Russian alliance into operation and then 'the civilized states of Europe would begin to tear one another to pieces'. Moltke said: 'This is the way things will and must develop, unless, one might almost say, a miracle takes place to prevent at the eleventh hour a war which will annihilate the civilization of almost the whole of Europe for decades to come.'

As a result of Moltke's memorandum, Bethmann Hollweg telegraphed to Count Pourtalès at 12.50 p.m. on 29 July: 'Kindly impress on M. Sazonov very seriously that further continuation of Russian mobilization measures would compel us to mobilize and that then European war could scarcely be prevented.' Stressing that this was 'not a threat but a friendly opinion', Pourtalès passed the message on to Sazonov at about 7 p.m., with consequences which can only be described as catastrophic. The Foreign Minister had spent the day engaged in an unending series of conversations with ambassadors and, in his muddled way, still seems to have had some hopes of preserving peace. While he was doing this, General Dobrorolski was getting the signature of the War Minister, Navy Minister and Minister of the Interior to the *ukaze* for general mobilization, while at Russian Army Headquarters the necessary telegrams were being prepared, ready for despatch to the farthest parts of the Empire. News of the bombardment of Belgrade by Austrian monitors came in that afternoon and, for the excitable and unstable Sazonov, Pourtalès' communication was the last straw. He immediately sought the Tsar's permission to call a conference with Sukhomlinov and Janushkevich to decide on mobilization, and the official diary of the Russian Foreign Ministry records:

After examining the situation from all points, both the Ministers [Sazonov and Sukhomlinov] and the Chief of the General Staff decided that in view of the small probability of avoiding a war with Germany it was indispensable to prepare for it in every way in good time, and that therefore the risk could not be accepted of delaying a general mobilization later by effecting a partial mobilization now. The conclusion reached at this conference was at once reported by telephone to the Tsar, who authorized the taking of steps accordingly. This information was received with enthusiasm by the small circle of those acquainted with what was in progress.

Between 9.30 and 10 p.m. on 29 July, General Dobrorolski was at the central telegraph office in St Petersburg ready to despatch the general mobilization order. He was just about to do so, when Janushkevich telephoned him to suspend it pending the arrival of a liaison officer. The latter reported that the Tsar had cancelled general mobilization and substituted partial mobilization instead. The Tsar's change of mind resulted from a telegram from the Kaiser received at 9.40 p.m., appealing for the Tsar's co-operation in averting a catastrophe. Saying, 'I will not be responsible for a monstrous slaughter', Nicholas insisted on the cancellation. The partial mobilization order was telegraphed to the relevant Military Districts at midnight. [. . .]

The last hopes of peace vanished on 30 July. At St Petersburg, Laguiche and Paléologue were gravely disturbed at the failure to order general mobilization and redoubled their clamour for warlike measures against Germany. A telegram despatched by Viviani [the French Prime Minister] from Paris at 7 a.m. on 30 July impressed on Paléologue that Russia should not immediately take any step which might offer Germany a pretext for a total or partial mobilization of her forces. It arrived too late to influence events and, in any case, was effectively throttled by the ambassador. During the day Sazonov, Sukhomlinov and Janushkevich exerted all the pressure in their power on the Tsar and on the afternoon of the 30th Sazonov won his reluctant consent to the proclamation of general mobilization. The significance of the Tsar's change of mind has been much exaggerated; the fatal Russian decision had been taken on 29 July, for partial mobilization would have led to war as surely as general mobilization.

The news of Russian partial mobilization was received in Berlin on the morning of 30 July, and during the next few hours Moltke's mood underwent a decisive change. Hitherto the attitude of the German Chief of Staff had been restrained; he had done nothing to hamper Bethmann Hollweg's belated attempt to put the brake on Austria and, at conferences on 29 July, he had not pressed for German mobilization. Even on the morning of the 30th he told Captain Fleischmann, the Austrian liaison officer with the German General Staff, that Russian partial mobilization was no reason for

German mobilization. Yet by 1 p.m. on the 30th Moltke was pressing Bethmann Hollweg for the immediate proclamation of *drohende Kriegsgefahr*, the first stage of general mobilization. He was unable to persuade the distracted Chancellor and returned from the interview in a state of 'great agitation'. [. . .]

There has been much speculation about the reasons for Moltke's change of mind. No doubt the increasing gravity of the general situation affected him considerably, but the decisive factor appears to have been news from Vienna that Conrad intended to adhere rigidly to Plan B, and did not propose to abandon that plan in the light of Russian partial mobilization. In a telegram to Berlin drafted at 7.30 p.m. on 30 July Conrad declared that Austrian general mobilization was imminent but the Austrian armies in Galicia would have a defensive rôle while the attack on Serbia would proceed; in a telephone message to Berlin on the afternoon of the 31st he confirmed that he intended to stand on the defensive against Russia and proceed with the punitive action against Serbia. These messages were preceded by a minute from the Austrian ambassador to Jagow on the afternoon of 30 July, and the implications for Germany were catastrophic. Unless Austria fully committed herself to Plan R^2 and launched a great offensive in Poland, the German Eighth Army in East Prussia would be overwhelmed by the Russian masses and the prospects for the success of the Schlieffen Plan would be hopelessly compromised. This explains the excited conversations between Moltke and Lieut-Colonel Bienerth, the Austrian military attaché, on the afternoon of 30 July and the frantic telegrams sent by them to Vienna that evening, urging immediate mobilization against Russia and promising unqualified German support in a European war which was declared to be 'the last means of preserving Austria-Hungary'.

The tone of these telegrams ran directly counter to the efforts which Bethmann Hollweg was then making to restrain Austria and persuade her to negotiate. On 31 July these contradictory exhortations drew the sarcastic comment from Berchtold [the Austrian Foreign Minister], 'who rules in Berlin, Moltke or Bethmann?' Berchtold said to members of the Imperial War Council that morning: 'I have sent for you because I had the impression that Germany was beating a retreat, but I now have the most reassuring pronouncement from responsible military quarters.' The Council then decided to submit the order for general mobilization to the Emperor Franz Joseph for signature.

Russian and Austrian general mobilization made a great war inevitable and Liddell Hart says: 'Henceforth the "statesmen" may continue to send telegrams, but they are merely waste paper. The military machine has completely taken charge.' As soon as Moltke learned of Russian general mobilization on the morning of 31 July, he not only insisted on the immediate proclamation of *Kriegsgefahr* in Berlin, but induced the Chancellor to despatch an ultimatum to St Petersburg demanding that Russia should cease all military measures against Germany and Austria-Hungary within twelve hours. In the absence of a reply, Germany declared war on Russia at 6 p.m. on 1 August. [. . .]

Notes

1. The Austrian Plan B ('Balkan') entailed a partial mobilization and offensive against Serbia with seven army corps, and an eventual defensive against Russia with nine corps if a general mobilization became necessary. It ran directly counter to the Schlieffen Plan.

2. According to Plan R ('Russia'), thirteen corps would take the field against Russia, while three would stand in readiness against Serbia.

B.   GERMANY'S AIMS IN THE FIRST WORLD WAR (extract)

Fritz Fischer

Source: *Germany's Aims in the First World War* (translation of *Griff nach der Weltmacht*, 1961) (Chatto and Windus, 1967), pp.87-92.

[. . .] There is no question but that the conflict of military and political interests, of resentment and ideas, which found expression in the July crisis [of 1914], left no government of any of the European powers quite free of some measure of responsibility — greater or smaller — for the outbreak of the war in one respect or another. It is, however, not the purpose of this work to enter into the familiar controversy, on which whole libraries have been written, over the question of war guilt, to discuss exhaustively the responsibility of the individual statesmen and soldiers of all the European powers concerned, or to pass final judgment on them. We are concerned solely with the German leaders' objectives and with the policy actually followed by them in the July crisis, and that only in so far as their policy throws light on the postulates and origins of Germany's war aims.

It must be repeated: given the tenseness of the world situation in 1914 — a condition for which Germany's world policy, which had already led to three dangerous crises (those of 1905, 1908 and 1911), was in no small measure responsible — any limited or local war in Europe directly involving one great power must inevitably carry with it the imminent danger of a general war. As Germany willed and coveted the Austro-Serbian war and, in her confidence in her military superiority, deliberately faced the risk of a conflict with Russia and France, her leaders must bear a substantial share of the historical responsibility for the outbreak of general war in 1914. This responsibility is not diminished by the fact that at the last moment Germany tried to arrest the march of destiny, for her efforts to influence Vienna were due exclusively to the threat of British intervention and, even so, they were half-hearted, belated and immediately revoked.

It is true that German politicians and publicists, and with them the entire German propaganda machine during the war and German historiography after the war — particularly after Versailles — have invariably maintained that the war was forced on Germany, or at least (adopting Lloyd George's dictum, made for political reasons, that 'we all stumbled into the war') that Germany's share of the responsibility was no greater than that of the other participants. But confidential exchanges between Germany and Austria, and between the responsible figures in Germany itself, untinged by any propagandist intent, throw a revealing spotlight on the real responsibility.

A few weeks after the outbreak of war, during the crises on the Marne and in Galicia, the Austrians asked urgently for German help against the superior Russian armies facing them. It was refused. Count Tisza [the Hungarian Prime Minister] then advised Berchtold to tell the Germans: 'That we took our decision to go to war on the strength of the express statements both of the German Emperor and of the German Imperial Chancellor that they regarded the moment as suitable and would be glad if we showed ourselves in earnest.'

Just three years later, on August 14, 1917, at the climax of a heated debate whether the war should be continued in the interest of Germany's war aims, Austria-Hungary's Foreign Minister, Count Czernin, told his German interlocutors excitedly: 'It was not Austria alone that began the war then.' Characteristically, the official German minutes in the Imperial Chancellery left Czernin's next sentence incomplete and passed over the retorts of the German statesmen, Michaelis, Kühlmann and Helfferich, but the minutes of the Army High Command (the OHL) gave the sentence in full: 'Germany demanded that the ultimatum to Serbia should be drawn up in those sharp terms.'

In February, 1918, again, Czernin asked Berchtold if he would object if he (Czernin) published a letter written by him to Tisza shortly before the outbreak of war, which showed: 'what strong efforts Germany was making at that time to hold us to a hard line, and how our alliance might have been in danger if we had given way'.

There is other evidence to confirm that the Central Powers in no way 'slid into war'. Josef Baernreither, an Austrian politician who was entirely well disposed towards the Reich and was a leading champion of the Mittel-europa idea during the war, made the following entry on the July crisis in his diary for December, 1914:

> The Germans were afraid that we would refuse to go with them if the war broke out over some question remote from us. At Algeciras we were still 'seconds': later, not even that; in the Morocco crisis we did not stand by Germany firmly. But war was bound to come, as things had developed, through the faults of German and Austro-Hungarian diplomacy. So when the Sarajevo murder took place, Germany seized her opportunity and made an Austrian grievance her signal for action. That is the history of the war.

Finally, on October 8, 1919, Czernin telegraphed to Karl H. von Wiegand (the Berlin correspondent of the *Herald and Examiner*) the following reply to questions addressed to him by Wiegand:

> Repeated conversations and interviews I had with Ambassador von Tschirschky could create no other impression than that his [the German] government expected warlike action on our part against Serbia. Especially a conversation I had with him during the early half of July convinced me that if we did not show this time that we were in earnest, then on the next occasion Berlin not only would not support us, but would in fact 'orient' itself in some other direction.
>
> What that would have meant for us, in view of the ethnographical composition of the Dual Monarchy and the territorial aspirations of our neighbour states, need not be explained.
>
> Tschirschky was informed about the material points in the ultimatum to Serbia before the final editing of the note and the textual contents were given to him two days before the Belgrade *démarche*.

Baernreither was confirmed in his view of the nature of the July crisis by a conversation which he had in November, 1915, with Otto Hoetzsch of Berlin, the historian of eastern Europe, leader-writer for the *Kreuzzeitung* and later German National deputy in the Reichstag. 'Then' (sc., after July 5, 1914), runs the entry in Baernreither's diary, 'the Emperor went off to Norway, knowing certainly that war would break out. Germany had arranged all this very cleverly, and had shown alertness and judgment in picking an occasion when she was certain of Austria's support in waging a war the inevitability of which had been becoming apparent for years past.'

A week later Hoetzsch's Berlin colleague, the economist Jastrow, confirmed the correctness of Hoetzsch's view to Baernreither.

Arthur von Gwinner, Director of the Deutsche Bank, again confirmed most clearly the will to risk war which existed in Germany, especially in the Foreign Ministry, in a conversation which he had on the July crisis at the end of August, 1914, with von Capelle, the Under-Secretary of State in the Reich Naval Office. He, too, stressed the factor of Austria's unreliability:

> The only reason why Lichnowsky was not informed was because here [in the Wilhelmstrasse] they were determined to force a conflict. When Capelle asked who had been the man behind this pressure, Gwinner answered, 'Herr von Stumm, in the Foreign Office, for example'. When Capelle expressed some doubt, he went on: 'Perhaps it was a whole group. They worked systematically to get Austria committed inextricably, as the first step, so as to be sure of her. The whole plan of campaign against Serbia was arranged in advance to make a conflict inevitable.'

This grave statement was published as early as 1926 by no less a man than Grand Admiral von Tirpitz, in his *Deutsche Ohnmachtspolitik* (Germany's Policy of Weakness), but it has, so far as the author knows, passed unnoticed.

Admiral Müller, commenting in his diary on the Entente's answer of December 31, 1916, to the German peace offer – a document which ascribed to Germany a substantial share of the guilt for the World War – wrote that it 'contained certain bitter truths on our doings at the outbreak of the war'.

Finally Albert Ballin, Bethmann Hollweg's and Jagow's intimate political confidant (he was sent to London by Jagow at the beginning of the crisis of July, 1914, in an attempt to secure Britain's neutrality, and was summoned to Berlin in the middle of 1915 to help draft Germany's note to the United States which was to decide on peace or war with America but was not received by Jagow after all), wrote at that date to the Secretary of State, out of his intimate knowledge of what had been done in July, 1914:

> I make every allowance for a man who is heavily incriminated, as Your Excellency is, and has to bear the frightful responsibility for having staged this war (*für die Inscenierung dieses Krieges*) which is costing Germany generations of splendid men and setting her back 100 years.

The official documents afford ample proofs that during the July crisis the Emperor, the German military leaders and the Foreign Ministry were pressing

Austria-Hungary to strike against Serbia without delay, or alternatively agreed to the despatch of an ultimatum to Serbia couched in such sharp terms as to make war between the two countries more than probable, and that in doing so they deliberately took the risk of a continental war against Russia and France. But the decisive point is that, as we now know – although for a long time it was not admitted – these groups were not alone. On July 5 and 6 the Imperial Chancellor, Bethmann Hollweg, the man in whom the constitution vested the sole responsibility, decided to take the risk and even over-trumped the Emperor when he threatened to weaken. That this was no 'tragic doom', no 'ineluctable destiny', but a deliberate decision of policy emerges beyond doubt from the diary of his private secretary, Kurt Riezler, who recorded in it his conversations with the Chancellor in the critical days (and, indeed, over many years). These diaries have not yet been published, but the extracts from them which have seen the light furnish irrefutable proof that during the July crisis Bethmann Hollweg was ready for war. More than this. Riezler's entry for the evening of July 8, after Bethmann Hollweg's return to Hohenfinow (where Rathenau was also stopping) shows what advance calculations the leaders of Germany were making in respect of the situation produced by the Sarajevo murder. According to his secretary, the Chancellor said: 'If war doesn't come, if the Tsar doesn't want it or France panics and advises peace, we have still achieved this much, that we have manoeuvred the Entente into disintegration over this move.'

In other words, Bethmann Hollweg reckoned with a major general war as the result of Austria's swift punitive action against Serbia. If, however, Russia and France were again to draw back (as in 1909 and 1911) – which he at first regarded as the less probable eventuality – then at least Germany would have achieved a signal diplomatic victory: she would have split Russia from France and isolated both without war. But war was what he expected, and how he expected its course to run we learn from his predecessor in the Chancellorship, Bülow, who had a long discussion with him at the beginning of August. Bethmann Hollweg told Bülow that he was reckoning with 'a war lasting three, or at the most, four months . . . a violent, but short storm'. Then, he went on, revealing his innermost wishes, it would, 'in spite of the war, indeed, through it', be possible to establish a friendly relationship with England, and through England with France. He hoped to bring about 'a grouping of Germany, England and France against the Russia colossus which threatens the civilisation of Europe'.

Bethmann Hollweg himself often hinted darkly during the war how closely Germany had been involved in the beginning of the war. He was less concerned with the 'staging' of it than to register the spirit of the German leaders who had made it possible for the war to be begun even after the premises for it had collapsed. The following bitter words are taken from his address to the Central Committee of the Reichstag at the beginning of October, 1916, during the sharp debate on the initiation of unlimited submarine warfare; they outline Germany's real 'guilt', her constant over-estimation of her own powers, and her misjudgment of realities:

> Since the outbreak of the war we have not always avoided the danger of under-estimating the strength of our enemies. The extraordinary develop-ment of the last twenty years seduced wide circles into over-estimating our own forces, mighty as they are, in comparing them with those of the rest of the world . . . in our rejoicing over our own progress (we have) not paid sufficient regard to conditions in other countries.

The July crisis must not be regarded in isolation. It appears in its true light only when seen as a link between Germany's 'world policy', as followed since the mid-1890s, and her war aims policy after August, 1914.

C.   STATESMEN VERSUS STRUCTURES: GERMANY'S ROLE IN THE OUTBREAK OF WORLD WAR ONE RE-EXAMINED (extract)

K.H. Jarausch

Source: *Laurentian University Review*, vol.5, no.3, June 1973, pp.137-42.

[. . .] On July 5 [1914], William II recalled Bethmann to Berlin to consider Francis Joseph's appeal for help, transmitted by the hawkish Austrian dip-lomat Count Hoyos. 'The Emperor received me and Undersecretary of State Zimmermann in the Park of the Neues Palais in Potsdam. No one else was present', the Chancellor later recalled. Having read the strongly worded Austrian memorandum, 'the Emperor declared that he could not deceive himself about the grave danger in which the pan-Serbian propaganda had placed Austria. But it was not up to us to advise our ally how to react to the bloodbath of Sarajevo. Vienna herself had to decide that.' William recom-mended a three-fold response: 'We should abstain from direct influence and advice, since we should work with all our means towards the goal of not letting the Austro-Serbian quarrel become an international conflict.' But 'Emperor Francis Joseph should know that we will not desert Austria-Hungary in this serious hour. Our own vital interests demand the preservation of Austria' as a great power. And following Berchtold's advice, 'he considered it desirable to draw Bulgaria [into the alliance] as long as that would not alienate Rumania'. Bethmann accepted this analysis since 'these opinions of the Emperor coincided with my own'. Later the same afternoon the hastily recalled military advisers of William minimized the gravity of the expected risk. Summarizing the informal discussions between Bethmann, Zimmermann, Minister of War Falkenhayn, and the chief of the military cabinet Lyncker, Adjutant General Plessen jotted into his diary: 'The opinion prevails that we should move against Serbia the sooner the better, and that the Russians — although friends of Serbia — will not intervene.' But Falkenhayn reassured Moltke, Chief of the General Staff: 'The Chancellor, who was also in Potsdam, seems to believe as little as I that the Austrian government is serious about its recently more forceful language.'

With such military encouragement, Bethmann gave the Austrian ambassador, Count Szögyény, one of the most momentous assurances of European history the following morning: 'Concerning Austria's relations with Serbia the German government believes that Vienna has to judge what has to be done to clarify this relationship; in this undertaking it can count safely on German support of the monarchy as ally and friend — whatever its decision.' To bolster the war party in Vienna, Szögyény concluded his despatch energetically: 'In the further course of the conversation, I realized that the Chancellor, like his imperial master, considers our immediate intervention against Serbia the most radical and the best solution of our Balkan difficulties.'

Why did Bethmann Hollweg depart so suddenly and fundamentally from his earlier policy of restraint towards Austria during the Balkan wars? The official documents contain no clue to his motivation. Conscious of Berchtold's desire for local war, the Chancellor gave more than a blank cheque. Prodded by William, Hoyos, and Zimmermann and encouraged by the generals, Bethmann formulated a coherent rationale, calling for a diplomatic offensive on the Balkans in which the Austrian punishment of Serbia would be just one part. Contrary to the tenor of the alliance with Rumania, Bethmann informed his ambassador in Bucharest that 'His Majesty understands that Emperor Francis Joseph considers reconciliation with Serbia impossible and attempts to counteract the dangers threatening his House and Empire from Belgrade through an alliance with Bulgaria'. The Sarajevo assassination gave Germany the historic chance for breaking the tightening vice of encirclement through a realignment of the south-eastern powers. The adherence of Bulgaria and Turkey to the Triple Alliance and the strengthening of dynastic ties with Rumania and Greece would isolate Serbia politically and militarily and eliminate Russian influence from the area. A quick diplomatic or if need be military triumph of Austria would restore the Central Powers' waning prestige. When the *Frankfurter Zeitung* predicted on July 9 that Vienna's 'diplomatic and political action' against Belgrade would 'probably be executed in short, swift strokes', Bethmann heartily agreed: 'Very good'.

Back in Hohenfinow after the momentous decision, the Chancellor explained the reasons for his reversal to Riezler 'at night on the veranda under the starry sky'. Bethmann pessimistically regarded the rumored 'Anglo-Russian negotiations for a naval agreement and a landing in Pomerania as the last link in a chain'. Although the British Admiralty publicly denied these reports, the increasing military cooperation among the Entente distressed the Chancellor. Bethmann feared that the German ambassador to the Court of St James, Prince Lichnowsky, was much too credulous and could easily be duped by the wily British. Recent general staff studies had reinforced Bethmann's fear of 'Russia's quickly growing military might. After the completion of their strategic railroads in Poland our position [will be] untenable.' Austria was growing 'weaker and more immobile' by the day. Vienna was 'increasingly undermined from north and south-east, at any rate incapable of going to war for German interests as our ally'. The Chancellor dismally concluded his military assessment: 'The Entente knows that we are, therefore, completely paralyzed.'

The crime of Sarajevo called for 'grave decisions'. 'Apparently, officially Serbia [is] incriminated. Austria wants to pull itself together', judging from 'Francis Joseph's mission to the Emperor inquiring about the *casus foederis*'. Now the Chancellor was confronted with our 'old dilemma at every Austrian action in the Balkans. If we encourage them, they say we pushed them into it. If we discourage them, they say we left them in the lurch.' Despairingly he predicted: 'Then they will throw themselves into the open arms of the Western powers and we lose our last important ally.' Fearing the break-up of the Dual Alliance, strained by German moderation in the Balkan wars, Bethmann considered his predicament 'worse than in 1912, because this time Austria is on the defensive against Serbo-Russian intrigues' and could not be restrained so easily. Backing Vienna entailed considerable risks as well: 'An attack on Serbia can lead to world war.' Any general conflagration 'however it ends [will lead] to a revolution of all existing conditions'. But inaction was worse: 'The future belongs to Russia which grows and grows, looming above us as an increasingly terrifying nightmare.' Under this heavy responsibility Bethmann decided on a leap forward. 'Perhaps the old Emperor [Francis Joseph] will prefer not to fight after all', the Chancellor consoled himself. 'If war comes from the east so that we have to fight for Austria-Hungary and not Austria-Hungary for us, we have a chance of winning.' And better yet, 'if war does not break out, if the Tsar is unwilling or France, alarmed, counsels peace, we have the prospect of splitting the Entente.'

Although uncertain about the likelihood of war, Bethmann resolved to run a calculated risk. Full support of Berchtold's desire for the punishment of Serbia could have three consequences: a local Balkan war, which could bring a diplomatic triumph, a realignment of the south-eastern states and a humiliation of the Entente. Equally likely seemed a continental war, engulfing Russia, Austria, France, and Germany. In such a conflict, the general staff promised a good chance of winning. Less desirable than a localized conflict, a continental struggle might ease the Russian pressure from the east, revitalize faltering Austria, regain the diplomatic initiative in the Balkans, and break up the enemy coalition. In Bethmann's mind only the last alternative was fraught with unacceptable danger: world war. The intervention of Britain or any other great power would upset the carefully balanced odds. Bethmann did not gamble frivolously, but because he considered 'our position desperate', hoping only, 'if war comes and the veils fall, the whole nation will follow, driven by necessity and peril'. Riezler longed for 'victory as liberation', since he was 'too young not to succumb to the lure of the new, the great movement'. But for Bethmann 'this action is a leap in the dark and as such the most serious duty'. While the pan-Germans were jubilant, the navy, army, and colonial leagues ecstatic, and the students feverish with misguided idealism, the ageing Chancellor entered on the uncertain course with great reluctance.

Bethmann's diplomatic gamble was not only endorsed but actively promoted by the other leaders of the Wilhelmine empire. The Emperor's only pro-war commitment prejudiced the issue before his Chancellor could advise differently. In the absence of the cautious Jagow, the energetic Zimmermann was swayed by Hoyos who considered the moment opportune for a war of revenge against Serbia, and when summarizing the Austrian memorandum Zimmermann counseled Bethmann to take resolute action. Only two months earlier Moltke had told Jagow: 'We must wage a preventive war to conquer our opponents as long as we still have a reasonable chance in the struggle.' The emotional impact of the murder on the sincere monarchist Bethmann at a time when he was still in mourning over the death of his wife was also severe. Those elements within the élites which like the navy and part of the business community (banking, trade and shipping interests) wanted to hold back were outshouted by the increasing chorus of chauvinist opinion, led by the imperialistic propaganda organizations such as the Pan-Germans and army and navy leagues. In the July of 1914 Bethmann believed that he acted in keeping with his earlier rejected letter of resignation in protest against the naval race: 'If war is forced upon us, we shall fight and, with God's help, not perish. But to conjure up a war ourselves without having our honor or vital interests imperiled, this I would consider a sin against Germany's destiny, even if human foresight would predict a total victory.'

After the fateful decision of July 5, Bethmann's chief concern became the smooth execution of the diplomatic offensive in the Balkans. The Chancellor remained in touch with Austrian intentions, but he did not intervene again until his return to Berlin during the climax of the crisis. 'Berchtold debates the timing, before or after Poincaré's visit to Petersburg. Better before, because then there is a greater chance that France, suddenly frightened by the spectre of war, will counsel peace in Russia', Riezler noted wishfully. 'Austria has decided on this course today but the Hungarian harvest has to be gathered first.' The Wilhelmstrasse, and more strongly the two ambassadors, Tschirschky and Szögyény, urged Berchtold to take speedy action, lest Europe intervene in the Austro-Serbian quarrel. Such pressure strengthened the war party in Vienna, but the time it took to persuade Tisza of the need for war, the Ballhausplatz's [Austrian Foreign Ministry's] slow collection of the crime dossier, and Chief of Staff Conrad's halting military preparations undermined Bethmann's rationale. Despite the possible complications, Jagow reaffirmed the German strategy after coming back from his honeymoon: 'In all circumstances, we want the conflict to be localized.' Berlin's proddings in Vienna and attempts to shield Austria diplomatically were directed towards a quick punitive strike, but not towards a continental or world war.

On the day of the Austrian ultimatum Bethmann began to contemplate the aftermath of the crisis. 'The Chancellor tells me that [Russian Foreign Minister] Sazonov said to [the banker] Robby Mendelssohn the other day: "Si l'Allemagne lache l'Autriche, je lacherai immédiatement après la France". He seems to toy with such possibilities. A lasting understanding with Russia would be preferable to an agreement with England. But its difficulties are far greater. Russia is far more exacting.' The alternative of sacrificing Vienna to a Russo-German accord was as quickly discarded as it had arisen. 'We must maintain Austria proper. Were Russia to unleash the South Slavs, we would be lost.' An agreement short of partitioning the Habsburg Empire would be at best an uneasy truce, and to begin negotiations with Sazonov now would only give him new weapons in London and Paris. 'If the Serbian quarrel passes without Russian mobilization, we can safely come to an understanding with the Tsar, [who will be] disappointed in the Western powers, once Austria is satisfied.' Despite such speculation, Bethmann reassured William II, 'It is improbable that England will immediately enter the fray.'

D. THE TRADITION OF APPEASEMENT IN BRITISH FOREIGN POLICY, 1865-1939 (extract)

P.M. Kennedy

Source: *British Journal of International Studies*, 2, 1976, pp.195-203.

If the policy of 'Appeasement' is inextricably associated in the historical consciousness with the efforts of Neville Chamberlain's government to preserve peace with the dictators in the 1930s, its origins have been recognized by numerous writers as going back many years before the immediate crises concerning the Sudetenland, Prague and the Polish Corridor. Some have traced its roots to the failure to prevent Japanese aggression in 1931 or Italy's attack upon Abyssinia in 1935; others, with more sense of the positive side of 'Appeasement', have focused upon the attitude of the British government and public towards Germany during and after the Versailles settlement; while Mr Gilbert, going a little further back in time, has argued that 'appeasement was born' at the moment of the British declaration of war in 1914. Few, if any, commentators have suggested that one should seek the beginnings of 'Appeasement' *before* that event, however.

It is the purpose of this paper, on the other hand, to argue that the real origins of the policy must be traced much further back, to the middle of the nineteenth century, and that the nature of British foreign policy did not greatly alter in its overall framework from that time until 1939; that there is, in fact, a British model of 'Appeasement' whose operation is detectable for some seventy-five years or so before Munich, and that it was only after that particular crisis that this model finally broke down. To maintain such an argument a great deal depends, as it always has done, upon the meaning of the very word 'Appeasement'. It may well be, as Professor Medlicott has urged, that the term is so contentious that it would be simpler to avoid its use altogether; but the fact remains that, since it has proved impracticable to banish the expression, the only alternative open to us is to define its meaning as clearly as possible. Throughout this paper 'Appeasement' will be held to mean *the policy of settling international (or, for that matter, domestic) quarrels by admitting and satisfying grievances through rational negotiation and compromise, thereby avoiding the resort to armed conflict which would be expensive, bloody, and possibly very dangerous*. It is in essence a *positive* policy, based upon certain optimistic assumptions about man's inherent reasonableness, as was clearly the case when executed by Gladstone in the 1880s or Lloyd George in 1919, but came increasingly to the fore in the 1930s and caused the word itself to take on a fully pejorative meaning. Indeed, until Munich or thereabouts, it may be said that the term 'Appeasement' was a perfectly respectable one, and that the changed meaning of the word was concomitant with the final collapse of the original policy.

The Model

'Appeasement' in the above sense, it is worth arguing, has been a particularly British form of diplomacy since the middle of the nineteenth century, and was rooted in the following distinguishable, although often interconnected, motives:

Moral Consideration. The application of the concepts of 'justice' and 'morality' to politics has been prominent in British thought from the time of the evangelical movement onwards and, although receiving many a set-back and much criticism from cynics, remained a strong feature among the formative political elements. Reinforcing this idea of the fair and pacific settlement of disputes, and the disapproval of the use (and, often, the existence) of armed force, was the Cobdenite vision of the world being a harmonious community. International arbitration, the abjuration of war as an instrument of national policy except in cases of self-defence, the emphasis upon conciliation and compromise, combined to produce a climate in which it was necessary for statesmen, particularly those favouring action which might lead to hostilities, to justify their policy in normal terms.

Economic Aspirations. As the so-called 'workshop of the world', mid-Victorian Britain was at the centre of a global economic system, importing raw materials and foodstuffs, exporting manufactured goods and coal, financing overseas developments, and providing services as a shipper, insurer and commodity-dealer. She had by this stage abandoned her previously successful mercantilist policy in favour of one based upon the calculation that Britain would gain the predominant share of an unlimited and ever-increasing world wealth through the free interchange of goods. Whilst this had many economic advantages, it also meant that she was, more than most other countries, a 'hostage' to the international boom. Any disruption of trade, whether by a temporary slump or, worse still, war, affected her economy more than those of her more protectionist neighbours. This basic situation did not alter by the turn of the century, when such states as the U.S.A. and Germany were overtaking Britain industrially, for she still maintained her dominance in 'invisibles'; and this trade was even more vulnerable to the collapse of the world economy (as was shown in 1929-33) than that in 'visibles', many of which could be disposed of domestically behind tariff walls. Most British statesmen were well aware that war would inevitably mean a reduction in exports, an increase in imports, a decrease in invisible earnings, and losses of manpower, shipping, etc. The preservation of peace was, for an economy such as Britain's (but not, say, for that of Nazi Germany), a vital national interest.

Furthermore, the relative industrial decline of Britain from the 1870s onwards meant that she had an ever-harder task in adjusting ends to means: that is to say, her national wealth was increasing too slowly to pay both for expensive social and economic reforms at home *and* for the 'fire insurance' of large defence forces in an uncertain world. An expensive arms-race with some foreign power, in addition to increasing the risk of eventual hostilities, also exacerbated this dilemma. For such a budgetary reason alone, British governments could normally be relied upon to seek to end an arms-race by diplomatic means, and thus to reduce defence spending.

Britain's Global Position. In contrast to the other Powers, Britain had interests in every part of the world. Even in the post-1815 period, when the Royal Navy's supremacy and the concentration of her rivals upon internal affairs made Britain more secure than ever before or since, her statesmen had to take into account their multifarious national obligations and could not devote all their attention or energies to one region. By the later nineteenth century, when other Powers were challenging the Royal Navy's mastery of the seas, when land power (in the form of mass armies, strategical railways, etc.) was gaining ground in relation to sea power, and when many more dangers to Britain's imperial position were arising, the government was beginning to perceive with alarm the increasing gap between the country's strength and its commitments. The British Empire was becoming, to use Liddell Hart's later expression, the greatest example of strategical over-extension in history. If all this tended to compel the government increasingly to consider which regions had priority and in which it might be necessary to give way gracefully, the simple existence of multifold dangers and obligations could occasionally 'paralyse' decision-making, for it was appreciated that if Britain concentrated too much in one region, she would have no strength to protect the others. Whether she clung on in all regions or escaped from some, her stretched global position was an enormously powerful reason for compromise with other states and for the pacific settlement of disputes with them – as, indeed, the government's defence and foreign policy advisers frequently pointed out.

The Domestic Situation. The steady extension of the franchise from 1867 onwards made politicians increasingly aware of the factor of 'public opinion', whether expressed by mass-circulation papers and interest-groups or by electoral results, and although the public could be excited upon a point of national honour or moral wrong, it was generally recognized as disliking wars, especially expensive ones, and as being a brake upon a belligerent foreign policy. Moreover, the electorate was ever more reluctant to deny itself social and economic reforms in deference to a large defence budget. The declaration of war had, therefore, to be 'popular'. In addition, the continuous need to introduce constitutional, social and economic reforms to reflect the changing demands and balance within this ever widening body politic was seen by most politicians as being their most vital task if they wished to stay in office. All but a few concentrated upon home affairs and regarded foreign complications as distractions which had to be settled as expeditiously and painlessly as possible.

To sum up, there were always such motives, moral, economic, strategic and domestic, operating in the public consciousness and prompting British governments from the mid-nineteenth century onwards to favour a foreign policy which was, with rare exceptions (e.g. 1878, 1911), pragmatic, conciliatory and reasonable. It was a policy predicated upon the assumption that, provided national interests were not too deleteriously affected, the peaceful settlement of disputes was much more to Britain's advantage than recourse to war. It was not merely in the 1930s, therefore, that 'Peace as National Interest' is a valid description of Britain's overall strategy.

But precisely because this policy was pragmatic, a compromise, a peculiar mixture of morality and calculated national interest, it attracted criticism from two groups who, from their opposing points of view, advocated different conceptions of the bases upon which British foreign policy should be constructed. The first was the 'Left' or the 'Idealists', both inexact terms but used here to describe that strong 'dissenter' tradition in British foreign policy, i.e. the Cobdenite, 'Little Englander' or later neo-Marxist viewpoint, which disliked overseas wars and entanglements as immoral, a drain upon the economy, a diversion from social reforms and a devious way of propping up an obsolete aristocratic or capitalistic system. Although in many ways this attitude was similar to that analysed in the 'model' above, it was more extreme and doctrinaire, and the Left was swift to criticize if it felt that the government was deviating from the straight and narrow paths: witness the Cobdenite isolationists' disapproval of *any* form of European entanglement even if it was advocated by Gladstone on behalf of the Concert of Europe; the criticism of Grey's foreign policy when it failed to secure a reconciliation with Germany; and the disapproval of post-1919 administrations for not fully embracing the ideals of the League of Nations. The realities of power, the constraints upon statesmen in office, the natural impetus towards 'continuity' in foreign policy, and the need felt even by radical-Liberal and Labour administrations to balance what was ideal with what was practicable, was rarely a problem for this group.

On the other side of the political spectrum was the 'Right' or the 'Realists', again an unsatisfactory term but used here to describe those who felt that the idea of a world living in permanent harmony was utopian, that might rather than right had usually had more influence upon international affairs, and that the governments should not flinch from the use of armed force to defend national honour and interests. This group rarely found the armed services adequate for all the country's obligations, was less prone to accept the assurances of foreign statesmen, regarded its own Left as being unrealistic or even traitorous, and expected to have most influence when a Conservative government was in office, although it was also willing to criticize its own party leaders for being too ready to compromise and conciliate.

The complete 'model', then, sees not only a basically pragmatic and reasonable tradition in British foreign policy since 1865, but also the existence of two non-governmental sentiments, one favouring more 'Appeasement' and the other less. It is a crude outline, and in reality the pattern varies, at least in its emphases, from one period to the next; but a brief examination of the course of British foreign policy since that date suggests that it might indeed be graced with the title of a 'tradition'.

The Tradition Established, 1865-1914

The year 1865 is significant here, of course, because it was not until Palmerston's death − and as a reaction to his internal and external policies − that his successors were able to initiate the tradition described above. Under Gladstone in particular, they adopted, firstly, a strategy of internal 'Appeasement', by which is meant that broad series of reforms in the structures of government so that they were more in line with the economic developments and social demands of the day; hence, following Disraeli's 1867 Reform Act came the sweeping changes in the army, education, civil service, Irish disestablishment, etc. instituted by the Liberals. Furthermore, they also executed a policy of external 'Appeasement', both as a corollary to their domestic reforms and because the Schleswig-Holstein affair had exposed the limitations of Britain's ability to intervene on the continent. This disengagement did not mean pure isolationism, but it did increase the government's preference for rational and peaceful solutions to international problems, the best examples here being Clarendon's attempts to secure mutual armed force reductions in Europe, with arguments based upon morality and political economy; the endeavours to persuade both France and Prussia to respect Belgian neutrality; and the agreement to abide by the *Alabama* tribunal's findings (a decision which Bismarck for one thought a sign of weakness and decadence).

As a consequence of the above, the government was criticized by the Left for getting entangled in European diplomacy, whereas the reaction from the Right was to display alarm at what it claimed was a policy of national weakness. Indeed, the pacific, cautious, mild-mannered handling of foreign affairs by Gladstone's first administration gave Disraeli the chance to secure for the Tories the patriotic 'card' which the Liberals had discarded after the death of Palmerston. In Disraeli's view, Britain should have had more say in the outcome of the Franco-Prussian war, should not have allowed Russia to abrogate unilaterally the Black Sea clauses of 1856, and should not have permitted the Dominions to sever their ties with the home-country. When in office, therefore, he demonstrated that mixture of assertiveness and concern which permeated his Crystal Palace speech, and deliberately — one might say, artificially — sought to adopt a muscular, non-appeaser stance (in the Eastern Crisis, the defence of India, the purchase of Suez Canal shares, a forward policy in West Africa, Zululand/Transvaal, and Afghanistan), all of which played into the hands of Gladstone in the latter's Midlothian campaign, the speeches of which, in their attitude to other states, were not far removed from those used by British statesmen in the 1920s and 1930s.

Gladstone's second administration represented, therefore, a deliberate attempt to return to what he believed was the traditional moral and pragmatic basis of British policy when it was not being 'debauched' by people like Palmerston and Disraeli. Encouragement was given to the concept of the 'Concert of Europe' (as opposed to the Bismarckian concept of power-blocs), and to the resolution of international problems through the friendly co-operation of the Great Powers; a retreat was made from Disraelian adventures in South Africa and Afghanistan; and this overall attitude of avoiding trouble and seeking a reasonable compromise with the demands of others could be seen in India (under Ripon's vice-royalty), in Ireland (the Land Act, Arrears Act and Liberal co-operation with Parnell) and at home (the third Reform Bill, and other reforms designed to accommodate the aspirations of the working classes).

This policy of sweet reasonableness again ran into problems, however, in a world still unconverted to Gladstonian principles, and the government felt itself compelled by events to occupy Egypt (to restore order), to extend the colonial empire (as a defensive measure against Franco-German annexations in 1884-5), and to take a harder line in Ireland (again, to restore order). But a detailed study of even these actions reveals men earnestly struggling to solve political problems on a rational and ethical basis. Predictably enough, their compromises were attacked on the one hand by the Radicals for not going far enough on the domestic side and for going too far over Egypt; and, on the other hand, by the Conservative opposition, the Whigs and the increasingly nervous middle-class intellectuals for going too far with internal reforms and not far enough in the defence of foreign and imperial interests and in the maintenance of maritime supremacy. 'Appeasement' in Ireland, i.e. Gladstone's conversion to Home Rule, brought much of this latter feeling to a head and led to the Liberal downfall.

Even in the period 1886-1914 (which can be treated as one because of the emphasis given then to 'continuity' in British foreign policy), the tradition may still be said to have been maintained, despite such manifestations to the contrary as the Boer War, the reconquest of the Sudan and the Fashoda confrontation, naval races with France and Russia and later with Germany, and patriotic press agitations. For, when one examines the *broad trends* in British foreign policy in these three decades, and especially the workings of the 'Official Mind', there is a strong case for arguing that the basic pattern, although upset by displays of bellicosity and somewhat lacking in the moral aspect of appeasement, remained the same.

In particular, the background factors affecting the formulation of policy intensified in these years. Domestically, politicians were having to respond more and more to democracy's demand for reforms in education, the Poor Law, national insurance and pensions, and thus the question of 'guns or butter' was being increasingly posed by the rival parties. Moreover, with the steady rise of a Labour Party *per se*, both Liberals and Conservatives recognized that they would have to tilt their electoral appeals more than ever to the 'working man'. On occasion a patriotic appeal would work (e.g. the 1900 election) but that was a short-lived and risky platform (as the 1906 election showed), and it would be fair to say that the growth of democracy favoured the 'Left' unless Conservatives were flexible enough to modify their principles and to make themselves attractive electorally to more than the middle classes. But all this meant that extreme caution had to be exercised over questions involving peace or war, and that the pressure upon financial resources intensified, defence budgets especially being a source of continual political controversy. Worse still, it was in these years that Britain's relative world position openly showed a decline occurring in industrial, commercial, colonial, naval and military terms. By the turn of the century, with such acute problems arising as those in South Africa, the Western Hemisphere, the Mediterranean and Near East, the approaches to India, and in China, with Britain eclipsed by newer states in steel, chemical and electrical production, with defence expenditures at new heights (despite the Navy proposing to abandon the 'Two-Power' standard and the Army's deficiencies exposed by the Boer War), there was a great deal of truth in Joseph Chamberlain's description of the 'Weary Titan, staggering under the too vast orb of his own fate'.

Secondly, the long-term pattern of foreign policy in this period was to solve problems by 'appeasing'. Faced with all these difficulties, British policy was bound to incline towards a reduction of commitments, the elimination of antagonisms, and the avoidance of confrontations which might lead to war, especially with a Great Power. Relations with the expanding United States furnish the best example here. War with such a fellow Anglo-Saxon country was regarded as particularly immoral and 'unnatural'; it would also be a disaster economically; it would give Britain's other rivals their opportunity elsewhere in the world; and the defence advisers were pessimistic as to its eventual outcome for the British Empire. Whether one emphasized the negative or the positive motives, everything pointed to a policy of 'Appeasement', which was in fact carried out. Washington's right to interfere in the Venezuela/British Guiana dispute was recognized; Britain abandoned her half 'share' in the future isthmian canal; Canada was given little support over the Alaskan boundary quarrel once London felt that Roosevelt was serious in his threats of action; and British naval and military forces were withdrawn from the Western Hemisphere, which became uncontestably an American sphere of influence.

Even the intractable question of Anglo-German relations after 1906 was not attended without frequent attempts at reconciliation which bear comparison with those of the 1930s. Hopes were placed in international agreements (the Hague Conferences) to reduce the burden of armaments. When this failed, proposals were made for bilateral arms reductions, such as Churchill's 'naval holiday' idea. Colonial concessions in the Middle East and Africa were suggested to Germany, in recognition for her claim for a fairer share of the world's raw materials. Binding military guarantees to France were avoided, lest this provoke controversy. Haldane's mission to Berlin in 1912 was a forerunner of frequent journeys by British statesmen there in the 1930s. And Anglo-German friendship societies, stressing common cultural and political ties, were set up and flourished. The size of the German fleet, and the prospect of a German defeat of France and the Low Countries, could never be ignored by London and ruled out any declaration of disinterest in what Berlin did; yet the natural response of the British government was to try to solve matters of dispute by compromise, rational discussion and mutual understanding, thereby avoiding the dreadful toll in men and material which the outbreak of a great war would bring. Between 1912 and 1914, the years of the so-called 'détente' in Anglo-German relations, it appeared that this policy was paying off.

Once again, too, the policy of pragmatic compromise attracted criticism from the Left and the Right. To the former, the British government's diplomacy still involved the country far too heavily in the game of power-politics, it diverted attention and funds from domestic affairs, and it encouraged the jingos. When relations with France or the United States or Russia were poor, a settlement of differences (usually at Britain's expense, despite the emphasis upon mutual goodwill and tolerance) was favoured; when Germany was the problem, it was urged that concessions should be made to her, the navy budget should be cut as a gesture of good faith, and no entangling commitments should be made with Germany's foes. The ideals of 'Peace, Retrenchment, Reform' made the Left unalterably opposed to foreign commitments and impatient when Liberal governments displayed too much caution and reserve in executing foreign policy along the lines of these high-minded principles.

For the Right, visibly alarmed not only at domestic developments but at the obvious signs of Britain's steady decline as a world power, the exact opposite was true. What they sought was an end to this policy of retreat, an indication that Britain would no longer be 'pushed around', a rejection of Left-wing policies which led to the disintegration and decay of the Empire, the United Kingdom and British society itself, and a thoroughgoing plan to counter all this by the regeneration of the whole body politic. And if Liberal administrations were most frequently the target, this did not mean that Conservative governments escaped unscathed: the Salisbury/Balfour administration of 1895/1905 was criticized, for example, for failing to protect British interests in China, for being too 'soft' towards France over Fashoda, for neglecting the maintenance of British naval supremacy, for the pathetic performance of the army during the Boer War, and for co-operating with Germany over Venezuela and Baghdad Railway matters.
[. . .]

8 ORIGINS OF THE RUSSIAN REVOLUTION

A. PROBLEMS AND PATTERNS OF RUSSIAN ECONOMIC DEVELOPMENT

Alexander Gerschenkron

Source: Alexander Gerschenkron (ed.), *Economic Backwardness in Historical Perspective* (The Belknap Press of Harvard University Press, 1962).

I

The emancipation of the peasantry stands at the threshold of the period under review. The question of whether, on the eve of the reform, the system of serfdom was disintegrating for economic reasons or whether its vitality and viability were still essentially unimpaired has been the subject of much controversy. But even those who, like the present writer, tend toward the latter view must admit that the development of the nonagrarian sectors of the economy was virtually premised upon the abolition of serfdom.

To say this, however, does not at all imply that promotion of economic development was a paramount objective of the emancipation. As was true of most of the agrarian reforms in nineteenth-century Europe, the authors of the Russian reform either considered industrialization undesirable or, at best, were indifferent to it. The actual procedures chosen reflected these attitudes. In many ways they were bound to hamper rather than facilitate economic growth. The emancipation involved, first of all, a determination of the land area to be given over by the landowner to peasants for permanent use. There is no question that over wide parts of the country (and particularly in the black-earth belt) the peasants received a good deal less land than had been customarily assigned to them prior to the reform. Second, there was the question of the magnitude of the quitrents (*obrok*) to be paid by the peasants as compensation for land allotments. It is true that once those rents were set, subsequent acquisition of land by the peasants (the so-called redemption procedure, by which the right of use was changed to the right of ownership) was rendered very easy and as often as not did not entail any *additional* burdens upon the peasantry. But the original rents were set far above the contemporaneous market prices of the land. [. . .]

It might be argued that the two features of the Russian reform just mentioned should have provided a favorable climate for subsequent industrialization; the inadequacy of the peasants' landholdings in conjunction with the considerable financial obligations imposed upon the peasants' households could have been expected to favor the flight from the country and thus to provide a large reservoir of labor supply to the nascent industry. Such might have been the consequences indeed, if the reform and the later legislative measures had not erected considerable barriers to land flight by strengthening the *obshchina*, the village commune, wherever it existed.

An English yeoman who found the cost of enclosing the land excessive could sell his farm and use the funds so obtained for business ventures outside agriculture or, at worst, for covering his transfer cost. A Russian peasant who wished to leave the village commune not only had to relinquish his rights in the land, but in addition had to pay, under the terms of the redemption procedures, what often were very sizeable sums before he could receive his release. A member of the household, rather than the head thereof, wishing to leave the village permanently also had to secure the consent of the head of the household. Where the periodic repartitions of land by the village commune were conducted on the basis of manpower at the disposal of the household, permanent departure of a family member was bound to reduce the extent of land to be made available to the household at the next repartition. In conditions of relative scarcity of land, the willingness of the head of the household to permit such departures could not be, and in general never was, very great. Nothing was more revealing of the irrational way in which the village commune functioned than the fact that the individual household had to retain the abundant factor (labor) as a precondition for obtaining the scarce factor (land). On the other hand, the readiness of the member of the household to sever for good his connection with the land and become firmly committed to non-agricultural pursuits naturally was adversely affected by these arrangements. [. . .]

While permanent migration to the city was rendered difficult, temporary moves on the part of the members of peasant households were much less so. Yet even in such cases, the permissive rights vested in the heads of the village administration and the heads of the household created various opportunities for impounding some portion of the earnings made in the city. The right to demand and to enforce the return to the village of the departed member certainly left much room for pressures and extortions of all kinds. If it is considered that age-long tradition and inveterate inertia would have hindered migration to industry under any circumstances, the Russian government by assigning to the *obshchina* and the *mir* such a strong role in the emancipation procedure and in the life of the post-emancipation village had created a considerable obstacle to the formation of a permanent industrial labor force in Russia.

If the double pressure to which the peasant economy was exposed – the inadequacy of land and the magnitude of the financial burdens – was prevented from causing a steady and considerable migration from the land, then that pressure itself was bound to assume the role of a retarding factor in the economic evolution of the country. The peasant economy was unable to increase its productivity because its income net of taxation and redemption payments did not permit sufficient investment; at times the low level of income even led to capital depletion. In addition, the prospect of repartitions militated against land improvements, even if and where they were financially possible; and the egalitarian nature of such repartitions prevented consolidation of landholdings assigned to individual households and precluded changes in cultivation methods and crop-rotation systems even where ignorance and inertia of the peasantry did not constitute an effective obstacle to such improvements.

In the long run, the scarcity of land available to the peasants in conjunction with the increase in population implied a steady deterioration in the economic position of the peasantry, despite purchases by village communes and individual peasants of gentry land and despite the formation, in the 1880s, of special institutions designed to finance such transactions.

It is true that the position of state peasants was more favorable than that of the former serfs in that their land allotments were somewhat larger and their financial burdens somewhat lighter, while the so-called imperial peasants were in between the two groups. Yet these differences, particularly in the long run, were not sufficiently large to warrant a different appraisal of the state and imperial peasantry. They too experienced the restrictive effects of the village commune, and the economic development of their farms also was restrained by the action of the government whose deliberate policy it was to bring their burdens in line with those imposed upon the former serfs.

It should be added that it would be a mistake to interpret the secular rise in land prices which characterized the period between the emancipation and the First World War as providing relief to the peasantry in the sense of reducing the real burden of their obligations. Over large areas of Europe market values of peasant land tended to be a good deal above the capitalized yield values. But in Russia that tendency was particularly strong. Land values moved upward even when prices of agricultural products were falling. The land hunger of the peasantry, stimulated by population growth, largely accounted for this discrepancy. Thus, the rise in land values, far from relieving the peasant economy, was an expression of its precarious position.

There is little doubt that the inhibitions upon the growth of output of the peasants' economy and the consequent limitations upon the peasants' purchasing power for industrial products were a serious obstacle to the industrialization of the country. They made it improbable from the outset that peasant demand for industrial goods could exercise a strong pull on industrial growth. This was clearly seen by a large number of Populist writers. Their conclusion was that industrial development in Russia was unlikely to start and, if started, was bound to founder in the shallowness of the 'internal market'.

This prospect left the Populists undismayed because of their aversion to industrialization and their fears of its social consequences. Yet the predictions did not come true. By 1914, Russia had taken very long strides along the road of industrial development. What had vitiated the Populists' predictions was their failure to see the manifold flexibilities and adjustabilities which are inherent in processes of economic development. The growing purchasing power of the peasant economy can be indeed important as a motive force of industrialization. Yet it is but one among a number of possible alternatives.

Economic development in a backward country such as Russia can be viewed as a series of attempts to find – or to create – substitutes for those factors which in more advanced countries had substantially facilitated economic development, but were lacking in conditions of Russian backwardness. Such 'substitutions' are the key to an understanding of the way in which the original disabilities were overcome and a process of sustained industrial growth was started in Russia. It is these acts of substitution that came to determine the specific pattern of industrial development.

But the process of industrialization is also a process of diminishing backwardness. In its course, factors that were lacking formerly tend to become evident and acquire increasing importance within the body economic. What was once in vain looked for to serve as a 'prerequisite' or a 'cause' of industrial development came into being as its effect. It is a fascinating pursuit in the history of modern industrializations to see to what extent the original 'substitutes' were thereby rendered obsolete and disappeared after having fulfilled their function; and to what extent they were preserved and continued to dominate the pattern of industrial development in its subsequent stages, even though the special need for them no longer existed. [...]

Over long stretches of the period under review, in manifold ways, in ever-changing forms, and at different levels, innovation and anachronism seem to coalesce and to separate, to follow and to displace each other. The remainder of this chapter will be devoted to an attempt to see the peculiarities of Russian industrialization in terms of these relationships.

II

The great spurt of Russian industrialization in the prerevolutionary period largely coincided with the decade of the 1890s. Thus, almost thirty years had passed [since emancipation] before the great effort could come about. This is not surprising. The peasant reform would have had to be very different if a direct and immediate impact upon industrial growth could have been expected from it. Moreover, even if the reform had been deliberately designed to favor industrialization rather than to obstruct it, a certain preparatory period of slow growth was almost inevitable. The judicial and administrative reforms which came in the wake of the emancipation were essential in creating a framework for modern business activity. But other changes, at least equally significant, were much slower in coming. Certainly a radical improvement in communications was crucial. One does not have to conjure up the dramatic and pathetic vision of a huge boiler being dragged by teams of oxen through the deep mud of the Ukrainian steppes on its way to the construction site of the first blast furnace in the *Donbas* in order to understand that some railroad building had to antedate the period of rapid industrialization. Railroads were indispensable to sustain a level of exports consonant with the needs of an industrializing economy. Railroad materials had to be imported from abroad, which in turn meant pursuit of a liberal foreign-trade policy with but a modicum of encouragement to domestic industry. Besides, a period of rapid growth does not materialize overnight simply because an institutional barrier to industrialization has disappeared. Such a period requires a simultaneous development of complementary efforts in many directions. The component elements of growth in the individual industrial branches must be adjusted to each other, and only when a number of such 'development blocks' [. . .] has been created is the stage set for the initiation of the great spurt.

There is little doubt that the decades following the emancipation can be conceived as such a period of preparation. And yet it is only in retrospect that they can be so viewed. The deficiency of the internal market, so untiringly stressed by the Populist writers, might have postponed the period of rapid growth until a far and indefinite future. The strategic factor in the great industrial upsurge of the 1890s must be seen in the changed policy of the government. The fear of industrialization, so much in evidence in the 1860s, was gone. Industrial development became an accepted and in fact the central goal. Once this happened, the problem of the peasant demand lost its previous significance, and its relation to industrialization was thoroughly reversed. It was as though a rotating stage had moved, revealing an entirely new scenery. The growth of peasant demand for industrial goods no longer was a prerequisite of successful industrialization. On the contrary, its curtailment became the objective. To reduce peasant consumption meant increasing the share of national output available for investment. It meant increased exports, stability of the currency, chances for larger and cheaper loans from abroad, and the availability of foreign exchange needed to service foreign loans.

The Russian state under Vyshnegradsky [Finance Minister, 1887-92] and Witte put the peasantry under very considerable fiscal pressure. It left the agricultural economy of the country to its own devices, satisfied that conversion of pastures into grain lands and some modest rise in productivity on those estates which were cultivated as such rather than leased to the peasants were sufficient to support the process of industrialization. Population of course was growing rapidly. In the closing years of the 1890s Russian agriculture produced less breadgrains per capita of the population than had been the case three decades earlier. If the increased exports are taken into consideration, the domestic availabilities were still smaller. A central principle of governmental policy was to impound a larger share of the peasants' output rather than to take active steps to raise that output.

Thus, the government's budgetary policy was effectively *substituted* for the deficiency of an internal market. The continuation of railroad construction on a large scale throughout the 1890s provided the government with convenient machinery for the maintenance of demand for industrial products. At the same time, in multifarious ways the government either supplied investment funds to industry directly or encouraged and facilitated investment in industry. Government action took the place of what in other countries was achieved by the pull of a growing free market, or by forced savings generated either by credit creation or by the impact upon current income of previously accumulated claims.

Those, however, were not the only processes of substitution that were taking place during the period of the great spurt of Russian industrialization. The Russian government, far from favoring all branches of industrial endeavor indiscriminately, concentrated its primary attention on the output of iron and steel and the machinery industries. The strategic interest in railroads and general political considerations certainly prompted the government in that direction. But as may be deduced from comparisons with other countries, this cannot be more than a part of the story. In a sense, this concentration upon certain branches of industry also was an emanation of substitutive processes.

Russia on the eve of its great industrial spurt suffered from many disabilities. Its entrepreneurs were far too few; their time horizon often limited, their commercial customs backward, and their standards of honesty none too high. The influx of labor to industry was inadequate because of the institutional framework that had been imposed upon agriculture. Such labor as was available was uneducated, restless and fitful in its habits, often trying to submerge the sense of frustration and loneliness in alcoholic excesses with consequent absenteeism, low productivity, and rebellion against the rules of the factory discipline. One of the few advantages that Russia, as many other backward countries in similar conditions, possessed was the possibility of borrowing technology from more advanced and more experienced industrial countries. In this field alone, Russia could equal, if not excel, them. It could concentrate on modern technology so that its factory equipment, though much smaller in the aggregate, could be much more up-to-date in its average composition. But the introduction on a large scale of technology from advanced countries, in its very nature, also meant a substitution of capital for labor. Far from being irrational in conditions of a backward country, it was the modern Western technology which enabled the Russian entrepreneurs to overcome the disability of an inadequate labor supply and very frequently also the inferior quality of that labor.

This is not to say that lack of suitable industrial labor in itself was not a hindrance to Russian industrialization. Introduction of a labor-saving process may mean lower cost per unit of the product; and still the entrepreneur may find the resulting saving insufficient to justify the effort of reorganization and modernization of the plant. His decision may be positive only if he feels that cost reductions will lead to a great expansion of output, thus increasing the total profits very considerably. But a sizeable expansion of output, even though the innovation is labor saving, will require a large increase in the labor force; accordingly, the decision may still fall against the innovation, unless the labor needed may be expected to come forth without too great a rise in wage rates. The point, therefore, is not that the difficulties which Russia experienced with the formation of an industrial proletariat were not a bothersome obstacle. The point rather is that the assurance of government demand for a considerable portion of the growing output in conjunction with the introduction of modern technology created a situation in which the quantitative and the qualitative inadequacy of the labor supply could be neutralized to an extent that still permitted a relatively high rate of industrial growth.

A historian of the period cannot fail to be impressed with two aspects of this process of assimilation of foreign technology. It may be taken for granted that throughout the nineteenth century technology tended to become more and more labor saving. This was true of the individual industrial branches, and even more so of industrial economies as a whole, because of the increasing share of those industries where technological progress led to particularly rapid increases in the capital-labor ratios. It is true of course that, broadly speaking, the Russian entrepreneurs had to accept Western technology such as it was. But if they had wanted to keep down the capital-labor ratios, they might well have tried to obtain secondhand equipment built in earlier phases of Western industrialization. The least they could do was to try to import technology from those countries where technological progress had been less rapid. In fact, the opposite was true. In the period of the great spurt of the nineties, it was no longer the English technology, but the more progressive German technology that came to dominate Russian imports; and increasingly, the eyes of engineers and factory managers turned toward the United States whence even more capital-intensive equipment was brought into the country. Thus alternatives were available, and there is no reason to assume that the choices made were not the rational ones.

On the other hand, it would be wrong to see the process of technological acquisition as one of mere imitation. True, in the last decade of the nineteenth century, the Russians had as yet very little opportunity for producing equipment which combined certain features of, say, American and German machinery (as began to happen several decades later). But they exercised discretion in the processes that were modernized and those that were left unchanged, often within the same plant. While the Russian blast furnaces were rapidly becoming bigger and technically more advanced, the processes of introducing the charge into the furnaces remained untouched by this development, and workers equipped with wheelbarrows still carried out the job. Where industrial work was still similar to that used in agriculture and capable of being performed by an unskilled and fluctuating labor force, it was allowed to continue to do so.

Finally, there is the problem of bigness. Bigness, in a broad sense, is of course inherent in the concept of a great spurt. But the industrialization in Russia, as in so many other backward countries in the nineteenth century, was also characterized by bigness both of individual plant and individual enterprise. There were many reasons for this. For one, the technology of the nineteenth century typically favored the large plants, and to accept the most advanced technology also meant accepting larger and larger plants. The state promoting industrial establishments, for good and not so good reasons, showed remarkably little interest in small businesses. Large enterprises were a much more lucrative source of graft; and the corruption of the bureaucracy tended to reinforce a tendency that was already present for weighty economic reasons. Similarly, the Russian government did little to check the strong cartelization movement within Russian industry which acquired momentum after the great spurt of the nineties. But what is of interest here is that the bigness of plant and enterprise, too, must be viewed as a specific substitution process. The lack of managerial and entrepreneurial personnel was compensated for by a scale of plants which made it possible to spread the thin layer of available talent over a large part of the industrial economy.

But what were the results and the aftermath of these developments? In purely quantitative terms, in terms of growth of industrial output, the spurt was truly a great one. The average annual rate of industrial growth during the nineties was around 8 per cent, and it was even better than that in the last years of the decade. None of the major countries in Western Europe had experienced a comparably high rate of change. The very rapidity of the transformation, however, was making for maladjustments of various kinds. The discrepancy between the industrial segment of the economy which was forging ahead and the relatively stagnant agricultural segment perhaps was the most crucial among those lags and tensions. But others were by no means unimportant.

The specific processes of substitution, which have been referred to above, tended to reinforce the heterogeneous character of the resulting economic structure. Contrasts between the new and the old appeared within the industrial group itself and within the individual plants and enterprises. Technology as a strategic factor in the industrial spurt implied modernization of some industrial branches and not of others. Within an industrial plant age-old processes based on tools used in the construction of the Pyramids were carried on side by side with methods representing the last word of the inventive genius of the nineteenth century. This inevitably was reflected in human contrasts within the labor force.

But the contrasts obviously transcended labor; they extended into the managerial group. The technical director, as the chief engineer frequently was called in a Russian factory, may have been indistinguishable from his Western counterpart. The commercial manager or the entrepreneur as likely as not was a much more complex phenomenon. He was able to understand and willing to exploit the economic advantages of the new technology, but at the same time he carried on attitudes and displayed forms of behavior which differed little, if at all, from those of preindustrial entrepreneurs in Russia. This was true of his relations to consumers, suppliers, credit institutions, and competitors. In addition, his relations with the governmental bureaucracy called for special, often very devious, actions. He had to be a different man in his way of dealing with a German firm which supplied his business firm with machinery and know-how, and in dealing with an official in the Ministry of Finance whence he obtained both subsidies and orders for deliveries. The great spurt in conditions of Russian backwardness could not fail to give rise to manifold stresses, tensions, and incongruities. [. . .]

All these disparities, created almost inevitably in the course of the great spurt, can be seen as problems for the phase of Russian industrial development that followed. However, overriding all of them in importance was the problem which the emancipation of the peasantry did not solve and the gravity of which was greatly enhanced precisely by the policy of rapid industrialization. Industrialization required political stability, but industrialization, the cost of which was largly defrayed by the peasantry, was in itself a threat to political stability and hence to the continuation of the policy of industrialization. The immediate effect of the basic substitution of the government's budgetary policies for the deficiency of the internal market was growth of industrial output. In the longer run, the effects were more complex.

III

What happened in Russia in the nineties of the last century was the great upsurge of modern industrialization. Nevertheless, certain aspects of it were not modern at all. Several times before in the course of Russian history, economic development seemed to follow a curious pattern: the military interests of the state induced the government to bring about a rapid spurt of economic growth. In the course of the process, heavy burdens were imposed upon the peasant population of the country, the enserfment of the Russian peasantry having been inextricably connected with the policies of economic development. So great were the burdens, and so heavy the pressure, that after a number of years the spurt tended to peter out, leaving an exhausted population to recover slowly from the stress and the strain that had been imposed upon it.

There is little doubt that military considerations had a good deal to do with the Russian government's conversion to a policy of rapid industrialization. True, no immediate military discomfiture preceded the initiation of the new policy. But the war of 1877 against the Turks was won on the battlefield in the Danube Valley and the Balkan Mountains, only to be lost in Berlin against the British and probably the Germans as well. In the course of the Berlin Congress, particularly during its dramatic moments, the Russian government had much opportunity and reason to reflect that it was not much better prepared for any military conflict with a Western power than it had been a quarter of a century earlier on the eve of the Crimean War. In the short run, Russian reaction consisted in shifting the direction of its expansionist policy away from Europe to Central Asia and the Far East. Taking a somewhat longer view and further prompted by the formation of military alliances in Central Europe, the government turned toward the goal of a drastic increase in the economic potential of the country.

In the 1890s, a renewed enserfment of the peasantry was, of course, not in the realm of practical politics. Nor was there any need for such a measure. The reforms of rural administration which had been introduced with the advent of reaction under Alexander III gave the central bureaucracy sufficient tax-exacting power over the peasantry; at least for some time it was possible to keep the peasantry in the state of docile compliance. The joint responsibility of the village commune for tax payments was helpful, though far from indispensable. The considerable shift to indirect taxation further increased the government's ability to pay for the industrialization in conditions of a relative price and currency stability. The fiscal policy of the government was able to perform the function which at an earlier age had been performed by the institution of serfdom.

The great spurt of the 1890s came to an end in 1900. The depression of that year was variously interpreted as an overproduction crisis, a financial crash, or a response to economic setbacks abroad, particularly in Central Europe. It is fairly clear, however, that below the surface phenomena lay the exhaustion of the tax-paying powers of the rural population. The patience of the peasantry was at its end. The following years were characterized by growing unrest in the villages until the folly of the war with Japan fanned the isolated fires into the flame of a widespread peasant rebellion in the course of the 1905 Revolution. All this was very much like the consummation of the traditional pattern of Russian economic development: a quick upsurge compressed within a relatively short period ending in years of stagnation. And yet there was a great deal more to the industrial spurt of the 1890s than simply a repetition of previous sequences of economic development. It would seem more plausible to view those similarities as the last emanations, in prerevolutionary Russia, of the traditional pattern. For the differences were fully as important as the similarities. Also in this broad sense, the new and the old appeared curiously commingled. Along with the resurrection of a specifically Russian past, there was also the assimilation of Russian economic development into a graduated but still general pattern of European industrialization.

Two, and perhaps three, factors stand out in distinguishing the upswing of the 1890s from similar episodes in the more remote past. One of them has just been mentioned. During the decade of the 1890s, the Russian government abstained from introducing for the sake of industrialization any far-reaching institutional change which, while aiding the process in the short run, would have become a serious obstacle to its continuation in the long run. Neither the institution of the *zemskii nachal'nik* [*zemstvo* chief] nor the additional steps taken in the 1890s to preserve and protect the village commune could of course compare in any way with the enserfment of the peasantry. That a government firmly committed to the policy of industrialization went out of its way to safeguard the *obshchina* [village commune] seemed paradoxical. But apart from the fiscal value of the arrangement, it was felt that its existence contributed to political stability within the country. Neither reason was persuasive. Satisfactory substitutes for joint responsibility for tax payments could easily have been found; and the events of the subsequent years showed clearly that the village commune nursed rebellious rather than conservative sentiments. The abolition of the commune still remained a problem of industrial policies in Russia, but it was one which antedated the period of rapid industrialization.

The other factor was positive. A modern industrialization based on the creation of fixed capital of considerable durability was not followed by periods of protracted stagnation as easily as had been the earlier, much more labor-intensive spurts of economic development ('stagnation' of course is to be understood simply in terms of a very low or even negative rate of growth). The recuperative power of a capital-intensive economy was greatly superior to that of its historical predecessors. And, finally, a modern industrialization is characterized also by a more substantial investment in human capital. In particular, it tends to bring about, over a relatively short period, a considerable change in entrepreneurial and managerial attitudes as well as, though to a lesser extent, in those of skilled labor. All this means that the effects of the great spurt reached out strongly into the future; that the process of industrialization could be resumed at diminished *faux frais* [expense] and in a form more efficient and less dependent upon the support of the state.

Such were the characteristic features of Russian industrial growth in the years between the 1905 Revolution and the outbreak of World War I. This, too, was a period of rather rapid growth (some 6 per cent per year), even though the rate of change remained below that of the 1890s. During those years industrialization could no longer be the primary concern of the government. War and revolution had greatly strained budgetary capabilities. The redemption payments (as well as the institution of joint responsibility) had disappeared under the impact of the revolution. [. . .] Railroad building continued, but on a much reduced scale. The execution of such armament plans as were conceived was being postponed from year to year. [. . .] But [. . .] Count Witte's fall and the abandonment of his policies did not prevent a renewed outburst of industrial activity.

Nothing underscores more clearly the changed attitude of the government than the fact that its most important action in the field of economic policy was Stolypin's legislation against the *obshchina*. In a radical reversal of the agrarian policies pursued only a few years earlier, Stolypin's reforms of 1906 and 1910 made it possible for the peasants to sever their connection with the *obshchina* through a simple and advantageous procedure, to acquire personal ownership of the land, and in the process often to swap the numerous strips of their former allotment for a single consolidated holding.

There is no question that many aspects of the reform were harsh and unfair to the less prosperous members of the village communes. There is also every evidence that the government's *volte-face* was caused by political considerations, that is to say, by the impressive lesson learned from peasant uprisings during the preceding revolution. The consequences of the reform for the process of industrial development were accidental from the government's point of view [. . .] .

Nevertheless, the potential positive effects of the reform on industrial development were indisputable. The authors of the reform, despite considerable opposition within the government, refused to accept the concept of family or household ownership; the ownership of peasants leaving the village commune was vested in the head of the household. For the first time, the road was open for an unimpaired movement to the city of peasant family members; for the first time large groups of Russian peasants could, like their counterparts in the West, sell the land and use the proceeds for establishing themselves outside agriculture. The war of 1914 necessarily cut short the implementation of the reform, but its initial effect was considerable. Both those peasants who had felt that leaving the commune would enable them to increase the productivity of their farms and those peasants who had been anxious to leave the village hastened to avail themselves of the separation procedure. It was a considerable step on the road of Russia's westernization.

And this is the aspect of the reform that is of primary importance from the point of view of the present discussion. [. . .] The withdrawal of the state after the upswing of the 1890s was marked by a measure which was designed to further rather than thwart industrial progress.

The westernization of Russian industrialization between 1906 and 1914 expressed itself in a large variety of ways. To use the previously adopted terminology, one could say that the pattern of substitutions was changing rapidly. To some extent banks stepped into the vacuum left by the state. In this way, credit-creation policies and some entrepreneurial guidance by the banks continued to substitute for the scarcity of both capital and entrepreneurship in Russia. But this mode of substitution tended to approximate the pattern of Russian development to that prevailing in Central Europe. The credit policies of the banks were still a substitute for an autonomous internal market, but there is little doubt that one of the consequences of the industrial creations of the nineties was the gradual emergence of such a market.

It may be quite tempting to view again the change between the period under review and that of the 1890s in terms of Erik Dahmén's dichotomy between development blocks in the state of full completion and development blocks in the beginning stage. The years 1906-1914 were characterized by the relative scarcities of coal, oil, and metals, in conjunction with the rapid forging ahead of metal-processing industries. There is a persistent and very much exaggerated tendency in present Russian historiography to present those scarcities as consequences of monopolistic policies in the basic-materials industries. It is probably more reasonable, still following Dahmén, to say that during the years preceding the First World War the structure of Russian industry was distinguished by specific disproportionalities and that once again, though on a much higher level, industry may have been passing through a period of dynamic preparation for another great spurt. Such a spurt, of course, never materialized. The point, however, is that considering the years 1906-1914 as a period of formation of new development blocks may help to explain why the rate of growth during those years was not higher than it was. It cannot explain the high growth that was actually attained in a situation where the outside aid to industry had manifestly declined to a fraction of its previous volume. It is more helpful, therefore, to regard this period as governed by the effects of diminished backwardness, and in this sense to view the whole stretch between the end of the 1880s and the outbreak of the war as consisting of two disparate and yet connected parts: the great spurt of the 1890s had prepared for the subsequent con-tinuation of growth under changed conditions.

Many of the tensions and frictions that could be so strikingly observed during the 1890s reappeared in the second period, if at all, in a considerably modified and tempered form. There is no question that great progress had taken place with regard to entrepreneurial attitudes. Without such progress and, in particular, without the general rise in trustworthiness of Russian businessmen, the banks could never have come to play a powerful role as suppliers of long-term credit to industrial firms. The general modernization of entrepreneurial attitudes no doubt made the complex of actions and relations of the individual entrepreneurs less heterogeneous. The decline in the importance of the government as an economic agent pointed in the same direction.

The years that had passed since the second half of the 1880s considerably increased the stock of permanent industrial labor in the country. At the same time, after 1905, more tangible improvements both in real wages and in working conditions became noticeable. The reduction in the importance of foreign engineers and foremen in factories and mines also tended to diminish friction. At the same time, the great pressure upon the peasantry had subsided. In contrast to the last decades of the nineteenth century, the quantity of breadgrain available for domestic consumption rose faster than did the population. The industrialization between 1906 and 1914 no longer offers a picture of a race against time and of progressive exhaustion, physically and mentally, of the population's power to suffer and to endure.

Those elements of relaxation and 'normalization' in the industrial process should not, however, disguise the fact that in other respects the great spurt of the 1890s, the industrial upsurge under conditions of extreme backwardness, still dominated the course of the development in the later period. The composition of the growing industry continued to favor the same branches as before. As in the earlier period, the stress on bigness was characteristic of both the productive and the organizational structure. The movement toward cartelization, which was mentioned before, must be regarded as a part of this continued emphasis on bigness. As was true in countries west of Russia, the policies of the banks tended to accelerate the process. In this sense they were the true heirs to the policies previously pursued by the bureaucracy. And like the latter, they tended to exaggerate and accelerate the process both for good and bad reasons. [. . .] Still [. . .] it was of utmost importance that the stress on large-scale business, the very essence of industrialization in conditions of backwardness and the basis for its successful implementation, could be preserved after the withdrawal of the state.

Russia before the First World War was still a relatively backward country by any quantitative criterion. The large weight of the agrarian sector of the economy and the low level of the nation per capita output placed her far below and behind neighboring Germany. Nevertheless, as far as the general pattern of its industrialization in the second period was concerned, Russia seemed to duplicate what had happened in Germany in the last decades of the nineteenth century. One might surmise that in the absence of the war Russia would have continued on the road of progressive westernization.

It is not entirely pointless to speculate on what might have happened in the course of such a development. Diminution of backwardness is a complex process. As has already been noted, certain paraphernalia of backwardness are shed fairly soon after the beginning of the process. Other elements are more resistant to change. Thus, the great school of industrialization tends to educate the entrepreneurs before it educates the workers; and it takes still longer before the influence of the industrial sector of the economy penetrates into the countryside and begins to affect the attitudes of the peasantry. In the latter respect, prerevolutionary Russia saw no more than the first modest traces of such an influence. Yet the likelihood that the transformation in agriculture would have gone on at an accelerated speed is very great. [. . .]

Russian industrial development around the turn of the century was frequently decried as 'artificial'. Count Witte used to reject the accusation with considerable vehemence as meaningless and irrelevant (probably with justice). For what matters is both the degree and the direction of 'artificiality' or 'spontaneity' in the process seen over an appropriately long time. Taking into consideration the economic conditions that prevailed in Russia prior to its great spurt of industrialization, it is difficult to deny that the Russian development fitted well into the general pattern of European industrialization, conceived, as it properly should be, in terms of a graduated rather than a uniform pattern.

The only purpose in speculating about the probable course of Russian economic development as it might have been, if not interrupted by war and revolution, is to try to cast more light on the general industrial trends that dominated the last period of industrialization in prerevolutionary Russia. Still the question remains whether war and revolution cannot be interpreted as the result of the preceding industrial development. Some Soviet historians certainly incline in that direction. If the Russian bourgeoisie could be saddled with the main responsibility for the outbreak of the war and if, in addition, it could be shown that in bringing about the war it had acted in response to the pressure of its economic interests — if, in short, the process of Russian industrialization carried in itself the seeds of the coming military conflict — then to abstract the war from the process in order to elucidate the course and prospects of Russian industrialization would mean to abstract the process as well. Some Russian manufacturers indeed may have welcomed the wartime orders for their products. Yet the precise mechanism through which such interests of the bourgeoisie were in fact translated into the decisions reached by the emperor and his government has remained altogether obscure.

The view just described seems to magnify the political significance of the Russian bourgeoisie out of all proportion and to substitute suppositions of various degrees of plausibility for historical evidence. It might be more persuasive to argue that the government saw a relatively short and victorious war as a chance to solidify the regime and to avert the danger of revolution. And the question then would be to what extent the preceding industrial development may be said to have been leading to another revolutionary cataclysm.

It is true, of course, that the social and political structure of the empire was shot through with manifold serious weaknesses. Opposition to the regime was nearly universal among the intelligentsia and certainly widespread among the industrial and mercantile groups. Since 1912, the year of the famous massacre in the Lena gold fields, the strike movement of the workers was again gaining momentum. And at the bottom of the social edifice there was the old resentment of the peasants who had never accepted the rightfulness of the gentry's ownership rights over the land. The peasantry's land hunger was a steady source of ferment. The sentiment in the villages was no doubt further exacerbated by the blows struck against the village commune and the threat of its dissolution. A new outbreak of revolutionary violence at some point was far from being altogether improbable.

And yet, as one compares the situation in the years before 1914 with that of the nineties, striking differences are obvious. In the earlier period the very process of industrialization with its powerful confiscatory pressures upon the peasantry kept adding, year in and year out, to the feelings of resentment and discontent until the outbreak of large-scale disorders became almost inevitable. The industrial prosperity of the following period had no comparable effects, however. Modest as the improvements in the situation of peasants were, they were undeniable and widely diffused. Those improvements followed rather than preceded a revolution and accordingly tended to contribute to a relaxation of tension. Stolypin's reforms certainly were an irritant, but after the initial upsurge their implementation was bound to proceed in a much more gradual fashion.

Similarly, the economic position of labor was clearly improving. In the resurgence of the strike movement economic problems seemed to predominate. It is true, of course, that in the specific conditions of the period any wage conflict tended to assume a political character because of the ready interventions of police and military forces on behalf of management. But this did not mean that the climate of opinion and emotion within the labor movement was becoming more revolutionary; as shown by the history of European countries (such as Austria or Belgium), sharp political struggles marked the period of formation of labor movements that in actual fact, though not always in the language used, were committed to reformism. There is little doubt that the Russian labor movement of those years was slowly turning toward revision and trade-unionist lines. As was true in the West, the struggles for general and equal franchise to the Duma and for a cabinet responsible to the Duma, which probably would have occurred sooner or later, may well have further accentuated this development. To repeat, I do not mean to deny that there was much political instability in the country. There clearly was. What matters here is that from the point of view of the industrial development of the country, war, revolution, or the threat thereof may reasonably be seen as extraneous phenomena. In this sense, it seems plausible to say that Russia on the eve of the war was well on the way toward a westernization or, perhaps more precisely, a Germanization of its industrial growth. The 'old' in the Russian economic system was definitely giving way to the 'new'. It was left to the regime that finally emerged from the 1917 Revolution, generated in the misery of the war and the shame of defeats, to create a different set of novelties and to mix them with old ingredients of Russian economic history in the strange and powerful infusion of Soviet industrialism. [. . .]

B.   THE BREAKDOWN OF THE TSARIST AUTOCRACY
George F. Kennan
(WITH 'COMMENT' BY HUGH SETON-WATSON)

Source: Richard Pipes (ed.), *Revolutionary Russia* (Harvard University Press, 1968), pp.1-22.

The discussion that follows proceeds from the premise that what occurred in Russia in February-March 1917 was, precisely, a *breakdown* of the autocracy under a fortuitous combination of momentary strains — not the overthrow of the existing order by revolutionary forces. In essence, the regime may be said to have collapsed because it was not able to muster sufficient support to enable it to withstand this sudden combination of strains. In quarters whose support would have been essential to enable it to do this, there was either distrust, indifference, outright hostility, or, in the particular case of the bureaucracy and the army, a mixture of disorientation, demoralization, and ineptness. The central question involved is therefore the question as to which of the regime's policies — that is, what elements of its behavior, what errors of commission or omission, or possibly what circumstances outside its control — were decisive or outstandingly important in bringing it to the helpless and fatal predicament in which it found itself at the beginning of 1917.

Such an inquiry presents special difficulty in view of the bewildering interaction of long-term and short-term causes. One is compelled to ask not just what were the long-term weaknesses that rendered the regime susceptible to the danger of collapse under relatively trivial pressures in the first place, but also what it was that caused the collapse to come at this particular moment.

I should like to begin with an examination of some of the long-term weaknesses and failures of the regime and then conclude with some brief reflections about the developments of the final wartime period just preceding its fall.

Long-term Weaknesses and Failures of the Regime

When one looks for those more basic mistakes and failings that undermined the tsarist autocracy and caused it to lose what the Chinese would call the 'mandate of Heaven', one is obliged first to deal with certain broadly held misimpressions on this score — misimpressions that Soviet historians, in particular, have been at no pains to dispel. One of these is that the autocracy lost the confidence and respect of the people because it failed to bring a proper degree of modernization to Russian society in the economic, technological, and educational fields — that it made no adequate effort to overcome Russia's backwardness. Another is that the regime was intolerably cruel and despotic in its treatment of the populace generally; and that a revolution was required to correct this situation. [. . .]

Let us take first the subject of industrialization. Here, it seems to me, we have one of those fields in which the tsar's regime had least to be apologetic about from the standpoint of responsibility for the modernizing of the country. The rates of industrial growth achieved in Russia in the final decades of tsardom would appear to compare not at all unfavorably with those achieved in Western countries at comparable stages of development. The 8 per cent growth rate that I understand to have been achieved in the 1890s, and the comparable 6 per cent figure for the period from 1906 to 1914, are respectable figures, to say the least. One must doubt that the pace of industrialization could have been pushed much further without producing adverse social consequences out of all proportion in seriousness to the gains involved. Nor does there seem to be any reason to suppose that if revolution had not intervened, and if the dynamics of growth observable in the final decades of tsardom had been projected into mid-century, the results achieved would have been significantly inferior to those that have actually been achieved under Soviet power. This is, of course, only another way of saying that if industrialization was the main concern then no revolution was needed at all: there were easier and no less promising ways of doing it.

It has often been pointed out by way of reproach to the tsar's regime — both at the time and since — that this growth was achieved only by an excessive acceptance of investment and equity participation by foreigners in Russian industry, as well as by excessive state borrowing from other governments. Certainly, the proportion of foreign equity participation in Russian industrial concerns was very high, particularly in mining and metallurgy; and it is perfectly true that the Russian government was the most heavily indebted, externally, of any government in the world at the time. But I am not sure how well these charges stand up as reproaches to the policies of the tsar's government. Whether the high rate of foreign industrial investment was a bad thing depends on whether one accepts the Marxist thesis that any important degree of such external financing represented a form of enslavement to the foreign investors. The experience of the United States, where foreign capital also played a prominent part in nineteenth century industrial development, would not suggest that this is the case. And as for the government borrowing: much of this, of course, found its way, directly or indirectly, into the process of industrialization, and particularly into the building of railways. But the main stimulus to such borrowing was not the need for industrial capital but rather the effort by the government to maintain a military posture, and to engage in military ventures, that were far beyond its means. These practices, and the heavy indebtedness to which they led, were indeed among the significant weaknesses of the regime; but they do not constitute a proper source of reproach to the regime in connection with its program of industrialization. Had the foreign borrowings of the government been restricted to what it required in order to do its share in the stimulation of the growth of industry, the resulting burden of debt would surely have been well within its means.

Another reproach often leveled at the tsar's government in this connection was that industrialization was given precedence over agriculture and that it was partially financed by the exploitation of the peasantry through such devices as high indirect taxation, rigged prices for agricultural products, forced exportation of grain, and so on. Certainly there is much substance in these charges. The program of rapid industrialization was indeed put in hand long before any attack of comparable vigor was made on the problems of the peasantry, and the peasant was made to contribute heavily to its costs. But these circumstances seem to me to be illustrative less of any error or unfeeling quality on the part of tsarist statesmen than of the cruelty of the dilemmas with which they were faced. Without at least a certain prior development of industry, and particularly without the construction of railway network, no modernization of Russian agriculture would have been conceivable at all. And while somewhat more might perhaps have been extracted from the upper classes through ruthless taxation, there is no reason to suppose that this could have changed basically the logic of the situation, which was that the cost of industrialization, to the extent it was not covered by foreign borrowing, had to be covered by limitations on consumption by the great mass of the Russian people— which meant, in fact, the peasantry. To have tried, through the device of heavy taxation, to switch this entire burden to the relatively well-to-do or property-owning classes would merely have tended to destroy existing possibilities for the accumulation of private industrial capital; but such private accumulation was precisely what the government was concerned, and for very respectable reasons, to stimulate and promote.

The truth is that the tsar's government, if it wished to get on in a serious way with the industrial development of the country, had no alternatives other than foreign borrowing and an extensive taxation of the peasantry. The claim that it should have avoided one or the other of these devices is thus equivalent to the allegation that it moved not too slowly but much too fast in the whole field of industrialization. For this there might be much to be said. But this is not the way the reproach is usually heard.

In the case of agriculture, the pattern is obviously more complex. Certainly, the reform of the 1860s left much to be desired: it was not properly followed through; the burdens resting on the peasantry down to 1905 were inordinate; the economic situation of large portions of the peasant population remained miserable. In all this there were just grounds for reproach to the regime; and I have no desire to minimize its significance. It seems reasonable to suppose that the additional burden of bitterness that accumulated in peasant minds in the final decades of the nineteenth century contributed importantly both to the peasant disorders of the first years of the new century, and to that spirit of sullen contempt for the dynasty, and indifference to its fate, that manifested itself at the time of the revolution.

Against these reflections must be set, however, two compensatory considerations. One has, first, the fact that the most important single factor involved in producing the land hunger and economic misery of the central-Russian village in these decades was nothing to do with governmental policy but simply the enormous increase in the rural population that occurred at that time — a doubling, and more, just in the years between the emancipation and the outbreak of the world war. Second, there is the fact that after 1906 the government did finally address itself vigorously, intelligently, and in general quite effectively to the problems of the Russian countryside. The fact that this effort came late — too late to be successful in the political and psychological sense — should not blind us to its imposing dimensions. What was achieved in those final years from 1907 to 1914 in a whole series of fields affecting the peasant's situation — in the purchase of land by small peasant holders, in the break-up of the peasant commune and the facilitating of the transition from communal to hereditary tenure; in the consolidation of strip holdings, with all the enormous labor of surveying and adjudication this involved; in resettlement and in colonization of outlying regions of the empire, in the development of the cooperative movement in the countryside — strikes me as impressive in the extreme.

One can truthfully say that the tsar's government deserved reproach for its failures in relation to the peasant throughout most of the nineteenth century. And there can be no doubt that the price of these failures figured prominently in the reckoning the autocracy had to face in 1917. No one would deny, in particular, the importance of the impact that the spectacle of all this rural misery and degradation had on the growth of the Russian revolutionary movement in the nineteenth century. And one can well say that such efforts as were made to improve the situation of the peasantry came much too late in the game. What one cannot say is that they did not come at all or that revolution was necessary because the tsar's government, as of 1917, had still done nothing effective about agriculture. The fact is that the revolution came precisely at the moment when the prospects for the development of Russian agriculture, the war aside, had never looked more hopeful.

Similar conclusions could be drawn, I should think, with relation to education. That Russia was slow in coming to popular education no one would deny. But that the progress made in this field in the final years of tsardom was rapid and impressive seems to me equally undeniable. If, as I understand to be the case, enrolments in primary schools throughout the empire more than doubled in the final two decades before 1914; if in this same period enrolments in institutions of higher learning more than tripled and those in secondary schools nearly quadrupled; or if, for example, the incidence of literacy among military recruits increased from 38 per cent in 1894 to 73 per cent in 1913 – then it may be argued, I think, that all this might have been done earlier; but it cannot be said that nothing consequential was being done at all. The official goal, as adopted five or six years before the outbreak of the world war, was the achievement of universal, compulsory primary school education. The tsarist authorities hoped to achieve this goal by 1922. The rate of progress made prior to the war suggests that it would probably have been achieved at the latest by the mid-1920s had not war and revolution intervened. This is certainly no later than the date at which it was finally achieved by the Soviet regime. Again, one simply cannot accept the thesis that the old regime kept the Russian people in darkness to the end and that a revolution was necessary in 1917 to correct this situation.

In all these fields of modernization, the pattern is in fact much the same: initial backwardness, long sluggishness and delay, then a veritable burst of activity in the final years. If it was in these fields that one was to look for the decisive failures of the autocracy and the reasons for revolution, then it would have to be said that there was much less reason for an overthrow of the regime in 1917 than there was in 1905. Had the 1905 Revolution succeeded, one might well have concluded that the tsar's regime had been overthrown because it failed to bring the Russian people into the modern age. To account for an overthrow coming in 1917, one has to look for other and deeper causes.

The first and most decisive of these causes seems to me to have been, unquestionably, the failure of the autocracy to supplement the political system in good time with some sort of a parliamentary institution — the failure, in other words, to meet the needs of the land-owning nobility and then, increasingly, of the new intelligentsia from all classes for some sort of institutional framework that would associate them with the undertakings of the regime, give them a sense of participation in the governmental process, and provide a forum through which they, or their representatives, could air their views and make their suggestions with regard to governmental policy. In the absence of any such institution, literally hundreds of thousands of people — student youth, commoners (*raznochintsy*), sons of priests, members of the national minorities, members of the gentry, even members of the land-owning nobility itself [. . .] found themselves, insofar as they did not become associated with the armed forces or the administrative bureaucracy, repelled by the regime, held at a distance from its doings and responsibilities, condemned either to a passive submissiveness in public affairs that did violence to their consciences as well as their energies or to the development of forms of association and political activity that could not, in the circumstances, appear to the regime as other than subversive. What was required, initially, was not a widely popular assembly. There was much to be said for the view that the Russian people at large were not yet ready for this. At any time in the nineteenth century, even a central assembly of the local government boards (*zemstva*) would have constituted an important safety valve, and in fact a very suitable one, insofar as it would have enlisted as collaborators in the tasks of government at the central level not mere theorists devoid of practical experience but people who had had the best sort of preparation: namely, experience at the local, provincial level in the fields of administration intimately connected with the lives and interests of the people. [. . .]

There was, of course, eventually, the Duma; and it was, as an institution, not really so bad as it has often been portrayed. Its initial members could [. . .] have made much better use of it than they actually did. The franchise was indeed a limited one, but it was not so severely limited as to prevent both First and Second Dumas from being violently oppositional, and even extensively revolutionary, in spirit. Nor can I develop any lively sympathy for the great unhappiness manifested by the Kadets over the fact that the Duma was not given the right to appoint and control the government. For an American, in particular, it is hard to regard a fusing of the legislative and executive powers as absolutely essential to a sound political system. But leaving aside the adequacy of the arrangements governing the constitution and functioning of the Duma, it is obvious that the granting of it by

Nicholas II came far too late and in precisely the wrong way — under pressure, that is, and with obvious reluctance and suspicion on his part. Given the situation that existed at that particular moment, it was natural enough for him to do so. There could have been no more than a minority of the members of the First Duma whose political aspirations, if satisfied, would not have ended in the violent destruction of the autocracy; and the tsar understood this very well. And yet it was Nicholas himself, his father, and his grandfather who were responsible for the fact that this was the way things were. Had they acted earlier — and the 1860s would not have been too soon — they might have had a different, more respectful, and less menacing sort of a parliamentary body before them. And the difference would, I think, have been decisive. The conservative and liberal intelligentsia, from which the dynasty really had something to hope, might have rallied to its side and the radical revolutionary movement, from which it could expect nothing good, would have been split. The effect of waiting forty years and establishing the Duma in 1906 instead of in the 1860s was just the opposite: it unified the radical-revolutionary movement against the regime and split the conservative and liberal intelligentsia, whose united support was essential if the dynasty was to survive.

It was true, of course, that to grant a parliamentary institution would have involved at any time on the tsar's part a readiness to share the power which the dynasty had previously exercised absolutely. But in the mid-nineteenth century, there were still people on the other side who would have been willing to content themselves with this sharing of supreme power. By 1906 there was practically no one left, not only in the revolutionary movement but among the liberals as well, who did not insist, by implication at least, on destroying the tsar's powers entirely rather than just sharing in them. It was the destruction of the autocracy as such, not really its limitation, that was implicit in the demands of the First Duma for a responsible government, for control in effect of the police, and above all for a general amnesty.

In the 1860s the dynasty might still have had before it, in a parliamentary institution, people who were anxious to see it succeed in its tasks and willing to help it do so. By 1906 it was confronted, in every political party to the left of the Octobrists and even partly in the ranks of that grouping, not by people who constituted a loyal opposition, not by people who really wanted the dynasty to succeed with the tasks of modernization to which I referred earlier on, not by people who wished to have a share in the dynasty's power, but by rivals for the exercise of that power, by people whose chief grievance against the regime was not that it was dilatory or incompetent but that it stood in their own path, whose complaint was not really that the autocracy misruled Russia, but that it prevented *them* from ruling – or misruling, as history would probably have revealed – in its place.

With Unkovskii and his associates [who had suggested the formation of a central *zemstvo* organ] in 1862, Alexander II might, it seems to me, have come to some sort of political terms. With [the Kadet] Miliukov and his associates, decorous and mild-mannered as they outwardly were, this same possibility no longer existed. It had become by that time a case of *kto kogo* (who whom) – either the tsar or they. Yet without their help, as February 1917 revealed, the dynasty itself could not be defended.

In the mid-nineteenth century, in other words, the autocracy could still have opted for the status of a limited monarchy. In 1906 this option no longer remained open to it. And the failure to accept it when it *had been* open left only one possibility, which was its final and total destruction.

This great deficiency – namely the denial of political expression– must be clearly distinguished from the question of physical cruelty and oppression in the treatment of the population. It was suggested, at the outset of this discussion, that it was a misimpression that the regime was intolerably cruel and despotic in this respect. This is, of course, a controversial statement; and I do not wish to make it unnecessarily so. I am well aware of the fact that the tsarist police and prison authorities, as well as the military courts, were guilty of many acts of stupidity, injustice, and cruelty. [. . .] But the standards of the present age are different from those of the latter – unfortunately so. The tsarist autocracy did not engage in the sort of prophylactic terror – the punishment of great numbers of the innocent as a means of frightening the potentially guilty – of which we have seen so much in our age. Its treatment of many individual revolutionaries [. . .] seems to have been, if anything, on the lenient side. The censorship was irritating and often silly, but it was not sufficiently severe to prevent the appearance in Russia of a great critical literature. Most important of all, one has to distinguish, when one speaks of police terrorism, between that element of it that is spontaneous and the element that is provoked. That the Russian revolutionaries behaved provocatively, and deliberately so, on countless occasions is something that few, I think, would deny. Now, it is a habit of political regimes to resist their own violent overthrow; it is something to be expected of them. Stolypin used harsh measures – yes – in suppressing the disorders of the period following the war with Japan, but measures no more harsh than the situation required from the standpoint of the regime. [. . .] In situations of this nature, where there is a constant interaction between the strivings of revolutionaries and the defensive efforts of a political regime, the question of responsibility for violence becomes a matter of the chicken and the egg. If one abstracts from the behavior of the regime in the administration of justice and in the imposition of political discipline that element that was provided by provocation from the revolutionary side, then the use of police terror cannot be regarded as more than a minor determinant of the alienation of great sectors of society that underlay the breakdown of 1917.

So much for the denial of parliamentary government and political liberty. A second crucial deficiency of the autocracy was one that it shared with a large part of upper-class Russian society, and with a portion of the lower classes as well, and that was for this reason not only much more difficult to recognize at the time but has been more difficult of recognition even in the light of history. This was extreme nationalism — that romantic, linguistic nationalism that was the disease of the age.

The spirit of modern nationalism was pernicious for the Russian autocracy for two reasons: first, because it reflected itself unfortunately on the treatment by the tsar's government of the national minorities; but second, because it led to an adventurous foreign policy, far beyond what the capacities of the Russian state at that time could support.

In an empire of which nearly half, or something more than one half (depending on where the Ukrainians were ranked) of the population was made up of national minorities, an absolute monarchy was confronted, in the age of nationalism, with a basic choice. It could make political concessions to the Great-Russian plurality and thus at least keep the strongest single national element firmly associated with it in an effort to hold down the minorities; or, if it did not wish to do this, it could employ a light touch with the minorities, do everything possible to reconcile them to the Russian state, and play them off against the potentially rebellious central Great-Russian group. The tsar's government did neither. Operating against the background of a sullen Russian peasantry, a frustrated Russian upper class, and a lower-class Russian intelligentsia veritably seething with sedition, it set about to treat the national minorities in the name of Russian nationalism with an utterly senseless provocation of their national cultures and feelings and a rigid repression of all their efforts to establish a separate national political identity. This was a policy calculated to make sure that if there were anyone among the minority elements who was not already alienated from the autocracy by virtue of its general social and political policies, he would sooner or later be brought into the opposition by the offense to his national feelings. Among the manifestations of this stupidity none was more serious than the anti-Semitism that set in after the murder of Alexander II — an aberration of policy that was at first simply clumsy and reactionary in an old-fashioned religious sense but then assumed, under Nicholas II, forms that were truly disgraceful and bespoke a profound perversion of political and philosophic understanding. This tendency was particularly unfortunate because it came at a period when, for the first time, a great many young Jews would have been prepared, given half a chance, to forget the specific circumstances of their religious and cultural origin and to become essentially russified. And this anti-Semitism was of course only a part of nationalistic policies that affected in some way and at some time practically every one of the minorities that lined the periphery of the empire. The revenge for this extraordinary blindness became apparent, quite naturally, in the form of the high percentage of members of the national minorities to be found in the revolutionary movement. It is impossible to say what 1917 would have been like without the Chkheidzes and Martovs, the Trotskys, Dzerzhinskiis, Radeks, Sverdlovs, Stalins, and Ordzhonikidzes; but certainly the non-Great-Russian component in the revolutionary opposition to tsardom was a great one, particularly after 1881, and it must be assumed to have added greatly to the difficulty of the predicament of the autocracy at that final moment.

The second manner in which the disease of extreme nationalism manifested itself in tsarist policy was, as already noted, in the field of foreign affairs. Particularly was this true under Nicholas II. The origins of the war with Japan were, from the Russian side, disreputable and inexcusable. There was no need for this involvement; it could easily have been avoided; the attendant military effort was clearly beyond the physical resources of the country at that moment of rapid economic and social transition; and the folly of the venture from the domestic-political standpoint was at once apparent in the events of the Revolution of 1905. And as though this war were not folly enough in itself, it had the further effect of making it more difficult than ever for Russia to resist involvement in the much greater and even more dangerous European war that was shortly to come. The financial distress in which the tsar's government finished the war with Japan left it more dependent than ever on the financial bounty of the French government and the French bankers and more helpless than ever before the French demands that Russia become in effect an instrument of French policy against Germany.

Whether this added element of financial dependence was decisive in bringing Russia into World War I may well be doubted. The same result would very possibly have been achieved by the nationalistic tendencies now raging unchecked among the Russian bureaucracy, the military caste, and the upper classes generally, coupled with the tsar's strange weakness for military adventurism. To people still imbued with a strong conviction of the iniquity of the kaiser's Germany or Franz Josef's Austria, it may seem strange to hear it suggested that the Russian monarchy might have done better, in the interests of its own preservation, to remain aloof from involvement in a war against Germany. In the light of the prevailing nationalistic emotionalism of the time, it would no doubt have seemed preposterous to suggest that Serbia should have been left to Austria's mercy and that Russian prestige, just recently so painfully injured in the crisis over the annexation of Bosnia and Herzegovina, should suffer another and perhaps even greater reverse of this nature. The fact remains that in 1914 Russia was in no condition to participate in a major war – the experience of the war with Japan had demonstrated this; and neither the fate of Serbia nor the question of control over the Dardanelles really represented for her a vital interest, comparable to what she stood to suffer by courting another domestic upheaval on the heels of the one she had just experienced in 1904-5.

The Franco-Russian alliance served, in Russia's case, a financial interest but not really a political one. The kaiser's Germany may have been a threat to Britain; it was not in great measure a threat to Russia. Some of the more sober statesmen, Witte and even the otherwise nationalistic Stolypin, saw this, and would have tried betimes to avoid the catastrophe to which this alliance, which took no proper account of Russia's internal condition, was leading. But it was the pervasive nationalism of the age that defeated them; and I am inclined, for this reason, to attribute to that nationalism a major role in the causes of the final collapse of the regime. A tsarist autocracy that saw things clearly and wished to exert itself effectively in the interest of its own preservation would have practised a rigid abstention from involvement in world political problems generally, and from exhausting foreign wars in particular, at that crucial juncture in its domestic-political development.

The third of the weaknesses of the autocracy that I should like to mention was the personality of the last Russian tsar himself. Poorly educated, narrow in intellectual horizon, a wretchedly bad judge of people, isolated from Russian society at large, in contact only with the most narrow military and bureaucratic circles, intimidated by the ghost of his imposing father and the glowering proximity of his numerous gigantic uncles, helpless under the destructive influence of his endlessly unfortunate wife: Nicholas II was obviously inadequate to the demands of his exalted position; and this was an inadequacy for which no degree of charm, of courtesy, of delicacy of manner, could compensate. It is ironic that this man, who fought so tenaciously against the granting of a constitution, had many of the qualities that would have fitted him excellently for the position of a constitutional monarch and practically none of those that were needed for the exercise of that absolute power to which he stubbornly clung. Time and time again, in the record of his reign, one finds the evidences of his short-sightedness and his lack of grasp of the realities of the life of the country interfering with the political process in ways that were for him veritably suicidal. [. . .]

So much for the leading and crucial weaknesses of the autocracy itself in the final decades of its power. Mention must be made, in conclusion, of the Russian revolutionary movement. It was, of course, not the revolutionary parties that overthrew the autocracy in 1917. Nevertheless, there were indirect ways in which their existence and activity affected the situation of the regime; and these must be briefly noted.

First of all, by providing a somewhat romantic alternative to any association with the governing establishment, the revolutionary movement drew many talented youths into an attitude of defiance and revolutionary disobedience to it, thereby impoverishing it in talent, energy, and intelligence. Every time that a young person of ability was drawn into the ranks of its revolutionary opponents, the bureaucracy, deprived of these sources of recruitment, became just that more stupid, unimaginative, and inept.

Second, there was the effect the revolutionary elements had on the development of governmental policy. They obviously had no interest in seeing the modernization of the country proceed successfully under tsarist tutelage, and they did as little as they could to support it. I find it significant that more useful social legislation appears to have been passed by the two final and supposedly reactionary Dumas than by the first two relatively liberal, and partially revolutionary, ones. But more important still was the influence of the revolutionaries in frightening the regime out of possible initiatives in the field of political reform. These revolutionary parties and groupings had, as a rule, no interest in seeing genuine progress made in the creation of liberal institutions. Their aim was generally not to reform the system but to cause it to fall and to replace it. For this reason, the more the regime could be provoked into stupid, self-defeating behavior, the better from their standpoint. They often found themselves, in this respect, sharing the same aspirations and purposes as the extreme right wing of the political spectrum, which also — though for other reasons — did not wish to see any liberalization of the autocracy. And in this respect one has to concede to the revolutionary movement a series of important successes. In one instance after another where there appeared to be a possibility of political liberalization or where the pressures in this direction were intense the timely intervention of revolutionary activity of one sort or another sufficed to assure that no progress should be made. One has only to recall, as examples, the effect of the Polish uprising of 1863 on the policies of Alexander II or the effect of his assassination in 1881 on the [cautiously reformist] projects then being entertained by Loris-Melikov [the Interior Minister].

The War and the Final Crisis

So much, then, for the major weaknesses, failures, and strains that entered into the undermining of the tsarist system of power. It remains only to note the manner in which the effect of all of them was magnified by the world war that began in 1914: magnified to a point where the system could no longer stand the strain. Wartime patriotic fervor, engulfing the liberal-parliamentary circles even more hopelessly than the government itself, brought them in at this point as critics of the government on new grounds: on the grounds that it was not *sufficiently* nationalistic, not *sufficiently* inspired and determined in its conduct of the war effort. And to this there was now added the quite erroneous but heady and dangerous charge that it was pro-German and even treasonable in its relations to the enemy. These charges were utilized by the liberal-parliamentary circles as the excuse for setting up new organizational entities, such as the various war industry councils, which were able to function as rival authorities to the governmental bureaucracy, to provide channels for political activity hostile to the regime, and eventually to contribute significantly to the circumstances surrounding its collapse. Meanwhile, the strictly military aspects of the war effort had a whole series of effects — such as the weakening by losses in battle of the loyal portion of the officers' corps, the stationing of undisciplined garrisons in the vicinity of the capital city, the removal of the tsar himself to field headquarters, and so on — that were to have important connotations, unfavorable to the security of the regime, at the moment of supreme trial. In a number of ways, furthermore, the war effort exacerbated relations between the government and members of the national minorities, who for obvious reasons did not always share the Russian emotional commitment to the war. Finally, not perhaps as a consequence of the war (this is hard to judge), but certainly simultaneously with it, there were the grotesque developments in the tsar's own personal situation, particularly the ripening and the dénouement of the Rasputin affair — developments that finally succeeded in alienating from his cause not only large elements of the immediate bureaucratic and military entourage that had constituted his last comfort and protection, but even a portion of the imperial family itself, thus completing his isolation and removing, or disqualifying his last potential defenders.

Conclusions

Prior to the undertaking of this review, I was inclined to feel that had the war not intervened, the chances for survival of the autocracy and for its gradual evolution into a constitutional monarchy would not have been bad. On reviewing once more the events of these last decades, I find myself obliged to question that opinion. Neither the tardiness in the granting of political reform, nor the excesses of an extravagant and foolish nationalism, nor the personal limitations of the imperial couple began with the war or were primarily responses to the existence of the war. None of the consequences of these deficiencies were in process of any significant correction as the war approached. The spectacle of the final years of tsardom prior to 1914 is that of an impressive program of social, economic, and cultural modernization of a great country being conducted, somewhat incongruously, under the general authority of a governmental system that was itself in the advanced stages of political disintegration. The successes in the field of modernization might indeed, if allowed to continue, have brought Russia rapidly and safely into the modern age. It is doubtful that they could for long have overbalanced the serious deficiencies of the political system or averted the consequences to which they were — even as war broke out — inexorably leading.

COMMENT ON KENNAN

Hugh Seton-Watson

To speak in reply to Mr Kennan is a great privilege. The paper we have heard combines all the clarity and eloquence that over many years we have learned to expect from him. It seems to me that the issues he raised are the important ones and that the ones he did not raise are less important. I also found myself agreeing very largely with his opinions. I shall, however, concentrate on those points on which I would differ from him in interpretation or in emphasis.

First, as regards modernization, I concur with what I take to be Mr Kennan's main thesis: the strains and stresses of nineteenth-century Russian society were largely due to the attempt by the state machine to modernize Russia from above. The process was in some ways mishandled, but the direction was on the whole the right one, and in the last ten years particularly impressive progress was made. In fact, it was not inability to confront the tasks of economic and cultural modernization that brought about the collapse. My general view would be the same, but I would like to comment on two important aspects of modernization — agriculture and education.

Mr Kennan observes that the cost of industrialization, to the extent it was not covered by foreign borrowing, had to be covered by limitations on consumption by the great mass of the Russian people, which meant, in fact, the peasantry. This is certainly true, not only of Russia, but of virtually all countries that have undergone industrialization, whether in modern times or, for example, in eighteenth-century England. But the Russian government's treatment of the peasants, if not absolutely unique, at least contrasted strikingly with the policy of many of the 'modernizing' countries. The essence of the Russian policy was that virtually none of the wealth that was taken from the Russian peasants was put back into agriculture. To compare Russia with Japan in the same period: the Japanese peasants, like the Russians, were squeezed by taxation, but part at least, even a rather large part, of the proceeds reverted to agriculture. Thus, the output per unit of arable land in Japan rose quite strikingly, whereas in Russia there was practically no improvement at all between the emancipation of the serfs and 1905, or at best the improvement was very slight. This lack was the real cause of the Russian peasants' misery. The rising population pressed on the same resources, whereas with a more intelligent policy the resources could have been greatly increased. The population pressure was not the fault of the government, but the government did nothing to cope with it. This population pressure was not absolute, but was caused by excessive population in relation to land incompetently cultivated. Land efficiently cultivated could have supported a much larger population. The government's failure to act was far more important as a cause of misery than the survival of large landed estates. One should remember that in 1914 the noble land owners' share of the arable land of Russia was between 15 and 20 per cent. That is a substantial share, of course, but it can hardly be said that Russian agriculture was dominated by noble landowners.

Second, education. As a general proposition, it seems to me that historical experience shows us that at the beginning of every process of modernization from above, willed by the ruler — of which Russia is an outstanding example and of which we have had many others in other parts of Eastern Europe, Asia, and the rest of the world in recent decades — there is bound to be a tremendous gap between the elite and the masses. This gap is bound to be a source of frustration to the new, modern, intellectual elite and a source of painful strain in the society as a whole. The gap can only be narrowed by raising the cultural level of the masses toward that of the intelligentsia — in other words, by the creation of a modern system of primary education. It was here that nineteenth-century Russia failed most abysmally. In education, nineteenth-century Russia had proud achieve-ments to show, but they were at the higher levels of the educational pyramid and in the upper social classes. In the first half of the nineteenth century, this situation was, I think, inevitable. Neither funds nor personnel were available to create a system of primary education. [. . .] By the 1880s, however, the situation was entirely different: then the funds and the personnel could have been found much more easily, but they were withheld. You will remember Delianov's circular of 1887, which recommended that secondary education should not be extended to the children of coachmen, servants, cooks, washerwomen, small shopkeepers and people of that sort. [. . .]

The picture of Russian primary education at the turn of the century is not only a shocking one, but one which could have been avoided with good will and intelligence. The truth is that the Russian government of the end of the century believed that the people were better off without education. This was retrogression from the time of Alexander I, or even of Peter the Great. [. . .]

After 1906 all this changed, as Mr Kennan has rightly stressed. Stolypin's peasant policy may or may not have been effective (opinions vary on this), but undoubtedly its aim was greater agricultural efficiency, and undoubtedly it put back into agriculture some of what was taken out in taxes. This was a new policy. Again, in education great progress was made. In 1913 the Ministry of Education received four times as much from the state budget as in 1900: it was still far too little, but it was real progress. It is true that the Council of State turned down the elementary education law of the Third Duma, but it was largely put into practice by government financial assistance to the *zemstva* and city councils, this of course being the exact reverse of the trend of the 1880s and 1890s, when the *zemstva* were actually impeded and obstructed. Education even during the war went ahead. Count Ignatiev, the penultimate minister of education, was an energetic, progressive man, who was able to achieve something, even in war conditions.

If then we look at the regime's policy from the point of view of economic and cultural modernization, we must conclude, I think, that progress had been made and that the orientation toward the end of the regime was rather intelligent.

It was not here that the failure lay. It was in the persistence of feelings of massive social and political discontent, which had their origins in the past century. These feelings resulted largely from the two great failures of the nineteenth century that I have mentioned — in agriculture and education. But the essence, I think, was not a feeling that Russia should be, and was not being, modernized but rather rage against the whole social and political system. Resentment grew not so much from a desire for modernization as from a passion for justice. This was true particularly of the intelligentsia, but to some extent it was true also of the people as a whole.

The non-Russian peoples, as Mr Kennan has well pointed out, were more and more resentful of Russian domination and more and more inclined to follow leaders who thought in terms of autonomy or even of independent states. The peasants were becoming politically conscious. It is a curious irony that, as the proportion of arable land held by the nobility diminished, so the resentment of the peasants against noble landowners, if anything, increased. The working class had the same reasons for discontent that working classes in the early stages of industrial development have had or have in all countries. And here, too, material improvements probably made for more discontent and more political radicalization. The emergence of a minority of skilled urban workers — quite a large minority by 1914 — who were materially much better off than the exploited, unskilled laborers of the 1880s provided cadres for political action by the workers.

But we should not, I think, exaggerate the importance of mass discontent. I think there is a point worth making here about the peasants. The peasants did not bring about the revolution. At the most, one can say that the peasants in uniform played their part in February 1917, but they did not operate as peasants, but as soldiers. Their motivation was military, not social, except in the most indirect way. The peasantry played an enormous part after February, but that is another story. [. . .] As for the workers, no one can deny their part in February. But workers' discontent, strikes and street demonstrations are things that any reasonably efficient government can normally handle. It is not enough to say that the workers made the February Revolution. The point is that the government was no longer reasonably efficient.

Here, two factors have to be considered: the impact of war and the alienation of the political class. Let us take the second factor first. The social and cultural conditions that had produced the original alienation of the intelligentsia from the regime were beginning to disappear in the last decade of the imperial regime, but the state of mind they had created for generations on end had not disappeared — it had hardly even begun to disappear. On the contrary, it had extended into wider sections of the upper and middle classes, into the business class, the bureaucracy, and probably into the officer class of the regular armed forces. [. . .]

Exasperation against the regime became more, rather than less, bitter in the last years of peace and in the war. [. . .] But [. . .], although the point is perhaps marginal, I differ from Mr Kennan about the issue of responsible government. It seems to me the matter was more important than he has allowed. The opposition of the Kadets was surely not due only to their insistence in 1906 on a doctrinaire imitation of some West European parliamentary system, with its responsibility of the executive branch to the legislative. They were not being offered, and dogmatically rejecting, an American-type presidential government with the executive and legislative branches separate but both subject to popular control. What they were being offered was the perpetuation of Nicholas II's autocracy, with the departments of the executive under the control of men chosen arbitrarily by him, with the representative assembly reduced to the status of a talking shop, quite unable to affect policy. Admittedly, for a time things worked out a little better than that. Stolypin at least was a real prime minister. Under him the Council of Ministers had a sort of embryonic unity, and the restricted-franchise Third and Fourth Dumas acted as some sort of a forum for political discussion. But I do not see how, in 1906, the Kadets could have anticipated this, or, if they had, could have accepted the prospect with equanimity, or indeed, how they could have acted otherwise than they did. With Mr Kennan's argument that the decisive chance was missed in the 1860s and that in 1906 it was too late, I am in absolute agreement, but I have rather more sympathy for such men as Miliukov than has become fashionable in recent times in the West.

And now the last point – the war. The actual impact of the war on the army and on the civil population [. . . was,] of course, decisive for the revolution. Without failure in war, even the regime of Nicholas II and [Premier] Goremykin might have carried on. There have been many examples in recent decades, in other countries besides Russia, of fantastically incompetent, tyrannical, and grotesque governments being able to carry on in peacetime if they are not subjected to external pressure. It is by no means impossible that even Nicholas II and [Premier] Goremykin could have stayed in power if there had not been a war. It is meaningless to make the observation that if there had not been a war when there was, there would still have been some sort of revolution some time: the revolution we know, with the consequences we know, would not have taken place.

However, the war was not just something which happened to Russia; it was brought on in large part by Russia's own policies. I am extremely glad that Mr Kennan stressed the importance of Russian official nationalism and anti-Semitism and their connections with the revolutionary movement in the sense that a disproportionately large number of Jews and non-Russians were recruited into the revolutionary groups. This consequence is not usually sufficiently stressed. I think, too, that he is right in suggesting a connection between these russifying policies and the Russian imperialism in foreign policy that contributed to the outbreak of the war. However, it must be admitted that Russia was not the only country whose government pursued policies of 'official nationalism' – that is, an attempt to use the state machine to force one nationality upon all the subjects of a multinational state. Official nationalism was to be found also in contemporary Prussia and Hungary. Anti-Semitism, too, was widespread (though not, it is true, officially sponsored as in Russia) in Austria and in the eastern provinces of Prussia and Hungary. Mr Kennan is surely right in linking Russian nationalism with a foreign policy that brought Russia to war, but I think he overrates Russia's responsibility for its outbreak. I would agree that the kaiser's Germany was not really a threat to Russia. But the war did not happen because Russia needlessly joined the conflict between Germany and Britain, the eventuality that, you will remember, was foreseen in Durnovo's famous memorandum of early 1914. The war happened because Austria was determined to take over the whole Balkan peninsula, and Germany backed her. Russia had the alternatives of letting this happen or going to war. If she had let it happen, then, leaving out any sentimental considerations about obligations of honor towards Serbia, whom she had twice already urged to give way — in 1909 and 1913 — she would have been serving notice to all that she was abdicating from great-power status [. . .]. No Russian government could have been expected to do so.

The counter-arguments are obvious enough. Russia's basic strength in manpower and economic resources was bound to assure her great-power status in the end. Political defeat in 1914 would at most have held her back for a decade or two. What did Serbia matter, or the Straits either, in comparison with the earth-shaking events of 1917? How pitiable the conflicts of the European powers in 1914 seem in the ages of Hitler and Stalin and Mao! How much more convenient it would be for us all if the war of 1914 had not come! We can all, from time to time, feel the force of such arguments, but it seems to me that they are unhistorical. In 1914 no one could think in these terms. In fact, Russia's decision to go to war in 1914 proved disastrous for the Russian imperial regime. But according to the conventional wisdom of 1914, there was no other choice. And if we must apportion blame, surely we cannot forget Austria. The Hapsburg monarchy gave its subjects better government, and perhaps a finer civilization, than the Russian autocracy, but it suffered from many of the same faults. Official nationalism in Budapest, *Schlamperei* in Vienna, an intellectual elite consumed with brilliant destructive criticism, rising national and social groups contemptuously excluded from a share in their own government, and occasional outbursts of futile rage from a ruling class that was on the way out, all these factors helped to turn Central Europe into a powder barrel. One may or may not prefer Vienna to St Petersburg, but one must note the similarity. Perhaps, in the late 1960s, one may have more sympathy with the predicament of declining rulers, elites, empires, and nations than an earlier generation of any English-speaking nation would have felt. But

one must also realize that these phenomena are likely to give rise to
dangerous and explosive situations.

C.   THE PROBLEM OF SOCIAL STABILITY IN URBAN RUSSIA, 1905-1917

Leopold Haimson

Source: *Slavic Review*, XXIII, no.4, December 1964, pp.619-42 (Part I)
and XXIV, no.1, March 1965, pp.1-22 (Part II).

I

When a student of the origins of 1917 looks back through the literature
that appeared on the subject during the 1920s and early 1930s, he is likely
to be struck by the degree of consensus in Soviet and Western treatments
of the problem on two major assumptions. The first of these, then almost
as widely entertained by Western as by Soviet historians, was that, just like
other 'classical' revolutions, the Revolution of 1917 had to be viewed, not
as a historical accident or even as the product of immediate historical circumstances, but as the culmination of a long historical process – stretching
back to the abolition of serfdom, if not to the appearance at the beginning
of the nineteenth century of the Russian revolutionary intelligentsia. The
second, balancing, assumption, which even Soviet historians were then still
usually prepared to accept, was that, notwithstanding its deep historical
roots, this revolutionary process had been substantially accelerated by the
additional strains imposed on the Russian body politic by the First World
War.

To be sure, even the sharing of these two assumptions allowed for a
range of conflicting interpretations and evaluations of the Revolution and
its background. Yet it made, however tenuously, for a common universe of
discourse, transcending the insuperable values that were already supposed
to separate 'Marxist' and 'bourgeois' historians. The years of the Stalin era
and the Cold War have seen the disappearance of this common universe of
discourse, and the emergence in its stead – particularly in Soviet and Western representations of the decade immediately leading up to the Revolution
of 1917 – of two almost completely incongruent, and almost equally
monolithic, points of view.

The first of these, which Soviet historians have advanced to demonstrate
the *zakonomernost'*, the historical logic (and therefore the historical legiti-

macy) of October, distinguishes in the years immediately preceding the First World War the shape of a new, rapidly mounting 'revolutionary upsurge'. According to the periodization that has become established for this stereotype, the first modest signs that the period of 'reaction' that had descended on Russian society with the Stolypin *coup d'état* had come to an end appeared as early as 1910-11. At first, the new revolutionary upsurge built up only very slowly, and it was only in April-May, 1912, in the wake of the Lena goldfields massacre, that it really began to gather momentum. From this moment on, however, the revolutionary wave is seen as mounting with such dramatic swiftness that by the summer of 1914 the country was ripe for the decisive revolutionary overturn for which the Bolsheviks had been preparing since the summer of 1913. In this scheme, obviously, the war is not viewed as contributing decisively to the unleashing of the revolutionary storm. On the contrary, it is held that by facilitating the suppression of Bolshevik Party organizations and arousing, however briefly, 'chauvinistic' sentiments among the still unconscious elements in the laboring masses, its outbreak temporarily retarded the inevitable outcome. It was only in late 1915 that the revolutionary movement resumed the surge which two years later finally overwhelmed the old order.

Partly as a response to this Soviet stereotype and to the gross distortions of evidence that its presentation often involves, we have witnessed during the past quarter of a century the crystallization in many Western representations of the origins of 1917 of a diametrically different, and equally sweeping, point of view. It is that between the Revolution of 1905 and the outbreak of the First World War a process of political and social stabilization was under way in every major sphere of Russian life which, but for the extraneous stresses that the war imposed, would have saved the Russian body politic from revolution – or at least from the radical overturn that Russia eventually experienced with the Bolshevik conquest of power.

It is important to note that not all the data on which these conflicting Western and Soviet conceptions rest are as radically different as their composite effects suggest. Indeed, as far as the period stretching from the Stolypin *coup d'état* to 1909-10 is concerned ('the years of repression and reaction', as Soviet historians describe them), it is possible to find in Soviet and Western accounts a rough consensus *on what actually happened*, however different the explanations and evaluations that these accounts offer of the events may be.

For example, even Soviet historians are prepared to recognize the disintegration that the revolutionary movement underwent during these years: the success, even against the Bolshevik underground, of the government's repressive measures; the 'desertion' of the revolutionary cause by so many of the hitherto radical members of the intelligentsia; the sense of apathy that temporarily engulfed the masses of the working class. Soviet historians also recognize the new rationale inherent in the Regime of the Third of June — the government's attempt to widen its basis of support by winning the loyalties of the well-to-do sector of the city bourgeoisie. And they emphasize, even more than is warranted, the willingness of these elements of the 'counterrevolutionary' bourgeoisie to seek, within the framework of the new institutions, an accommodation with the old regime and its gentry supporters. To be sure, Soviet historians are less prepared than their Western *confrères* to concede the progress that was actually achieved during the Stolypin period in the modernization of Russian life. But the basic trends that they detect during these years — in both government policy and public opinion — are not, for all that, so drastically different.

Where the minimal consensus I have just outlined completely breaks down is in the interpretation of the period stretching from 1910-11 to the outbreak of the First World War. What is basically at stake, as we have seen, is that while Soviet historiography discerns, beginning in the waning days of the Third Duma, the onset of a new, rapidly mounting, revolutionary upsurge, most Western historians are not prepared to concede the validity of any such periodization. On the contrary, with the growing impact of the Stolypin reforms in the Russian countryside and the increasing vitality displayed by the *zemstvo* and other institutions of local self-government, they find the processes of modernization and westernization which they see at work in the earlier period now sweeping even more decisively into the rural and provincial corners of national life. To be sure, many Western historians do recognize the alarming note introduced on the eve of the war by the growing clash between the reactionary attitudes of government circles and the liberal expectations of society [. . .] . But most of them are drawn to the conclusion that in the absence of war this crisis could and would have been resolved without deep convulsions, through the more or less peaceful realization by the liberal elements of Russian society of their long-standing demand for genuine Western parliamentary institutions.

Oddly enough, the completely different representations entertained by Western and Soviet historians of the immediate prewar years rest, in part, on inferences drawn from a phenomenon on which both schools of thought concur — the fact that beginning in 1910-11, the industrial sector of the Russian economy recovered from the doldrums into which it had fallen at the turn of the century and underwent a new major upsurge. Soviet historians are less apt to emphasize the more self-sustained and balanced character that this new industrial upsurge assumes in comparison with the great spurt of the 1890s, and they are less sanguine about its long-range prospects, but

they do not deny the fact of the spurt itself. On the contrary, they consider
it the major 'objective factor' underlying the revival of the Russian labor
movement and the recovery of the Bolshevik Party that they distinguish
during these years.

It is here that we come to the root of the disagreement between Western
and Soviet historians on the dynamics of the prewar period and, more
broadly, on the origins of the Russian Revolution. Even as cautious and
sophisticated a historian as Alexander Gerschenkron sees in Russia's
economic development on the eve of the war, in contrast to the admittedly
socially onerous industrial growth of the 1890s, a factor making for social
and political stabilization. And what is really the crux of the issue — if only
because it involves the core of the Soviet historians' case — Gerschenkron
and other Western commentators find this stabilizing effect of Russia's
economic progress on the eve of the war reflected in a perceptible lessening
of social and political tensions in both the countryside and the working-
class districts of the cities. 'To be sure', he concedes, 'the strike movement
of the workers was again gaining momentum' since April, 1912. But the
economic position of labor was clearly improving, and 'in the resurgence
of the strike movement, economic problems seemed to predominate'.
Gerschenkron recognizes that 'in the specific conditions of the period any
wage conflict tended to assume a political character because of the ready
interventions of police and military forces on behalf of the management.
. . . But this did not mean that the climate of opinion and emotion within
the labor movement was becoming more revolutionary. As shown by the
history of European countries (such as Austria and Belgium), sharp political
struggles marked the period of formation of labor movements that in actual
fact, though not always in the language used, were committed to reformism.
There is little doubt that the Russian labor movement of those years was
slowly turning toward revision and trade unionist lines.'[1]

Against this alleged background of the growing moderation of the
Russian labor movement, the picture that Western accounts usually draw
of the fortunes of the Bolshevik Party during the immediate prewar years
is a dismal one. Thus, for example, Leonard Schapiro's treatment of this
period lays primary stress on the state of political paralysis to which Lenin
and his followers appear to have driven themselves by July, 1914; on the
isolation of the Bolshevik faction within the political spectrum of the
RSDRP [Russian Social Democratic Labour Party]; [. . .] on the havoc
wrought in Bolshevik Party cadres by periodic police arrests, guided by
Okhrana agents successively hidden at all levels of the party apparatus; on
the alleged permanent loss of popularity that the Bolsheviks suffered among
the workers beginning in the fall of 1913 as a result of their schismatic

activity, particularly in the Duma; on the ultimate blow to the Bolsheviks' prestige inflicted by the exposure of their most popular spokesman in Russia, Roman Malinovsky, as just another *agent provocateur*. 'There was more unity now [. . .] on the non-bolshevik side than ever before', Schapiro concludes:

> With the weight of the International behind them there was more likelihood than there had been in 1910 that the menshevik leaders would find the necessary courage to break with Lenin for good if he persisted in his policy of disunity at all costs. If Lenin were isolated in his intransigence, there was every chance that many of his 'conciliator' followers, who had rejoined him in 1912, would break away again. The bolshevik organization was, moreover, in a poor state in 1914, as compared with 1912. The underground committees were disrupted. There were no funds, and the circulation of *Pravda* had fallen drastically under the impact of the split in the Duma 'fraction'.

In substance, like many other Western historians, Schapiro considers that by July, 1914, a death sentence had been pronounced against the Bolshevik Party, which but for the outbreak of war would shortly have been carried out.

The contrast between this picture and the accounts of Soviet historians is, of course, quite startling. It is not only that their conception of the twenty-seven months leading up to the war is dominated by the image of a majestically rising strike movement which month by month, day by day, became more political in character and revolutionary in temper. It is also that they see this movement as one dominated, in the main, by a now mature, 'class conscious', hereditary proletariat, hardened by the experience of the Revolution of 1905 and the years of reaction, and directed by a revived Bolshevik Party to whose flag, at the beginning of 1914, 'four-fifths of all the workers of Russia' had rallied. To be sure, the party was faced in its unswerving drive toward revolution by the opposition of various factions of Russian Social Democracy. But according to the Soviet view, these factions represented by the summer of 1914 little more than empty shells resting mainly on the support of 'bourgeois opportunist' *intelligenty* in Russia and the emigration. The correctness of the party's course since [. . .] 1912 [. . .] of rejecting any compromise with these 'bourgeois opportunist' elements, of combining economic and political strikes and mass demonstrations in a single-minded drive toward an 'all-nation political strike leading to an armed uprising' — is considered amply confirmed by the evidence that in July, 1914, such an all-nation strike was already 'under way' and an armed uprising 'in the offing'. Indeed, Soviet historians allege, the revolutionary upsurge had reached such a level by the beginning of 1914 that even the leading circles of the 'counterrevolutionary' bourgeoisie had come to realize the irreparable 'crash' of the Regime of the Third of June.

What are the realities submerged beneath these harshly conflicting representations? Any careful examination of the evidence in contemporary primary sources suggests, it seems to me, that the vision advanced by some Western historians of the growing moderation of the Russian labor movement can be even partially upheld only for the period stretching from the Stolypin *coup d'état* to the spring and summer of 1912. This, almost up to its conclusion, was a period of relative labor tranquillity, as in a context of economic stagnation the masses of the Russian working class relapsed into apathy, after the defeat of their great expectations of 1905.

It was in this ultimately deceptive setting of labor peace, and of the futile and increasingly degrading spectacle of the Bolsheviks' collapsing underground struggle [. . .], that the leaders of the Menshevik faction began to articulate the philosophy and programs of an open labor party and labor movement. The current task of Social Democracy, they insisted, was not to pursue in the underground, under the leadership of a handful of intelligentsia conspirators, now clearly unattainable maximalist objectives. It was to outline for the labor movement goals, tactics, and organizational forms which, even within the narrow confines of the existing political framework, would enable the masses of the working class to struggle, day by day, for tangible improvements in their lives and to become through the experience of this struggle 'conscious' and responsible actors — capable of making their own independent contribution to the vision of a free and equitable society. Not only did the Menshevik 'Liquidators'[2] articulate this vision of an open labor party and labor movement during these years but they appeared to be making progress in erecting the scaffolding of the institutions through which the vision was to be realized. They were seeking to organize open trade unions, cooperatives, workers' societies of self-improvement and self-education, and workers' insurance funds: organs intended not only to help the worker but also to enable him to take his life into his own hands. Even more significantly, the Menshevik 'Liquidators' appeared to be succeeding during this period in developing, really for the first time in the history of the Russian labor movement, a genuine workers' intelligentsia animated by their own democratic values, which, it seems, would have been far more capable than any self-appointed intelligentsia leadership of eventually providing an effective bridge between educated society and the masses of the workers. [. . .]

To be sure, in 1910-11, the Mensheviks' workers' intelligentsia still appeared very thin, and the number and size of their open labor unions pitifully small in comparison with the size of the labor force, or indeed with the level that the organization of the working class had reached [in 1906]. And even these puny shoots were being periodically cut down by the authorities, with only the feeblest echoes of protest from the still somnolent labor masses.

Thus even in this early (and in certain respects most successful) period of the Mensheviks' struggle for a Europeanized labor movement one must distinguish a considerable gap between vision and tangible achievement. The private correspondence of Menshevik leaders during 1909, 1910, and 1911 is replete with despondent statements about the 'depression' and 'fatigue' prevailing among the older generation of the Menshevik movement at home and in the emigration, about the failure to draw new members into the movement, about the negligible number of *praktiki* [activists]. [. . .] What chiefly kept up their spirits during these lean years was the expectation that things were bound to improve, once Russian society emerged, as it necessarily would, from its current state of political apathy. [. . .]

Once the expected political revival occurred, was it not to be expected that a more progressive Duma, supported by an aroused public, would legislate the necessary legal safeguards for the open labor organizations from which a massive and yet self-conscious and self-disciplined workers' movement would at long last emerge? [. . .] Martov discerned the approach of such a turning point in the movement of opinion as early as November, 1909: 'The signs are multiplying' that 'the counterrevolution is ending', he then wrote [. . .]. 'And if the course of events is not artificially forced, and if, as is almost unquestionable, two to three years of industrial upsurge lie before us, the time of the elections [to the Fourth Duma] can provide the occasion for the turning point [*perelom*].'

Martov's forecast actually proved too conservative. It was not in the fall but in the spring of 1912 that the break he awaited occurred, under the immediate impact of the Lena goldfields massacre. The news of the massacre provoked a great outburst of public protest and, what was more important, a veritable explosion in the Russian working class. Between April 14 and 22, close to 100,000 workers struck in Petersburg alone, and the total number of strikers in the country as a whole probably reached about 250,000. This wave of protest strikes and demonstrations persisted almost without interruption through mid-May. May Day, 1912, saw nearly half a million workers out on the streets, the highest number since 1905 [. . .]. Even the official statistics compiled by the Factory Inspectors of the Ministry of Trade and Industry, which undoubtedly were seriously underestimated, recorded that close to 550,000 workers had participated in political strikes during 1912, a level well below that of the revolutionary years 1905-6 but much higher than that of any other previous years in the history of the Russian labor movement. [. . .]

The strike statistics for 1913 would in fact reveal a further upsurge of the labor movement, though not one of quite the dimensions [of 1905]. The yearly compilations of the Factory Inspectors showed but a relatively modest rise in the total number of strikes and strikers, and indeed indicated a small drop in the number of those listed as political. However, the monthly breakdowns of these figures registered such a drop only in April and May, for which a much smaller number of political strikes and strikers were listed than for the corresponding months of 1912 — the exceptionally agitated aftermath of the Lena goldfields massacre. Thus it would be questionable to infer that there occurred in the course of 1913 a general decline of political unrest among the Russian working class. The prevailing opinion among contemporary observers was that the year had instead been marked by a rise in the intensity of both political and economic strikes.

The correctness of this diagnosis was to be confirmed by developments in the following year. The first half of 1914 would witness an unprecedented swell of both political and economic strikes. Even the overconservative estimates of the Factory Inspectors reported for this period a total of 1,254,441 strikers. Of these, 982,810 were listed as political — a figure almost as high as that for 1905, the previous peak year, even though the calculations for 1914 covered only the first six months of the year, and excluded for the first time the highly industrialized Warsaw *gubernia* [province].

What realities do these statistical aggregates actually reflect? To justify their belief in the increasingly reformist character of the Russian labor movement on the eve of the war, some Western writers have argued that the very distinction drawn in the reports of the Factory Inspectors between political and economic strikes is artificial: economic strikes were quick to assume a political character when they ran up against brutal police interference, and were often listed as such in the reports of the Factory Inspectors. This is a correct observation, often noted in contemporary reports of the labor scene. But as Menshevik commentators continuously emphasized, the opposite was just as often the case. Strikes ostensibly economic in character often demonstrated by the unrealistic character of their objectives and the impatience and violence of the tactics with which they were conducted that they merely provided an excuse for the expression of political unrest. This appears to have been true even in 1913, the one year of the 'upsurge' in which, according to official statistics, economic motifs were predominant in the strike movement. [. . .]

Indeed, it appears that from the Lena massacre to the outbreak of war,

the progress of the strike movement was characterized by an almost continuous flow in which political and economic currents were inextricably
mixed: quite often, even the ostensible objectives of individual strikes
combined political and economic demands; and even more notably, the
individual waves of 'economic' strikes and 'political' strikes and demonstrations proved mutually reinforcing, each seemingly giving the next additional
impetus, additional momentum. By the beginning of the summer of 1914,
contemporary descriptions of the labor scene forcibly suggest, the workers,
especially in Petersburg, were displaying a growing spirit of *buntarstvo*
[rebelliousness] — of violent if still diffuse opposition to all authority —
and an instinctive sense of class solidarity, as they encountered the repressive measures of state power and what appeared to them the indifference
of privileged society.

However, the most telling evidence against the thesis that beneath the
surface the Russian labor movement was actually developing a reformist
and trade unionist orientation, is the reception that the workers gave, as
the war approached, to Bolshevik as against Menshevik appeals.

In the first months of the new upsurge, Menshevik commentators had
naturally been heartened by the impressive revival of the labor movement.
Writing shortly after the 'grandiose political strikes' of April and May,
1912, Fedor Dan called them not only a 'turning point in the Russian
labor movement' but also 'the beginning of the liquidation of the Regime
of the Third of June'. [As he saw it] the workers were now opposing themselves to the rest of society and the working-class movement was generally
assuming 'a much more sharply defined class character' than it had had in
1905. This, Dan observed, was merely a reflection of the growing maturity
and organization of the proletariat and an indication of the successful work
that the Menshevik 'Liquidators' had conducted during the years of reaction.
[Furthermore,] if the workers were now opposing themselves to society, so
society was now opposing itself to the workers:

> To the growing class maturity of the proletariat corresponds a similar
> growing class maturity of the bourgeoisie. And the 'support' that now
> surrounds the labor movement has little in common with the foggy
> romantic support which in 1905 impelled *Osvobozhdenie* to exclaim:
> 'How enchanting the workers are' and Mr Struve to declare triumphantly:
> 'We have no enemies to the left.' ... The proletariat has ceased to be
> 'enchanting' in the eyes of bourgeois society [...].

In this passage Dan was describing approvingly what would indeed become
one of the major conditioning factors in the development of the labor

movement during the new upsurge — the break in the fragile and tenuous psychological ties that had been so painfully built up between the workers and the opposition circles of educated society during the decade leading up to the Revolution of 1905. But if the Mensheviks were originally inclined to consider this mutual confrontation of workers and society a positive indication of the growing class maturity of both, they were soon to change their minds.

The first signs of alarm were sounded within a few months, with the returns, in the fall of 1912, of the elections to the Fourth Duma. In these elections, as Lenin and his followers untiringly emphasized thereafter, Bolshevik candidates won in six of the nine labor *curiae* in Russia, including all six of the labor *curiae* in the major industrial provinces. In their published commentaries on the election returns the Menshevik leaders pointed out (most often quite accurately) the major flaws in the Bolshevik claims to a sweeping victory, but in their private correspondence, they conceded more readily that, whatever the extenuating circumstances, the results of the elections in the labor *curiae* had been a definite setback. [. . .]

The developments on the labor scene in 1913, and especially during the first six months of 1914, would amply confirm [. . .] the significance of these election returns. Not only were these eighteen months generally characterized by a steady rise in the spirit of *buntarstvo*, of the elemental, revolutionary explosiveness of the strike movement, particularly in the capital. Not only were they marked by a growing responsiveness on the part of the amorphous and largely anonymous committees in charge of the strikes, as well as of the workers' rank and file, to the reckless tactics of the Bolsheviks and to their 'unmutilated' slogans of a 'democratic republic', 'eight-hour day', and 'confiscation of gentry lands'. They also saw the Mensheviks lose control of the open labor organizations they had struggled so hard to build. From the spring and summer of 1913, when the Bolsheviks [. . .] began to concentrate their energies on the conquest of the open labor organizations, the pages of the Mensheviks' journals and their private correspondence were filled with the melancholy news of the loss of one position after another [. . .]. [By] July, 1914, when the Bolsheviks laid their case before the Bureau of the Socialist Internationale for being the only genuine representatives of the Russian working class, they claimed control of 14½ out of 18 of the governing boards of the trade unions in St Petersburg and 10 out of the 13 in Moscow.

To be sure, the Mensheviks' situation in the two capitals was far bleaker, and the Bolsheviks' far brighter, than anywhere else in the country. But even with this reservation, their position gave the Mensheviks little ground for comfort. As early as September, 1913 [. . .] Martov foresaw the further catastrophes that were likely to befall the Menshevik cause. [He wrote,] 'It is altogether likely that in the course of this season our positions in Petersburg will be squeezed back even further. But that is not what is awful [*skverno*]. What is worse is that from an organizational point of view, Menshevism — despite the newspaper [the Mensheviks' Petersburg organ, *Luch'*, launched in late 1912], despite everything that has been done during the past two years — remains a weak little circle [*slaben'kii kruzhok*].' And at a meeting of the Menshevik faction in the Duma, in late January, 1914, the Georgian deputy, Chkhenkeli, observed in an equally catastrophic vein that the Mensheviks appeared to be losing all of their influence, all of their ties, among the workers.

Bitterest and most desperate of all were the complaints of the Menshevik trade unionists, the representatives of their now defeated workers' intelligentsia. In March, 1914, Fedor Bulkin, one of the Menshevik *praktiki* driven out of the governing board of the Union of Metalworkers six months earlier, exclaimed in the pages of *Nasha zaria* [*Our Dawn*]:

> The masses which have recently been drawn into the trade union movement are incapable of appreciating its great significance for the proletariat. Led by the Bolsheviks, they have chased the *Likvidatory* [Liquidators], these valuable workers, out of all leading institutions. . . . The experienced pilots of the labor movement have been replaced by ones who are inexperienced, but close in spirit to the masses . . . for the time being, the *Likvidatory* are suffering and, in all likelihood, will continue to suffer, defeat. Bolshevism — *intelligentskii* [intellectual], narrowly fractional, jacobin — has found its support in the masses' state of mind.

In the concluding passage of this statement, Bulkin was reiterating the thesis (which he had already spelled out in an earlier article) that the Bolsheviks' victories had been largely attributable to the sway that the Social Democratic intelligentsia -- with its narrow dogmatism, its intolerance, its factional spirit — still continued to hold over the workers' minds. Once the proletariat freed itself from this pernicious influence of the intelligentsia and grew to affirm its own independent spirit, its own self-consciousness, the Bolsheviks' strength would evaporate into thin air.

Naturally, the editors of *Nasha zaria* could not allow this argument [. . .] to appear without an answer. [. . .] Martov, in the same issue of the journal, wrote a fulgurant reply. It was all too easy for Bulkin to assert that Bolshevism was an intelligentsia influence grafted onto the body of the hapless Russian working class. [. . .] Where was the Bolshevik intelligentsia which supposedly still 'stood on the shoulders of the proletariat'? It simply was no longer there. All of the major figures in the Bolshevik intelligentsia — Bogdanov, Lunacharsky, Rozhkov, Pokrovsky, Bazarov, and so many others — had deserted Leninism. All that was left was 'a handful of people with literally no names, or names it would be inexpedient to mention'.

If the culprit was not the pernicious influence of the intelligentsia, to what source was the new mood of the labor movement to be traced? The Bolsheviks had a simple explanation: the workers' new mood was merely a reflection of the growth to consciousness of a now mature hereditary Russian proletariat — recovered from the defeats of 1905, hardened by the years of reaction, and rallied solidly behind the Bolshevik Party. Needless to say, Menshevik commentators found this explanation wanting. Indeed, in their writings of the period we find them groping for precisely an opposite answer: the laboring masses which had crowded into the new labor movement during the years of the new industrial upsurge — and of the new explosive strike wave — were in the main no longer the class-conscious, mature proletariat of 1905. Some of the most acute Menshevik observers (Martov, Levitsky, Gorev, Sher) pointed specifically to the social and political effects of the influx into the industrial working class of two new strata.

The first of these was the younger generation of the working class of the cities, the urban youths who had grown to working age since the Revolution of 1905 [...]. It was these youths, 'hot-headed and impulsive', 'untempered by the lessons of the class struggle', who now constituted the intermediary link between the leading circles of the Bolshevik Party and the laboring masses. It was they who now provided, in the main, the correspondents and distributors of Bolshevik newspapers, who instigated the workers' resolutions and petitions in support of Bolshevik stands, and who dominated the amorphous, *ad hoc* strike committees which were providing whatever leadership still characterized the elemental strike wave. More recently, in the spring and summer of 1913, it had been these green youths who had begun to flow from the strike committees into the open trade unions and had seized their leadership from the older generation of Menshevik trade unionists. 'Here', noted one observer, 'the representatives of two different periods, [men] of different habits, different practical schools — two forces of workers, "young" and "old" — have encountered one another for the first time ... [the takeover] which occurred extremely quickly, for many almost unexpectedly, took place in an atmosphere of patricidal conflict.'

Of course, the cadres of the new generations of the hereditary working class of the cities would have remained leaders without followers had it not been for the influx into the labor force of a second, much more massive, new stratum. These were the recruits, usually completely unskilled, who, from 1910 on — the year of the 'take-off' of the new industrial upsurge and of the turning point in the Stolypin agrarian reforms — had begun to pour into the labor armies of the cities from the countryside. It was these many thousands of ex-peasants, as yet completely unadapted to their new factory environment, 'driven by instincts and feelings rather than conscious-ness and calculation', who gave the mass movement 'its disorganized, primitive, elemental character', noted Martov's younger brother, Levitsky. Naturally, these 'unconscious' masses proved most responsive to the ex-tremist objectives and tactics advocated by the Bolsheviks: to their demands for 'basic' as against 'partial' reforms, to their readiness to support any strikes, regardless of their purpose and degree of organization. Above all, the Bolshevik 'unmutilated' slogans of an eight-hour day, 'complete demo-cratization', 'confiscation of gentry lands' — and the basic vision underlying these slogans of a grand union of workers and peasants arrayed against all of society, 'from Purishkevich to Miliukov' — were calculated to sound a deep echo among these new elements of the working class, which combined with their current resentments about factory life the still fresh grievances and aspirations that they had brought from the countryside.

Indeed, by the early months of 1914, the influx of these ex-peasant masses into the cities had led not only to a striking rise in the Bolshevik fortunes but also to a still relatively modest and yet notable revival among the workers of Left Populist tendencies. Commenting on this revival of Left Populism, which now threatened to replace Menshevism as the chief opposition to the Bolsheviks, Martov emphasized in a series of articles 'the swilling mixture of anarchist and syndicalist tendencies with remnants of peasant urges and utopias' which appeared to animate the Left Populists' adherents. These workers might have physically left the village, he observed, but they had by no means broken their psychological ties with it: 'As they face the hardships, the darkness of city life, they hold onto their dream of returning to a patch of land with their own cow and chickens . . . and they respond to the slogans of those who promised them the fulfilment of this dream.'

To what extent can one support with statistical evidence the emphasis that the more discerning Menshevik observers of the labor scene laid on the role played in the industrial unrest of the period by the younger generation of urban industrial workers and the recruits to the labor force from the countryside? We know, of course, that the increasingly explosive strike wave broadly coincided with an industrial upsurge which saw the Russian industrial labor force grow from some 1,793,000 in January, 1910, to approximately 2,400,000 in July, 1914, a rise of over 30 per cent. And obviously this sharp and sudden increase in the labor force could be achieved only [with a] massive inswell into the urban labor market of landless and land-poor peasants, freed of their ties to the land by the Stolypin legislation [. . .] . The literature of this period is replete with reports of the influx of these raw recruits into the industrial army. But let us refine the analysis, and focus our attention on those sectors of the Russian labor force which appear to lead the contemporary strike movement, and especially those strikes which bear a distinctly political character. One can easily distinguish two such sectors. The first of these may be defined geographically: it is the labor force of the province and particularly the city of Petersburg and sub-urbs, which in the first six months of 1914 contributed close to 50 per cent of the total of 1,254,000 strikers estimated for the country as a whole, and almost two-thirds of the 982,000 strikers listed as political. Secondly, when one compares strike statistics for different industries (as against different regions) it becomes apparent that by far the heaviest incidence of strikers, particularly of political strikers — in Petersburg just as in the country as a whole — is to be found among the workers in the metalwork-ing industry.

It is notable, and undoubtedly significant, that these two sectors of the labor force [. . .] grew by an average of roughly 50 per cent as against the national average of less than 30 per cent. If we consider the necessity of allowing for replacement as well as increases in the labor force, we may assume that by 1914 well over half of the workers in Petersburg, as well as in the metalworking industry in the country as a whole, were persons who at best had undergone a very brief industrial experience. It has already been noted that while some of these recruits were urban youths who reached working age during these years, most had to be drawn from outside the cities. In this connection, one further observation appears relevant: it is that since the beginning of the century a marked shift in the pattern of labor recruitment from the countryside into the Petersburg labor force had been taking place. As the labor supply available in Petersburg province and in other provinces with relatively developed manufacturing or handi-craft industries declined, a growing percentage of the recruits into the Petersburg labor force had to be drawn from the almost purely agricultural, overpopulated, central provinces of European Russia — the very provinces in which the dissolution of repartitional tenure [. . .] was making itself most heavily and painfully felt.

A vast mass of workers who combined with their resentments about the painful and disorienting conditions of their new industrial experience a still fresh sense of grievance about the circumstances under which they had been compelled to leave the village. A new generation of young workers of urban origin to lead them — impatient, romantic, singularly responsive to maximalist appeals. Our puzzle would appear to be resolved if it were not for a disconcerting fact. The conditions I have so far described, except perhaps for the presence of a somewhat lower percentage of young workers of urban origin, also largely obtained in other areas and sectors of the Russian labor force, which remained, however, less animated than the ones we have singled out by the spirit of *buntarstvo* of which we have been seeking the roots. These conditions probably obtained, for example, almost as much in the Donbas as in Petersburg; and for workers in chemicals as much as for those in the metalworking industry. This is why we necessarily have to add one further element which, for obvious reasons, was generally absent in most contemporary Menshevik analyses: the role exercised by Bolshevik party cadres — workers and *intelligenty* alike. If the Petersburg workers displayed greater revolutionary explosiveness, and especially greater responsiveness to Bolshevik appeals, than the workers of the Donbas, it was undoubtedly in part because of the Petersburg workers' greater exposure to Bolshevik propaganda and agitation. Similarly, if the workers in the metalworking industry were so much more agitated politically than the workers in other industries, it was partly because the labor force in the metalworking industry consisted of a peculiar combination of skilled and unskilled, experienced and inexperienced, workers — the older and more skilled workers contributing in their contacts with the young and unskilled a long-standing exposure to revolutionary, and specifically Bolshevik, indoctrination. [. . .]

This is not to say that during these years the Bolshevik Party cadres in Petersburg, and especially their underground organizations, bore even a faint resemblance to the depictions of them currently offered by some Soviet historians. Penetrated from top to bottom by agents of the secret police [. . .] they were experiencing serious difficulties in replenishing their ranks, depleted periodically by arrests [. . .].

Yet even under these conditions the Bolshevik Party apparatus managed to survive, to retain some old and recruit some new members: younger workers, but also older workers, with a background of participation in the revolutionary underground, who in many cases had left the party during the years of reaction but were now returning to the fold; survivors of the older generation of the Bolshevik intelligentsia, but also fresh recruits from those elements in the intelligentsia youth who for temperamental reasons or because of adverse material circumstances were not attracted by the Bolsheviks' maximalist appeals. These recruits were, to be sure, not very numerous, nor was their mood representative of that of the intelligentsia as a whole. Indeed, many of them were animated by a new kind of anger and bitterness [. . .] whose strident quality often appeared to reflect not merely outrage about the betrayal of the revolutionary cause by the 'opportunist' majority of the intelligentsia, but also a sharp sense of social antagonism: the antagonism of the young for the older and more established, of the less favored for the more fortunate members of society.

And all this anger and bitterness now struck a responsive chord in the masses of the working class. Given this correspondence of mood, given the even more precise correspondence between the image of state and society that the Bolsheviks advanced and the instinctive outlook of the laboring masses, the Bolshevik Party cadres were now able to play a significant catalytic role. They succeeded, as we have seen, in chasing the Menshevik 'Liquidators' out of the existing open labor organizations. They transformed these organizations into 'fronts' through which they managed to absorb, if not to control, the younger workers who headed the Petersburg strike movement. Through the pages of *Pravda*, through the verbal appeals of their deputies in the Duma, by leaflet and by word of mouth, they managed to stir up and exploit the workers' embittered mood. Thus, it seems fair to say that by the outbreak of war the Bolshevik center in Petersburg, and particularly its open organizations, had developed into an organism whose arms, while still very slender and vulnerable, were beginning to extend into many corners of the life of the working class.

In January, 1914 [. . .] the Menshevik leader Martov [. . .] gloomily noted the correspondence between the Bolsheviks' appeals and the workers' contemporary state of mind. The threat presented by Bolshevism, he argued, lay not in the handful of *intelligenty* and semi-*intelligenty* that it still managed to attract, but rather in the response that it had evoked, the roots that it had unquestionably sunk, among the masses of the workers themselves. Against whom had the workers struck in their spirit of *buntarstvo*? Martov [asked.] Against the 'Liquidators', against the scaffold of the open European-type party that had been erected between 1907 and 1911 by those proletarian elements that had been genuinely indoctrinated with Marxism — in substance, against their own workers' intelligentsia [. . .]. And if the workers had done so under the [Bolsheviks], Martov concluded, it was because, of all the demagogical groups in Russian society, this one, at least for the time being, was best attuned to the workers' own mood.

If I might summarize my own, and to some degree, Martov's argument, it is that by 1914 a dangerous process of polarization appeared to be taking place in Russia's major urban centers between an *obshchestvo* [society] that had now reabsorbed the vast majority of the once alienated elements of its intelligentsia (and which was even beginning to draw to itself many of the workers' own intelligentsia) and a growing discontented and disaffected mass of industrial workers, now left largely exposed to the pleas of an embittered revolutionary minority.

This is not to suggest that by the outbreak of war the Bolshevik Party had succeeded in developing a secure following among the masses of the working class. The first year of the war would show only too clearly how fragile its bonds to the supposedly conscious Russian proletariat still were. Indeed, it bears repeating that the political threat of Bolshevism in 1914 stemmed primarily not from the solidity of its organizations nor from the success of its efforts at ideological indoctrination, but from the workers' own elemental mood of revolt. [. . .]

The elements of strength and weakness in the Bolshevik leadership of the labor movement on the eve of war and the relative significance of this movement as a revolutionary force are graphically illustrated by the contrast between the general strike which broke out in the working class districts of Petersburg in the early days of July, 1914, and the nature of the mutual confrontation of the workers and educated society that had characterized the high tide of the Revolution of 1905. On the earlier historical occasion – in September and October, 1905 – the workers of Petersburg and Moscow had rejoined, however briefly, the world of Russian educated and privileged society. Flocking out of their tawdry factory districts, they had descended into the hearts of the two capitals to join in society's demonstrations, to shout its slogans, to listen in the amphitheaters of universities and institutes to the impassioned speeches of youthful intelligentsia agitators. This had been the background of the awesome spectacle of the truly general strikes which paralyzed Petersburg and other cities of European Russia during the October days, driving the frightened autocracy to its knees.

In July, 1914, in protest against the brutal suppression by police detachments of a meeting of the Putilov workers called in support of the strike in the Baku oil fields, a strike as massive and explosive as any that had erupted among the workers in 1905 swept the outlying working-class districts of Petersburg. [. . .] By [July 7], according to official estimates, over 110,000 workers had joined in the strikes. Almost all the factories and commercial establishments in the working-class districts of the city were now closed, and many thousands of workers were clashing in pitched battles with Cossacks and police detachments. [. . .] [But] the heart of the capital remained largely still.

By the morning of July 9, the Bolsheviks' Petersburg Party Committee, sensing that the strike was doomed 'due to inadequate party organizations' and 'lack of weapons', decided to call on the Petersburg proletariat to go back to work. But it quickly discovered that it could not control the strike movement. The workers had now 'gone berserk', according to police reports, and were 'not even willing to listen' to those orators who asked them to call off the strike. Whatever element of leadership the strike still maintained would now be assumed by younger and more impatient hands. [. . .] Despite the dispatch to the working-class districts of the capital on July 11 of a whole cavalry brigade from Tsarkoe Selo, the strike movement lurched forward, in an atmosphere of increasingly violent conflict and despair. [. . .] It was not until July 15, four days before the outbreak of the war, that order in the factory districts of Petersburg was fully restored.

II

The four-day interval between the last gasps of the Petersburg strike and the outbreak of war may not altogether dispose of the thesis of Soviet historians that only the war prevented the strike movement of July, 1914, from turning into a decisive attack against the autocracy: after all, it may be argued that even before the war actually broke out the rapidly gathering international crisis acted as a brake on the revolutionary wave. Yet surely much of the conviction of this argument pales in the light of the two glaring sources of political weakness that the strike revealed from its very inception – weaknesses that had caused its original Bolshevik leadership to seek to bring it to an end at least five days before it at last petered out.

One of these sources of impotence had been the failure of the clashes in Petersburg to set off anything like the all-national political strike which even the Bolshevik leaders had considered (probably excessively) a necessary condition for the armed assault against the autocracy. The unfolding of the Petersburg strike had given rise to sympathy strikes and demonstrations in other industrial centers: in Moscow and Warsaw, Revel, Riga, and Tallin, Kiev, Odessa, even Tiflis. But nowhere, not even in Warsaw and Moscow, had these strikes displayed a degree of massiveness and revolutionary intensity comparable to that of the Petersburg movement.

Yet another factor was even more crucial: the inability of the Petersburg workers to mobilize, in time, active support among other groups in society. [. . .] No demonstrations, no public meetings, no collective petitions – no expressions of solidarity even barely comparable to those that Bloody Sunday had evoked were now aroused. Thus, in the last analysis, the most important source of the political impotence revealed by the Petersburg strike was precisely the one that made for its 'monstrous' revolutionary explosiveness: the sense of isolation, of psychological distance, that separated the Petersburg workers from educated, privileged society.

Where does this analysis leave us with respect to the general problem of political and social stability in Russian national life on the eve of the war that we posed at the beginning of this discussion? Clearly, it seems to me, the crude representations to be found in recent Soviet writings of the 'revolutionary situation' already at hand in July, 1914, can hardly be sustained. Yet when one views the political and social tensions evident in Russian society in 1914 in a wider framework and in broader perspective, any flat-footed statement of the case for stabilization appears at least equally shaky.

It isn't so much, as some of the soberer Soviet accounts suggest, that the Bolshevik Party Congress scheduled for the summer of 1914 was likely to stimulate at long last the broad organization and coordination of party activities required for the conduct of a successful all-nation political strike. Or even, as Lenin firmly expected, that the continuation of the new industrial upsurge was calculated to bring workers in other industrial centers, in fairly short order, to the same pitch of revolutionary unrest as their Petersburg 'vanguard'. The first development was conceivable; the second, even likely. But it is probable that Lenin and his followers assigned to both somewhat exaggerated importance. If the February revolution revealed what could be achieved with a minimum degree of organization, the October seizure of power would show how decisively an overturn in Petersburg could affect the rest of the country.

A far more important source of the explosiveness of the revolutionary tendencies at work in Imperial Russia on the eve of war lay, rather, I believe, in a phenomenon which has been substantially underestimated by many Soviet and Western commentators. It is that by July, 1914, along with the polarization between workers and educated, privileged society that we outlined in the first part of this essay, a second process of polarization – this one between the vast bulk of privileged society and the tsarist regime – appeared almost equally advanced. Unfolding largely detached from the rising wave of the labor movement, this second process could not affect its character and temper but was calculated to add a probably decisive weight to the pressure against the dikes of existing authority. By 1914 this second polarization had progressed to the point where even the most moderate spokesmen of liberal opinion were stating publicly, in the Duma and in the press, that an *impasse* had been reached between the state power and public opinion, which some argued could be resolved only by a revolution of the left or of the right.

Perhaps the most dramatic symptom of this growing political crisis was the progressive disintegration of existing intra- and inter-party alignments, particularly on the political spectrum of the liberal center. This political *bouleversement*, which finally came to general public notice in late 1913 and early 1914 as 'the crisis of the parties', actually appears to have been developing, largely behind the scenes, from the opening days of the Fourth Duma.

[. . .] A split between [. . .] the 'bourgeois' and '*raznochintsy*-radical' wings of the Kadet Party [. . .] developed at this time: from the fall of 1912 onward the joint meetings of the Kadet Party's Central Committee and the Kadet deputies in the Fourth Duma began to witness increasingly bitter clashes between the representatives of the new coalescing center and right wings of the party, headed by Miliukov, and the Left Kadets, usually led by Nekrasov.

The very fact that the Center and Right Kadets, who had been so bitterly divided since the first two Dumas, should now have been impelled to combine forces suggests that a completely new issue, overshadowing their old personal and political differences, had become paramount. According to Miliukov, the new issue that, even at this early stage, had come so dramatically to the fore was whether the Kadet Party should now adopt a 'revolutionary' or an 'evolutionary' orientation [towards the] resolution of the conflict between the tsarist regime and the liberal majority of educated society. [. . .]

The conflict came to a head, according to Miliukov, over the issue whether the Kadet deputies should be permitted to contribute to the quota of signatures that the deputies of the leftist parties needed to raise their usually incendiary parliamentary questions. Nekrasov, himself a frequent signer, strongly supported this practice. Miliukov opposed it with equal vehemence on the ground that it seriously strained the Kadets' relations with their more conservative Octobrist allies, and on this issue he formally won a majority of the party to his side. But this was a hollow victory. In defiance of party discipline, Kadet deputies continued to endorse the requests for parliamentary questions of their Trudovik and Social Democratic colleagues (thereby making possible many a parliamentary *skandal*), and as time progressed a growing number of deputies of the Progressist Party joined them in this practice.

The Progressist Party, recruited in the waning days of the Third Duma from a combination of the old *Partiia mirnogo obnovleniia* [Party of Peaceful Renewal] and dissatisfied Octobrist and Right Kadet deputies, was, at least in its leadership, preeminently a party of big businessmen and industrialists. That representatives of this party, theoretically well to the right of those moderate elements in the Kadet ranks that were making such an issue of the matter, should now be prepared to endorse the requests for parliamentary questions of Socialist deputies clearly suggested that a major political realignment was in the making. This realignment saw the leadership of the Progressist Party move so sharply to the left *in its tactical course* that by early 1914 it had established close contact with representatives of the major parties of the radical left, including the Bolsheviks. [. . .] Even if, largely due to Lenin's reticence, the Bolsheviks ultimately failed to cash in on [an offer of cooperation by the Progressists,] by 1914 [a crisis of the parties had developed] and [. . .] responsible figures in Russian liberal circles were now prepared to take [risks] in their search for a revolutionary solution to the current political deadlock. For the pages of the Bolshevik press all too clearly suggested that Lenin and his followers had now set their sights on the emergence from the expected revolutionary overtures of nothing short of a 'genuine', Bolshevik-led, 'democratic regime of the working class and peasantry'.

Indeed, by the beginning of 1914 any hope of avoiding a revolutionary crisis appeared to be evaporating even among the more moderate representatives of liberal opinion. Under the impact of the blind suicidal course pursued by the government and its handful of supporters, the Octobrist Party had split at the seams. Commenting on the decision of the sixteen Left Octobrist deputies to revolt against their party leadership and to oppose any suggestion of reconciliation with the existing regime, A. S. Izgoev, himself a proponent of political moderation, [. . .] now trumpeted in the pages of *Russkaia mysl'* [*Russian Thought*] :

> The failure of the 'Left Octobrists' is not their personal failure. It has marked the crash of a whole conception. Russia's renovation cannot be accomplished by the forces of the gentry class. Its best people are helpless. 1861 will not be repeated. The resolution of society's tasks is being turned over to other hands. 'Democracy is on the march.'

In a long wail of despair, Peter Struve, the most eloquent spokesman in Russian liberalism for an 'evolutionary orientation', described in the same issue of *Russkaia mysl'* the course of collision with society which the government and its fanatic supporters appeared to be setting. Ever since the failure of the Stolypin experiment, he recalled, the state power had been engaged in an increasingly bitter struggle against the very legal order that it had sanctioned with the October Manifesto. The state power recognized the legal existence of the Duma; yet with every weapon at their command its agents sought to stifle the existence of the majority of the parties represented in it. It purportedly recognized society's right to representation; yet its bureaucracy zealously struggled to suppress society's organs of local self-government. Given these basic contradictions in the Russian body politic, there was a superficial logic to the 'shameless propaganda' now circulating in higher official circles about the need for new violations of the Fundamental Laws, for a counterrevolution of the right which at a minimum should reduce the Duma to a purely consultative organ. But the pursuit of such a course, Struve desperately argued, would inevitably lead in short order to a radical revolutionary overturn. The only real salvation for the state power lay in its own restoration to health, a restoration which could be achieved only through the abandonment of its suicidal struggle against society. [. . .] Yet one way or another, Struve concluded, on a new militant note, the country would have its way [and his] willingness [. . .] at least to contemplate the unleashing of the very revolutionary Antaeus against which he had warned so eloquently but five years earlier was perhaps the most dramatic indication of how far by 1914 the polarization between state and educated society had actually progressed.

To be sure, one could still encounter [. . .] the observation, so frequently repeated in later émigré memoirs, that 'the frustrating atmosphere' that enveloped one in Petersburg evaporated when one got but '*100 versty* [60 miles] from the large centers'. 'There everything is quiet', observed the moderate Kadet commentator Gessen in his annual review for *Riech'* [*Speech*] in January, 1914. 'There nonetheless a complex process of adjustment is taking place; the wall between city and country is breaking down.'

Indeed, many signs of economic and social progress could be found in the Russian province of the year 1914 — the introduction of new crops, new techniques and forms of organization in agriculture, and the industrialization of the countryside; the growing literacy among the lower strata and invigorated cultural life among the upper strata of provincial society. But no more than in the major cities were these signs of progress and change in the localities to be viewed as evidence of the achievement or indeed the promise of greater political stability. [. . .] An article published by S. Elpatevsky in *Russkoe bogatstvo* [*Russian Wealth*] in January, 1914, strikingly described the two almost hermetically separated worlds that were now apparent in most provincial towns:

There is taking place a kind of gathering on the opposing sides of the wall which is dividing Russia. On one side have gathered the united *dvorianstvo* [gentry], the united bureaucracy, office-holders — generally the people who, in one way or another, 'are feeding at the public trough'. On the other side have gathered the plain citizens [*obyvateli*], the crowd of provincial society.

To be sure, Elpatevsky recognized, the division between 'official' and 'unofficial' Russia was of long standing, but in the years since the 1905 Revolution, it had become far sharper than ever before. 'Twenty-five years ago, provincial liberal or cultured society was [still] a mixed society. It included office-holders who were considered to have the liberalism or enlightenment required for membership in cultivated society.' But most of the middle and small gentry had now given up their distinctive gentry traditions and had been incorporated into educated society. And by the same token, 'the ranks of the office-holders [had] long since been purged of anyone endowed with a civic sense'.

Thus it was that 'official' and 'unofficial' Russia had now turned into two worlds completely sealed off one from the other. The inhabitants of these two worlds still met more or less peacefully – at the theater, on the boulevard, in the public park. But they now belonged to different clubs, attended different public lectures, were no longer welcome at each other's soirées. [. . .] 'In the camp of official Russia', there now prevailed 'a mood of hostility against those who recognize[d] the October Manifesto, against those of other nationalities and faiths, against those who believe[d] differently and worship[ped] differently.' On the other side, 'desires [had] become clearer and more definite', and 'thoughts, more agitated and intense'. 'Official Russia [had] learned nothing and forgotten nothing'; it had 'outgrown nothing', and 'become adjusted to nothing'. And, for its own part, society 'had long since ceased to expect the realization of its aspirations from above'.

Thus, Elpatevsky discerned in Russian provincial life, by the beginning of 1914, the same signs of the polarization of opinion as in the center of the political arena where 'the government, after seeking to reach an understanding with the Kadets, then with the Octobrists, [had] now moved over to the right-wing parties', while on the other side of the fence 'all expectations within the Duma of any [possible] legislative work with the government [were] steadily declining'. The crisis had now become so acute that revolution or counterrevolution appeared the only way out: 'Even some of the Octobrists [were] now being heard to say that there was no longer any sense in trying to safeguard the Duma', while the right-wing factions, which for a year now had been loudly warning of 'impending conflict', 'revolution', and 'repetition of 1905', had managed to persuade themselves of the inevitability of a 'catastrophic confrontation'. From all this Elpatevsky concluded [. . .] that the tensions in national life were rapidly approaching the breaking point [. . .] .

One paradoxical aspect of the polarization between state and society under these gathering clouds of revolution and counterrevolution deserves to be considered further [. . .] . It is clear that in many respects the Russian state – on the eve of the First World War just as in February, 1917 – was ripe, indeed overripe, for a takeover by a new *pays réel*: by new would-be ruling groups and institutions ready to assume formal control of national life.

[The tsarist regime was in an] advanced state of decomposition [and], at the same time, it appeared that in the proliferating organs of self-expression and independent activity of educated society — in the political and journalistic circles surrounding the State Duma and the local organs of self-government, in the cooperative societies of city and country, in the various societies of public enlightenment and the now more militant associations of big business and industry — a whole organized structure of order and potential authority had now crystallized, far better prepared to take and effectively exercise power than had been the case, say, of any of their institutional counterparts on the eve of the French Revolution.

Yet, [one] is likely to be struck by the frequent note of despondency, sounded even by temperamentally sanguine observers, about the sense of confusion and malaise pervading the political and social scene. [Gessen wrote in 1914:]

Much of [society's] activism is [expended] in tensions between groups and within groups . . . [on] useless conversations about the formation of blocs, about [the conclusion of] agreements. The same is true of intra-party relations. The most striking example in this respect is Social Democracy, in which the conflict between Bolsheviks and Mensheviks has consumed everything else. [But] the same is generally true of other parties.

Seeking an explanation for 'this unhealthy situation', [. . .] Gessen found it in 'the general decline of morals', and 'the unappeasable hunger for sensations' in contemporary society — the standard reaction of an *intelligent* of the old school to all of the untoward, novel phenomena of the day.

It is likely that the political and social *anomie* that Gessen myopically discerned had more to do with the impact on public opinion of the deadlock between the state power and educated society than with any of Sanin's sexual orgies. As we have already noted, the essence of the 'crisis of the parties' was that every responsible political figure now had to decide for himself whether to abandon the frustrating path of reform and risk the unleashing of a new revolution. Not only was the confrontation of this issue calculated to cause a reshuffle in all existing political alignments; it also brought the realization that the very organisms of the more moderate parties were not suitably organized for, or adaptable to, the pursuit and exploitation of a revolutionary situation.

Yet even this does not appear an adequate explanation for the sense of frustration and futility that Gessen detected among the leaders of the parties of the center and moderate left. Its chief source, I believe, lay in an often inarticulate but widely shared feeling that these parties were not sufficiently broadly gauged, that they were representative at best of the *tsenzovye elementy*, the privileged sector of society, and were woefully lacking support among its lower strata — most emphatically, of course, among its now politically aroused industrial workers. This feeling [. . .] made for the realization in circles of 'advanced opinion' that existing political combinations were no longer adequate to turn the corner successfully: to carry off a revolution and yet keep under control the 'elemental' instincts that such a revolution was likely to unleash among the urban and rural masses. [Hence] the yearning, so widely expressed by representatives of 'advanced opinion' on the eve of the war, to recapture somehow the spirit and the thrust of the old, pre-1905 Liberation movement — to establish anew a broad political combination, capable of mobilizing the support of all politically significant and potentially significant sectors of Russian society, through the medium of new personal contacts and associations, through the thread of new informal links between the representatives of the liberal center and the radical left.

It is in this same perspective, I believe, that we should interpret and weigh the character of that still shadowy phenomenon of Russian political and social life in the immediate prewar period, the contemporary revival of Masonry. [. . .]

[And] in this same perspective [too], it may perhaps not be difficult to outline a set of hypothetical circumstances under which Russia might have undergone — even in the absence of the specific additional strains induced by the war, though maybe under the immediate stimulus of some other, purely domestic crisis — the kind of radical overturn on which Lenin was already gambling by late 1913-early 1914 and which Russia actually experienced with the October Revolution.

However, I would rest my case on somewhat more modest, and more solid, grounds: on the prosaic, but often ignored, proposition that *the character, although not necessarily the gravity*, of the political and social crisis evident in urban Russia by the eve of the war is more reminiscent of the revolutionary processes that we shall see at work during Russia's second revolution than of those that had unfolded in Russia's first. [. . .] What the war years would do was not to conceive, but to accelerate substantially, the two broad processes of polarization that had already been at work in Russian national life during the immediate prewar period.

On the one hand, these years would witness not only a sharpening of the dissatisfaction of educated society with the inept, helpless tsarist regime but also the further crystallization — in the State Duma, the Zemskii Soiuz [Union of *Zemstvos*], Soiuz Gorodov [Union of Towns], the War-Industrial

Committees, and other central and local organs of public expression and activity — of a seemingly effective network of new organization, new order, new authority, fully prepared to take over and hold the reins of power as soon as the old state power fell.

But these same years witnessed as well the further progress of the other process of polarization that we have already observed in the prewar period — the division between the educated, privileged society and the urban masses — a process which would sap the new regime of much of its potential effectiveness, its authority, its legitimacy, even before it actually took over. Underlying the progress of this second polarization were not only the specific economic deprivations caused by the war but also the substantial acceleration of the changes in the character and temper of the industrial working class that we already noted in the immediate prewar years: the influx at an even more rapid tempo of new elements into the industrial army under the impact of the war boom and of the army's drafts.

Some of these new workers were women, some were adolescent or under-age boys, some (in the metalworking industry, for example) were older industrial workers shifted from nonstrategic to strategic industries, but most, we presume, continued to be drawn to the industrial army from the countryside — in the first order, from the overpopulated agricultural provinces of Central European Russia, which in 1913-14 had already provided such suitable recruits for Bolshevik agitation. The experience of 1917 would show only too clearly, if admittedly under the stresses of war, what a few more months of this agitation could do.

To be sure, the experience of the first eighteen months of the war temporarily obscured the workings of these disruptive processes. These months witnessed an indubitable crack-up of the Bolshevik Party under the combined blows of police arrests and of the draft of Bolshevik Party workers. Indeed, they saw a brief rally of public opinion under the spell of the national emergency which unquestionably affected not only educated society but also substantial elements of the 'laboring masses'. Even more notably, this period saw an accentuation, or at least a sharper articulation, of the desire already displayed in the prewar period by the older, Menshevik-oriented, labor intelligentsia to rejoin the framework of national life. Left momentarily at the center of the Russian labor scene, many of the most prominent figures in this workers' intelligentsia now joined the Labor Groups of the War-Industrial Committees. Some did so with the undivided purpose of supporting the war effort; others, admittedly, with a more complex mixture of 'defensist' sympathies and revolutionary hopes — both elements, however, articulating and solidifying by their participation in these organs of 'society' more conciliatory attitudes toward the liberal elements represented in them.

But the political and social significance of these phenomena was proven, all too quickly, to be ephemeral. By late 1915-early 1916, some of the leaders of 'advanced opinion' already resumed, this time in earnest, plots for the overthrow of the tsarist regime. By 1916, the wave of labor unrest once again began to swell. And within another year, the Menshevik workers' intelligentsia, whose stature had been so suddenly and dramatically magnified by the special conditions of war, would demonstrate an equally dramatic inability to influence, even minimally, the course of events. One of the most notable phenomena of 1917, which became evident almost from the very first days of the Revolution, was the failure of any of the leaders of the Workers' Group in the Central War-Industrial Committee to strike any responsive chord among the rank and file of their own working class, and to play a political role even comparable to that of their nonproletarian, but more radically inclined, *confrères* in the Menshevik Party. By this time the wall of mutual incomprehension that had come to separate this workers' intelligentsia from the rank and file of the laboring masses rose almost as high as the wall that these masses perceived between themselves and 'bourgeois' society. This was to be one of the most startling features of 1917, the sorry outcome of the Mensheviks' long effort in the aftermath of 1905 to build in Russia a genuinely Europeanized labor movement.

As a historian's eyes follow the unfolding of the revolutionary processes that have been outlined in this essay, they may well search for the illumination to be derived from comparative historical perspectives — from the comparisons that we have already implicitly drawn of the revolutionary situations in Russia in 1905, 1914, and 1917; from comparisons between the character of the labor disorders in Petersburg on the eve of the First World War and that of contemporary labor unrest in other European capitals; from the even bolder and broader comparisons that might be drawn between the prehistory of the great Revolution of 1917 and that of the great Revolution of 1789. Yet, it seems to me, the differences that any of these comparisons might bring out would loom far larger than the similarities.

There is an obvious singularity about the decade leading up to 1917 in the perspective of contemporary Western experience. This singularity lies, at least in part, in the fact that these years incorporate and compress to such an extraordinary degree the two sharply distinct revolutionary processes that I have discussed — processes which in the history of other European countries are not to be found coinciding, with such intensity, in any single phase of historical development. The nearest equivalent to the political and social attitudes displayed by the Russian workers in 1914 is probably to be found on the prewar European scene among elements of the French working class, which manifested at least a comparable sense of alienation from the existing political order and the prospering world of other strata of French society. But even if this state of affairs had led by the eve of the war to a serious crisis in the system of the Third Republic, the crisis was not further complicated and aggravated by the remaining presence on the stage of substantial vestiges of an old order and an Old Regime. By the same token, if vestiges of an Old Regime may be argued to be far more visible on the German political and social scene of 1914, and to have contributed to an unresolved deadlock between the Imperial Government and the Reichstag, it surely would be difficult to claim that the social attitudes that the German working class contributed to this crisis are even barely comparable to those of the stormy Russian proletariat.

If we view the prehistory of 1917 in the perspective of the decade in Russia's development leading up to 1905, its singularity does not lie so much in the range of groups and attitudes represented among the opposition and revolutionary forces. After all, the all-nation movement which finally emerged in October, 1905 — only to disintegrate even more quickly than it had come together — was marked by an even greater heterogeneity of constituent elements: gentry, professional men, and belatedly aroused big businessmen and industrialists; workers and peasants, or, more precisely, would-be representatives of a peasant movement; Bolsheviks, Mensheviks, Socialist Revolutionaries, and that grab bag of political tendencies gathered under the umbrella of the Soiuz Osvobozhdeniia [Union of Liberation] .

And all these groups and tendencies were animated by quite different underlying attitudes toward the economic and social processes that were at work in national life. Some were driven to revolutionary opposition by their impatience for a clearer and fuller articulation in Russian life of the values and institutional forms attendant on their vision of a modern world. Others were filled with resentment largely by the very forces that were at work in this modernization, or at least by the forms that this modernization had assumed during the Witte experiment: by the sufferings and deprivations that weighed on the countryside, the darkness and strangeness of life in the barracks and hovels of the industrial slums, the gross and offensive sight of the new rule of money. And even the members of the intelligentsia, who had contributed so much to patching this coalition together, had temporarily succeeded in doing so precisely because so many of them — drawn as they were from many of these sharply separated corners of Russian society — actually combined in themselves, beneath the flimsy logical constructions of ideologies, the malestrom of chaotic and conflicting attitudes represented in national life.

While this heterogeneity of the constituent groups in the all-nation opposition to absolutism at the beginning of the century, and of the underlying attitudes of the members of the intelligentsia who led them (Liberals, Marxists, and Populists alike), ultimately accounts for the rapidity of the disintegration that this coalition underwent in the crucible of 1905, it also explains, of course, the irresistible power that it briefly manifested. If only for a flickering historical moment, the autocracy was confronted by the outline of a new and seemingly united nation. For this flickering moment, the intelligentsia, which had emerged as the prototype – the microcosm – of this united nation, managed to induce the groups under its sway to bury the long-standing differences of interests, outlook, and values that had separated them and to agree to a common set of discrete political objectives, to a common vision, however partial and abstracted, of Russia's immediate future if not of her ultimate destiny.

The potential significance of this achievement of getting different groups to agree on a limited set of political objectives – of finding a common denominator for some interests and suspending, postponing the clash of others – should not be underestimated, since it constituted the essential prerequisite for the successful launching of that great French Revolution of 1789 whose image possessed the political imagination of so much of Russia's intelligentsia in 1905: for in the prerevolutionary years 1787-88 the opposition to the *ancien régime* drew much of its strength not only from the 'progressive' aspirations of the Third Estate but also from the resentments of nobles and churchmen rebelling, in the name of thinly disguised feudal liberties, against the administrative innovations of a haltingly modernizing state. To be sure, in the France of 1789, the balance between 'progressive' and 'reactionary' forces had been far more heavily weighted in favor of the former than turned out to be the case in the Russia of 1905. Still, if any even partially valid historical analogy is to be sought between the French and Russian prerevolutionary experiences, it should be drawn, it seems to me, between the French prerevolution and the years in Russian life leading up to 1905, not to 1917.

Indeed, it is difficult to escape the conclusion that the failure of Russia's first revolution, and the repudiation that it induced among so many in the intelligentsia of their traditional revolutionary ethos, substantially contributed to the character and pattern of the second. For if the intelligentsia's sense of messianic mission [. . .] had unquestionably contributed to the growth of revolutionary tendencies and thus to the instability of the existing political order, it had also made – particularly from the 1890s, when both Populists and Marxists had been converted to the cause of political freedom – for the translation of the new feeling of mobility in national life into a somewhat greater sense of social cohesion; for the bridging, however slow and precarious, of the psychological chasms that had hitherto divided Russia's society of estates.

By the same token, it may well be argued that the failure of the intelligentsia to secure these bridges in 1905 − even in the minimal form of a political and social framework temporarily acceptable to a broad spectrum of Russian society − and the decline in subsequent years of its sense of messianic mission substantially contributed to the character and gravity of the divisions in Russian life that we have examined in this essay. For, as it turned out, a brief historical interval, the partially reformed political order gained a new lease on life. But this brief measure of *political stability* was achieved in part at the price of the promise of greater *social cohesion*, greater *social stability*, which, for urban Russia at least, had been contained in the turbulent years leading up to 1905. The tensions and strains which earlier had been largely contained in the channels of common political objectives would eventually be polarized into separate revolutionary processes, each adding to the pressures against the tsarist regime but also contributing − by their separation − to the eventual disintegration of the whole fabric of national life.

Thus it was that 1917 would witness the collapse of an ancient old order at the same time that it would see an industrial working class and eventually a peasant mass, impelled by an amalgam of old and new grievances, combine against a stillborn bourgeois society and state. Thus it was, finally, that in the throes of these two separate revolutions, Russia would not manage for many years to recover a new historical equilibrium − to find its own Thermidor.

Notes

[1. Alexander Gerschenkron, 'Problems and patterns of Russian economic development', reprinted in this volume, pp. 193-210.]

2. The term of opprobrium that the Bolsheviks applied to those whom they accused of advocating the 'liquidation' of the revolutionary underground.

9 DOMESTIC CENSORSHIP IN THE FIRST WORLD WAR

Deian Hopkin

Source: *Journal of Contemporary History*, vol.5, no.4, 1970, pp.151-69.

Studies in Britain in the twentieth century have tended to omit or barely mention one of the most vital factors in the political and social framework of that society, the mass media. The topic is encumbered by great obstacles. The usual problems of quantification and analysis are complicated by the ambiguity of concepts such as 'public opinion' and 'propaganda', and the prolific quantities of newspaper material make its examination extremely laborious. Not only is it difficult in retrospect to relate editorial comment to events; it is even more difficult to penetrate the impersonal facade of the newsprint and examine the writers and editors, who are, in reality, the newspapers. The greater part of this groundwork awaits preparation. Some aspects of the topic can however be examined at the present, and one of the more important, if peripheral, of these is the development of censorship during the First World War. The unexpectedly early release, in 1966, of certain classes of documents at the Public Record Office casts new light both on the attitudes of government officials to the idea of censorship, and also on its operation, especially in the field of domestic newspapers and journals. The censorship of cables and wireless falls into a different category. One of the first acts of the British government when war was declared in 1914 was to cut the cables between Germany and the United States, and throughout the war a close watch was maintained on telegraphy and wireless communication. But this lay in the area of open war where the enemy was easily distinguishable. Much more difficult was the task of classifying and controlling opinion and information presented in the domestic press. Here the problem was not of discovering an enemy, but of assessing degrees of dissidence.

A number of problems arose from the publication of news and opinion in wartime. There was the usual danger of publishing information that might be useful to the enemy. This was by no means a new problem but it was magnified in the late nineteenth century by the development of the popular press, with its keen awareness of competition and circulation figures. Moreover, the new press had created a new reading public, by all accounts more impressionable than the traditional newspaper public. And, above all, the authorities were soon aware that Britain was fighting a total war on a scale hitherto inconceivable. While there was a great need to muster the country's resources, to mobilize the nation's manpower, and to channel the people's aspirations into support for the Allies, there was soon need to sustain Britain's morale as well. While patriotism was easily engendered at the outbreak of war, when a quick victory seemed certain, the illusions were equally easily dispelled as the prospect of victory receded. The press acquired a new and lasting significance. War psychology had arrived. But if the logical connotation of this was war propaganda, the first step in the process was censorship.

The question of censorship had already been raised some time before the outbreak of the war in an attempt to solve the perennial problem, the leakage of valuable information to a prospective enemy. In January 1899, not long after the establishment of the first popular newspaper, the War Office had urged the Home Office to consider the need for a general control over the press in wartime. It was suggested that the danger of leakage had grown commensurate with the growth of the popular press, but the government as a whole was less impressed by the hypothesis, and the Boer War passed without the introduction of any of the recommended censorship. In 1904 the matter was again raised, this time by the Prime Minister, Balfour. A draft bill providing some measure of control was prepared, but the Conservatives were preoccupied with other things, and the bill was shelved. The change of government in 1906 did little to speed up the progress of the proposed legislation, but the matter was not entirely forgotten. At the end of 1906, the Committee of Imperial Defence voiced the opinion that 'the means of applying such power should not be delayed until the outbreak of war'. But it made no immediate proposals, and no further draft was prepared until the end of 1908. This time a new obstacle arose which undermined the whole scheme. Representatives of the newspaper proprietors announced their unremitting hostility to the whole idea of censorship by statute. They did, however, agree to the establishment of a Joint Standing Committee in which they would co-operate with representatives of the Admiralty and War Office in regulating the conduct of the press on a purely voluntary basis.

The establishment of the principle of voluntary participation set the pattern for the normal relationship between the press and the government in matters of control and censorship, and it worked surprisingly well. In urging some form of control the government partly anticipated its need not only in times of actual war, but also in the more frequent periods of diplomatic tension. In 1912, shortly after the Committee was established, the press were asked not to report on the progress of certain work being carried out by the Ordnance Survey Department. The press acceded to this request, as they did on subsequent occasions. In 1914, therefore, a mutually acceptable principle for press control which fell short of actual censorship was already in being.

When war broke out, however, the government was no longer willing to accept the principle of voluntary control. The Joint Committee was superseded by a new organization in which the newspaper press played no part. An official Press Bureau was established on 7 August 1914 headed by a civilian but consisting largely of naval and military officers. At first its work was hampered not only by poor working conditions but also by the administration. The first Director, F.E. Smith, stayed for barely a month; he was succeeded by Stanley Buckmaster, with whom, it seems, it was difficult to work. In May 1915, therefore, the Bureau was reorganized. The Home Secretary took responsibility for its activities and Buckmaster, who had become Lord Chancellor, was succeeded by two joint directors, one a distinguished colonial administrator, Sir Frank Swetenham, and the other, Sir Edward Cook, a well-known journalist and former editor of the *Daily News*. The establishment was increased from 50 to 122. The main functions of the Bureau were two-fold. One department controlled the supply and distribution of information from the Admiralty and the War Office to the newspapers, while a second department examined every telegram and cable sent and received by each newspaper. Any other material which the press normally used might be submitted voluntarily to the Press Bureau for its opinion. Although the Bureau exercised a considerable measure of control, it also sought to establish a high level of co-operation with the press. And, up to a point, the press responded. As early as 27 July 1914, the major Fleet Street editors had agreed not to publish details of British military dispositions, and, for its part, the Bureau was prepared to define to editors the limits beyond which they should not go. To this effect it issued periodical directives, known as 'D' notices, giving specific advice on the treatment of news. Furthermore, in order to foster good relations with at least the major newspapers, the Bureau kept a list of fifty editors to whom confidential information could be relayed.

Though publication of facts was the Bureau's chief concern, at times its interest extended beyond this. As embarrassing to the government as the leakage of information, if not equally dangerous, was the tendency of the press to exaggerate the extent of Allied successes. It is perhaps significant that on the very day the establishment of the Bureau was announced, the *Daily Mail*, in a special edition, gave a plausible and detailed account of an entirely fictitious British naval victory. It was against this kind of euphoria that the Bureau came to direct itself. In March 1915 the press were warned against being over-optimistic in their reporting. As the war ground to a halt in the muddy trenches of Northern France, so the psychology of the nation had to be reoriented. The press had a valuable role to play in this and the Bureau was well aware of that potential. By 1917 it was said to be secretly instructing the press to play down the extent of any British victories in order to prepare the public for a prolonged war.

But if the press were prepared to accept limitations on their news reporting, and even to comply with the Bureau's directives on matters of balance and form, they were less prepared to tolerate the attitude which the Bureau adopted towards them. From early in the war the level of co-operation between the two was marred by a 'spirit of hostility'. To a certain extent this was due to an unavoidable conflict of outlook, which is perhaps not surprising in view of the small number of journalists employed by the Bureau. However powerful the patriotism of a newspaper, its chief object was to obtain the swiftest possible publication of newsworthy material, and, since competition between newspapers continued, time was, as always, the critical factor. The Bureau, for its part, was anxious to assess the possible implications of publishing such material, and this was a time-consuming exercise. Moreover, it was easier, and much safer, for the Bureau simply to delay sending on material until it ceased to be noteworthy. Such delays became common, and throughout the war the press was hampered by a dearth of news from the Bureau. Some sections of the press retaliated. 'Some papers', complained the Bureau in September 1915, 'especially those published in places remote from London, seldom submit matter to the Bureau'. Others ignored the 'D' notices and in 1915 some thirty-five socialist and pacifist newspapers were removed altogether from the 'D' list for this offence. But the non-statutory censorship exercised by the Press Bureau was generally very effective. A newspaper could do little without news. Not every section of the press, however, relied on a steady supply of news. A considerable number of journals of opinion used little immediately fresh news and to this section belonged the pacifist journals. Since the pacifists were among the most voluble of the government's critics, the failure of the Press Bureau to control these journals was doubly irritating. Moreover, the non-pacifist journals and newspapers also expressed critical opinions, and in consequence the jurisdiction of the Bureau had to be reinforced by a more formal form of censorship.

This was provided in the regulations of the Defence of the Realm Act (DORA), an act which, among other things, established the government's right to impose a statutory limit on the freedom of the press. Some journalists approved. One prominent editor, A.G. Gardiner, maintained that 'there comes a time when even the freedom of the press must give place to the safety of the State'. But others disagreed. Convinced of the value of their work as guardians of the public interest, especially in wartime, the majority of editors chafed at the new regulations. Chief among them was Lord Northcliffe who had, ironically enough, earlier advocated government control of the press in wartime. During the war, however, he used his news-papers to make and unmake politicians, and to attack government policies of which he disapproved. Despite public reprobation, he continued to voice his own peculiar brand of patriotism, and was finally kept in check only when Lloyd George brought him into the government.

But Northcliffe was an exception to almost every rule, and the Defence of the Realm Act was primarily directed at those whose patriotism was not so manifest. It conferred on the government sweeping powers to legislate, by decree and regulation, on matters concerning every aspect of life. One clause in the act referred to the need to 'prevent the spread of false reports or reports likely to cause disaffection to His Majesty or to interfere with the success of His Majesty's forces by land or sea or to prejudice His Majesty's relations with foreign powers'.

Subsequently several regulations were enacted to deal with various points arising from this. Regulation no. 18 prohibited the obtaining and com-munication of naval and military information. This covered most aspects of the work done by the official Press Bureau and gave the 'voluntary' censorship the support of statutory compulsion. Opinion was most easily dealt with by regulation 27, which reiterated the intention to prevent the spread of 'false reports' likely to cause 'disaffection'. The regulation was interpreted very liberally and proved the most frequently used in prosecut-ing dissidents. In addition, regulation 51 enabled the authorities to enter premises suspected of being used for publishing or distributing dissident literature. These regulations were widely used throughout the war against newspapers of all sizes and all shades of opinion, from the *Jewish Times* to the *Morning Post*, the *Globe* to the *Worker*, the *North London Guardian* to the *Glasgow Forward*.

G.P. Gooch who, as editor of the *Contemporary Review*, saw censorship at first hand, claimed that the authorities strictly enforced their admonition against offending Britain's allies. The decision to prosecute a newspaper was, however, often governed by political considerations. In November 1915, the *Globe*, which had already embarrassed the government by its rancorous attack on Prince Louis of Battenberg, First Lord of the Admiralty, was suppressed under DORA for reporting the imminent resignation of Lord Kitchener. The paper threatened political harmony, at best never more than tenuous, within the government, and it was felt necessary to make an example of the paper to prevent yet more serious incidents. The regulations were enforced against other patriotic papers, however, only on the few occasions when they inadvertently published dangerous information. But it was more difficult to invoke the regulations as a measure of repression against pacifists. Throughout the war, the authorities proved extremely reluctant to prosecute anti-war newspapers and journals. In the first place minority groups, as the pacifists were, probably stood to gain from any publicity given them by a court case. Herbert Samuel, the Home Secretary in 1916, thought that 'prosecutions, which would have to be numerous if a policy of repression was once decided upon, would cause more harm than good. They would . . . have the effect of advertising speeches and publications which are now for the most part left in obscurity . . . they would probably not succeed in preventing the repetition of the offences.' Sir Ernely Blackwell, head of the legal department at the Home Office, outlined the dilemma by pointing out that 'whilst the . . . movement remains small, prosecution would do more harm than good . . . If the movement grows to considerable dimensions prosecution will not repress it.' But the authorities were also concerned with their image at home and abroad. To some extent government officials were sensitive to the enormous powers they enjoyed during the war. Commenting on the power to enter premises conferred by regulation 51, the Director of Public Prosecutions suggested that they were 'of so drastic a character as too closely to approach the application of martial law at a time when the civil law had not been suspended'. Herbert Samuel was more worried that a policy of repression against the pacifists would 'give rise to an agitation damaging to our cause in America and elsewhere, based on the charge that His Majesty's Government was using the power of the executive to prevent freedom of speech and to conceal important facts from the nation'.

The government's continuing liberalism was not the only factor shielding the pacifists. If anything, the process by which prosecutions could be instituted was too vague to be effective. Part of the problem was the difficulty of establishing the illegal character of pacifist propaganda. One official at the Home Office regretted that in most pacifist writing 'there is not a passage which is capable of direct and absolute contradiction'. 'The method applied', complained another official in the same department, 'is a cunning and malevolent distortion of the facts which cannot be met with direct denial.' And serious doubts were expressed whether a case would stand up in court under these circumstances. Sir Ernely Blackwell doubted 'whether general peace propaganda and advocacy of early negotiations can be successfully dealt with under Regulation 27', and added that 'the meaning of "giving aid and comfort" to the enemy, can hardly be used to cover advocacy of peace, however mischievous it may be'. Their experiences in court helped to confirm the authorities' fears. In August 1915 the Salford police had raided the premises of the National Labour Press, the publications organization of the Independent Labour Party, and seized specimens of their publications to prepare for a prosecution. A similar raid took place in London but, although the London magistrates found in favour of the police, the Salford magistrates were not convinced of the illegality of the seized literature. In consequence, the prospect of losing even the occasional case was sufficient deterrent for the police, and in June 1916 the Home Office issued a circular to all police authorities discouraging action against any publication except those against which a conviction had already been obtained. Herbert Samuel concluded that 'the points at issue are less for courts of law to determine than for Parliament and public opinion'.

The authorities still sought legal alternatives, however. One solution resorted to was to try cases *in camera*, but there is no evidence that this was particularly effective. Temporary suppressions for technical infringements were more effective. In 1915 *Britannia*, the suffragette paper, was suppressed and the following year two other papers, the Glasgow *Forward* and Birmingham *Forward*, were dealt with in the same way. But these were temporary expedients and the authorities were never able to find a satisfactory way of silencing the dissidents. The whole struggle is, perhaps, epitomized by the continuing appearance, throughout the war, of the most important of all the pacifist newspapers, the *Labour Leader*.

The *Leader* was saved from probable extinction by the First World War; as the war dragged on, its fortunes improved. By 1917, the Home Office had to concede that its power was 'considerable, and its influence far-reaching amongst the labouring classes'. Its opinion was regarded as significant if almost treasonable. One Home Office official thought it was doubtful 'whether if the *Labour Leader* was produced in Berlin it could advertise or further the German case better'. Conflicting views regarding the nature of the paper were held, however, by various officials. Some felt that it was 'more or less a business concern started before the war which merely advocates views which it believes to be popular with its readers', while others were convinced that the publishers of the paper were 'misguided fanatics'. This gave rise to a vicious circle. Some officials challenged the value of prosecuting the paper which was 'after all, a genuine newspaper . . . when leaflets and pamphlets written expressly for the purpose, are allowed currency'. Others were equally convinced that it was 'little use suppressing pamphlets if the *Labour Leader* is allowed free scope'. But several factors contributed to prevent suppression. Attempts were made on several occasions to construct a case against the paper, but each time the difficulty arose 'of fastening on to any article which in itself would render the paper liable to conviction'. Moreover it was the *Labour Leader* that had been involved in the abortive Salford case in 1915 and the authorities were doubly careful for that reason.

Above all, however, the *Labour Leader* acquired a new significance after December 1916. Lloyd George invited Arthur Henderson, the leader of the Labour Party, to join his new government. It was a vital moment in British politics and, what is more to the point, for Lloyd George himself. Everything seemed to hang on the approval of the Annual Conference of the Labour Party due to meet on 27 January. Just at this time the Home Office had finally resolved to prosecute the *Labour Leader*, but when Lloyd George, on Henderson's urging, argued against it, the matter was dropped. The decision of the Labour Conference was far too important to Lloyd George to be endangered by what was, after all, a minor matter. Henderson expected he would have a tough job convincing the conference of the importance of joining the new coalition and, he claimed, 'all arguments would be futile if, as would be the case, the attention of the Conference was directed to the proceedings which we had instituted against the paper and the spirit thereby aroused would defeat all our efforts'. By 1917, then, the *Leader* was regarded as much a part of the labour as of the pacifist movement, and although the immediate argument of December 1916 ceased to apply once the Labour Conference endorsed their leaders' co-operation with Lloyd George, the authorities still felt it necessary to placate Labour opinion by tolerating the publication of the *Labour Leader*.

The paper had one other factor in its favour. Like other pacifist journals. it was a part of the press, which enjoyed something of a corporate status. The authorities' awareness of this is reflected in their belief that there existed among newspapers of all political creeds a certain bond. For example, one reason given for not prosecuting the *Labour Leader* was that 'it might attract the sympathy of more reputable papers'. One Cabinet member believed that 'the solidarity of the press was so strong that it was practically impossible to prevent an almost unanimous outcry by all newspapers in the event of any further interference'. Although the member was referring to leading daily newspapers, the reasoning was easily applicable to lesser newspapers like the *Labour Leader*, which after all was the organ of an established Parliamentary party.

But if pacifist publications were shielded from permanent suppression, the authorities went to considerable lengths to minimize their influence and restrict their circulation. The Home Office set up a special unit to examine all sorts of pacifist literature, in particular the *Labour Leader*. In June 1916, after it was discovered that the enemy were using materials from the *Leader* for propaganda purposes, the export of the paper and several others was prohibited and the authorities ordered the seizure of any pacifist papers found in Post Office mailbags. Neither of these bans was entirely successful. The export ban became the subject of a heated parliamentary debate when it was discovered that a similar ban had been placed on the *Nation*, an established Liberal newspaper. Moreover, in January 1917 the Germans were found to be broadcasting material from the *Labour Leader* which had been inadvertently reproduced in the *Morning Post*. As a result, the Press Bureau was obliged to supplement the ban by instructing editors to avoid referring in any way to pacifist journals. The GPO ban was even less successful. On 12 March 1917 a snap search of the mails to seize copies of the *Tribunal*, the journal of the conscientious objectors, unearthed only 859 of the estimated 7000 that should have been there, and the authorities were forced to admit that the No-Conscription Fellowship was foiling them by using sealed envelopes.

More effective were the raids made by the police and military authorities on premises used by pacifists. Although few court cases arose out of these raids, they inflicted considerable inconvenience on the organization of the pacifist movement. Between September and November 1917, for example, twenty-four raids were carried out and a considerable quantity of literature seized. Even if nothing else came of these raids, they at least prevented the distribution of literature. And the police might also discover materials for a case. In January 1918 a special committee was set up under Mr Justice Shearman to examine material seized in this way, and its work was facilitated by the issue of a new regulation dealing with pamphlet literature. In the past the authorities had had great difficulty in tracing the printers of pamphlets. In November 1917 a regulation was issued requiring all leaflets and pamphlets to bear the name and address of both author and printer and to be submitted to the Press Bureau for approval at least 72 hours before publication. This had a considerable effect on both the tone and content of much pacifist propaganda. By April 1918, the Independent Labour Party were publishing nothing to which the Press Bureau could take exception. On the other hand they capitalized on the situation to a certain extent by franking their leaflets 'Passed by the Press Censor' in an attempt to boost sales by associating their propaganda with government approval.

The police had found from experience that a threat against a printer's equipment was one of the most effective ways of halting the publication of pacifist literature. In 1917 the police, by threatening to damage linotype machinery worth £16,000, exacted an agreement from the Director of the National Labour Press to stop publishing *Tribunal*. The threat was a serious one. One printer of *Tribunal*, Mr S.H. Street, was raided by the police in April 1918 and machinery worth £500 was damaged in the process. Moreover, when this proved insufficient warning, the police arraigned him on several technical offences and he was fined a total of £300. Even if the damage wilfully inflicted on printing equipment was illegal, no printer could afford to be without his machines for any length of time, and the process of recovering damages was both long and hazardous.

Beyond the printing shop lay a great network of pacifist groups who organized meetings and speaking tours, as well as distributing literature. And if the need for the censorship of literature was great, the need to curb the vocal propaganda being carried out all over the country was greater still. But it was often harder to pin down an individual propagandist than to arraign a newspaper. The tradition of free speech had an even firmer foundation than the idea of a free press. Furthermore, during the Boer War Lloyd George himself had addressed numerous anti-war meetings. In 1917, as in 1900, the law could do little to prevent such meetings. Speakers were circumscribed by a multitude of laws that governed conduct in public places and defined the slender boundary between meeting and mob. But this line was not often crossed, and the authorities were unable to curtail public meetings without an evident breach of the law. It was easy to convict a member of the No-Conscription Fellowship when he had refused a clear directive to enlist. It was a different matter to prosecute one of its members for publicly expressing his objections to the war. In 1916, the government issued a regulation giving a Secretary of State power to prohibit meetings which threatened to give rise to 'grave disorder', but this regulation was seldom used. The authorities relied instead on other methods for controlling meetings.

Their best ally was the pro-war public. At the beginning of the war, the bulk of the population considered pacifism an utterly detestable phenomenon. Within a week of the declaration of the war, 'undisciplined jingoes' were breaking up peace rallies in Edinburgh, and in Aberdare howling mobs drowned Keir Hardie's peace meetings. Throughout the war, meeting after meeting was wrecked by mobs composed very often of uniformed soldiers, and the patriotic press supported them all the way, led by the *Daily Express*, which delighted in its daily vituperation against the 'pasty-faced peace cranks'. Sometimes there was open violence, but more often meetings were simply abandoned. It was convenient for the authorities simply to stand aside and let the tide of public opinion do the work they could not easily do themselves. Pacifists found it increasingly difficult to hire halls without the guarantee of police protection. In some cases the pacifists got together and bought meeting halls, but such arrangements were few and far between. More often they doggedly moved from hall to hall, town to town, trying to keep one step ahead of the patriots. And at meetings which were quiet there was usually a plain-clothed policeman in attendance, surreptitiously recording the speeches. The authorities then considered whether these transcripts provided grounds for prosecution. Meantime, the patriots were active not only during meetings. Many busily denounced individual pacifists to the police. If the pacifists had been quick to denounce the war, the patriots had been equally quick off the mark in denouncing the pacifists. In August 1914, a Monmouthshire collier complained about the activities of a fellow-worker, and in Newton-le-Willows, a vicar vigorously denounced a 'pro-German English socialist of the most rabid type' who was 'far more dangerous than any German spy'. Miss Boston, a member of the Independent Labour Party, walked out in disgust from a meeting addressed by her leader, Ramsay MacDonald, whose speech, she claimed, was 'mischievous, calculated to do vast damage'. Parishioners complained against their priests, Catholic and Unitarian, and anonymous patriots denounced the activities of their neighbours. Many complained about the literature which the pacifists so assiduously distributed. The quantities of pamphlets, leaflets, and even books were substantial. According to the police one Lancashire man who expressed an interest in pacifism was showered with 5000 pamphlets, '100 bound volumes, as well as many thousands of leaflets'. The postage alone came to £21.

During the first two years of war prosecutions against individual pacifists were numerous. According to the returns of one county, Glamorgan, prosecutions were instituted from the beginning of the war up to 1 January 1917, and the penalties inflicted ranged from fines of £30 to several months' imprisonment. But from 1917 onwards, the number dropped sharply, although the number of cases considered rose. In the first nine months of 1917, the Glamorgan Constabulary recommended 40 prosecutions compared with 54 for the previous two-and-a-half years. The Director of Public Prosecutions, however, recommended only one case for prosecution. The Chief Constable was dismayed. Pointing out that for two years the police had been diligently tracking the pacifists, he argued that his committee 'are beginning to demur about paying the bills seeing that the authorities in London refuse to authorize prosecutions in cases which we consider very strong'. From Leicester, too, the complaint came that the work of the patriots would be hampered if there were no more prosecutions. The reasons for the decline in the number of cases is not clear, but there are indications that by 1917 the Cabinet were beginning to recognize that the pacifists had important points to make. Admitting the vigour of the pacifists' campaign which 'had the field to itself', several Cabinet members, including Sir Edward Carson, pointed out that the peace movement was gaining ground largely because the Allied war aims were so unclear. When these aims were at last formulated, the government were urged to issue a full statement of them in order to gain a psychological effect. Certainly the authorities were aware that the pacifist movement was gaining ground, and feared that it was spreading among the military. It was less important, therefore, to prosecute individual pacifists than to tackle the whole movement, and this required above all a counter-offensive on the part of the patriots and the government. In 1917 the authorities' attitude towards the pacifists changed. Pacifism was regarded less and less as a criminal activity, and the emergence of Lord Lansdowne as a forthright advocate of a negotiated peace helped to confirm the thesis that the pacifists were a respectable body of sincere critics. The government began to put more and more effort into arguing its own case, and in the last year of the war it developed an efficient propaganda machine. The hitherto haphazard publication of propaganda by a variety of departments and unofficial bodies was now co-ordinated by the creation of a single department, headed by a highly successful press magnate, Lord Beaverbrook. In January 1918 the Cabinet was urged to accept the fact that 'the government had become definitely and officially responsible for propaganda'. Soldiers and civilians were henceforth organized into a publicity machine for the government's war policies.

But the government retained its powers of censorship until the end of the war. Moreover, patriots continued to break up meetings and denounce pacifists to the very end. But the defeat of Germany was becoming politically less relevant than the impending struggle with a new enemy, Bolshevism. Long before the end of the war, intelligence reports spoke of growing Boshevik and revolutionary activity, and the events of 1917 seemed to herald the dawn of a new era. In Britain, the fiery Leeds Conference of socialists seemed to pose a huge threat to the British establishment and the authorities were disturbed by the resurgence of left-wing activity on the Clyde and in South Wales. Pacifism benefited from this in two ways. The revolutionary groups sought to associate themselves with general peace propaganda, thus augmenting the pacifist movement. On the other hand the authorities recognized that pacifism was less threatening than Bolshevism, and this may in part account for the general relaxation of measures taken against individual pacifists. Nevertheless the authorities wished to control the activities of both pacifists and Bolsheviks and used the same machinery to do so.

At the end of the war, then, the authorities were reluctant to dismantle either the machinery for censorship or that for the organization of propaganda. One official claimed that 'the abolition of censorship will deprive ... the government of most important sources of information'. But if the war had produced a threat, albeit an ineffective one, to the idea of free speech, the end of the fighting made the challenge irrelevant. If four years of war had altered the political structure of Britain and reshaped the political balance of power, it had not seriously eroded any of the traditional liberties. The mood of elation at victory and at the prospect of a future without war, and the confident prediction of some experts that even Bolshevism was a dying star, rendered futile any arguments for the retention of the wartime restrictions on speech and publication. And so at midnight on 24 July 1919, censorship disappeared imperceptibly. Nothing had changed except that the idea of a free press and free speech had, if anything, been enhanced.

10 INTRODUCTION TO *MAN, THE STATE AND WAR*

Kenneth N. Waltz

Source: *Man, the State and War: A Theoretical Analysis* (Columbia University Press, 1959), Chapter 1, 'Introduction', pp.1-15.
By permission of the author and publisher.

Asking who won a given war, someone has said, is like asking who won the San Francisco earthquake. That in wars there is no victory but only varying degrees of defeat is a proposition that has gained increasing acceptance in the twentieth century. But are wars also akin to earthquakes in being natural occurrences whose control or elimination is beyond the wit of man? Few would admit that they are, yet attempts to eliminate war, however nobly inspired and assiduously pursued, have brought little more than fleeting moments of peace among states. There is an apparent disproportion between effort and product, between desire and result. The peace wish, we are told, runs strong and deep among the Russian people; and we are convinced that the same can be said of Americans. From these statements there is some comfort to be derived, but in the light of history and of current events as well it is difficult to believe that the wish will father the condition desired.

Social scientists, realizing from their studies how firmly the present is tied to the past and how intimately the parts of a system depend upon each other, are inclined to be conservative in estimating the possibilities of achieving a radically better world. If one asks whether we can now have peace where in the past there has been war, the answers are most often pessimistic. Perhaps this is the wrong question. And indeed the answers will be somewhat less discouraging if instead the following questions are put: are there ways of decreasing the incidence of war, of increasing the chances of peace? Can we have peace more often in the future than in the past?

Peace is one among a number of ends simultaneously entertained. The means by which peace can be sought are many. The end is pursued and the means are applied under varying conditions. Even though one may find it hard to believe that there are ways to peace not yet tried by statesmen or advocated by publicists, the very complexity of the problem suggests the possibility of combining activities in different ways in the hope that some combination will lead us closer to the goal. Is one then led to conclude that the wisdom of the statesman lies in trying first one policy and then another, in doing what the moment seems to require? An affirmative reply would suggest that the hope for improvement lies in policy divorced from analysis, in action removed from thought. Yet each attempt to alleviate a condition implies some idea of its causes: to explain how peace can be more readily achieved requires an understanding of the causes of war. It is such an understanding that we shall seek in the following pages. To borrow the title of a book by Mortimer Adler, our subject is 'How to Think about War and Peace'. The chapters that follow are, in a sense, essays in political theory. This description is justified partly by the mode of inquiry — we proceed by examining assumptions and asking repeatedly what differences they make — and partly by the fact that we consider a number of political philosophers directly, sometimes in circumscribed fashion, as with St Augustine, Machiavelli, Spinoza, and Kant, and sometimes at length, as with Rousseau. In other places we shall concentrate on a type of thought, as in the chapters on behavioral scientists, liberals, and socialists. But what is the relevance of the thoughts of others, many of them living far in the past, to the pressing and awful problems of the present? The rest of the book is an answer to this question, but it is well at the outset to indicate the lines along which we shall proceed.

Why does God, if he is all-knowing and all-powerful, permit the existence of evil? So asks the simple Huron in Voltaire's tale, and thereby confounds the learned men of the church. The theodicy problem in its secular version — man's explanation to himself of the existence of evil — is as intriguing and as perplexing. Disease and pestilence, bigotry and rape, theft and murder, pillage and war, appear as constants in world history. Why is this so? Can one explain war and malevolence in the same way? Is war simply mass malevolence, and thus an explanation of malevolence an explanation of the evils to which men in society are prey? Many have thought so.

> For though it were granted us by divine indulgence to be exempt from all that can be harmful to us from without [writes John Milton], yet the perverseness of our folly is so bent, that we should never cease hammering out of our own hearts, as it were out of a flint, the seeds and sparkles of new misery to ourselves, till all were in a blaze again.

Our miseries are ineluctably the product of our natures. The root of all evil is man, and thus he is himself the root of the specific evil, war. This estimate of cause, widespread and firmly held by many as an article of faith, has been immensely influential. It is the conviction of St Augustine and Luther, of Malthus and Jonathan Swift, of Dean Inge and Reinhold Niebuhr. In secular terms, with men defined as beings of intermixed reason and passion in whom passion repeatedly triumphs, the belief has informed the philosophy, including the political philosophy, of Spinoza. One might argue that it was as influential in the activities of Bismarck, with his low opinion of his fellow man, as it was in the rigorous and austere writings of Spinoza. If one's beliefs condition his expectations and his expectations condition his acts, acceptance or rejection of Milton's statement becomes important in the affairs of men. And, of course, Milton might be right even if no one believed him. If so, attempts to explain the recurrence of war in terms of, let us say, economic factors, might still be interesting games, but they would be games of little consequence. If it is true, as Dean Swift once said, that 'the very same principle that influences a bully to break the windows of a whore who has jilted him, naturally stirs up a great prince to raise mighty armies, and dream of nothing but sieges, battles, and victories', then the reasons given by princes for the wars they have waged are mere rationalizations covering a motivation they may not themselves have perceived and could not afford to state openly if they had. It would follow as well that the schemes of the statesman Sully, if seriously intended to produce a greater peace in the world, were as idle as the dreams of the French monk Crucé — idle, that is, unless one can strike at the roots, the pride and petulance that have produced the wars as they have the other ills that plague mankind.

There are many who have agreed with Milton that men must look to man in order to understand social and political events, but who differ on what man's nature is, or can become. There are many others who, in effect, quarrel with the major premise. Does man make society in his image or does society make him? It was to be expected, in a time when philosophy was little more than a branch of theology, that the theologian-philosophers would attribute to human agency what many philosophers before and since have described as the effects of the polity itself. Rousseau, among many who could be mentioned, makes a clean break with the view that, man being a social animal, one can explain his behavior in society by pointing to his animal passion and/or his human reason. Man is born and in his natural condition remains neither good nor bad. It is society that is the degrading force in men's lives, but it is the moralizing agency as well. And this latter effect Rousseau was unwilling to surrender even had he thought it possible for men to retreat to the state of nature. This is his position, consistently reflected in his various works, though the myth persists that he believed the savage noble and lamented the advent of society. Man's behavior, his very nature, which some have taken as cause, is, according to Rousseau, in great part a product of the society in which he lives. And society, he avers, is inseparable from political organization. In the absence of an organized power, which as a minimum must serve as the adjudicating authority, it is impossible for men to live together with even a modicum of peace. The study of society cannot be separated from the study of government, or the study of man from either. Rousseau, like Plato, believes that a bad polity makes men bad, and a good polity makes them good. This is not to say that the state is the potter and man a lump of clay posing no resistance to the shape the artist would impart. There are, as Rousseau recognized, similarities among men wherever they may live. There are also differences, and the search for causes is an attempt to explain these differences. The explanation of consequence — whether one is worried about the recurrence of theft or of war — is to be found in studying the varying social relations of men, and this in turn requires the study of politics.

Can man in society best be understood by studying man or by studying society? The most satisfactory reply would seem to be given by striking the word 'or' and answering 'both'. But where one begins his explanation of events makes a difference. The Reverend Thomas Malthus once wrote that, 'though human institutions appear to be the obvious and obtrusive causes of much mischief to mankind; yet, in reality, they are light and superficial, they are mere feathers that float on the surface, in comparison with those deeper seated causes of impurity that corrupt the springs, and render turbid the whole stream of human life'. Rousseau looked at the same world, the same range of events, but found the locus of major causes in a different ambit.

Following Rousseau's lead in turn raises questions. As men live in states, so states exist in a world of states. If we now confine our attention to the question of why wars occur, shall we emphasize the role of the state, with its social and economic content as well as its political form, or shall we concentrate primarily on what is sometimes called the society of states? Again one may say strike the word 'or' and worry about both, but many have emphasized either the first or the second, which helps to explain the discrepant conclusions reached. Those who emphasize the first in a sense run parallel to Milton. He explains the ills of the world by the evil in man; they explain the great ill of war by the evil qualities of some or of all states. The statement is then often reversed: if bad states make wars, good states would live at peace with one another. With varying degrees of justification this view can be attributed to Plato and Kant, to nineteenth-century liberals and revisionist socialists. They agree on the principle involved, though they differ in their descriptions of good states as well as on the problem of bringing about their existence.

Where Marxists throw the liberals' picture of the world into partial eclipse, others blot it out entirely. Rousseau himself finds the major causes of war neither in men nor in states but in the state system itself. Of men in a state of nature, he had pointed out that one man cannot begin to behave decently unless he has some assurance that others will not be able to ruin him. This thought Rousseau develops and applies to states existing in a condition of anarchy in his fragmentary essay on 'The State of War' and in his commentaries on the works of the Abbé de Saint-Pierre. Though a state may want to remain at peace, it may have to consider undertaking a preventative war; for if it does not strike when the moment is favorable it may be struck later when the advantage has shifted to the other side. This view forms the analytic basis for many balance-of-power approaches to international relations and for the world-federalist program as well. Implicit in Thucydides and Alexander Hamilton, made explicit by Machiavelli, Hobbes, and Rousseau, it is at once a generalized explanation of states' behavior and a critical *point d'appui* against those who look to the internal structure of states to explain their external behavior. While some believe that peace will follow from the improvement of states, others assert that what the state will be like depends on its relation to others. The latter thesis Leopold Ranke derived from, or applied to, the history of the states of modern Europe. It has been used to explain the internal ordering of other states as well.

Statesmen, as well as philosophers and historians, have attempted to account for the behavior of states in peace and in war. Woodrow Wilson, in the draft of a note written in November of 1916, remarked that the causes of the war then being fought were obscure, that neutral nations did not know why it had begun and, if drawn in, would not know for what ends they would be fighting. But often to act we must convince ourselves that we do know the answers to such questions. Wilson, to his own satisfaction, soon did. He appears in history as one of the many who, drawing a sharp distinction between peaceful and aggressive states, have assigned to democracies all the attributes of the first, to authoritarian states all the attributes of the second. To an extent that varies with the author considered, the incidence of war is then thought to depend upon the type of national government. Thus Cobden in a speech at Leeds in December of 1849:

Where do we look for the black gathering cloud of war? Where do we see it rising? Why, from the despotism of the north, where one man wields the destinies of 40,000,000 of serfs. If we want to know where is the second danger of war and disturbance, it is in that province of Russia — that miserable and degraded country, Austria — next in the stage of despotism and barbarism, and there you see again the greatest danger of war, but in proportion as you find the population governing themselves — as in England, in France, or in America — there you will find that war is not the disposition of the people, and that if Government desire it, the people would put a check upon it.

The constant interest of the people is in peace; no government controlled by the people will fight unless set upon. But only a few years later, England, though not set upon, did fight against Russia; and Cobden lost his seat in 1857 as a result of his opposition to the war. The experience is shattering, but not fatal to the belief; for it relives in the words of Wilson, for example, and again in those of the late Senator Robert Taft. In the manner of Cobden but in the year 1951, Taft writes: 'History shows that when the people have the opportunity to speak they as a rule decide for peace if possible. It shows that arbitrary rulers are more inclined to favor war than are the people at any time.' Is it true, one wonders, that there is a uniquely peaceful form of the state? If it were true, how much would it matter? Would it enable some states to know which other states they could trust? Should the states that are already good seek ways of making other states better, and thus make it possible for all men to enjoy the pleasures of peace? Wilson believed it morally imperative to aid in the political regeneration of others; Cobden thought it not even justifiable. Agreeing on where the causes are to be found, they differ in their policy conclusions.

But what of those who incline to a different estimate of major causes? 'Now people', President Dwight Eisenhower has said, 'don't want conflict — people in general. It is only, I think, mistaken leaders that grow too belligerent and believe that people really want to fight.' Though apparently not all people want peace badly enough, for, on a different occasion, he had this to say: 'If the mothers in every land could teach their children to understand the homes and hopes of children in every other land — in America, in Europe, in the Near East, in Asia — the cause of peace in the world would indeed be nobly served.' Here the President seems to agree with Milton on where cause is to be found, but without Milton's pessimism — or realism, depending on one's preconceptions. Aggressive tendencies may be inherent, but is their misdirection inevitable? War begins in the minds and emotions of men, as all acts do; but can minds and emotions be changed? And, if one agrees that they can be, how much and how fast can whose minds and feelings be changed? And, if other factors are relevant as well, how much difference would the changes make? The answers to these questions and to those of the preceding paragraph are not obvious, but they are important. How can they best be sought?

Some would suggest taking possible answers as hypotheses to be investigated and tested empirically. This is difficult. Most English liberals at the time of the First World War argued, as did Wilson, that the militarist and authoritarian character of the German state prompted Germany to seek the war that soon spread to most of the world. At the same time some liberals, most notably G. Lowes Dickinson, argued that no single state could be held guilty. Only by understanding the international system, or lack of system, by which the leaders of states were often forced to act with slight regard for conventional morality, could one understand and justly assess the processes by which the war was produced. Dickinson was blasted by liberals and socialists alike for reversing the dominant inside-out explanation. Acceptance or rejection of explanatory theses in matters such as this most often depends on the skill of the pleaders and the mood of the audience. These are obviously not fit criteria, yet it would be foolish to argue that simply by taking a more intensive look at the data a compelling case could be built for one or the other explanatory theory. Staring at the same set of data, the parties to the debate came to sharply different conclusions, for the images they entertained led them to select and interpret the data in different ways. In order to make sense of the liberals' hypothesis we need somehow to acquire an idea of the interrelation of many possibly relevant factors, and these interrelations are not given in the data we study. We establish or, rather, assert them ourselves. To say 'establish' would be dangerous, for, whether or not we label them as such, we cannot escape from philosophic assumptions. The idea we entertain becomes a filter through which we pass our data. If the data are selected carefully, they will pass like milk through cheesecloth. The recalcitrance of the data may cause us to change one filter for another, to modify or scrap the theory we hold — or it may produce ever more ingenious selection and interpretation of data, as has happened with many Marxists trying to salvage the thesis that with the development of capitalism the masses become increasingly impoverished.

If empirical investigations vary in incidence and in result with the ideas the empiricists entertain, it is worth asking ourselves if the ideas themselves can be subjected to scrutiny. Obviously they can be. The study of politics is distinguished from other social studies by concentration upon the institutions and processes of government. This focuses the political scientists' concern without constituting a self-denying ordinance against the use of materials and techniques of other social scientists. On the latter point there is no difficulty for the student of international relations; there is considerable difficulty on the former, for international relations are characterized by the absence of truly governmental institutions, which in turn gives a radically different twist to the relevant processes. Yet there is a large and important sense in which traditional political philosophy, concentrating as it does upon domestic politics, is relevant for the student of international relations. Peace, it is often said, is the problem of the twentieth century. It is also one of the continuing concerns of political philosophers. In times of relative quiescence the question men put is likely to be: what good is life without justice and freedom? Better to die than live a slave. In times of domestic troubles, of hunger and civil war, of pressing insecurity, however, many will ask: of what use is freedom without a power sufficient to establish and maintain conditions of security? That life takes priority over justice and freedom is taken to be a self-evident truth by St Augustine and Luther, by Machiavelli, Bodin, and Hobbes. If the alternative to tyranny is chaos and if chaos means a war of all against all, then the willingness to endure tyranny becomes understandable. In the absence of order there can be no enjoyment of liberty. The problem of identifying and achieving the conditions of peace, a problem that plagues man and bedevils the student of international relations, has, especially in periods of crisis, bedeviled political philosophers as well.

R.G. Collingwood once suggested that the best way to understand the writings of philosophers is to seek out the questions they were attempting to answer. It is here suggested that the best way to examine the problems of international political theory is to pose a central question and identify the answers that can be given to it. One may seek in political philosophy answers to the question: where are the major causes of war to be found? The answers are bewildering in their variety and in their contradictory qualities. To make this variety manageable, the answers can be ordered under the following three headings: within man, within the structure of the separate states, within the state system. The basis of this ordering, as well as its relevance in the world of affairs, is suggested in the preceding pages. These three estimates of cause will subsequently be referred to as images of international relations, numbered in the order given, with each image defined according to where one locates the nexus of important causes.

Previous comments indicate that the views comprised by any one image may in some senses be as contradictory as are the different images *inter se*. The argument that war is inevitable because men are irrevocably bad, and the argument that wars can be ended because men can be changed, are contradictory; but since in each of them individuals are taken to be the locus of cause, both are included in the first image. Similarly, acceptance of a third-image analysis may lead to the false optimism of the world federalists or to the often falsely defined pessimism of a *Realpolitik* position. Since in all respects but one there may be variety of opinion within images and since prescription is related to goal as well as to analysis, there is no one prescription for each image. There are, however, in relation to each image-goal pairing, logical and illogical prescriptions.

One can say that a prescription is wrong if he can show that following it does not bring about the predicted result. But can one ever show that a prescription was actually followed? One often hears statements like this: 'The League of Nations didn't fail; it was never tried.' And such statements are irrefutable. But even if empirical disproof were possible, the problem of proving a prescription valid would remain to be solved. A patient who in one period of illness tries ten different medications may wonder just which pill produced the cure. The apportioning of credit is often more difficult than the assigning of blame. If a historical study were to show that in country A increases in national prosperity always followed increases in tariffs, to some observers this might seem to prove that high tariffs are a cause of prosperity; to others, that both of these factors are dependent on a third; and to still others, nothing at all. The empirical approach, though necessary, is not sufficient. The correlation of events means nothing, or at least should not be taken to mean anything, apart from the analysis that accompanies it.

If there is no empirical solution to the problem of prescription verification, what solution is there? Prescription is logically impossible apart from analysis. Every prescription for greater peace in the world is then related to one of our three images of international relations, or to some combination of them. An understanding of the analytical terms of each of the images will open up two additional possibilities for accepting or rejecting prescriptions. (1) A prescription based on a faulty analysis would be unlikely to produce the desired consequences. The assumption that to improve men in a prescribed way will serve to promote peace rests on the further assumption that in some form the first image of international relations is valid. The latter assumption should be examined before the former is made. (2) A prescription would be unacceptable if it were not logically related to its analysis. One who suffers from infected tonsils profits little from a skilfully performed appendectomy. If violence among states is caused by the evilness of man, to aim at the internal reform of states will not do much good. And if violence among states is the product of international anarchy, to aim at the conversion of individuals can accomplish little. One man's prognosis confounds the other man's prescription. If the validity of the images themselves can be ascertained, the critical relating of prescription to image becomes a check on the validity of prescriptions. There is, however, an additional complicating factor. Some combination of our three images, rather than any one of them, may be required for an accurate understanding of international relations. We may not be in a situation where one can consider just the patient's tonsils or his appendix. Both may be infected but removing either may kill the patient. In other words, understanding the likely consequences of any one cause may depend on understanding its relation to other causes. The possible interrelation of causes makes the problem of estimating the merit of various prescriptions more difficult still.

What are the criteria of merit? Suppose we consider again the person who argues that 'bad' states produce war, that 'good' states would live peacefully together, that therefore we must bring states into accord with a prescribed pattern. To estimate the merit of such a series of propositions requires asking the following questions: (1) Can the final proposition be implemented, and if so, how? (2) Is there a logical relation between prescription and image? In other words, does the prescription attack the assigned causes? (3) Is the image adequate, or has the analyst simply seized upon the most spectacular cause or the one he thinks most susceptible to manipulation and ignored other causes of equal or greater importance? (4) How will attempts to fill the prescription affect other goals? This last question is necessary since peace is not the only goal of even the most peacefully inclined men or states. One may, for example, believe that world government and perpetual peace are synonymous, but one may also be convinced that a world state would be a world tyranny and therefore prefer a system of nation-states with a perpetual danger of war to a world state with a promise of perpetual peace. [. . .]

11 THE GENERAL STRIKE (extract)

G.A. Phillips

Source: *The General Strike* (Weidenfeld and Nicholson, 1976), Chapter XII, pp.264-74; and pp.293-5.

The expressions of outrage which greeted the end of the General Strike had been fully and fearfully anticipated. 'We shall be told we have betrayed the miners. We will get it in the neck, sure', Tillett told Herbert Samuel on the eve of its termination. When the news was relayed to the strikers in the country, Eccleston Square was exposed to a barrage of phone calls and messages from local organizations, at first apprehensive, then increasingly accusatory. The fierceness of the reaction was greater because, in some cases, the conclusion of the stoppage had been interpreted as a sign that a victory had been secured. When the worst news was confirmed, deputations were sent to London from as far away as Newcastle to confront those responsible for the capitulation.

Widespread and emotional as this popular condemnation was, however, it was not clearly focussed nor without certain qualifying nuances. In the first place criticism did not usually lead — except from Communist sources — to a demand for the renewal of the General Strike. The firm allegiance of local strike bodies to the TUC was, to this extent, unaffected by the decision of the latter to call off the stoppage. The miners' leadership did not attempt to resist the resumption of work, and while their lodges across the country might have been more disposed to urge an unofficial prolongation of sympathetic action, the geographical isolation of the miners' organizations curtailed the possibility of their influencing other workers. Moreover, the circumstances in which the stoppage had ended diverted attention from the General Council itself to its constituent unions, who were made responsible for the return to work — and thus from the desertion of the miners to the terms and conditions imposed upon strikers by their own employers. Union branch meetings were apt to direct their displeasure against their own leadership rather than against the TUC. Significantly, too, the protests reaching the General Council itself, which were partially analyzed by its research department, were found to be levelled more frequently at its failure to secure guarantees against victimization than at any other alleged delinquency. The rank and file of his own union, Bevin asserted later, were not much concerned about 'who was right and who was wrong at the General Council [but] ... whether we could have got them back better'.

Few union executives joined the chorus of denunciation — most preferring to observe, as long as possible, a diplomatic silence on the circumstances of the strike's conclusion. The principal exception was the Amalgamated Society of Woodworkers, which adopted a resolution on 13 May, circulated subsequently to all the affiliates of the TUC, expressing 'grave concern at the instruction received from the Trades Union Congress that the General Strike initiated by that body with the full approval of the affiliated unions had been called off without the consideration of the unions concerned', and demanding an immediate reconvention of the special executive conference. This view was endorsed by the Electrical Trades Union and NATSOPA, but by no other organization of importance.

The General Council and its Critics

The indictment of the General Council depended primarily, of course, on the strength of the miners' case. But their attack was also, for various reasons, inconsistently pursued and relatively ineffectual. Its conduct was left, at least initially, largely in the hands of Arthur Cook, whose outspoken public speeches after the stoppage were supplemented by the publication, early in June, of his own account of the strike in the pamphlet, *The Nine Days*. Cook's denunciatory rhetoric exposed him, however, to counter-charges of distortion, self-contradiction and personal animus, discrediting his argument at least in official quarters. But the other miners' leaders, like their fellow-executives, were reluctant to engage in open recriminations — though their word might in some cases have carried more weight — both because of the damage likely to be sustained by the movement in the process of internal conflict, and more particularly because of their continued dependence on the TUC and its constituents for a measure of financial and moral support during the lock-out. The Federation's council did not finally publish their own statement on the crisis until immediately before the conference of union executives in January 1927. Even in making this belated submission, moreover, they still revealed a certain uncertainty over whether to fashion their criticisms to appeal to the prejudices of the officers of other organizations — which implied emphasizing the largely constitutional issue raised by the woodworkers of the impropriety of the method by which the strike had been ended — or to concentrate upon their own sectional grievances, especially the unacceptability of the Samuel memorandum, at the risk of appearing unduly self interested. In the end their case was weakened by the element of ambiguity, even of disingenuousness, which it displayed.

It was however the miners' delay in launching their attack, not its inherent lack of conviction, which did most to diminish its force. Faced with the popular outcry against its treachery and incompetence after the

strike, the General Council itself favoured recalling the conference of
executives without delay to endeavour to rebut the accusations directed
against it. As soon as the reports of its various subcommittees had been
drafted and approved, therefore (and a document prepared, based on that
of the Negotiating Committee, for distribution to the executive delegates)
the Council summoned the meeting of its constituents for 25 June. But at
its session on the seventeenth the MFGB representatives, Smillie and
Richards, urged their colleagues that the issue of the TUC statement at this
point 'would be most damaging to the Miners' cause'. The date of the conference was discussed again on 22 June, when a considerable section of the
Council still wished to see it take place and a motion to send out the official
report was declared 'not carried' after twelve votes had been cast for and
against. That evening the Council eventually agreed with the miners' officials
to postpone the conference, on condition that Cook's pamphlet was withdrawn from sale, that public attacks on their own members ceased and that
the Federation refrained from advocating further an embargo on coal or a
financial levy without the consent of other unions.

The rule of silence thus enacted was not wholly observed. At the TUC
in September, for example, miners' and left-wing delegates shouted down
John Bromley, the ASLEF secretary, who had written a fierce attack on
the MFGB leadership and policy in his union journal. But further controversy was successfully damped down both by Pugh's circumspect presidential
address and by the General Council's insistence that any debate on the
strike be left to the delayed conference of executives. A Communist motion
objecting to this decision, unsupported by the miners, received only three
quarters of a million block votes.

By the time the trade union executives assembled to consider the General
Strike (and the General Council's activities during the mining lock-out
which followed) there was a natural inclination to avoid opening old wounds.
Except in the coal industry itself the effects of the struggles of the past year
had been less drastic than previously feared. A broad 'capitalist offensive'
still showed no signs of materializing; even the unemployment and victimization which had followed the General Strike had been reduced to modest
proportions. On the other hand both the necessity of concerting resistance
to the apprehended Conservative legislation on trade disputes, and equally
the anxiety not to dissipate the political success which recent by-election
gains promised to the Labour Party, sustained a desire for unity. The miners'
executive, for its part, was increasingly reluctant to associate itself with the
more extreme viewpoint of Communist critics who had lambasted the
Federation's own retirement from the battle with the mine-owners the
previous month. Nor, of course, was it any longer apparent what tangible

benefit the miners themselves would gain from the inquisition which they now chose to advocate.

The miners' attack on the General Council can be broken down into a number of separate charges, at least three of which had also been made by the woodworkers and other disaffected members of Congress:

1. That the TUC leadership had failed to undertake the preparations necessary to ensure the effective organization of the General Strike.
2. That the Council had exceeded its authority in accepting the terms of settlement without referring them to the conference of executives for approval.
3. That it had failed to obtain guarantees protecting the strikers against victimization.

For those accusations concerning their own maltreatment by the General Council, the miners had little overt support except from the unofficial left:

4. That the MFGB representatives had been insufficiently consulted during the Council's negotiations with the government immediately before the stoppage, or the talks with Samuel during it.
5. That the Samuel memorandum had been accepted without any assurance of the government's readiness to observe its terms.
6. That those terms, in acquiescing in the necessity of wage reductions, were themselves inconsistent with the resolution empowering the Council to order a general strike.

The General Council's own report to the conference, much longer than the Federation's statement, consisted chiefly of a detailed narrative of its various diplomatic activities between 1 and 12 May. It afforded *explicit* answers only to the last two of the charges set out above, though the defence it offered on other counts was either implicit in its rendering of the history of the negotiations, or else was provided by its spokesmen in the course of the conference debate. To the six articles of indictment, the response, direct or indirect, was thus as follows:

1. Elaborate preparations for a general strike were impractical in view of the limited constitutional authority and financial resources of the General Council; to have undertaken them would simply have led to further counter-measures on the government's part and impeded negotiations.

2. The General Council regarded the first conference of union executives as having given it full powers to negotiate a settlement provided it respected the main principles of the memorandum submitted to it (*The Coal Crisis*), and treated the withdrawal of the mining lock-out as a *sine qua non*. In effect this charge was thus met by the defence of the Samuel memorandum. The Council also argued that 'If . . . the strike was to be terminated with a maximum of advantage to the miners and the other unions, a decision [had to be] reached whilst the unions remained both strong and disciplined'; procedural delays were clearly undesirable.

3. The avoidance of victimization, like the implementation of the orders to strike in the first instance, was, according to Arthur Pugh, a responsibility which individual unions could not constitutionally delegate. Furthermore, only a handful of replies were received to Citrine's telegram of 13 May instructing affiliated organizations to seek negotiations with their employers 'and report forthwith'. It was to ease the problem of reinstatement, Thomas noted, that the Council had urged the miners, without effect, to resume work alongside other unions.

4. The Council did not meet the miners' specific complaints, that they had no representatives present at its meetings during the strike, or at the majority of the conversations with Sir Herbert Samuel. But this issue hinged on a larger one: by turning down successive 'bases of negotiation' worked out with Samuel, the Federation had asserted a *de facto* power to decide collective policy on behalf of the TUC which it did not rightfully possess. An absolute veto, indiscriminately exercised, made 'consultation' futile.

5. The Council, as has been shown, maintained that the acceptance of the Samuel memorandum by the miners would have brought about a situation in which the government would have felt obliged to adopt it; but they did not answer the miners' further point, that since they were aware of the Federation's objections to the memorandum on 12 May, they were dishonest in claiming to other unions that an understanding involving the withdrawal of the lock-out had been reached and remained intact.

6. The Council admitted, as it was bound to do, that it had agreed in principle to a reduction in the miners' wages. 'Every Executive here has always set out, and always will set out, in wage negotiations with a certain programme', said Thomas, 'but every Executive . . . knows perfectly well that they must and do reach a point where they have got to determine on balance what is best.' At the same time, it was

contended that the terms of the Samuel memorandum were consistent in all essentials with the statement submitted to the union executive conference on 29 April (*The Coal Crisis*), and with the proposals drafted by the Council's subcommittee in co-operation with the miners' officials on 3 May. *The Mining Dispute* contained an elaborate appendix setting out in parallel columns the corresponding clauses of the three documents (together with those of the government offer of 14 May). The willingness of the Council to require the miners to accept a revision in wages was justified partly by reference to the jointly devised terms of 3 May, and partly, once again, by Herbert Smith's eve-of-strike statements on his attitude to the Royal Commission report.

Manifestly the General Council could not acquit itself fully of charges of betraying, or at least misleading, both the miners and its own constituent unions. It omitted to mention the discussions which had taken place in the Negotiating Committee on the subject of strike preparations; gave only the briefest indication of the concern which it had felt about the durability of the stoppage and none of its fear of indiscipline; and not surprisingly disguised its own confusion over the status of the Samuel memorandum. If its arguments nonetheless prevailed, this was probably for two overriding reasons. Firstly, most union executives accepted its view, without need of elaborate demonstration, that a continuation of the General Strike would have brought it no nearer to success, but rather entailed its defeat 'by a process of attrition which would have disorganised the Trade Union movement . . . completely established the reactionary elements in the country, and damned any possibility of getting a fair consideration of the miners' case'; and that in these circumstances the terms of the Samuel memorandum, however unofficial, represented a reasonable basis of negotiation. Secondly, what rested on the endorsement of the Council's judgements was not just its prestige, but its legitimacy as a representative organ of the movement. The miners were regarded as having denied its powers of determining the general interest, and their claim to have done so in the name of some higher court, or in accordance with some original and binding contract, were in the end seen to be untenable.

Such hopes as the miners may have entertained of carrying the conference with them were dispelled by the character and course of the debate. The chairman, George Hicks, appealed to the participants to avoid a display of animosity, and his plea was uniformly obeyed. There was on this occasion none of the visible ill-feeling seen at the meeting of Congress four months earlier. Arthur Pugh, opening the case of the General Council, created an atmosphere of sobriety, and even of torpor, by reading the whole of the official report to the delegates. In the exchanges which followed, the contrasting dialectical skills of Bevin, Thomas and Citrine far excelled those of Smith and Cook. But since more attention was devoted on both sides to the course of the conversations at Eccleston Square and Downing Street during the nine days, than to the major issues allegedly in dispute, the union representatives present were unlikely to have been swayed from an initial predisposition to vindicate the Council and to put an end to an unwanted controversy. The miners' proposal to refer the General Council's report to the membership of its affiliated organizations for further discussion offered no resolution, and cast doubt on the capacity of the executives to make up their own mind. It received the support of the woodworkers and a few small unions, but was easily defeated, soon after the conference had entered its second day, by 2,840,000 votes to 1,095,000.

The General Strike Interpreted

In retrospect, and to the detached observer, the discussion which followed the General Strike appears irritatingly superficial and the lessons drawn from this experience disappointingly unperceptive. Most union leaders remained, in the aftermath, unwilling to admit the inherent deficiencies of this industrial weapon or their own error in resorting to it. The stoppage continued to be measured as a triumph of solidarity and organization without regard to its tactical and industrial objectives. Within a few weeks of its termination, two of the General Council's members, Hicks and Purcell – endeavouring perhaps to restore their reputation as left-wingers – were writing that the rank-and-file response to the strike call represented a union victory in itself, and that the continued concentration of capitalist forces might necessitate a repetition of the effort. Even those more noted for their moderation expressed similar opinions. In his presidential address to the Bournemouth TUC Pugh suggested a view of the General Strike little altered by the experience:

> When the unions combined their forces last May, they were not invoking any new principle of industrial action, but simply asserting more effectively on a large scale the traditional Trade Union refusal to accept dictated terms of employment whether from employers or the Government. As a means of resisting such settlements in industrial disputes, the weapon used by the unions last May will not be left unused when it is sought to enforce upon any section of the workers terms which have not been made the subject of negotiation and collective agreement.

The expression of these sentiments no doubt reflected a wish among leading trade unionists to undo the psychological damage of defeat, but they were not for that reason insincere. And the explanation of the failure of the General Strike which may be distilled from them, facile though it was, suffered no private or retrospective criticism. According to this inter-pretation, the unhappy outcome of the stoppage was to be attributed, firstly to the obstinacy of the miners, and secondly to the prominence given by the government to the factitious question of constitutional security. The Conservative administration, according to *The Mining Dispute*, ' ingen-iously obscured their own position as a third party in the dispute by raising constitutional issues and treating a sympathetic strike on industrial issues as a political movement'. At the September Congress Arthur Pugh had earned applause from his audience for making this same point: 'It was not the unions but the Government which endeavoured to convert an industrial struggle into a political conflict, and sought to make party capital out of it. Nothing but the restraint, forbearance and good sense of our members prevented the agents of the Government fomenting a revolutionary temper and plunging the country into conditions of civil war.' Even some of those who claimed to have opposed the declaration of a general strike, like J.H. Thomas, appear to have subscribed to the same view, that the fate of the stoppage was sealed by the 'constitutional issue' being 'falsely raised' and 'unfairly used'.

For a greater logic and a more decisive verdict it is necessary to look outside the trade union movement, to socialist politicians of left and right. After the event, and from their differing vantage points, both Labour and Communist Party leaders affirmed that the General Strike was *inherently* a political act, that the General Council's enduring assumption that 'industrial' and 'political' objectives would be rigidly separated was fundamentally mistaken, that, accordingly, *any* government faced by an attack of this kind would be bound to adopt an unyielding stance. To the spokesmen of the Parliamentary Labour Party this conviction precluded any resort to a general strike for conventional union purposes. 'We learned', avowed J.R. Clynes, 'that a national strike could not be used as a weapon in a trade dispute . . . There is one way, and one only, to alter unfair conditions in Britain. It is through the ballot box, and not through violence or resistance.' And MacDonald, in the *Socialist Review*, wrote in similar vein:

The General Strike is a weapon that cannot be used for industrial purposes. It is clumsy and ineffectual. It has no goal which when reached can be regarded as victory. If fought to a finish as a Strike, it would ruin Trade Unionism, and the Government in the meantime could create a revolution; if fought to a finish only as a means to an end, the men responsible for decisions will be charged with betrayal. . . . The real blame is with the General Strike itself and those who preached it without considering it and induced the workers to blunder into it. It was not (because of its nature it could not be) of help to the miners. . . . I hope that the result will be a thorough reconsideration of Trade Union tactics. Large industrial operations of either offence or defence cannot be planned by platform speeches. If the wonderful unity in the Strike which impressed the whole world with the solidarity of British labour would be shown in politics, labour could solve mining and similar difficulties through the ballot box.

The Communist *Theses on the General Strike*, presented to their October Congress, were *mutatis mutandis* equally definite about the futility of the General Council's conception of it.

The fact that every mass strike is a political strike was clearly revealed in spite of the denials of the General Council. The basic industries were stopped, not to coerce the mineowners, but to coerce the Government. The General Council was objectively decreeing that no newspapers should be printed, that no food should be transported without its permission, or that of its local organizations, that no person could travel to or from work by the recognized public means. To render these prohibitions effective, its local organs had to enter into conflict with the emergency organizations of the Government. It had to call upon the workers to be loyal to their unions, which was in effect to be disloyal to the Government, which was locked in conflict with those unions. The germs of alternative Government were apparent. . . .

The technical weakness of the strike plan followed from the General Council's attitude. They believed that the Government in the existing situation was impregnable and sought for an excuse to call off the strike. When the Government raised the cry of 'The Constitution in danger', they weakly denied that they were challenging the Government (which, if true, would have made the strike purposeless). The strike was either aiming at coercing the Government, representing the capitalists as a whole, or it was nothing.

Whilst these strictures had an undoubted plausibility, however, such *post hoc* wisdom did nothing to *explain* the confusion which it discerned in the behaviour of the General Council, still less to demonstrate an alternative course of action which would obviously have brought greater success. The

TUC leadership was indeed vacillating and confused. But its critics failed to appreciate that the economic and political situation to which it was responding was itself obscure and ambiguous. Thus on the one hand the memory of a 'capitalist offensive' against organized labour during the post-war depression was still fresh in the minds of the union leadership, whilst on the other, outside the mining industry, the evidence of an immediate threat to working-class standards in 1926 was slight; the General Strike was the echo rather than the voice of class war. This receding memory also explains why the General Council were on the one hand impelled to resort to a general strike by rank-and-file enthusiasm for and faith in this tactic, but on the other hand lacked the means of sustaining that enthusiasm. There may have been 'a great wave of emotion and resentment against the attempt to use the weapon of [the] lock-out to starve the miners into submission'; but unending sacrifices could not be demanded from sympathy and nothing more. By the very act of involving other unions in the conflict the Council highlighted differences of interest, for not all organizations were equally involved nor all combatants equally resilient, nor all wage-earners equally assured of reinstatement. Finally, whilst on the one hand the Conservative Government did display some partiality for the views of the mine-owners during the crisis, on the other hand it could not credibly be portrayed as an administration of pure reaction, nor even of blatantly capitalist sympathies; in consequence, its overthrow could never be seen by the majority as a *sine qua non* of the winning of concessions on the mining question. In short, it is obvious that the General Strike had specific and substantial causes more potent than the 'muddled philosophy' of its leadership; but that these causes were, of their very nature, certain to moderate the goals in view and to inhibit the manner of its conduct. Only in the light of these complex circumstances can one understand the paradox, that the General Council entered the strike with the utmost reluctance yet remained, after the event, sure that the enterprise had been morally justified. [. . .]

Conclusion

Only in a very modest and unspectacular fashion, therefore, did the General Strike alter the ideas or the behaviour of the union movement. It reinforced a trend towards industrial peace that was already under way, and it confirmed a long-established faith in a regulated system of voluntary collective bargaining. Its chief effect, however, was simply to change the movement's rhetorical style, the tone of its public discourse. This meant that to some extent the unions presented a different and more acceptable image to the outside world. It also entailed an adjustment, more significant but more difficult to assess, in the relations of the union leadership with its rank and file. The attention now given to maintaining the morale of the membership, and perhaps to encouraging their active involvement in organizations that were democratic at least in aspiration, appears to have diminished. Even so, the degree of alienation which resulted is demonstrable only in the case of that organized left-wing movement within the unions whose criticisms of officialdom were probably too extreme to be widely accepted and whose militancy was too undiscriminating to be generally popular. In the long run it is possible that the decline of a conspicuous idealism, the loss of a radical aura, did affect the motives which caused men to join trade unions and the extent to which members participated in their affairs. Yet so broad a judgement is not only resistant to proof, but risks doing injustice to the diversity of character and outlook which the movement still accommodated.

In the end the General Strike merits historical study less for what it changed in the labour movement, than for what it revealed of the unchanging. It was the product of a trade unionism which, though it seemed to contain many inconsistent features, was still too stable a compound to be transformed by so short a process. The union movement was so durable in its make-up, as it revealed on this occasion, because it was predominantly defensive in its objectives, disinclined to state its purposes in ideological terms, concerned primarily with the achievement of an effective organization and internal discipline, not with any long-term programme of social and political reconstruction. Not only was the General Strike justified by reference to these relatively unambitious standards in the first instance; it could also be reckoned subsequently, on the same basis, by no means a total failure. The relations of the unions with the social system of which they were part were similarly difficult to disturb. The conditions to which the organized working class were subject were far from uniform and the social resentments they created were equally variable. But in every case — even in the coal industry — hostility to the capitalist order was moderated by the very fact of the survival of a powerful trade union organization. Moreover the crisis of 1926 served to indicate how far the leaders and members of these institutions shared, especially in the political sphere, the values of their fellow-citizens: the belief in constitutional modes of government, in the virtues of legality, in a pragmatic and conciliatory approach to potentially disruptive social issues. Neither the grievances which had brought about the General Strike nor the inhibitions which had limited its scope and shortened its course were much affected by the experience of it; one or even two generations later they were scarcely less in evidence.

12 RUSSIA: 'SOCIALISM IN ONE COUNTRY'

Alec Nove

Source: *Stalinism and After* (Allen and Unwin, 1975), pp.29-37.

The Great Debate: Socialism in One Country

> Oh ye, whose task it is
> To put between high banks of concrete
> Our country's stormy and anarchic waters,
> More severe, even more grim than he,
> You follow Lenin's road.

In these words the poet Esenin addressed Lenin's heirs. Esenin himself loved old peasant Russia, and was shortly to commit suicide. Yet he felt instinctively what was to be done, and the coercive logic of the situation.

Let us look at the problems faced by Stalin, or by any other Bolshevik who happened to be in power. If, even in the briefest sketch, things look complicated, the reason is that they *were* exceedingly complicated. Yet to understand what Stalinism was all about, it is necessary to dwell on the problems of the twenties. To see him merely as a power-hungry despot is to see only one aspect of the truth.

There was the problem of *industrialisation*, begun under the Tsars, and disrupted by war and revolution. New and large investments were necessary to carry Russia forward, beyond reconstructing the industries which already existed in 1913. How were the necessary resources to be obtained? There were now no landlords, no large capitalists. Foreign capital was unlikely to be forthcoming, since the Bolsheviks had repudiated past debts. Accumulation and sacrifice would be at the expense of the people, and the bulk of the people were peasants.

Industrialisation had two other aspects. One was military: Russia had a feeble war industry and lacked steel and machinery-making capacity. Yet there she was, isolated in a hostile world. Security considerations provided a sense of urgency. The other aspect was political. Bolshevism rested on the idea of a working-class dictatorship. The working class was small. The survival of the regime in the long run, i.e. its political security, required a much larger proletariat, a large industry. Lenin once put the point vividly: 'Either the political conquests of Soviet power will perish, or we will place them upon an economic foundation. This does not now exist.'

The *peasant problem* was intimately linked with these considerations. The peasants, having seized the landlords' land in 1917-18, were now a conservative or at least non-socialist force, interested in higher prices for food and not in the least interested in financing industrial development. The land was being cultivated in fragmented smallholdings, many of them divided into strips in medieval style, and by antique methods. The traditional peasant communal institution, known as the *mir* or the *obshchina*, controlled the use of the land and in effect ran the villages, rendering the local Soviets largely powerless, especially as the Party had few members in rural areas. Again this raised the issue of political security. But perhaps more important still was the contradiction between peasant agriculture and the needs of industrialisation. The peasants ate better, but sold less of their produce. This was a consequence of the elimination of landlords and of most large peasant (*kulak*) holdings by the revolution, as these had specialised on production for the market instead of their own subsistence.

True, the more enterprising peasants were once again consolidating their holdings, leasing their poorer neighbours' land, setting up as mini-capitalists. This more commercial attitude was economically desirable, no doubt, but appeared politically dangerous to the regime. Tons of ink were devoted to earnest argument about the *kulak* menace. Might it not lead to the domination of the countryside by men whose class interests were anti-Soviet? (It was hoped that the poorer peasants would show more sympathy for Soviet power.) But industrialisation requires more marketings of farm produce, to feed the growing towns and for export. How was it to be obtained?

These problems and dilemmas were an inescapable consequence of the seizure of power by the Bolsheviks in a predominantly peasant country, under conditions of international isolation. Less clear was the choice of a way out.

One group, led by Trotsky, and whose chief theorist was Preobrazhensky, analysed the situation with skill and clarity, but was driven to the conclusion that to 'build socialism' in Russia alone was impossible. They urged a speed-up in industrial investment, greater pressure on the better-off peasants, accused the Stalin group of being soft on *kulaks*, but argued that revolutions in other major countries could alone bring victory. They denounced Stalin's tactics in China, in Germany and elsewhere as inimical to the success of the world communist movement.

The other wing of the Party was most clearly represented by Bukharin, with whom Stalin chose at that time to ally himself. Bukharin believed in NEP, and in an alliance with the bulk of the peasantry. He was conciliatory to the better-off peasants, whom he wished to encourage to grow more produce for the market. This logically called for increased production (and imports) of industrial goods which the peasants wanted. In the long run he expected socialism to be built. 'Socialism in one country' was possible, he asserted, but by cautious stages, 'at the speed of the peasant nag'. To go faster was to endanger the alliance with the peasants and thereby to threaten the stability of the whole Soviet regime. He denounced Trotsky's policy as adventurist, and as lacking faith in Russia.

Trotsky's career has been the subject of a good biography in three volumes by Isaac Deutscher. He was a man of brilliant intellect and eloquence, who rose to prominence as chairman of the St Petersburg Soviet during the disorders of 1905, and subsequently took an independent line, disagreeing with Lenin on many issues. He helped devise the so-called theory of 'permanent revolution', in which the process of revolution not only spreads over the world but must occur continuously within each country. During the First World War, in exile, he took a position similar to Lenin's and soon after his return to Russia in 1917 he joined the Bolshevik Party and was a leading co-worker of Lenin's during the seizure of power, becoming first Commissar of Foreign Affairs and the Commissar for War. In the latter capacity he played a major role in organising the Red Army in the civil war. Despite his eminence, or because of it, he was never 'accepted' by other Bolshevik leaders, and his somewhat arrogant manner did not help. As soon as Lenin's health failed, they tried by every means to discredit Trotsky. His past disagreements with Lenin were magnified, his doctrine of 'permanent revolution' presented as a threat to a hard-won respite; the masses had had enough of revolution.

Stalin accepted the principle of *socialism in one country*, and used Bukharin in the fight to destroy Trotsky and Zinoviev (who, when it was too late, joined Trotsky in defying his ex-ally Stalin). He never went as far as Bukharin in enunciating a pro-peasant policy, but preferred to bide his time, creating meanwhile a politically impregnable position, so that when the clash with Bukharin came the latter had no choice but meek surrender.

Stalin's doctrine had a ready appeal to Party members. Revolution in the West was unlikely for many years to come. What business had the Bolsheviks to rule Russia unless they at least claimed to be building socialism? It was all very well for Trotsky to quote Lenin's words about world revolution and Russia's backwardness. The difficulties faced by an isolated backward Russia were a fact. Yet what was the ruling party to make of its power? The Mensheviks and the Western Social Democrats had criticised them for seizing power 'prematurely', in a situation 'unripe' for socialism. Most Party members must have yearned for a leadership which would confirm their belief that their efforts were not in vain, that success, though difficult, was possible. Stalin could appeal also to a latent nationalism: Russia would show the world a new way of living. This theme too had deep roots: poets like Blok and Voloshin during the revolution, and in past centuries the religious ideologists of 'Moscow the Third Rome'. Truth and righteousness would come to the world from Soviet (or Holy) Russia.

Against such an appeal to political self-preservation, national tradition and harsh realities, Trotsky was powerless. Even without the clever manipulation by Stalin of the party machine, he had lost and he knew it. He saw himself the victim of the self-interest of the party-state bureaucracy, and of the weariness of the people, who had suffered much and were unwilling to listen to prophets of still more (indeed 'permanent') revolution. Stalin also proved himself to be a master of intrigue and political manoeuvring, arts in which Trotsky proved to be incompetent. So we must see his defeat as due to a combination of adverse circumstances and personal qualities and deficiencies, with the circumstances as the decisive factor.

By 1926, Trotsky, Zinoviev and the so-called 'left-opposition' were helpless and isolated in the Party. They persisted in playing to the rules, keeping disagreements within the Party which was now controlled by their enemies. For them the Party was all that mattered. Or maybe they understood too well that the mass of the people were hostile to all Bolsheviks, and so an appeal to the (peasant) majority against the ruling caucus made no sense. Anyway, it was not until November 1927 that a few desperate oppositionists went out into the streets to demonstrate, to appeal at least to the city 'proletariat', to their Party comrades. They were speedily silenced, many were exiled, Trotsky was sent to Alma Ata, in distant Central Asia, and was then exiled from the USSR to Turkey, whence he wandered helplessly until a Stalinist assassin finished him with an ice-pick in distant Mexico in 1940.

Up to 1927, Stalin was in alliance with Bukharin, Bukharin had succeeded Zinoviev as the head of the Communist International, which in these days still seemed to matter, at least to the faithful. Rykov, an ally of Bukharin, was prime minister. Tomsky, also of the Bukharinist persuasion, was boss of the trade unions. Through cronies such as Molotov, Stalin controlled the Party Secretariat, but his control was not yet absolute. The supreme body at the top of the party, the Politbureau, could decide against him. Lenin's testament was known to them. They — or rather the Stalin-Bukharin majority — had decided to keep it secret, but it could be revived, and Stalin still could not afford to offend his allies, certainly not until Trotsky, Zinoviev and their friends were totally destroyed politically, and even then he had to tread warily. We must surmise that he deeply resented these limitations on his power and bided his time; later he would create and seize opportunities to rid himself of men on whose loyalty he could not rely, and who were intellectually his superiors. Bukharin was a man of undoubted brilliance, charm, eloquence, held in great affection and esteem by many party members (as Lenin had said). He was, however, no match for Stalin in political in-fighting.

While on one level Stalin could be seen as wanting the Bukharin group out of the way in order that he should achieve supreme power, it is true and perhaps more important to see that they clashed over policy. So we must return to the 'great debate', and go on looking at the very real dilemmas which faced the Bolsheviks in the mid-twenties.

NEP seemed to be a great economic success. By 1926 Soviet industry had reached the production levels of 1913. So now they had to move on, to plan the future economic development of Russia. Discussions raged about how best to proceed, at many levels, including the economic-technical one. How fast? In what direction? Should investments be channelled to agriculture, so as to buy modern machinery from the West, paying for it with farm exports? Or should Russia aim to make her own machinery at the earliest possible moment? Should industrial investment concentrate primarily on consumer goods industries or on heavy industry? Since there was much unemployment, might it not be wiser to invest in industries using a great deal of labour? What kind of planning should there be? What role should be reserved for prices and market forces, which were of major importance under NEP? In trying to cope with these and other questions, Soviet economists can be said virtually to have invented development economics, anticipating many arguments which were first heard in the West when development and growth became fashionable, i.e. after the Second World War.

Economics as such is not our concern, but it is easy to see that many of the above questions had political aspects of the very highest importance. 'How fast' meant: 'how hard is it desirable or feasible to squeeze the peasants?' Bukharin, as has already been pointed out, wanted to avoid conflict with the peasants, which meant being content with a modest rate of capital accumulation and thereby slow growth. Priority for heavy industry not only meant the creation within Russia of the sinews of future growth, and of the basis of a modern arms industry, but also multiplied the sacrifices (no one can eat or wear steel or machine-tools) and once again brought the peasant question to the fore. A decision in favour of centralised planning and against market forces would — and did   change the political as well as the economic scene, impelling it towards what came to be called totalitarianism. So political issues, the personal power struggle and economic difficulties were all of great significance, and interpenetrated each other. This had some tragic results. Thus a non-Party 'technical' economist who advised that more should be invested in consumer goods industries could be labelled an ally of the Bukharinist faction and, when repression grew, he might be arrested and never seen again.

But this is to run ahead. Mass terror was still in the future. Party leaders who spoke their minds in 1926 did not expect to be jailed, and Stalin still had not the power to jail them.

Stalin was a secretive man, and his published works and speeches give us less insight into his real thoughts than is usual with politicians. Indeed he lied on a prodigious scale. Consequently we do not know when he made up his mind to part company with Bukharin and steal the policy clothes of the Trotskyist opposition. The most likely explanation is that he always regarded NEP as a forced, temporary compromise, that he preferred ruthless strong-arm methods to accommodation, that he wished to launch a major industrialisation drive as soon as it was practicable; therefore he had mis-givings about Bukharin's line. We do know that when Bukharin went so far as to launch the slogan 'get rich' (i.e. encouraging the *kulaks* to produce more for the market), Stalin said: 'This is not our policy.' However, tactical exigencies, and the country's weakness and vulnerability, inclined him to play along with the Bukharin group until Trotsky was eliminated. In 1927 he became strong enough to act on his own, though he still had to play his cards with caution. The party congresses in 1925 and 1927 had gone on formal record in favour of industrialisation and also of the growth of collectives in agriculture. But these resolutions were not controversial. Questions of tempos and coercion were.

Already in 1926-7 a speed-up in investment began, and grain prices were kept low. Very quickly this caused trouble, and Stalin's reactions to the resultant crisis showed how his mind was working.

The Great Turning-Point

People first became aware of a crisis in connection with grain procurements. Grain in Russia was then, and still is to some extent, 'the staff of life', and also a major export. In the winter of 1927-8 it became apparent that the peasants were not willing to sell enough grain at the official price. Many hoarded it to await higher prices, or fed their livestock better. In doing so, they behaved as economic men. It is absurd to 'blame' them though Stalin treated them as conspirators.

At the same time investments were increasing, some major construction projects were begun, ambitious versions of a five-year plan, the first in history, were being drafted. The impact of this on the economy was to create goods shortages. The reason for these shortages was that the new investments diverted resources into major construction projects, increasing at the same time the incomes of those working on them, while the supply of consumer goods could not match the increases in purchasing power. This, in a free-market economy, would have been reflected by inflationary price rises, but the state tried to keep prices low by strict controls, and this led to an imbalance between supply and demand. The NEP traders and petty manufacturers could cash in, by selling scarce goods at high prices. Increasingly they were treated by Party officials as black-marketeers; they were taxed arbitrarily, refused licences, denied materials and transport. This took time, but NEP was beginning to break up in the winter of 1927-8, with Stalin's evident approval, even though in all official speeches the principles of NEP continued to be exalted. Bukharin had every cause to be worried.

Then came the flashpoint. Defying the Party's own rules, ignoring the Politbureau, acting directly through his cronies in the Party machine, Stalin dealt with the grain procurement problem by violence. Disregarding the law, the police set up road-blocks, seized peasant produce en route to the (legal) markets, confiscated 'surplus' and 'hoarded' grain. Stalin himself went to the Urals and Siberia to supervise the operation in those areas, and called this extortion technique 'the Urals-Siberian method'. In the light of subsequent arbitrariness and brutality, this might seem to us to be 'normal' behaviour. But in terms of NEP it was an outrage. Local officials were taken aback. Many thought that laws should be observed. Stalin reprimanded them: 'Suppose this is an emergency measure. What of it? . . . As for your prosecuting and judicial officials, they should be dismissed!'

Force, not economic means, not persuasion, had been used against the peasants. Not just against *kulaks* or other real or imagined class enemies, but also against millions of so-called 'middle peasants', ordinary smallholders. NEP was doomed. A new coercive era was beginning.

Bukharin was horrified. A row blew up in the Politbureau. Stalin admitted excesses, retreated in words, allowed the publication of a resolution which apparently censured over-zealous application of policies designed to meet an emergency. But he kept his grip firmly on the apparatus of power, began a campaign to isolate and discredit the so-called 'right-wing deviationists', the name given by Stalin to anyone who sought to avoid a clash with the mass of the peasantry. He repeated the policy of requisitions. The helpless Bukharin saw at last — why did he not see it before? — what was coming to him. In despair he turned even to his old party enemy Kamenev, friend of Zinoviev and ally (in 1926-7) of Trotsky, and spoke with horror of this 'Genghis Khan', who would destroy them all. (Genghis Khan was a Tartar potentate who conquered China and terrorised much of Asia. His name is a byword in Russia for cruelty and massacre.) At last Bukharin saw that he had much more in common with the oppositionists he had helped to destroy than with his formidable ex-ally. It was much too late. He went under without being able to put up any fight.

The year 1928 saw the removal of moderate economic advisers. The able and original minds who were pioneers of economic development theory nearly all lost their jobs, and not long afterwards some of them were arrested. Kondratiev, Vainshtein, Feldman, Bazarov . . . the list is a long one. A few hardy individuals survived to be released after the death of Stalin. (I met one of these few in Moscow in 1969.)

This was also the first year of 'show trials', the much publicised morality-story court cases in which the accused plead guilty to unlikely but politically 'convenient' offences. Various engineers confessed to plots and sabotage on behalf of foreign powers. But these were not yet Party men. That was to come later.

It was the last year in which open discussion of controversial issues was possible in the Party. It was in September of that year that Bukharin's 'Notes of an economist' was published, a carefully worded plea for moderation and balance in industrial planning. From then on, neither he nor any other Party leader — Stalin and his henchmen excepted — would get his thoughts into print. They could still gather and grumble, exchange letters, perhaps even conspire. But the last remaining vestige of the Party as a policy discussion forum faded away never to return, as Stalin consolidated his power and began to impose his conception of how Russia should be ruled.

In April 1929 the sixteenth Party Conference adopted the maximum version of the first five-year plan. This envisaged a huge leap forward in industrial construction. Industrial output was to rise by 180 per cent, investment by 228 per cent, consumption by almost 70 per cent, agricultural output by 55 per cent. All warnings that such figures were unrealistic were rejected as 'right-deviationist' heresy, if not treason. Stalin may or may not have believed that this plan was realisable. After all, there was no precedent in the world's economic history, and he may have genuinely thought that, by mobilising the Party and people to a supreme effort, there really were 'no fortresses the Bolsheviks cannot take', to cite a slogan of the period. Alternatively he may have believed that by these methods more could be achieved than by a balanced growth strategy, even if many of the targets were indeed unreal. Finally, he must have seen in this sort of approach great political virtues: it mobilised under his leadership a mass of Party members, to storm the heavens, to create a modern industrial society. Let us not underestimate the genuine enthusiasm which this policy generated, especially among the younger of the faithful. Whether consciously or subconsciously, Stalin must have welcomed the logic of this strategy: discipline, struggle, repression, organisation. He was at home in such a setting.

The year 1928, then, was a great turning-point. The realisation of this did not happen suddenly, it only gradually dawned even on well-informed citizens that a momentous turn was in progress. The more so as the tightly controlled press pretended that policy was unchanged, that NEP was still the basis of the Party line. Yet 'the revolution from above' was already beginning.

13 PARTY AND STATE IN SOVIET RUSSIA AND NAZI GERMANY

Aryeh L. Unger

Source: *Political Quarterly*, vol.36, part 4, 1965, pp.441-59.

The purpose of this inquiry is to review the relationship between the apparatus of the party and the apparatus of the state in two régimes which are widely regarded as prototypes of modern totalitarian government — Soviet Russia and Nazi Germany. Prevailing opinion among scholars appears to look upon party control of state organs as a necessary requisite of totalitarianism. This view, it seems to me, disregards some fundamental differences between Soviet and Nazi practices and consequently places undue emphasis upon the totalitarian imperatives for party control over the administration of the state.

The Threat of Bureaucratic Control

If there is a 'totalitarian' case for party control over the state apparatus, it would, I suppose, be founded on what might be called the threat of bureaucratic virtues. It is not difficult to see that such essential ingredients of efficient bureaucracy as stability, order and rationality — not to mention objectivity — can easily become revolutionary vices. Max Weber already argued that the existence of modern bureaucracies 'makes "revolution" in the sense of the forceful creation of entirely new forms of authority more and more impossible . . . it substitutes *coups d'état* for "revolutions"'. He even went so far as to say that absolute rulers were 'powerless' against their bureaucratic experts. It might reasonably be argued that it is precisely the determination of totalitarian rulers not to allow their revolutions to founder on the rocks of bureaucratic norms which explains the need for party control over the state apparatus.

Indeed, both the Bolsheviks and the Nazis soon after coming to power seemed to perceive the need to counteract the 'static administration' of the state by means of the 'dynamic leadership' of the party. Lenin was forever preoccupied with the evils of bureaucratic inertia and repeatedly warned 'not to divorce the administration from politics'. At the 10th Congress of the Soviet Party in 1921 he gave an unadorned exposition of the totalitarian rationale as regards the state apparatus when he stressed that, the apparatus must be subordinated to politics . . . politics call for resolute changes, flexibility and skilful moves. . . . A firm apparatus should be fit for every manoeuvre. But if firmness is transformed into ossification, if it hinders change, a struggle is inevitable. . . . As an auxiliary the firmer the apparatus the better. . . . But if it is unable to manoeuvre it is fit for nothing.

And Hitler declared in his Proclamation to the 1935 Congress of the NSDAP in connection with the Nuremberg racial legislation:

I should like to make it quite clear that . . . wherever the formal bureaucracy of the state should prove itself incapable of solving a problem, there the nation will bring into play its own, more living organisation in order to clear the way for the realisation of its vital necessities . . . that which can be solved by the state will be solved by the state, but any problem which the state by its essential character is unable to solve will be solved by means of the movement.

Yet, however desirable the juxtaposition of party leadership and state administration might have seemed in theory, in practice the distinction proved exceedingly elusive. Both Nazi and Soviet experience have shown that what were intended to be separate components of an interlocking structure invariably became subject to a variety of pressures leading either to virtual fusion or constant friction. Either way, the purposes of both leadership and administration were adversely affected. The party's own dynamism was impaired as its administrative responsibility expanded and as its organs assumed the 'static' features inherent in all bureaucracies, while the state apparatus was constantly harassed by party 'leadership' which obstructed and obscured the channels of command, inhibited the intiative of state officials and generally undermined the stability and discretion which are essential for administrative efficiency. The result has been that 'shapelessness' of the totalitarian structure so often noted by outside observers: not the control of one (state) bureaucracy by means of a vigilant party, but the erection of another (party) bureaucracy which has competed with that of the state in some fields and obstructed it in others and not infrequently conspired with it to shield both against the central authority.

If this is the price of party control over the state it may be assumed that totalitarian rulers will pay it only with reluctance. Administrative efficiency is a high-priority item on the value scale of most modern régimes; there is no reason to believe that totalitarian régimes would forego it lightly.

Certainly both the Nazis and the Bolsheviks were aware of the consequences of the party's involvement in state-administrative functions. But whereas the Nazis were able to treat its cause by restricting party control of the state administration, the Bolsheviks were confined to treating the symptoms. Just as the Nazis anticipated that the party's preoccupation with matters belonging to the realm of the state apparatus would 'divert the party from its real tasks of leading, educating, watching, stimulating [and] striving forward', so the Soviet leaders realised the 'danger of party bodies becoming severed from the masses and being transformed from organs of political leadership . . . into something in the nature of managing institutions, incapable of counter-acting parochial, narrow-departmental and other anti-state tendencies . . .'. The difference was, however, that while the Nazis, maintaining that 'without a proper administration the leadership is power-less', drew the conclusion that 'to be effective the state, too, must be independent' and that the 'direct intervention' of the party was therefore 'state-hostile' (*staatsfeindlich*), the Communists could merely warn the party not to confuse leadership with administration, 'not to replace' the state organs but 'to guide' them.

Bolshevik Distrust of State Power

Soviet practice was determined primarily by the ideological predispositions with which the Bolsheviks embarked on the revolution of 1917 and the political circumstances in which the revolutionary drama was enacted. The Marxist teaching had left the Bolsheviks with a general distrust of state power and a specific injunction to 'smash' the pre-revolutionary state structure and to replace it by a broadly administered 'Commune state' which would bear the seeds of its ultimate extinction within itself. The revolution placed the Bolsheviks in possession of a state apparatus which was discredited in the eyes of the public, demoralised as a result of a disas-trous war and weakened by the agitation of the revolutionary parties and the conflict with the soviets which had sprung up after February in town and country. Moreover, the overwhelming majority of former state officials was implacably hostile to the Bolsheviks. In the circumstances, to use the existing state apparatus as an instrument of Bolshevik government would have been politically inexpedient as well as ideologically unorthodox.

Indeed, the revolutionary régime made no effort to maintain the crumbling authority of the former state organs but on the contrary pro-ceeded to demolish it altogether with a recklessness that was sanctioned in Marxist doctrine and sustained by the conviction that the fate of the revolution hung by the speed with which the principal fortress of bourgeois society was destroyed. Yet, while the demolition of the old state could be accomplished swiftly and relatively smoothly, the erection of its successor posed problems of a different magnitude. The new repositories of state power, the soviets, rapidly proved themselves incapable of shouldering the vast tasks of administration that presented themselves to a régime aiming at a drastic transformation of society against a background of civil war and economic chaos. Not only did the 'armed people' lack the necessary administrative and technical experience to build the new order on the ruins of the old; the radically democratic character of the soviets also rendered them extremely cumbersome and unreliable tools of revolutionary government. Revolutions, as Marx had already warned, cannot be fought by democratic assemblies. And this was especially true when, as in Russia, the revolutionary régime was in the hands of a minority party. The administrative and technical incompetence of the mass organs quickly necessitated the restoration of the centralised bureaucratic machinery staffed with non-Communist and even counter-revolutionary professionals. The political unreliability of the Soviet structure — now increased further by the employment of former Tsarist officials — just as quickly necessitated the imposition of party controls. What remained, or rather, what became of the original vision of a broadly based, mass-administered, proletarian 'half-state', was a rigidly co-ordinated system of power in which the popular assemblies provided little more than a façade for a highly centralised state bureaucracy controlled at all levels 'in the name of the proletariat' by parallel organs of the party. In November 1918 Lenin had confidently declared that 'the entire mass of the workers, not only its leaders and foremost representatives, but really the broadest strata, know that they themselves are building socialism with their own hands'. Less than two-and-a-half years later he was engaged in persuading his followers that it would be necessary 'to build communism with the hands of non-communists'. If power was not to slip from the precarious grasp of the Bolshevik régime in the process, far-flung party controls were essential.

The Role of the Communist Party

Looking back, this sequence of events seems to have unfolded with inexorable logic. Given the men they were — Marxists, harbouring an ideologically determined suspicion of state organs, and professional revolutionaries, endowed with a highly developed sense of practical politics, a compulsive urge for power and an ardent faith in the party as the supreme instrument of proletarian emancipation — and the circumstances in which they found themselves, there was probably little else the Bolsheviks could have done if they wished to retain their hold on the country. Yet, although the path that led from the dictatorship of the proletariat to the dictatorship of the party apparatus was traversed swiftly – and, perhaps, predictably – it had by no means been charted out in advance. There was certainly no sanction in Marxism for the party-state duopoly; indeed, the party is not mentioned by either Marx or Engels in the context of the proletarian state. Lenin devoted a single sentence to the party in his *State and Revolution*, the one work in which he set out to depict the practices of the future proletarian government. It is only in retrospect that the reference to the party's task as that of 'directing and organising the whole order, of being the teacher, guide and leader of all the toilers', attains a degree of ominous significance; the general argument of *State and Revolution* is uncompromisingly dedicated to the proposition that the Marxist 'Commune state' could and would be made to work in Russia.

It would be greatly under-estimating Lenin's political perspicacity were one to assume that the space allotted to the party in *State and Revolution* accurately reflected the importance which he attached to its role in the future state. To the man who had taught and practised the principles of authoritarian leadership in creating the disciplined 'party of a new type' it must have been obvious all along that the problems involved in applying the Marxist revolutionary prescription to a society in which the proletariat was numerically insignificant as well as culturally and politically backward, would be well-nigh insurmountable without the active intervention of the 'professional revolutionaries'. But in 1917 Lenin did not, and probably could not, anticipate the precise forms and extent which party intervention would take. He counted on the party *members* to conquer and lead the soviets; he did not count on the party *apparatus* to control the state apparatus at all levels. At the time of the revolution a party apparatus proper could hardly be said to have existed. By inspired improvisation a skeleton staff barely managed to conduct the internal administration of the party and to maintain its agitational activities. In many of the more distant localities there were no party organisations at all and for those that existed communication with the centre was sporadic and unreliable. That the party was able to function at all was due in the main to the organisational genius of the party secretary, Sverdlov, and to the fact that the long years of underground activity had created a nucleus of *komitetchiki* [committee members] who more often than not thought and acted in unison without formal directives. Certainly this was not a machine which could undertake to control the administration of Russia. Indeed, throughout the first year of the Bolshevik régime power was exercised primarily through the soviets. It was only after the 8th Congress of the party in 1919 that steps were taken to construct a party apparatus which could ensure that Bolshevik power would not be dismantled by hostile 'bourgeois specialists', on the one hand, and intractable as well as incompetent mass assemblies on the other.

By the end of the civil war party control over the activities of state agencies had become general practice. A routine of government had been established which has not been shaken by subsequent developments. The upheaval of industrialisation and collectivisation in the late 1920s reproduced with only minor changes the conditions of the October revolution. It, too, was a 'revolution from above' in which the régime once more found itself isolated from the mass of the people in the countryside as well as from the specialist cadres in the towns. Communism was still being built 'with the hands of non-communists', and party control both over the state administration in general and over economic construction in particular was more essential than ever.

Changes in Soviet Society

Since then the situation has in many ways been fundamentally transformed. There can be no doubt that the present leadership of the Soviet Union is no longer as isolated from the people it governs as was Stalin's personal tyranny. Not only was the majority of 'class enemies' liquidated in the course of the Stalinist terror, but a new generation of Soviet-born and Soviet-educated state officials, engineers, economists, army officers, etc., has grown up in and around the party. However much the individual or group interests and predilections of the new leading strata may be at variance with specific features and policies of the régime, one would have thought that its members could be relied upon to execute the goals and directives of the central power without the close institutional control of the party apparatus that had been necessary in the first two decades of Bolshevik rule. There is today, and has been for some time past, a substantial exchange of personnel between the apparatus of the party and that of other institutions. As a type, the party *apparatchik* may still be distinct from other power-holders, but such distinctions as there are relate to personality rather than to political loyalty, class origin, or 'ideological firmness'. The distinction frequently made between the generalists of the party and the specialists of other institutions also seems to me to have lost a great deal of its former validity. The recent emphasis on the 'secular' training of party functionaries attests to the régime's awareness of the fact that if the party apparatus is to maintain its relative position in the Soviet order it will have to employ the kind of personnel capable of coping with the sophisticated problems of a modern economy. Clearly the zealous but untutored party boss who could bully the 'bourgeois specialist' is at a decisive disadvantage when confronted by the Soviet engineer or administrator who combines superior technical expertise with an impeccable party record.

Why then is there no sign of the party relinquishing its hold over the administration of the Soviet Union? To attempt to answer this is to enter into the realm of conjecture. It should first be remembered, however, that there had in fact been such signs during the second world war and again towards the end of Stalin's reign. It seemed then that the party's ascendancy was being substantially curtailed not only in relatively unobtrusive practice but also in widely proclaimed theory. When articles and books extolling the state as 'chief instrument in the construction of communism' began to appear, there was indeed reason to believe that the party's demotion from its former position of unchallenged supremacy over the state apparatus was, if not an accomplished fact, at least an imminent prospect. Whether it was an attempt at rationalising the governmental machinery or merely an aspect of the power-technique of a single ruler who sought to play off the two hierarchies against one another and used the ubiquitous secret police as final arbiter, the fact remains that it was possible to make a start in dismantling party control without visibly diminishing the totalitarian stature of the Soviet regime.

Party Supremacy in USSR

There remains, however, the indisputable reassertion of the party's primacy which has been an outstanding feature of the Khrushchev era. Any number of explanations may be advanced for this 'regressive' development, all of them necessarily speculative. It may, of course, be no more than a reflection of the victory of Khrushchev, the supreme representative of the party, in the struggle for Stalin's succession. Possibly, too, Khrushchev was seriously seeking ways and means of ushering in the long-promised 'withering away' of the state, in which case the replacement of the apparatus of the state by that of the party might conceivably have presented itself as an attractive and harmless solution. Soviet theoretical pronouncements of recent years have certainly done a good deal to retrieve the prospect of the stateless society from the limbo into which Stalin's dialectical exercises had consigned it; and there have been some steps to transfer state functions to social organisations operating under party direction. Perhaps the most likely single explanation must be sought simply in the belief of the Soviet leadership that the system cannot afford a relaxation of the party's grip over the administration of the state, especially now that the deterrent of a terroristic police has been removed from the forefront of the scene. But whatever factor or combination of factors is responsible for the restoration of party control, it would seem to lie in Soviet reality rather than in any independent totalitarian imperatives.

The Nazi Contrast

In this respect the contrast with Nazi Germany is most instructive. The Nazis had no ideological prejudice against the state as such. They assumed power unburdened by any theory of the state beyond a number of generalisations which in line with the racial doctrine of the preservation of the *Volk* derived the origins and functions of the state from that primary purpose. There was certainly nothing in Nazi doctrine which was in any way inconsistent with the desirability of a strong power. For Hitler the 'true state' was 'a mighty weapon which everyone has to obey. . . .'. Like the Bolsheviks the Nazis regarded the state as an instrument — of the *Volk*, to be sure, and not of a class — but unlike them they were committed neither to the immediate destruction of the pre-revolutionary state nor to the gradual abolition of a post-revolutionary 'half-state'. The influence of ideological texts on totalitarian action is questionable at best, and if the sporadic utterances of the Nazis on the state deserve mentioning in the context of this necessarily brief outline it is only because in Nazi Germany, as in Soviet Russia, political expediency and ideological predisposition reinforced each other in determining the party's role in the administration of the state.

It should be noted that, unlike Lenin, Hitler assumed power at the head of a party that had been built up not only with a view to the seizure of power but also to its administration. Already in *Mein Kampf* he had 'no doubt that the future institutions of this [the national socialist] state must grow out of this movement . . .'. In the long years of waiting for power the party had erected a formidable apparatus of its own with central departments that closely paralleled those of the state and a network of subordinate organs that spread across the length and breadth of Germany. Whatever the professional competence of this apparatus, there can be no doubt that the Nazis were far better equipped to launch an extensive system of party control over state agencies in 1933 than the Bolsheviks had been in 1917.

The German Bureaucracy's Attitude

On coming to power, however, the Nazis found a state apparatus that was firmly entrenched, universally respected and fully prepared to administer the new order. A judicious personnel policy and a general tightening of the state structure which destroyed the last remnants of autonomy in regional and local administration, were all that was required in order to transform the existing state organs into efficient and trustworthy instruments of totalitarian government. The notion of an authoritarian state, moreover, was familiar and acceptable to most sectors of German public opinion;

certainly, the ill-fated interlude of the Weimar Republic had done little to strengthen the faith of the people in democratic institutions.

These two factors, the existence of a state apparatus that was both willing and competent as well as the ready acceptance of its authority by the community at large, might in themselves have sufficed to restrict the potential role of the party in the administration of the state. There were other, more important disincentives. In sharp contrast to the Bolshevik revolution, the Nazi *Machtergreifung* [seizure of power] was the product of an alliance with some of the nation's most powerful institutions. It was the collaboration of the military and economic 'establishments', above all, which helps to explain not only the remarkable swiftness with which the *Machtergreifung* was accomplished, but also the régime's considerable, if short-lived, successes at home and abroad. No one was better aware of this than Hitler himself. When in 1936 he boasted of having succeeded in 'circumnavigating the most difficult cliff of every revolution', Hitler referred specifically to the support of the armed forces, but he knew that the substance of his claim applied in equal measure to other pre-revolutionary power factors. He fully acknowledged the trend of his political tactics when he went on to say:

I have always held the conviction that in the last instance a new revolution can only succeed if it manages not only to incorporate these institutions in the new state but also to bind them for better or for worse to the new state. That is, alas, a more difficult task than that of simply destroying such instruments. It is far more difficult to carry out a revolution and to place these instruments, in even strengthened form, in the service of the new idea.

Difficult or not, there can be no doubting the success with which Hitler accomplished the task of harnessing these institutions to the fate of the Third Reich. But while both the army and the economic leaders welcomed the creation of an authoritarian state apparatus and fully co-operated with it, they would most certainly have been opposed to a more vigorous intrusion of the party into the administration of the state in general and into the realm of their own affairs in particular. Whether the Nazi vessel would have run aground in consequence of such opposition must remain an open question. It was a risk, at any rate, which Hitler, for one, was not prepared to take, the less so, as he had no reason to mistrust either the ability or the readiness of the civil service, the army and the economy to execute policies for which they were professionally qualified and with which they were in basic agreement. There never was much doubt after 1933 that national socialism was being built with the hands of national socialists.

The party that burst upon the German scene after January 30, 1933, intoxicated as it still was with the slogans of the *Kampfzeit* [time of struggle], may have expected to see 'heads roll' as part of a revolutionary upheaval in which the 'rotten structure' of Weimar would be swept away and the foundations laid for the new, national socialist edifice, growing, as its leader had promised, 'out of this movement'. But Hitler and his allies in the commanding heights of German public life clearly had other plans. The reign of the 'brown battalions' which marked the first phase of the seizure of power was necessary in order to provide an outlet for the pent-up energies of a party trained in violence, which, if denied all its prey, might well have turned to devour its masters, and useful in creating a climate of intimidation in which the régime could eliminate opposition and consolidate its hold on the levers of power. There were some revolutionary 'cliffs' — notably rival parties and trade unions — which Hitler had no intention of 'circumnavigating'. By the summer of 1933 the immediate revolutionary objectives of the Nazis had been secured. An impressive display of force, skilfully blended against a background of pseudo-legality, had shown the nation who was master in the land. The time had now come to apply the brakes to the party's revolutionary ardour and to reassert the authority of the state. Thus in sharp contrast to the Bolshevik leaders who in a resolution of the 8th Party Congress, less than a year-and-a-half after the October rising, called upon the party to 'win for itself undivided political mastery in the soviets and practical control over all their work', Hitler warned the newly appointed *Reichstatthalter* (provincial governors) in July 1933 that party organisations must not be allowed to 'assume the functions of government' for 'the party has now become the state'. And Frick, in his capacity as Minister of the Interior, followed up Hitler's warning in a circular letter to the *Reichstatthalter* ordering them 'to guard the authority of the state under all circumstances'.

To be sure, in theory the party's supremacy over the state was almost as firm in Nazi Germany as it was in Soviet Russia. There had been some confusion in the period following the Nazi seizure of power, with spokesmen for the party and the state advancing conflicting claims to superior status. The theoretical quarrel was largely settled, however, after Hitler's unequivocal declaration at the 1934 Party Congress that 'it is not the state which gives orders to us, but we who give orders to the state! It is not the state which has created us; we have fashioned ourselves our state.' One year later, at the 1935 Congress of the Nazi party, Hitler referred to the state 'as only one of the forms of organisation of national life . . . set in motion and dominated by the immediate expression of the national will to live, the party, the national socialist movement'. Henceforward, the party's status as 'the leadership, in fact the legislature' was a recurrent theme of Hitler's pronouncements, faithfully echoed by the majority of Nazi theorists.

The Separation of Party and State

In practice, however, the régime saw to it that the 'leadership' of the party remained separate from the administration of the state and deprived of the power to control the activities of the state apparatus. Party officials, who on the strength of Hitler's statement at the 1934 Congress proceeded to issue orders to civil servants were quickly disabused of their misconceptions. The party 'orders the state', they were told, through its appointees in the state apparatus. It does 'not intervene in the state directly but rather utilises the administration itself in order to bring its influence to bear upon it'. As one writer put it, the *Fuehrer*'s statement must be understood as meaning 'not that party organs are to give instructions to state organs but that the life of the state is to be conducted in the spirit of the movement'. Another writer sought to console party functionaries, who had been 'disappointed' at the limited powers granted to them in comparison with the authority exercised by their former colleagues who had transferred to state service, by the assurance that 'the party itself fashions this state but this is not a programme for today or tomorrow; it is a programme for a generation if not for several generations'.

The Nazi Party's Sphere of Control

Such party control as emerged from the turmoil of the first months of Nazi rule and was built into the routine processes of government, was confined to personnel appointments and promotions, and to the 'political education' of state officials. Party-state relations in all other spheres were conducted on the basis of consultations through the party's regional offices, the *Gauleitungen*, at the intermediate administrative level – the *Gauleiter* occupied parallel state and party offices in personal union – and through the Deputy Leader's Staff – later the Party Chancellory – at the national level. Complaints and suggestions of party organisations had to be forwarded through the same channels. To be sure, this did not prevent local party functionaries from attempting to interfere in the affairs of the state adminis-tration; nor were such attempts always successfully rebuffed by the state apparatus. The archives of the Third Reich contain countless instances of party intervention in cases ranging from the administration of justice to the issue of business licences. Whether or not party intervention was effective depended on the aggressiveness of the party functionary and the authority and standing of his opposite number in the state hierarchy. It must be emphasised that where party intervention did not take the form of a blatant attempt at dispensing patronage, it was usually prompted by the complaints of citizens with *prima facie* genuine grievances against the state bureaucracy. General political intervention arising out of impersonal policy matters was relatively rare at all but the very highest levels. None of this approached the institutional provisions for party direction and supervision which form part of the Soviet system of government.

For its part, the Nazi leadership discouraged the initiative of local party zealots to meddle in matters outside the party's immediate responsibilities. At the 1935 Party Congress Hitler authoritatively delineated the respective spheres of party and state. 'The function of the state', he declared, 'is the continuation of the administration as it has arisen and developed in the course of history . . . within the framework and by means of the law.' As to the party, its primary function in regard to the state apparatus was the political training of civil servants and the 'transfer of those who have been so trained to the state to be its leaders and staff'. But once trained and transferred, civil servants came under the exclusive jurisdiction of the state in all matters pertaining to their official duties: 'For the rest the principle of mutual respect and the observance of competencies remains. That is the goal.'

In the following year Hitler again affirmed that for him 'all the requisites for a government closely bound up with the people', were fulfilled by the fact 'that the entire personnel which determines the actions of the state and Reich runs from base to summit through this movement'. And in his speech to the Reichstag of February 20, 1938, he once more declared that 'there is in Germany no problem of the relationship between the national socialist state and the national socialist party. . . . In this Reich everyone who holds a responsible position is a national socialist.'

The Pillars of the Nazi Régime

Hitler did not, of course, evaluate the political reliability of the generals, industrialists or professional state servants on a par with that of his veteran party leaders. His public protestations of the unity of the pillars that supported the Third Reich were designed as much to allay the fears of his conservative collaborators as to restrain the revolutionary ambitions of his party followers. In private both he and other party leaders gave frequent vent to their distrust and resentment of the 'reactionary diehards' (*die Ewiggestrigen*). Indeed, Hitler's last-quoted speech came in the wake of a reshuffle and purge in the Cabinet and the top leadership of the army, and probably reflects a desire to ward off possible opposition to which the action might have given rise.

Yet although they harboured suspicions of certain individuals and even groups in the armed forces, the economy and the state apparatus, the Nazis did not regard these institutions as a whole in any light other than that of collaborators. Unlike the Soviet party, the NSDAP was from the outset not an isolated column advancing into hostile territory, but part of a broad front, of which other national socialist units occupied different sectors. There were rivalries, jealousies, suspicions and recriminations, but there was also a common basis of agreement concerning the immediate, if not also the ultimate, objectives of the campaign. It was only in the last years of the Second World War that the common front began to crack and the party found itself progressively isolated. It was then, too, that it began, in the words of the *Voelkischer Beobachter* of December 18, 1943, 'to deal with matters that reach into the state administration. . . . The administrative channel is shortened and the initiative of the party probes more deeply and more tangibly into . . . the very structure of the state.'

The War Years in Germany

The complex web of party-state relations that developed during the latter years of the war cannot be described here. As a broad generalisation it would be true to say that the opportunities for party intervention in the realm of state affairs multiplied in proportion as popular morale deteriorated and regular communications were disrupted. When emergency situations called for prompt, unrehearsed decisions and the civil servant, conditioned as he was to work within a strictly centralised administrative order, found himself unable to refer back to his superiors, the man with the greater political authority on the spot often stepped in and assumed responsibility for activities ranging from the re-allocation of labour, to the distribution of food, the evacuation of refugees and the building of fortifications. For their part, state officials seemed relieved to disassociate themselves from the crumbling structure of the Third Reich and to abdicate powers which they were in any case not equipped to exercise. But the pattern varied from region to region, and it evolved in response to the mounting pressure of events rather than as part of a centrally inspired design.

If there had been an official policy to involve the party in the administration of the state and to raise party organisations to agencies of control over the state apparatus, one would have expected to find its foremost representatives in the Party Chancellory. Yet as late as October 29, 1943, Bormann wrote to Rosenberg that the latter's proposal to increase the powers of party functionaries in the occupied Eastern territories would 'obliterate the existing and necessary boundaries between the competencies of party and state and burden the party with matters alien to its nature.

The party's task is the leadership of men (*Menschenfuehrung*) . . .'. A Party Chancellory directive of August 7, 1942, had already affirmed the premise that any 'consideration of the pros and cons of personal union must start with the tasks of the NSDAP as the organisation which has to lead and take care of all German people politically, ideologically and culturally', and concluded that 'to burden the party with the functions of the executive would necessarily render the implementation of these tasks . . . more difficult and even impossible'.

Even in those fields of party activity which were opened up by the circumstances of the war and bordered on the sphere of *Menschenfuehrung*, the 'initiative of the party to probe more deeply' into the state administration, was severely circumscribed. One such field was the mobilisation of labour. On April 22, 1942, the newly installed General-Plenipotentiary, Sauckel, himself a veteran party leader, appointed the party's *Gauleiter* as his regional representatives and explicitly instructed them to employ their subordinate party organisations to render direct assistance in the mobilisation of additional labour reserves. At the same time, however, he charged the *Gauleiter* to pay 'the strictest attention' that 'offices of the NSDAP, its organisations, formations and affiliated associations neither assume functions for which agencies of the state, the armed forces or economic institutions are competent and responsible, nor arbitrarily interfere in administrative processes, which according to the *Fuehrer*'s will fall outside the party's competence'.

Indoctrination of the Armed Forces

As Sauckel's directive intimates, what has been said hitherto of the party's relationship to the civil state apparatus applies in at least equal measure to the armed forces and to economic institutions. Indeed, such powers as the party exercised over the civil service – in respect of personnel appointments and political training – did not extend to the military. It was only with the introduction of the National Socialist Guidance Officers (NSFO in German initials) after December 22, 1943, that the party attained a measure of control over political indoctrination in the armed forces. The regulation of the economy was the exclusive responsibility of the state, aided by the various institutions of 'self-government'. The party exercised a measure of indirect influence, especially through its control over personnel appointments to state agencies and economic chambers, but neither national economic planning nor the routine processes of production and distribution fell within the purview of party activity. The Central Economic Commission of the NSDAP confined itself to internal party-economic matters. The task of the Economic Advisers attached to the regional (*Gau*) and district (*Kreis*) party offices was to see to it that 'national socialist economic conceptions were taken into account', but they had 'no direct influence over the every-day questions of economic life'.

Conclusion

Enough has been said to show that the Nazi party at no point attained the effective supremacy over the administration of the state which the Soviet party established in the early years of the Bolshevik revolution. Was Nazi Germany therefore in some important aspects less 'totalitarian' than Soviet Russia? If party control over the state apparatus is regarded as an essential trait of totalitarianism the answer must clearly be in the affirmative. For myself, I would hold that the Nazis operated a governmental machinery whose totalitarian capability derived from within rather than from party controls imposed from without. That they were able to do so and the Soviet Communists were not, was due above all to the fact that, unlike the latter, they could assure themselves from the outset of the support of some of the most powerful institutions in German public life. There was no need for party control on anything like the Soviet scale so long as that support was freely forthcoming. The Nazis thus avoided a dilemma which has pursued the Soviet régime from its earliest days: the vicious circle that leads from political control to administrative or technical responsibility (if only because the politically significant decisions of civil servants, economic managers, army officers, etc., are primarily administrative, economic, military, etc.), and thence to further controls. The result in the Soviet Union has been that proliferation of control instruments which Professor Fainsod aptly described as the 'institutionalisation of mutual suspicion'. Suspicion is inherent in the totalitarian method of government and sooner or later it is bound to become institutionalised. But the experience of Nazi Germany would seem to indicate that where there is no basic divergence between the functionaries of the party and the leading personnel of other institutions as regards political reliability, the essential purposes of 'institutionalised suspicion' can be met without direct party control over the administration of the state.

14 ORIGINS OF THE COLD WAR

Arthur Schlesinger, Jr

Source: *Foreign Affairs*, vol.46, October 1967, pp.22-52.

I

The Cold War in its original form was a presumably mortal antagonism, arising in the wake of the Second World War, between two rigidly hostile blocs, one led by the Soviet Union, the other by the United States. For nearly two somber and dangerous decades this antagonism dominated the fears of mankind; it may even, on occasion, have come close to blowing up the planet. In recent years, however, the once implacable struggle has lost its familiar clarity of outline. With the passing of old issues and the emergence of new conflicts and contestants, there is a natural tendency, especially on the part of the generation which grew up during the Cold War, to take a fresh look at the causes of the great contention between Russia and America.

Some exercises in reappraisal have merely elaborated the orthodoxies promulgated in Washington or Moscow during the boom years of the Cold War. But others, especially in the United States (there are no signs, alas, of this in the Soviet Union), represent what American historians call 'revisionism' – that is, a readiness to challenge official explanations. No one should be surprised by this phenomenon. Every war in American history has been followed in due course by skeptical reassessments of supposedly sacred assumptions. [. . .] It is not to be supposed that the Cold War would remain exempt.

In the case of the Cold War, special factors reinforce the predictable historiographical rhythm. The outburst of polycentrism in the communist empire has made people wonder whether communism was ever so monolithic as official theories of the Cold War supposed. A generation with no vivid memories of Stalinism may see the Russia of the forties in the image of the relatively mild, seedy and irresolute Russia of the sixties. And for this same generation the American course of widening the war in Viet Nam – which even non-revisionists can easily regard as folly – has unquestionably stirred doubts about the wisdom of American foreign policy in the sixties which younger historians may have begun to read back into the forties.

It is useful to remember that, on the whole, past exercises in revisionism have failed to stick. [. . .] But this does not mean that one should deplore the rise of Cold War revisionism. For revisionism is an essential part of the process by which history, through the posing of new problems and the investigation of new possibilities, enlarges its perspectives and enriches its insights. [. . .]

II

The orthodox American view, as originally set forth by the American government and as reaffirmed until recently by most American scholars, has been that the Cold War was the brave and essential response of free men to communist aggression. Some have gone back well before the Second World War to lay open the sources of Russian expansionism. Geopoliticians traced the Cold War to imperial Russian strategic ambitions which in the nineteenth century led to the Crimean War, to Russian penetration of the Balkans and the Middle East and to Russian pressure on Britain's 'lifeline' to India. Ideologists traced it to the Communist Manifesto of 1848 ('the violent overthrow of the bourgeoisie lays the foundations for the sway of the proletariat'). Thoughtful observers (a phrase meant to exclude those who speak in Dullese about the unlimited evil of godless, atheistic, militant communism) concluded that classical Russian imperialism and Pan-Slavism, compounded after 1917 by Leninist messianism, confronted the West at the end of the Second World War with an inexorable drive for domination.

The revisionist thesis is very different. In its extreme form, it is that, after the death of Franklin Roosevelt and the end of the Second World War, the United States deliberately abandoned the wartime policy of collaboration and, exhilarated by the possession of the atomic bomb, undertook a course of aggression of its own designed to expel all Russian influence from Eastern Europe and to establish democratic-capitalist states on the very border of the Soviet Union. As the revisionists see it, this radically new American policy — or rather this resumption by Truman of the pre-Roosevelt policy of insensate anti-communism — left Moscow no alternative but to take measures in defense of its own borders. The result was the Cold War.

These two views, of course, could not be more starkly contrasting. It is therefore not unreasonable to look again at the half-dozen critical years between June 22, 1941, when Hitler attacked Russia, and July 2, 1947, when the Russians walked out of the Marshall Plan meeting in Paris. Several things should be borne in mind as this re-examination is made. For one thing, we have thought a great deal more in recent years [. . .] about the problems of communication in diplomacy — the signals which one nation, by word or by deed, gives, inadvertently or intentionally, to another. [. . .] We must strive to see how, given Soviet perspectives, the Russians might conceivably have misread our signals, as we must reconsider how intelligently we read theirs.

For another, the historian must not overindulge the man of power in the illusion cherished by those in office that high position carries with it the easy ability to shape history. [. . .] The physical course of the Second World War – the military operations undertaken, the position of the respective armies at the war's end, the momentum generated by victory and the vacuums created by defeat – all these determined the future as much as the character of individual leaders and the substance of national ideology and purpose.

Nor can the historian forget the conditions under which decisions are made, especially in a time like the Second World War. These were tired, overworked, aging men: in 1945, Churchill was 71 years old, Stalin had governed his country for 17 exacting years, Roosevelt his for 12 years nearly as exacting. During the war, moreover, the importunities of military operations had shoved postwar questions to the margins of their minds. All – even Stalin, behind his screen of ideology – had become addicts of improvisation, relying on authority and virtuosity to conceal the fact that they were constantly surprised by developments. [. . .] None showed great tactical consistency, or cared much about it; all employed a certain ambiguity to preserve their power to decide big issues; and it is hard to know how to interpret anything any one of them said on any specific occasion. This was partly because, like all princes, they designed their expressions to have particular effects on particular audiences; partly because the entirely genuine intellectual difficulty of the questions they faced made a degree of vacillation and mind-changing eminently reasonable. [. . .]

III

Peacemaking after the Second World War was not so much a tapestry as it was a hopelessly raveled and knotted mess of yarn. Yet, for purposes of clarity, it is essential to follow certain threads. One theme indispensable to an understanding of the Cold War is the contrast between two clashing views of world order: the 'universalist' view, by which all nations shared a common interest in all the affairs of the world, and the 'sphere-of-influence' view, by which each great power would be assured by the other great powers of an acknowledged predominance in its own area of special interest. The universalist view assumed that national security would be guaranteed by an international organization. The sphere-of-influence view assumed that national security would be guaranteed by the balance of power. While in practice these views have by no means been incompatible (indeed, our shaky peace has been based on a combination of the two), in the abstract they involved sharp contradictions.

The tradition of American thought in these matters was universalist

— i.e. Wilsonian. Roosevelt had been a member of Wilson's subcabinet; in 1920, as candidate for Vice President, he had campaigned for the League of Nations. It is true that, within Roosevelt's infinitely complex mind, Wilsonianism warred with the perception of vital strategic interests he had imbibed from Mahan. [. . .] But in principle he believed in joint action and remained a Wilsonian. His hope for Yalta, as he told the Congress on his return, was that it would 'spell the end of the system of unilateral action, the exclusive alliances, the spheres of influence, the balances of power, and all the other expedients that have been tried for centuries — and have always failed'.

Whenever Roosevelt backslid, he had at his side that Wilsonian fundamentalist, Secretary of State Cordell Hull, to recall him to the pure faith. [. . .] Remembering the corruption of the Wilsonian vision by the secret treaties of the First World War, Hull was determined to prevent any sphere-of-influence nonsense after the Second World War. He therefore fought all proposals to settle border questions while the war was still on [. . .].

In adopting the universalist view, Roosevelt and Hull were [. . .] expressing what seems clearly to have been the predominant mood of the American people, so long mistrustful of European power politics. [. . .]

It is true that critics, and even friends, of the United States sometimes noted a discrepancy between the American passion for universalism when it applied to territory far from American shores and the pre-eminence the United States accorded its own interests nearer home. Churchill, seeking Washington's blessing for a sphere-of-influence initiative in Eastern Europe, could not forbear reminding the Americans, 'We follow the lead of the United States in South America', nor did any universalist of record propose the abolition of the Monroe Doctrine. But a convenient myopia prevented such inconsistencies from qualifying the ardency of the universalist faith.

There seem only to have been three officials in the United States Government who dissented. One was the Secretary of War, Henry L. Stimson, a classical balance-of-power man, who in 1944 opposed the creation of a vacuum in Central Europe by the pastoralization of Germany and in 1945 urged 'the settlement of all territorial acquisitions in the shape of defense posts which each of these four powers may deem to be necessary for their own safety' in advance of any effort to establish a peacetime United Nations. Stimson considered the claim of Russia to a preferred position in Eastern Europe as not unreasonable [. . .]. Acceptance of spheres of influence seemed to him the way to avoid 'a head-on collision'.

A second official opponent of universalism was George Kennan, an eloquent advocate from the American Embassy in Moscow of 'a prompt and clear recognition of the division of Europe into spheres of influence and of a policy based on the fact of such division'. Kennan argued that nothing we could do would possibly alter the course of events in Eastern Europe; that we were deceiving ourselves by supposing that these countries had any future but Russian domination; that we should therefore relinquish Eastern Europe to the Soviet Union and avoid anything which would make things easier for the Russians by giving them economic assistance or by sharing moral responsibility for their actions.

A third voice within the government against universalism was (at least after the war) Henry A. Wallace. As Secretary of Commerce, he stated the sphere-of-influence case with trenchancy in the famous Madison Square Garden speech of September 1946 which led to his dismissal by President Truman [. . .] .

Stimson, Kennan and Wallace seem to have been alone in the government, however, in taking these views. They were very much minority voices. Meanwhile universalism, rooted in the American legal and moral tradition, overwhelmingly backed by contemporary opinion, received successive enshrinements in the Atlantic Charter of 1941, in the Declaration of the United Nations in 1942 and in the Moscow Declaration of 1943.

IV

The Kremlin, on the other hand, thought *only* of spheres of influence; above all, the Russians were determined to protect their frontiers, and especially their border to the west, crossed so often and so bloodily in the dark course of their history. These western frontiers lacked natural means of defense — no great oceans, rugged mountains, steaming swamps or impenetrable jungles. The history of Russia had been the history of invasion, the last of which was by now horribly killing up to twenty million of its people. The protocol of Russia therefore meant the enlargement of the area of Russian influence. Kennan himself wrote (in May 1944), 'Behind Russia's stubborn expansion lies only the age-old sense of insecurity of a sedentary people reared on an exposed plain in the neighborhood of fierce nomadic peoples', and he called this 'urge' a 'permanent feature of Russian psychology'.

In earlier times the 'urge' had produced the tsarist search for buffer states and maritime outlets. In 1939 the Soviet-Nazi pact and its secret protocol had enabled Russia to begin to satisfy in the Baltic states, Karelian Finland and Poland, part of what it conceived as its security requirements in Eastern Europe. But the 'urge' persisted, causing the friction between Russia and Germany in 1940 as each jostled for position in the area which separated them. Later it led to Molotov's new demands on Hitler in November 1940 — a free hand in Finland, Soviet predominance in Rumania and Bulgaria, bases in the Dardanelles — the demands which convinced Hitler that he had no choice but to attack Russia. Now Stalin hoped to gain from the West what Hitler, a closer neighbor, had not dared yield him.

It is true that, so long as Russian survival appeared to require a second front to relieve the Nazi pressure, Moscow's demand for Eastern Europe was a little muffled. Thus the Soviet government adhered to the Atlantic Charter (though with a significant if obscure reservation about adapting its principles to 'the circumstances, needs, and historic peculiarities of particular countries'). Thus it also adhered to the Moscow Declaration of 1943, and Molotov then, with his easy mendacity, even denied that Russia had any desire to divide Europe into spheres of influence. But this was guff, which the Russians were perfectly willing to ladle out if it would keep the Americans, and especially Secretary Hull (who made a strong personal impression at the Moscow conference) happy. 'A declaration', as Stalin once observed to Eden, 'I regard as algebra, but an agreement as practical arithmetic.'

The more consistent Russian purpose was revealed when Stalin offered the British a straight sphere-of-influence deal at the end of 1941. Britain, he suggested, should recognize the Russian absorption of the Baltic states, part of Finland, eastern Poland and Bessarabia; in return, Russia would support any special British need for bases or security arrangements in Western Europe. There was nothing specifically communist about these ambitions. If Stalin achieved them, he would be fulfilling an age-old dream of the tsars. The British reaction was mixed. [. . .] Churchill seemed evenly poised between the familiar realism of the balance of power, which he had so long recorded as an historian and manipulated as a statesman, and the hope that there must be some better way of doing things. His 1943 proposal of a world organization divided into regional councils represented an effort to blend universalist and sphere-of-influence conceptions. His initial rejection of Stalin's proposal in December 1941 as 'directly contrary to the first, second and third articles of the Atlantic Charter' thus did not spring entirely from a desire to propitiate the United States. On the other hand, he had himself already reinterpreted the Atlantic Charter as applying only to Europe (and thus not to the British Empire), and he was, above all, an empiricist who never believed in sacrificing reality on the altar of doctrine.

So in April 1942 he wrote Roosevelt that 'the increasing gravity of the war' had led him to feel that the Charter 'ought not to be construed so as to deny Russia the frontiers she occupied when Germany attacked her'. Hull, however, remained fiercely hostile to the inclusion of territorial provisions in the Anglo-Russian treaty; the American position, Eden noted, 'chilled me with Wilsonian memories'. Though Stalin complained that it looked 'as if the Atlantic Charter was directed against the U.S.S.R.', it was the Russian season of military adversity in the spring of 1942, and he dropped his demands.

He did not, however, change his intentions. A year later Ambassador Standley could cable Washington from Moscow: 'In 1918 Western Europe attempted to set up a *cordon sanitaire* to protect it from the influence of bolshevism. Might not now the Kremlin envisage the formation of a belt of pro-Soviet states to protect it from the influences of the West?' It well might; and that purpose became increasingly clear as the war approached its end. Indeed, it derived sustenance from Western policy in the first area of liberation.

The unconditional surrender of Italy in July 1943 created the first major test of the Western devotion to universalism. America and Britain, having won the Italian war, handled the capitulation, keeping Moscow informed at a distance. Stalin complained:

> The United States and Great Britain made agreements but the Soviet Union received information about the results . . . just as a passive third observer. I have to tell you that it is impossible to tolerate the situation any longer. I propose that the [tripartite military-political commission] be established and that Sicily be assigned . . . as its place of residence.

Roosevelt, who had no intention of sharing the control of Italy with the Russians, suavely replied with the suggestion that Stalin send an officer 'to General Eisenhower's headquarters in connection with the commission'. Unimpressed, Stalin continued to press for a tripartite body; but his Western allies were adamant in keeping the Soviet Union off the Control Commission for Italy, and the Russians in the end had to be satisfied with a seat, along with minor Allied states, on a meaningless Inter-Allied Advisory Council. Their acquiescence in this was doubtless not unconnected with a desire to establish precedents for Eastern Europe.

Teheran in December 1943 marked the high point of three-power colla-boration. Still, when Churchill asked about Russian territorial interests, Stalin replied a little ominously, 'There is no need to speak at the present time about any Soviet desires, but when the time comes we will speak.' In the next weeks, there were increasing indications of a Soviet determination to deal unilaterally with Eastern Europe [. . .].

The Red Army continued its advance into Eastern Europe. In August the Polish Home Army, urged on by Polish-language broadcasts from Moscow, rose up against the Nazis in Warsaw. For 63 terrible days, the Poles fought valiantly on, while the Red Army halted on the banks of the Vistula a few miles away, and in Moscow Stalin for more than half this time declined to co-operate with the Western effort to drop supplies to the Warsaw Resistance. [. . .] The Russians, it is evident in retrospect, had real military problems at the Vistula. [. . .] None the less, Stalin's indifference to the human tragedy, his effort to blackmail the London Poles during the ordeal, his sanctimonious opposition during five precious weeks to aerial resupply, the invariable coldness of his explanations ('the Soviet command has come to the conclusion that it must dissociate itself from the Warsaw adventure') and the obvious political benefit to the Soviet Union from the destruction of the Home Army − all these had the effect of suddenly dropping the mask of wartime comradeship and displaying to the West the hard face of Soviet policy. In now pursuing what he grimly regarded as the minimal re-quirements for the postwar security of his country, Stalin was inadvertently showing the irreconcilability of both his means and his ends with the Anglo-American conception of the peace.

Meanwhile Eastern Europe presented the Alliance with still another crisis that same September. Bulgaria, which was not at war with Russia, decided to surrender to the Western Allies while it still could; and the English and Americans at Cairo began to discuss armistice terms with Bulgarian envoys. Moscow, challenged by what it plainly saw as a Western intrusion into its own zone of vital interest, promply declared war on Bulgaria, took over the surrender negotiations and, invoking the Italian precedent, denied its Western Allies any role in the Bulgarian Control Commission. In a long and thoughtful cable, Ambassador Harriman medi-tated on the problems of communication with the Soviet Union. 'Words', he reflected, 'have a different connotation to the Soviets than they have to us. When they speak of insisting on "friendly governments" in their neigh-boring countries, they have in mind something quite different from what we would mean.' The Russians, he surmised, really believed that Washington accepted 'their position that although they would keep us informed they had the right to settle their problems with their western neighbors unilater-ally'. But the Soviet position was still in flux: 'the Soviet Government is not one mind.' The problem, as Harriman had earlier told Harry Hopkins, was 'to strengthen the hands of those around Stalin who want to play the game along our lines'. The way to do this, he now told Hull, was to

be understanding of their sensitivity, meet them much more than half way, encourage them and support them wherever we can, and yet oppose them promptly with the greatest of firmness where we see them going wrong. . . . The only way we can eventually come to an understanding with the Soviet Union on the question of non-interference in the internal

affairs of other countries is for us to take a definite interest in the solution of the problems of each individual country as they arise.

As against Harriman's sophisticated universalist strategy, however, Churchill,
increasingly fearful of the consequences of unrestrained competition in
Eastern Europe, decided in early October to carry his sphere-of-influence
proposal directly to Moscow. Roosevelt was at first content to have
Churchill speak for him too and even prepared a cable to that effect. But
Hopkins, a more rigorous universalist, took it upon himself to stop the
cable and warn Roosevelt of its possible implications. Eventually Roosevelt
sent a message to Harriman in Moscow emphasizing that he expected to
'retain complete freedom of action after this conference is over'. It was
now that Churchill quickly proposed — and Stalin as quickly accepted —
the celebrated division of southeastern Europe: ending (after further
haggling between Eden and Molotov) with 90 per cent Soviet predominance
in Rumania, 80 per cent in Bulgaria and Hungary, fifty-fifty in Jugoslavia,
90 per cent British predominance in Greece.

Churchill in discussing this with Harriman used the phrase 'spheres of
influence'. But he insisted that these were only 'immediate wartime arrangements' and received a highly general blessing from Roosevelt. Yet, whatever
Churchill intended, there is reason to believe that Stalin construed the
percentages as an agreement, not a declaration; as practical arithmetic, not
algebra. For Stalin, it should be understood, the sphere-of-influence idea
did not mean that he would abandon all efforts to spread communism in
some other nation's sphere; it did mean that, if he tried this and the other
side cracked down, he could not feel he had serious cause for complaint.
[. . .]

It is not unreasonable to suppose that Stalin would have been satisfied
at the end of the war to secure what Kennan has called 'a protective glacis
along Russia's western border', and that, in exchange for a free hand in
Eastern Europe, he was prepared to give the British and Americans equally
free hands in their zones of vital interest, including in nations as close to
Russia as Greece (for the British) and, very probably — or at least so the
Jugoslavs believe — China (for the United States). In other words, his initial
objectives were very probably not world conquest but Russian security.

V

It is now pertinent to inquire why the United States rejected the idea of
stabilizing the world by division into spheres of influence and insisted on
an East European strategy. [. . .]

The first reason is that they regarded this solution as containing within itself the seeds of a third world war. The balance-of-power idea seemed inherently unstable. It had always broken down in the past. It held out to each power the permanent temptation to try to alter the balance in its own favor, and it built this temptation into the international order. It would turn the great powers of 1945 away from the objective of concerting common policies toward competition for postwar advantage. [. . .] The Americans were perfectly ready to acknowledge that Russia was entitled to convincing assurance of her national security — but not this way. 'I could sympathize fully with Stalin's desire to protect his western borders from future attack', as Hull put it. 'But I felt that this security could best be obtained through a strong postwar peace organization.'

Hull's remark suggests the second objection: that the sphere-of-influence approach would, in the words of the State Department in 1945, 'militate against the establishment and effective functioning of a broader system of general security in which all countries will have their part'. The United Nations, in short, was seen as the alternative to the balance of power. Nor did the universalists see any necessary incompatibility between the Russian desire for 'friendly governments' on its frontier and the American desire for self-determination in Eastern Europe. [. . .] The American criteria were [. . .] that the government 'should be dedicated to the preservation of civil liberties' and 'should favor social and economic reforms'. A string of New Deal states — of Finlands and Czechoslovakias — seemed a reasonable compromise solution.

Third, the universalists feared that the sphere-of-influence approach would be what Hull termed 'a haven for the isolationists', who would advocate America's participation in Western Hemisphere affairs on condition that it did not participate in European or Asian affairs. Hull also feared that spheres of interest would lead to 'closed trade areas or discriminatory systems' and thus defeat his cherished dream of a low-tariff, freely trading world.

Fourth, the sphere-of-interest solution meant the betrayal of the principles for which the Second World War was being fought — the Atlantic Charter, the Four Freedoms, the Declaration of the United Nations. Poland summed up the problem. Britain, having gone to war to defend the independence of Poland from the Germans, could not easily conclude the war by surrendering the independence of Poland to the Russians. Thus, as Hopkins told Stalin after Roosevelt's death in 1945, Poland had 'become the symbol of our ability to work out problems with the Soviet Union'. [. . .]

Fifth, the sphere-of-influence solution would create difficult domestic problems in American politics. Roosevelt was aware of the six million or more Polish votes in the 1944 election; even more acutely, he was aware of the broader and deeper attack which would follow if, after going to war to stop the Nazi conquest of Europe, he permitted the war to end with the communist conquest of Eastern Europe. [. . .] Roosevelt believed that no administration could survive which did not try everything short of war to save Eastern Europe, and he was the supreme American politician of the century.

Sixth, if the Russians were allowed to overrun Eastern Europe without argument, would that satisfy them? Even Kennan, in a dispatch of May 1944, admitted that the 'urge' had dreadful potentialities: 'If initially successful, will it know where to stop? Will it not be inexorably carried forward, by its very nature, in a struggle to reach the whole — to attain complete mastery of the shores of the Atlantic and the Pacific?' His own answer was that there were inherent limits to the Russian capacity to expand — 'that Russia will not have an easy time in maintaining the power which it has seized over other people in Eastern and Central Europe unless it receives both moral and material assistance from the West'. [. . .]

Most of those involved [. . .] rejected Kennan's answer and stayed with his question. If the West turned its back on Eastern Europe, the higher probability, in their view, was that the Russians would use their security zone, not just for defensive purposes, but as a springboard from which to mount an attack on Western Europe, now shattered by war, a vacuum of power awaiting its master. [. . .] If a row with Russia were inevitable, every consideration of prudence dictated that it should take place in Eastern rather than Western Europe.

Thus idealism and realism joined in opposition to the sphere-of-influence solution. The consequence was a determination to assert an American interest in the postwar destiny of all nations, including those of Eastern Europe.

VI

For better or worse, this was the American position. It is now necessary to attempt the imaginative leap and consider the impact of this position on the leaders of the Soviet Union who, also for better or for worse, had reached the bitter conclusion that the survival of their country depended on their unchallenged control of the corridors through which enemies had so often invaded their homeland. They could claim to have been keeping their own side of the sphere-of-influence bargain. [. . .] In overt political matters the Russians were scrupulously playing the game. They had watched in silence while the British shot down communists in Greece. In Jugoslavia Stalin was urging Tito (as Djilas later revealed) to keep King Peter. They had not only acknowledged Western pre-eminence in Italy but had recognized the Badoglio régime; the Italian Communists had even voted (against the Socialists and the Liberals) for the renewal of the Lateran Pacts.

They would not regard anti-communist action in a Western zone as a *casus belli*; and they expected reciprocal license to assert their own authority in the East. But the principle of self-determination was carrying the United States into a deeper entanglement in Eastern Europe than the Soviet Union claimed as a right (whatever it was doing underground) in the affairs of Italy, Greece or China. When the Russians now exercised in Eastern Europe the same brutal control they were prepared to have Washington exercise in the American sphere of influence, the American protests, given the paranoia produced alike by Russian history and Leninist ideology, no doubt seemed not only an act of hypocrisy but a threat to security. [. . .]

So Moscow very probably, and not unnaturally, perceived the emphasis on self-determination as a systematic and deliberate pressure on Russia's western frontiers. Moreover, the restoration of capitalism to countries freed at frightful cost by the Red Army no doubt struck the Russians as the betrayal of the principles for which *they* were fighting. 'That they, the victors', Isaac Deutscher has suggested, 'should now preserve an order from which they had experienced nothing but hostility, and could expect nothing but hostility . . . would have been the most miserable anti-climax to their great "war of liberation".' By 1944 Poland was the critical issue [. . .]. While the West saw the point of Stalin's demand for a 'friendly government' in Warsaw, the American insistence on the sovereign virtues of free elections [. . .] created an insoluble problem in those countries, like Poland (and Rumania), where free elections would almost certainly produce anti-Soviet governments.

The Russians thus may well have estimated the Western pressures as calculated to encourage their enemies in Eastern Europe and to defeat their own minimum objective of a protective glacis. Everything still hung, however, on the course of military operations. The wartime collaboration had been created by one thing, and one thing alone: the threat of Nazi victory. So long as this threat was real, so was the collaboration. In late December 1944, von Rundstedt launched his counter-offensive in the Ardennes. A few weeks later, when Roosevelt, Churchill and Stalin gathered in the Crimea, it was in the shadow of this last considerable explosion of German power. The meeting at Yalta was still dominated by the mood of war. [. . .]

Harriman still had the feeling before Yalta that the Kremlin had 'two approaches to their postwar policies' and that Stalin himself was 'of two minds'. One approach emphasized the internal reconstruction and development of

Russia; the other its external expansion. But in the meantime the fact which dominated all political decisions – that is, the war against Germany – was moving into its final phase. In the weeks after Yalta, the military situation changed with great rapidity. As the Nazi threat declined, so too did the need for co-operation. The Soviet Union, feeling itself menaced by the American idea of self-determination and the borderlands diplomacy to which it was leading, skeptical whether the United Nations would protect its frontiers as reliably as its own domination in Eastern Europe, began to fulfil its security requirements unilaterally.

In March Stalin expressed his evaluation of the United Nations by rejecting Roosevelt's plea that Molotov come to the San Francisco conference, if only for the opening sessions. In the next weeks the Russians emphatically and crudely worked their will in Eastern Europe, above all in the test country of Poland. They were ignoring the Declaration on Liberated Europe, ignoring the Atlantic Charter, self-determination, human freedom and everything else the Americans considered essential for a stable peace. 'We must clearly recognize', Harriman wired Washington a few days before Roosevelt's death, 'that the Soviet program is the establishment of totalitarianism, ending personal liberty and democracy as we know and respect it.' [. . .]

The atmosphere of mutual suspicion was beginning to rise. In January 1945 Molotov formally proposed that the United States grant Russia a $6 billion credit for postwar reconstruction. With characteristic tact he explained that he was doing this as a favor to save America from a postwar depression. The proposal seems to have been diffidently made and diffidently received. Roosevelt requested that the matter 'not be pressed further' on the American side until he had a chance to talk with Stalin; [. . .] the proposal was renewed in the very different political atmosphere of August. This time Washington inexplicably mislaid the request during the transfer of the records of the Foreign Economic Administration to the State Department. It did not turn up again until March 1946. Of course this was impossible for the Russians to believe; it is hard enough even for those acquainted with the capacity of the American government for incompetence to believe; and it only strengthened Soviet suspicions of American purposes.

The American credit was one conceivable form of Western contribution to Russian reconstruction. Another was lend-lease, and the possibility of reconstruction aid under the lend-lease protocol had already been discussed in 1944. But in May 1945 Russia, like Britain, suffered from Truman's abrupt termination of lend-lease shipments – 'unfortunate and even brutal', Stalin told Hopkins, adding that, if it was 'designed as pressure on the Russians in order to soften them up, then it was a fundamental mistake'.

A third form was German reparations. Here Stalin in demanding $10 billion in reparations for the Soviet Union made his strongest fight at Yalta. Roosevelt, while agreeing essentially with Churchill's opposition, tried to postpone the matter by accepting the Soviet figure as a 'basis for discussion' — a formula which led to future misunderstanding. In short, the Russian hope for major Western assistance in postwar reconstruction foundered on three events which the Kremlin could well have interpreted respectively as deliberate sabotage (the loan request), blackmail (lend-lease cancellation) and pro-Germanism (reparations). [. . .]

The Cold War had now begun. It was the product not of a decision but of a dilemma. Each side felt compelled to adopt policies which the other could not but regard as a threat to the principles of the peace. Each then felt compelled to undertake defensive measures. Thus the Russians saw no choice but to consolidate their security in Eastern Europe. The Americans, regarding Eastern Europe as the first step toward Western Europe, responded by asserting their interest in the zone the Russians deemed vital to their security. The Russians concluded that the West was resuming its old course of capitalist encirclement; that it was purposefully laying the foundation for anti-Soviet régimes in the area defined by the blood of centuries as crucial to Russian survival. Each side believed with passion that future international stability depended on the success of its own conception of world order. Each side, in pursuing its own clearly indicated and deeply cherished principles, was only confirming the fear of the other that it was bent on aggression.

Very soon the process began to acquire a cumulative momentum. The impending collapse of Germany thus provoked new troubles: the Russians, for example, sincerely feared that the West was planning a separate surrender of the German armies in Italy in a way which would release troops for Hitler's eastern front, as they subsequently feared that the Nazis might succeed in surrendering Berlin to the West. This was the context in which the atomic bomb now appeared. Though the revisionist argument that Truman dropped the bomb less to defeat Japan than to intimidate Russia is not convincing, this thought unquestionably appealed to some in Washington as at least an advantageous side-effect of Hiroshima.

So the machinery of suspicion and counter-suspicion, action and counter-action, was set in motion. But, given relations among traditional national states, there was still no reason, even with all the postwar jostling, why this should not have remained a manageable situation. What made it unmanageable, what caused the rapid escalation of the Cold War and in another two years completed the division of Europe, was a set of considerations which this account has thus far excluded.

VII

Up to this point, the discussion has considered the schism within the war-time coalition as if it were entirely the result of disagreements among national states. Assuming this framework, there was unquestionably a failure of communication between America and Russia, a misperception of signals and, as time went on, a mounting tendency to ascribe ominous motives to the other side. It seems hard, for example, to deny that American postwar policy created genuine difficulties for the Russians and even assumed a threatening aspect for them. All this the revisionists have rightly and usefully emphasized.

But the great omission of the revisionists – and also the fundamental explanation of the speed with which the Cold War escalated – lies precisely in the fact that the Soviet Union was *not* a traditional national state. This is where the 'mirror image', invoked by some psychologists, falls down. For the Soviet Union was a phenomenon very different from America or Britain: it was a totalitarian state, endowed with an all-explanatory, all-consuming ideology, committed to the infallibility of government and party, still in a somewhat messianic mood, equating dissent with treason, and ruled by a dictator who, for all his quite extraordinary abilities, had his paranoid moments.

Marxism-Leninism gave the Russian leaders a view of the world according to which all societies were inexorably destined to proceed along appointed roads by appointed stages until they achieved the classless nirvana. More-over, given the resistance of the capitalists to this development, the existence of any non-communist state was *by definition* a threat to the Soviet Union. [. . .]

Stalin and his associates, whatever Roosevelt or Truman did or failed to do, were bound to regard the United States as the enemy, not because of this deed or that, but because of the primordial fact that America was the leading capitalist power and thus, by Leninist syllogism, unappeasably hostile, driven by the logic of its system to oppose, encircle and destroy Soviet Russia. Nothing the United States could have done in 1944-5 would have abolished this mistrust, required and sanctified as it was by Marxist gospel [. . .] So long as the United States remained a capitalist democracy, no American policy, given Moscow's theology, could hope to win basic Soviet confidence, and every American action was poisoned from the source. So long as the Soviet Union remained a messianic state, ideology compelled a steady expansion of communist power.

It is easy, of course, to exaggerate the capacity of ideology to control

events. The tension of acting according to revolutionary abstractions is too
much for most nations to sustain over a long period [. . .] . As any revolution grows older, normal human and social motives will increasingly reassert
themselves. In due course, we can be sure, Leninism will be about as
effective in governing the daily lives of Russians as Christianity is in governing the daily lives of Americans. [. . .]

Paradoxically, of the forces capable of bringing about a modification of
ideology, the most practical and effective was the Soviet dictatorship itself.
If Stalin was an ideologist, he was also a pragmatist. If he saw everything
through the lenses of Marxism-Leninism, he also, as the infallible expositor
of the faith, could reinterpret Marxism-Leninism to justify anything he
wanted to do at any given moment. No doubt Roosevelt's ignorance of
Marxism-Leninism was inexcusable and led to grievous miscalculations.
But Roosevelt's efforts to work on and through Stalin were not so hopelessly naive as it used to be fashionable to think. With the extraordinary
instinct of a great political leader, Roosevelt intuitively understood that
Stalin was the *only* lever available to the West against the Leninist ideology
and the Soviet system. If Stalin could be reached, then alone was there a
chance of getting the Russians to act contrary to the prescriptions of their
faith. The best evidence is that Roosevelt retained a certain capacity to
influence Stalin to the end; the nominal Soviet acquiescence in American
universalism as late as Yalta was perhaps an indication of that. It is in this
way that the death of Roosevelt was crucial – not in the vulgar sense that
his policy was then reversed by his successor, which did not happen, but in
the sense that no other American could hope to have the restraining
impact on Stalin which Roosevelt might for a while have had.

Stalin alone could have made any difference. Yet Stalin, in spite of the
impression of sobriety and realism he made on Westerners who saw him
during the Second World War, was plainly a man of deep and morbid
obsessions and compulsions. [. . .] A revisionist fallacy has been to treat
Stalin as just another Realpolitik statesman, as Second World War revisionists see Hitler as just another Stresemann or Bismarck. But the record
makes it clear that in the end nothing could satisfy Stalin's paranoia. His
own associates failed. Why does anyone suppose that any conceivable
American policy would have succeeded?

An analysis of the origins of the Cold War which leaves out these factors
– the intransigence of Leninist ideology, the sinister dynamics of a totalitarian society and the madness of Stalin – is obviously incomplete. It was
these factors which made it hard for the West to accept the thesis that
Russia was moved only by a desire to protect its security and would be
satisfied by the control of Eastern Europe; it was these factors which

charged the debate between universalism and spheres of influence with apocalyptic potentiality.

Leninism and totalitarianism created a structure of thought and behavior which made postwar collaboration between Russia and America — in any normal sense of civilized intercourse between national states — inherently impossible. The Soviet dictatorship of 1945 simply could not have survived such a collaboration. Indeed, nearly a quarter-century later, the Soviet régime, though it has meanwhile moved a good distance, could still hardly survive it without risking the release inside Russia of energies profoundly opposed to communist despotism. As for Stalin, he may have represented the only force in 1945 capable of overcoming Stalinism, but the very traits which enabled him to win absolute power expressed terrifying instabilities of mind and temperament and hardly offered a solid foundation for a peaceful world. [. . .]

15 EUROPEAN INTEGRATION

A. TOWARDS A HISTORY OF EUROPEAN INTEGRATION (extract)

Walter Lipgens

Source: 'Towards a history of European integration: projected volumes of the EUI Florence', *Journal of Common Market Studies*, vol.XVII, no.1, September 1978, pp.83-9.

Soon after its inauguration in October 1976, the European University Institute decided, as one of its major projects of research, to promote a series of volumes of documents covering the History of European Integration and a multi-volume description of the History of European Integration. To so many outstanding colleagues in contemporary history, assembled from most countries of the European Community, it needs no explanation that, in the age of world wars, and especially between 1943 and 1949, the completely new world structure in which we are living today came into being; and that historical science must do justice to its rôle in society by clarifying from the sources the way of that process, and the consequences.

There are at least *three* major factors that undoubtedly *distinguish* the world political situation after the two world wars from the pre-1914 world: the fact that the two former flanking powers of Europe, the USA and the Soviet Union, have developed into the dominating world powers of the second half of the twentieth century, each of them a continental union in itself with powerful resources; the fact that the 'Third World' countries previously administered as colonies by Europeans have attained independence; and the fact that in Europe, as an answer to its catastrophic decline in a single generation, a political idea, previously developed by a few individuals, became an organized European unification movement that succeeded in inducing parties and governments in the larger Western part of Europe, which in the American sphere of influence had retained the freedom to do so, to take the first steps towards a policy of unification. The process thereby begun of European integration led to the foundation of supranational organizations, and has maintained itself, despite severe setbacks, as the dominating theme of European post-war history after the East-West conflict, and is now moving forwards to the first direct election of a European Parliament.

It is this third fact that provides the historiographical task of our research project. The European integration that has begun and that differentiates

Europe after the Second World War clearly from pre-war Europe means that 'European history' thereafter takes two forms: a continuation of the national histories, with their specific problems, institutions and archives, and in new forms a common European history of the efforts towards economic and political integration, of the joint West European institutions founded to that end and their archives, the historiographical treatment of which will call for multinational cooperation. [. . .]

I

The basic fact of development since the First World War and particularly in the decade from 1941 to 1950 was the decline of Europe on the one hand and the rise of the new world powers on the other hand. The European States that before 1914 had, because of cultural and technical competitive advantages, dominated the world directly or indirectly for a good three centuries, had in two world wars that began within Europe mutually ruined themselves and rendered themselves impotent. Russia and America, on the other hand, took up independent leadership rôles in world politics, each as the bearer of a world programme of its own. Measured against the rise of these two continental unions, each of which had capacities that exceeded those of the European States taken together, the European States had already become medium or small States in the inter-war period; the renewed decline into reactionary nationalism ended in 1945 with the new world powers meeting on the soil of the devastated old continent and formally restoring 26 small sovereign States in Europe, while *de facto* dividing the old continent between themselves into spheres of influence. The capacities of these continental unions showed a scale of technical and political power that had outgrown units of the size of the European nation States: none of them can any longer fulfill the most primitive function of a State by giving security against foreign conquest (as almost all of them – except Britain – had demonstrated in collapse and years of occupation). Between the two new world powers, which together controlled some 90 per cent of the military potential of the world, Europe was now, as Arnold Toynbee with his tireless accuracy formulated it, a huge power vacuum. The European cultural unit, geographically reduced in the East and losing its colonial areas, had now, on the world political scale of the post-war era, become a balkanized intermediate area between the new world powers.

In response to the decline that was already apparent following the First World War, an increasing number of authors had in the inter-war years already called on the European peoples to overcome their internal disputes and unite, in view of their economic impoverishment and the rise of extra-European powers.

These plans in the inter-war years and also those made in exile during the Second World War, had mentioned the need for closer cooperation and for its guarantee by some institutions similar to confederation of States. The real break-through to the federal concept was achieved in face of the continental cataclysms of the years 1941-2, notably in the future plans of the non-communist resistance movements on the continent: only a voluntary federal integration of the European peoples into a federal State could meet the needs. In these resistance texts the following themes are to the fore:

1. The basic, central justification mentioned by most authors for their plans for European federation was formulated as an ideological rejection of 'L'idolisation des Etats', as 'Défense de la France', 'la fausse nécessité du totalitarisme, nécessité forgée de toutes pièces par un nationalisme exaspéré'. The nation State system that had brought so much suffering to the European people and reduced itself to absurdity in the excesses of the fascisms, was felt to be no longer tenable. Instead, the point was to protect the real values, individual freedoms, religious and political human rights against these *étatiste* nationalisms through a European federation that would have the task of preventing the return of nationalism and fascism in the member States.

2. Just as basic a justification, mentioned by almost all the authors in the midst of the sufferings of the war, was that European integration should finally prevent these nation States from plunging the European population into a new war in each generation. The League of Nations of the inter-war period had not been able with its purely inter-governmental machinery to carry out its task of preventing war. The League of Nations failed, as Léon Blum put it in 1941 in the Vichy jail in a text that was influential in the whole of the French resistance, 'because it was not a great autonomous power, independent of the national sovereignties and above them; because to carry out its decisions it possessed neither a political authority nor a material force that would have priority over those of the States'. It was only European federative integration that could put a final end to 'European civil wars' and bring about the definitive guarantee of peace in Europe. Not a renewed loose League of Nations but only a supra-national federal authority could finally overcome the warring nationalisms.

3. The resistance authors shared the worldwide concern to make impossible any repetition of German aggression; however, faced with the question of how this could be done without breeding a new German nationalism

through one-sided impositions, occupation and reparations etc., and without creating an economic disaster area in the centre of Europe, to the detriment of the whole, by demolitions and constant reduction of the industrial level, they answered it quite differently from the planners of nation State provenance, by asserting that the 'German problem' could genuinely be solved only by the complete integration of Germany into a European federation.

4. Most texts did speak of the economic necessity for a common market. What 'Liberté', for instance, had said already in 1941 was often repeated: Europe was 'the smallest continent, with 28 nations side by side in it. The international division of labour that makes each nation dependent on the other, and the development of means of communication, make these boundaries intolerable. They must be removed.' However, this was regarded as proven already by the economic crisis of 1930, and in resistance texts was generally brought forward only as an addition to arguments 1 to 3.

Immediately after liberation in 1944-5, in all the countries of the area of continental collapse, there arose organized groups of federalists, mostly under the leadership of erstwhile resistance leaders, who proclaimed the need for the integration of the European peoples from these motives and for these reasons. But any possibility of extension, far less realization, of this concept was initially blocked by the two victorious world powers, whose troops were in Europe and who decided all questions of importance; they had provided for the restoration of the European nation States and the creation of a global order for peace. The Soviet Union had categorically insisted on the elimination of any hint of the integration of European countries from allied post-war planning, and the USA under Roosevelt agreed so as to guarantee lasting Russian-American friendship — a bipolar world in which Europe could no longer count as a power on its own. Faced with this unanimity the proponents of European integration had to endure, from summer 1945 to summer 1946, a year of bitter hopelessness and in-effectiveness, while nation State ideas and bureaucracies won back ground. It was only when during the summer of 1946 the differences between the world powers became increasingly clear and the fear gained ground that the USA and the Soviet Union might come to conflict that the European federalists were able, with increasing response, to offer the idea of European federation with a new approach as a contribution to solving the problem. Now, a full awareness of the weakness and fragmentation of Europe between the new world powers and a growing consciousness of the main lines of development mentioned at the beginning came to the fore as a fifth theme: that the European peoples, between the new world powers, could only win back an independent future and a say in affairs by integration.

After a preliminary congress in Hertenstein, which declared that Europe wished to 'solve the problems of its destiny itself in the spirit of federalism' and thereby 'make its contribution to reconstruction and to a world confederacy of peoples', all these groups gradually united in the 'Union Européenne des Fédéralistes' (UEF, founded in Paris in 1946), which was the element of the future 'European unification movement' with the highest membership. All their programmes started from the idea of an all-European integration from Warsaw to Paris, as a 'bridge between East and West', often called the 'third force'. The UEF working session in mid-April 1947 in Amsterdam was still stating as its goal 'qu'une Entente Fédérale Européenne est indispensable pour surmonter la politique des blocs, et éviter ainsi un nouveau conflit qui résulterait inévitablement du partage du monde en zones d'influence'. But actual development led to two decisive limitations:

1. The Soviet Union, oriented under Stalin towards direct imperialist rule over the Eastern third of Europe occupied by it and in its Western policy guided by the principle 'divide et impera', refused any positive cooperation in European integration; it also compelled the rejection of the European idea in the countries it occupied and bound the communist parties in Western Europe to a reactionary nationalism.

The USA on the other hand, unwilling in the face of Stalinist expansion to allow all Europe's helping power to fall into Russian hands, took up the idea of European integration positively. During the decisive Foreign Ministers' conference in Moscow, when its failure was already becoming clear, the US Senate and House of Representatives resolved on March 31, 1947 'that the Congress favours the creation of a United States of Europe within the framework of the United Nations'. Two months later, Secretary of State Marshall offered the Europeans large resources for economic reconstruction, on the condition that they 'combine their forces'.

In August 1947, the UEF took the difficult decision 'to start where it is possible . . ., where the peoples still have a certain freedom of decision', in Western Europe, and provisionally to abandon cooperation with East Europe and accept the Marshall plan. Thus the European unification movement was not able itself to select the way to realization; for the duration of the East-West conflict between the two world powers it became a functional element of Western self-assertion in that conflict.

2. In the Western European negotiations that were beginning it proved

immediately that Britain was not yet ready to follow the idea of European integration in the sense of the combination and communitarization of erstwhile state areas of competence, but insisted on institutionalized co-operation between autonomous governments as for the moment the only acceptable step towards a 'Western Union'. This corresponded to the still unbroken (in 1948) self-confidence of the country that, thanks to the entry of Russia and the USA, had, in contradistinction to almost all the countries of the continent, survived the war without the experience of collapse, and which still saw itself as the centre of a Commonwealth. Britain managed to bring it about that the ERP aid did not serve the construction of a common market, but was invested in the restoration of the national economies, against the egoisms of which the economic cooperation machinery of the OEEC (from April 1948), which aimed at unanimity, had to begin a laborious struggle, often subject to setbacks from vetoes by individual countries.

Likewise, the call for the convocation of a European constituent assembly, put forward in 1948 by 190 British MPs and large majorities in the Belgian and French Parliaments, was reduced by the British government's resistance in governmental negotiations to the status of a purely consultative Council of Europe, adopted in May 1949 — to the regret also of so many British friends.

Following these two limitations and disappointments, the federalists and the parliamentary majorities of the Western European continental States came in 1950 to the resolve to make a real start on the work of integration in a still narrower area, intially without Britain and Scandinavia, but finally with a supra-national approach. 'The addition of sovereign States meeting in a council will not create an entity.' The real Europe must be striven for 'through the setting up of joint economic bases and at the same time by creating new authorities, recognized by the states' — these were the words with which on May 3, 1950 Jean Monnet justified his proposal to Foreign Minister Robert Schuman to take a direct step aimed at an important point and start by bringing coal and steel under a supra-national authority. This was the second start by the method of supra-national functionalism, and on the realization of the Coal and Steel Community by great majorities in the countries of the Six. The premature attempt to extend it to a defence community failed in 1954. Instead, the Rome treaties brought its extension to the whole of the economy, leaving the question open of how to get to political union from there. But our attempt to write the history has first of all to deal with the start and with the historiographical problems of the first decade. [. . .]

B.   OF BLIND MEN, ELEPHANTS AND INTERNATIONAL INTEGRATION

Donald J. Puchala

Source: *Journal of Common Market Studies*, vol.X, no.3, 1972, pp.267-84.

The story of the blind men and the elephant is universally known. Several blind men approached an elephant and each touched the animal in an effort to discover what the beast looked like. Each blind man, however, touched a different part of the large animal, and each concluded that the elephant had the appearance of the part he had touched. Hence, the blind man who felt the animal's trunk concluded that an elephant must be tall and slender, while his fellow who touched the beast's ear concluded that an elephant must be oblong and flat. Others of course reached different conclusions. The total result was that no man arrived at a very accurate description of the elephant. Yet, each man had gained enough evidence from his own experience to disbelieve his fellows and to maintain a lively debate about the nature of the beast.

The experience of scholars who have been conceptually grappling with contemporary international integration is not unlike the episode of the blind men and the elephant. More than fifteen years of defining, redefining, refining, modeling and theorizing have failed to generate satisfactory conceptualizations of exactly what it is we are talking about when we refer to 'international integration' and exactly what it is we are trying to learn when we study this phenomenon. Part of the problem stems from the fact that different researchers have been looking at different parts, dimensions or manifestations of the phenomenon. Furthermore, different schools of researchers have exalted different parts of the integration 'elephant'. They have claimed either that their parts were in fact whole beasts, or that their parts were the most important ones, the others being of marginal interest. Added conceptual confusion has followed from the fact that the phenomenon under investigation — international integration and all it involves — has turned out to be more complex than anyone initially suspected. Consequently, uncertainty *within* schools of researchers currently compounds dissension *between* the schools. Alas, the 'elephant' grew in size and changed in form at the very moment that the blind men sought to grasp it! Finally, many of those who have tried to describe and explain international integration have been influenced in their intellectual efforts by normative preferences. As a result we have all too often found international integration discussed in terms of what it *should be* and what it *should be leading toward* rather than in terms of what it really is and is actually leading toward. In light of the reigning conceptual confusion in the realm of integration studies it is difficult to see why the field has acquired a reputation for theoretical sophistication. Rather, I should think that those of us in the field would be rather embarrassed at the fact that after fifteen years of effort we are still uncertain about what it is we are studying.

This paper is about international integration, about what it is, and about what it is not. My problem: what is actually taking place 'out there' in the empirical world when we say that something we call international integration is taking place? Since questions of definition and description continue to pose barriers to cumulative research and theoretical synthesis in integration studies, what I offer here is yet another tilt at the definitional windmill. [. . .]

I The Inadequacies of Conventional Conceptualizations

One of the most difficult intellectual feats to accomplish is to confront an essentially new phenomenon, recognize its novelty, and then go on to describe and explain this novelty without destroying it with blunt and inappropriate analytical instruments. More specifically, I believe that I can make a fairly strong case for the assertion that those clusterings of events we label 'international integration' are essentially new happenings peculiar to the post-World War II era. Contemporary international integration is a product of forces, interests and attitudes peculiarly prevalent in the post-1945 world. It consequently embodies structures and processes and thrives in an attitudinal environment characteristic of this new postwar world. Despite this, however, we in integration studies have continually insisted upon analyzing cases of this new phenomenon as if they were instances of more familiar and time-tested patterns. That is, instead of asking 'what is contemporary international integration?' and thereby opening our minds to its novelty, we have asked, 'is it federalism?' 'is it nationalism?' 'is it functionalism?' or 'is it old-fashioned power politics?' As it has turned out, after some fifteen years of research, contemporary international integration is none of these, nor of any combination of them. Therefore, conventional analytical models reflecting traditional familiar phenomena do not accurately describe, do not satisfactorily explain, and do not even raise very productive questions about the new, unfamiliar, and rather unconventional phenomenon, contemporary international integration. For example:

(1) *Contemporary International Integration is not Federalism*. At least it is not classical federalism. Thus far, the patterns of political — economic interaction in different regions of the world — Western Europe, Central America, East Africa, Eastern Europe — which have attracted the attentions of

students of international integration, have not by and large resembled patterns suggested by the federalist model. For example, no new central governments have been established to assume functions traditionally allotted to federal governments. Not even in Western Europe are new central authorities representing groups of states in international relations. On the occasions when the Commission speaks for the Six internationally, as in the case of the Kennedy Round negotiations or with regard to association agreements, its positions symbolize multi-lateral diplomatic compromises among six governments much more than they represent the policies of any central or 'federal' government. In addition, even when the Commission intermittently speaks for the 'Six' each member-state continues to speak for itself in world councils and capitals. Then, too, let us not forget that all international integration arrangements currently in existence, including the Western European system, are functionally limited mostly to economic concerns, and therefore poorly approximate the functionally diffuse systems implicit in the federalist model.

In fairness, it is true that analysts using federalist models as guides to inquiry have looked upon contemporary international integration as 'emergent' rather than 'mature' federalism. Nevertheless, the point is that they have been preoccupied (if not obsessed) with questions about the degree of central authority present, the degree of state sovereignty relinquished, and the parcelling of prerogative, power and jurisdiction among national and international authorities. Moreover, these same analysts have tended to equate 'progress' or 'success' in international integration with movement toward central government.

Such analysis is of course legitimate. But it has not been very productive. Most obviously it has not turned up very much federalism in contemporary international integration. But more importantly, conceptualizing and conducting inquiry in terms of the federalist model has tended to blind analysts to a number of interesting questions. Most broadly, is it really true that no progress toward international integration in various parts of the world has been made simply because little movement in the direction of regional central government has been registered? More provocatively perhaps, to what extent does participation in an international integration arrangement actually enhance rather than undermine national sovereignty? Relatedly, to what extent does an international integration arrangement preserve rather than supersede an international state system? Clearly, the analyst in the federalist mode is not prompted to ask these latter sorts of questions. Is he missing something of significance?

(2) *Neither is International Integration Actually 'Nationalism' at the*

Regional Level. So ingrained has the nationalism model become in Western political thinking and analysis, that we find it difficult to conceive of a non-national international actor, or a political system uncomplemented by an underlying community of people or peoples. Naturally, then, when talk of and movement toward regional unity in different parts of the world attracted the attentions of scholars, a good many assumed that movement toward international integration had to be progress toward the social and cultural assimilation of nationalities — i.e. toward *nationalism* at the regional level. For example, cued by historical precedents we looked for evidence of integration in Western Europe in the 'Europeanization' of Frenchmen, Germans and Italians, much in the way that historians sought and found evidence of national integration in the Frenchifying of Normans, the Germanization of Bavarians and the Italianization of Neopolitans. The nationalism model led us to focus upon the assimilatory impacts of inter-actions and transactions among diverse peoples manifested in enhanced familiarity, responsiveness, and mutual identification, as well as emergent in-group/out-group consciousness. But though we were guided by validated and operational theories of nationalism, and despite the fact that we wielded the most sophisticated methodological tools of modern social science, our researches turned up few 'Europeans', even fewer 'Central Americans' and 'East Africans' and no 'East Europeans', at all. This lacking evidence of progress toward the social and cultural assimilation of nationalities led some analysts to conclude that contemporary international integration was more myth than reality — no nationalism therefore no integration! Others, however, cherished evidence drawn from youth studies and concluded that regional nationalism, at least in Western Europe, was present after all, and that the heyday of European community would arrive as the current younger generation gained maturity and as its members acquired positions of influence and responsibility. Still others, convinced that assimilation simply had to be a component of contemporary international integration, worded and reworded survey questions until 'regional nationality' did at last emerge in poll results, irrespective of whether it existed in respondents' attitudes.

Credit goes to the nationalism analysts for recognizing that contemporary international integration requires a particular kind of attitudinal environment. However, the environment they seek has failed to materialize. Problems in using the nationalism model as a guide to analyzing contemporary international integration are similar to those involved in using the federalism model. First, testing the model against reality in Western Europe, in Central America and elsewhere produces negative results. Regional nationalism, as noted, turns out not to be a component of international integration. Second, as with the federalist case, asking the analytical questions suggested by the nationalism model, deters thinking about a range of interesting alternative questions. For example, the analyst guided by the nationalism model is directed toward asking questions about people-to-people interactions and transactions, about similarities and differences in peoples' life styles, value systems and cultural norms, and especially about their attitudes toward one another and attendant percep- tions of 'we-ness'. But are these really the appropriate questions to ask about the attitudinal environments supportive of inter-governmental co- operation and international institutionalization? Does it really matter what peoples think about one another? Or, rather, does it perhaps matter more what these people think about international cooperation and about supra- national decision-making? The point here is that while the analyst guided by the nationalism model has been primarily concerned with links and bonds among peoples, he has by and large ignored links and bonds between peoples and their governments and between peoples and international organizations and processes. Is he missing something of significance?

(3) [*Functionalist Analysts*] have achieved greater descriptive accuracy than others grappling with contemporary international integration. Part of this accuracy, of course, must be accounted for by the fact that architects of international integration in Western Europe and elsewhere were directly influenced by functionalist thinking and therefore constructed their systems from functionalist blueprints. Still, let us give credit where credit is due. Functionalist analysts have accurately located the origins of inter- national cooperation in realms of functional interdependence; they have pinpointed the significance of sector approaches; they have grasped the importance of non-governmental transnational actors.

Yet, very little in contemporary international integration has actually 'worked' the way the functionalist design said that it would. Most reveal- ingly, national governments have remained conspicuous and pivotal in internationally integrating systems, quite in contrast to the functionalist model which shunts these to the periphery of action. Leadership, initiative and prerogative have by and large remained with national governments. They have not gravitated to technocrats, bureaucrats and non-governmental actors. Moreover, national governments participating in international integration schemes have proven far more interested in 'welfare' pursuits and far more restrained in 'power' pursuits than functionalist theorizing would have led us to believe. Equally significant, functional task-areas in international economics, communications, science and technology, which the functionalist model stipulates immune from international politics, have in fact turned out to be the central issue-areas in the lively international politics of international integration. There are simply no non-political issues in relations among states!

Most important, the functionalist model misses the essence of the growth and expansion of international regime during international integration. So concerned are functionalist analysts with sector-to-sector task expansion, that many have failed first to recognize that this sectoral 'spillover' is but one possible variety of expansion or growth during international integration. It is also, incidently, the variety of growth that is least in evidence in existing cases. But, at least two other varieties can be monitored. First, there is expansion in the volume of internationally coordinative activities within given functional sectors. In addition, and much more important, there is possible expansion in the *political system* brought into being when functional sectors are integrated internationally. Such systemic expansion is evidenced by the entrance of increasing numbers of actors and interests into international program-planning and policy-making.

Second, neither have functionalist analysts been fully cognizant of the fact that sector-to-sector task expansion, spillover or its variants index integrative progress only if one assumes that 'functional federation' or multi-sector merger is the end product of international integration. Here again, we are evaluating the present in terms of a hypothetical future which may never come about. If multi-sector merger is not the end product of international integration, if integration does not really go very far beyond the nation-state, then other varieties of systemic growth which reflect activity and complexity rather than extension might be the more telling indicators of healthy and productive international integration.

In sum, the functionalist analyst too has been partially strait-jacketed by his framework for thinking about international integration. He asked how men may achieve international cooperation by circumventing politics among nations. But, he has not asked how international cooperation is in fact achieved during international integration in the very course of international politics. Then, he has asked how functional integration spreads or spills over in the direction of federal government. But, in light of what has actually come to pass in Western Europe, might it not have been more productive to ask how a program of transnational sectoral merger fits into and becomes an integral part of a broader pattern of intraregional international relations? That is, what if the termination state for international integration in fact resembles Western Europe, *circa* 1970? Why do some sectors get merged and others do not? More significantly, what kind of international politics results in a system where some functional sectors are transnationally merged and others are not? Impressionistically speaking, it would seem that this 'broader pattern of intraregional international relations', this complex of merged and unmerged sectors and the aggregation of associated governing authorities of one type or another begins to approximate what we are really talking about when we speak of contemporary international integration. Does the functionalist analyst really recognize this? Is he missing something if he does not?

(4) *Nor, Finally, Is Contemporary International Integration Simply Power Politics.* The school of analysts who have looked upon and thought about international integration within the framework of 'Realist' or *Macht Politik* models have fallen short of understanding what the phenomenon is or involves. To these analysts, international integration is a process of mutual exploitation wherein governments attempt to mobilize and accumulate the resources of neighboring states in the interest of enhancing their own power. Power is to be enhanced so that traditional ends of politics among nations may be accomplished — i.e. international autonomy, military security, diplomatic influence and heightened prestige. In Realist thinking, international organizations created in the course of international integration are but instruments to be used by national governments pursuing self-interests. They are made at the convergent whims of these governments, and flounder or fossilize as their usefulness as instruments of foreign policy comes into question. Over all, the Realist analyst argues that what we are observing 'out there' and calling international integration are really international marriages of convenience, comfortable for all partners as long as self-interests are satisfied, but destined for divorce the moment any partner's interests are seriously frustrated. Hence, international integration drives not toward federalism or nationalism or functionalism, but toward disintegration. It never gets beyond the nation-state.

The wisdom of the Realist model is that it conceives of international integration as a pattern of international relations and not as something above, beyond or aside from politics among nations. But the shortcoming in the model is that it conceives of international integration as *traditional international relations* played by traditional actors, using traditional means in pursuit of traditional ends. So convinced is the political realist that 'there is nothing new under the sun' in international relations that he never seriously asks whether international actors other than national governments may independently influence the allocation of international rewards. Nor does he ask whether actors committed to international integration may be pursuing any other than the traditional inventory of international goals — autonomy, military security, influence and prestige. Do these really remain important goals in contemporary international relations? Nor, finally, does the realist ask how actors committed to integration agreements in fact define their self-interests. Could it be that actors engaged in international integration actually come to consider it in their own self-interest to see that their partners accomplish their goals? In sum, by assuming that international politics remains the 'same old game' and that international integration is but a part of it, the realist analyst is not prompted to ask what is new in contemporary international relations? Is he missing something of significance?

II Toward a New Conceptualization

If there has been a central theme running through my review of analytical models, it is that our conventional frameworks have clouded more than they have illumined our understanding of contemporary international integration. No model describes the integration phenomenon with complete accuracy because all the models present images of what integration could be or should be rather than what it is here and now. Furthermore, attempts to juxtapose or combine the conventional frameworks for analytical purposes by and large yield no more than artificial, untidy results. Clearly, to surmount the conceptual confusion we must set aside the old models, and, beginning from the assumption that international integration could very well be something new that we have never before witnessed in international relations, we must create a new, more appropriate, more productive analytical framework. I contend that this new model must reflect and raise questions about what international integration *is* in Western Europe, Central America, East Africa, etc., *at present*. We must, in other words, stop testing the present in terms of progress toward or regression from hypothetical futures since we really have no way of knowing where or how contemporary international integration is going to end up. The remainder of this essay is a very preliminary step in the direction of a new conceptualization of contemporary international integration.

Is It Really An 'Elephant' After All?

Complexity of Structure. I will hypothesize, though I cannot argue the case as convincingly as I would like to at this moment, that *contemporary international integration can best be thought of as a set of processes that produce and sustain a Concordance System at the international level.* 'Concordance', according to dictionaries I have consulted, means, 'agreement' or 'harmony', and 'concord', its root, refers to 'peaceful relations among nations'. A 'Concordance System' by my definition is an international system wherein actors find it possible consistently to harmonize their interests, compromise their differences and reap mutual rewards from their interactions. I selected the term 'Concordance System' primarily because I found it necessary to have a name for what I believe I see coming into being 'out there' in the empirical world. But what we call this product of international integration is not very important; how we describe it is centrally important.

What does a Concordance System look like? First, states or nation-states are among the major component units of the system, and national governments remain central actors in it. While it can and will be argued that contemporary international integration does in fact go 'beyond the nation-state' both organizationally and operationally, it nonetheless does not go very far beyond. It certainly does not drive the state into oblivion, economic, political or otherwise. Neither does it relegate the national government to obscurity. Whatever may be the indeterminate future of present-day regional common markets, harmonization agreements and other varieties of integrative ventures here subsumed under the label 'Concordance System', these are presently clusters of cooperatively interacting states. For all we know now, 'international integration' may never be more than this. Therefore, what we are really talking about when we speak of contemporary international integration are neither federations, nor nationalities, nor functional latticeworks, but *international state systems* of a rather interesting kind.

Hopefully having made the point that national governments remain important actors in Concordance Systems, it now must be said that one of the most interesting features of these systems is that national governments are not the only important actors. In fact, the most complex Concordance Systems may include actors in four organizational arenas – the subnational, the national, the transnational and the supranational. In contrast to familiar federal systems, there is no prevailing or established hierarchy or super-ordination-subordination relationship among the different kinds of actors in the system. Instead, each of the actors remains quasi-autonomous (more or less so depending upon issues in question), all are interdependent, and all interact in pursuit of consensus that yields mutual rewards. [. . .] The Concordance System, then, is a pluralist system. But because it includes four organization levels or arenas rather than two as is the case in conventional pluralist models it is a much more complex system than that which we are accustomed to analyzing. Nevertheless, let us bear in mind that despite its complexity and despite the novelty of some of its actors (for example, transnational interest groups) the Concordance System is basically an international system. Certainly, it is not the exclusively government-to-government or 'billiard ball' system of traditional world politics. But it is essentially a system of relations among sovereign states and separate peoples. It is a new kind of international system first created by Europeans to meet European needs in the post-World War II era. Its popularity has spread.

Novelty in Process. Aside from complexity of structure, a number of other distinctive features characterize the Concordance System. Some of these have to do with the nature of interaction processes within the system. First, the Concordance System tends to be a highly institutionalized system wherein actors channel the bulk of their transactions in all issue-areas through organizational networks according to routinized procedures. That is, the process of international interaction within the Concordance System is much more bureaucratic than it is diplomatic. 'Bureaucratic' as I use it here is not meant belittlingly. Quite to the contrary, just as efficient bureaucracy tends to reflect advanced civilization, 'bureaucratic international relations' reflects ordered, standardized, planned, efficient problem-solving in relations among nations. In the Concordance System conflict is effectively regulated and cooperation is facilitated via institutionalized, constitutional, precedential or otherwise standardized, patterned procedures which all actors commit themselves to use and respect. In a way, we can say that the Concordance System characteristic of contemporary international integration is the farthest thing removed from the traditional anarchy of international politics, but which is yet not a state, nation-state or federation. Let it be noted, however, that a Concordance System need not be institutionally centralized. Transactions are channeled through institutions, to be sure, but the Concordance System may include any number of functionally specific organizations and any number of standardized procedures, while it includes nothing even vaguely resembling an overarching central government. In this way, again, the Concordance System remains essentially an international system.

By looking at processes within the Concordance System somewhat more abstractly, we are able to note two further distinctive features of the system. First, political conflict is an integral part of the international interaction pattern. It occurs within and between all action arenas. But, quite in contrast to the modalities of traditional international relations, and accordingly baffling to analysts of the Realist school, most conflict within the Concordance System follows from divergent views about 'ways to co-operate' rather than from fundamental incompatibilities in the interests of the various actors. That is, common, convergent, or at least compatible ends among actors are prerequisites for the emergence of a Concordance System, if these are not present no Concordance System will develop. What actors within the system tend to disagree about most often are the kinds of procedures they will commit themselves to as they bureaucratize their international relations. Therefore, in observing Concordance Systems we should expect to find conflict, we should expect this to be initiated over questions of establishing new harmonizing procedures, and we should expect it to be terminated in agreements on new procedures acceptable to all actors. In this sense, conflict may well be functional to the Concordance System. But to be sure, incompatibilities in actor's basic interests and questions about ultimate ends and goals do intermittently crop up within Concordance Systems, as they certainly did during Charles de Gaulle's challenges to the EEC system in Western Europe. When such questions do emerge and are openly contested, they become disfunctional to the continuation of the Concordance System and could lead to its deterioration.

Second, *bargaining among actors* toward the achievement of convergent or collective ends is the predominant style of interaction within the Concordance System. This bargaining, with exchanged concessions and ultimate compromises, tends to characterize interactions within and between all action arenas. As such, coercion and confrontation are both alien to the Concordance System, are considered illegitimate by actors and occur infrequently. In the vocabulary of the Theory of Games, primitive confrontation politics and resultant constant-sum gamesmanship are alien to Concordance Systems. Much more typical is the variable-sum game pattern which rewards all actors for their cooperative behavior and penalizes them for competitive behavior. Moreover, the game as played in the Concordance System is a 'full information' game where players readily learn of rewards from cooperation and penalties from competition by communicating openly with one another. In short, there is no premium on secrecy and deception in the politics of the Concordance System as there often tends to be in more traditional diplomacy. Of course, none of this is to say that lapses into confrontation politics, attempts at punishment and retaliation, and zero-sum gamesmanship are completely extinguished in Concordance Systems. Again, however, to the extent that these vestiges of traditional international politics enter into interaction patterns of the Concordance System, the system itself comes into jeopardy.

Some Attributes of Atmosphere. The Concordance System survives and thrives in a distinctive attitudinal environment. Four features of this psychological setting are especially notable.

First, pragmatism is the prevailing political doctrine of the Concordance System. If the term pragmatism sounds overly formal, call it 'down-to-earthism'. What it means is that international social, economic and political problems are looked upon by actors involved first as real, second as soluble and third as approachable by whatever means seem most promising of rapid, efficient solution. Pragmatism does not cherish any cosmic first principles, such as those that found socialism, nationalism, communism or liberalism, nor does it project utopian visions. It rather equips its adherents to pour themselves into problem-solving without anxiety about doctrinal purity. Lerner and Gordon admirably capture the pragmatic atmosphere of the present-day Western European Concordance System:

> The collapse of traditional ideologies has made the European élites into pragmatists. They have tried to face the new realities of their postwar situation in ways that work. . . . They can now work more effectively with each other on problems of common interest even when they do not share a common ideology that tells them how to talk about these problems. . . . This is what we call, 'the new pragmatism'.

Second, and perhaps relatedly, the Concordance System is supported by perceptions of international interdependence, or, if not this, then at least by perceptions of national inadequacy. Again, after Lerner and Gordon, and with respect to Western European élite thinking:

> Indeed, there has been a convergent consensus in Europe over the last decade (1955-1965) that national options are not viable and that trans-national choices are the only realistic alternatives.

One of the first steps toward a Concordance System, perhaps, is the emergence of the realization on the part of governments and peoples that they need one another in vital ways. But, let it be noted that such perceptions of national inadequacy and international interdependence as are found among élites (and masses also) within Concordance Systems are not negotiations of the nation-state, nor are they reflections of a new cosmopolitanism. They are rather recognitions of modern economic and technological forces that transverse national frontiers, recognitions that states can no longer relieve internal pressures by external imperialism, and indeed affirmations that nation-states can be preserved as distinct entities only through the international pooling of resources to confront problems that challenge their separate existence.

Third, and again probably relatedly, the 'atmosphere' within the Concordance System, especially in councils where common programs are formulated and decided upon, is one of high mutual sensitivity and responsiveness. To begin with, actors within the system tend to possess a good deal more information about one another and about one another's goals, objectives, preferences and needs than is common in more traditional diplomacy where emphasis is upon one's own needs and upon ways to fulfill these regardless of what the other fellow may want. But even more important, actors within the Concordance System feel some compulsion to see to it that their partners' needs as well as their own are fulfilled in decisions made and programs executed. All of this may sound rather strange to the student of traditional international relations. Nevertheless, it is precisely this atmosphere of shared compulsion to find mutually rewarding outcomes, this felt and shared legitimacy in concession-making, and this reciprocal sensitivity to needs that markedly distinguishes between the new international politics of the Concordance System and the traditional politics of the Machiavellian world.

Fourth, and finally, the Concordance System includes people, or, better stated, peoples. These are the mass populations of the nation-states within the system. What is distinctive about these peoples is that they accord legitimacy to the structures and processes of the system. For one thing, they accept the subnational-national-transnational-supranational political environment that surrounds them, and they defer to the outcomes of the bargaining processes in the multi-arena system. Put more simply, the mass populations of the Concordance System see the system itself as legitimate, and its decisional outputs as authoritative. They comply accordingly. Again, this is a far cry from traditional international relations in the age of integral nationalism! In addition, let it be underlined that mass populations within the Concordance System need not be assimilated into a supranationality. In fact, they may not even like one another very much. They do, however, recognize, accept and bow to the necessities of international cooperation in an age of interdependence, and they support international integration accordingly. [. . .]

16 POLISH SOCIETY (extract)

Jan Szczepański

Source: *Polish Society* (Random House, 1970), pp.33-42, 109-16, 124-8, and 130-8.

On September 1, 1939, Hitler's forces invaded Poland. After a desperate and heroic fight of only a few weeks against the superior German war machine, the Polish army was defeated. When Soviet troops invaded eastern Poland on September 17, the fate of the independent Polish state was sealed. The western provinces were incorporated into the Reich, the eastern part into the Ukrainian and Byelorussian Soviet republics, and central Poland was transformed into a German-ruled *Generalgouvernment* (province). The Nazis looked down on the Poles as an 'inferior race' to be destroyed or turned into a reservoir of 'cheap slave labor'. The military defeat had not, however, crushed the morale of the Polish people. The war went on in Western Europe. Nobody believed in a final victory for the German armies. In the first weeks after the partition, groups of underground armed forces began their operations. A Polish government-in-exile was set up in Paris, and after the collapse of France, it was transferred to London. After 1941, when German armies invaded the Soviet Union, the Polish government-in-exile established relations with the Soviet government, but these relations deteriorated in 1943 and before long were completely severed. In 1942, a new Communist party was organized in Poland, known as the Polish Workers party, and Polish Communists in the Soviet Union established a new political organization, the Union of Polish Patriots, a counterpart to the Polish political group in London.

The Polish armed forces fought on all fronts in the war: in Norway, France, Libya, Russia, Great Britain, Italy, and Poland. There were over 230,000 Polish soldiers in Western Europe; the underground home army had 380,000 soldiers, and the people's army also had tens of thousands – both armies fighting a partisan war in Poland. The first Polish army, organized in the Soviet Union, left that country to join Allied forces in the Middle East and went from Egypt to Libya and Italy, fighting in the ranks of British armies. The second Polish army, organized by the Union of Polish Patriots, joined the Soviet forces and fought from October 1943 until they finally entered Berlin in 1945.

The history of the war will not be repeated here, but an attempt will be made to sum up the major changes it brought about in the structure and life of Polish society, for World War II proved to be a great turning point in Polish history.

The Elements of Change

First, the Polish population suffered an enormous loss of life. Poland paid the highest price of all the belligerent nations: of the 35 million prewar citizens of Poland, over 6 million perished; that is, 220 out of every 1,000 people were killed. (Corresponding figures for other Allied countries were: for Yugoslavia, 108 out of every 1,000; for the USSR, 40; for Czechoslovakia and France, 15; for the United Kingdom, 8; and for the United States, 1.4.) Only about 660,000 Poles, however, were killed in active battle. The rest died in bombed cities, in prisons, and, above all, in concentration camps. Of the 1.2 million inhabitants in Warsaw alone, about 800,000 were killed in the siege of 1939 and in the uprisings in 1943 and 1944. It must be stressed that in the war Poland lost the most valuable segments of her population, because the most determined, most able, and most courageous were engaged in the underground struggle, serving in the armed forces, and otherwise carrying out the resistance. The intelligentsia paid the highest toll in lives: some 35 per cent of the educated strata perished. As General Halder of Germany had stated, 'The Polish intelligentsia must be prevented from establishing itself as the governing class.'

A second important fact is the shift of Polish boundaries from east to west. As a consequence of agreements made at Teheran and Yalta (where no representative of any Polish government was present), Poland lost 69,290 square miles of territory in the east, and gained 39,587 square miles in the west, so that the area now totaled 120,359 square miles. Thus, Poland once again had almost exactly the same frontiers as it did in the second half of the tenth century when it first emerged on the European political scene. But, in addition to loss of territory, there were many other consequences. Millions of Poles were moved from the eastern to the western territories immediately after the armistice, at a time when transport facilities were almost completely destroyed. This move was therefore made under conditions that entailed great hardship and suffering.

When the idea of new Polish boundaries arose in 1943 at the Teheran Conference, it was Winston Churchill who suggested the formula accepted there: 'It is sought in principle that the home of the Polish nation should be between the so-called Curzon line and the line of the Oder, including for Poland East Prussia (as defined) and Oppeln; but the actual tracing of the frontier line requires careful study, and possibly disentanglement of population at some points.' The problem of new Polish boundaries had to be settled among the Allies, because the Soviet Union did not intend to

Figure 16.1: Interwar and Postwar Frontiers

Source: Clifford R. Barnett, *Poland* (New Haven, Conn.: Hraf Press, 1958).

withdraw from the territories occupied in 1939; thus, compensation for Poland had to be sought in the west. The transfer of German populations had been envisaged by President Roosevelt as early as 1943, and finally at Potsdam, in 1945, the United States, the Soviet Union, and Great Britain agreed. 'The three Governments, having considered the question in all its aspects, recognise that the transfer to Germany of German populations, or elements thereof, remaining in Poland, Czechoslovakia and Hungary, will have to be undertaken. They agree that the transfers that take place should be effected in an orderly and humane manner.' To carry this out, an Allied Commission was set up to supervise the transfers. In 1946 and 1947, about 2.2 million Germans were transferred to Germany, following the more than 5 million who had left these territories previously, on the orders of German authorities, when Russian troops entered Germany in the winter of 1944-5. About 1.5 million Poles, whose forebears had lived in this area since the Middle Ages, remained.

The ensuing mass migrations brought almost every third Polish family into a new ecological setting. Millions of people moved into the western territories, émigrés returned from Western Europe, as did Polish populations from eastern sections of the Soviet Union and from German concentration and forced labor camps. But several hundred thousand remained abroad. The peasants moved into destroyed and deserted towns. All these occurrences made the problem of integration especially acute. In the western and northern territories there was a population of about 1.5 million Poles who had been separated from Poland for over 600 years (since 1335) and who, while they had preserved the Polish language and Polish cultural traditions, were accustomed to a quite different way of life than other Poles. Therefore, their adjustment to the ways brought in by the new Polish settlers was not easy. There was also the problem of integration of the new territories into the rest of the country. These were territories in ruins. In 1945, the following percentages of buildings were destroyed in the western cities: Wrocław (Breslau), 65; Szczecin (Stettin), 45; Kołobrzeg, 80; Legnica (Liegnitz), 65; and Gdańsk (Danzig), 55. But in the twenty years that have passed, the problems of integration have been solved. The cities and villages have been rebuilt, and so has the economy of these territories. Industrial output is now three times as great as it was in 1936. The milestone year of these territories was 1964, when the first children of the second-generation settlers were born there. In these twenty years, over 4 million Polish children have been born on this soil. Integration is now an accomplished fact.

But the changes of paramount importance were those in political and economic organization. Rather than entering into the complicated and tragic political history of Poland during the war, I will limit myself to stating that the Polish territory was liberated by the Soviet army and the Polish units fighting in its ranks. The struggle between two opposing Polish political orientations ended with the victory of the Soviet-supported pro-communist side, the Great Powers giving their final support to the new government formed in Poland and withdrawing recognition of the government-in-exile. Thus, Poland changed its political order and became a state referred to by Western political scientists, politicians, and journalists as a 'communist society'.

The new political order is based on Marxist-Leninist ideology and recognizes itself as a revolutionary social order aimed at the 'construction of a socialist society'. Thus, the assuming of political power by the Marxist-Leninist political party had as its consequence the establishment of a socialized economy, planned changes of the social class structure, and planned reconstruction of cultural institutions according to the new ideological principles. The assuming of power by the Polish Workers party — which, as the leading political force, had concentrated in its hands the key positions and was thus able to carry out all reforms considered necessary from the ideological point of view — proved to be the most significant political result of the war. It is true that the war had destroyed the very fabric of the interwar society, but that society would still have been capable of resurrection after the war. The new political order prevented this resurrection and out of the disorganized and profoundly shaken society, a new type of Polish nation emerged, based on those social classes that, throughout the whole of Polish history, had been regarded as inferior.

This new social order was founded on a socialized economy. Nationalization of all enterprises employing more than fifty employees was ratified by the Sejm in 1946 — although, in practice, these enterprises had been taken over by the state in 1944 and 1945 — and were operated under the control of governmental or workers' organizations. Many of the former owners had perished during the war or had left the country and were not in Poland at the time of nationalization. Smaller enterprises were socialized in subsequent years. The agricultural estates were parceled out and allotted to farm laborers, small peasants, or repatriates coming back to the old country.

The socialization of the economy has proved to be the most important long-run factor in changing the character of the nation. It has had a far-reaching impact on people's life chances, career opportunities, and personality development, as well as on the character of the labor force, on the participation of citizens in economic activities, and on work motivation. For its operation, a nationalized economy requires a special kind of motivation in which social and moral motives are as valid as economic incentives; it replaces personal initiative with the initiative of planning institutions; and it requires a complicated system of planning and management institutions having a highly differentiated structure but also a high level of operational efficiency. For all these reasons, socialization of the economy has had the most profound impact on the whole life of the nation, although social scientists and other observers have been fascinated mainly by the impact of the political order and political activities. It is true that the new economic order was created by political decisions, but 'the economic front' became the main concern of party authorities at the very beginning.

Society After the War

How did the war change the social composition of the society? [. . .] The landowning class will be the first social class considered. This sector disappeared almost completely under the German occupation, when all the estates in the provinces incorporated into the Reich (*die eingegliederten Ostgebiete*) were expropriated and taken over by Germans, and the owners were expelled to central Poland or imprisoned. Expropriation was also carried out in the eastern territories occupied by Soviet troops, where the estates were transformed into collective farms or state farms. By 1945, therefore, only small remnants of the landowning class remained on their estates. Land reform, following expulsion of the Germans, allotted the land to farm laborers and small peasants or turned estates into state farms. Thus, the possibility of revival of this class, which for almost a thousand years had been the leading social force in the nation, was nullified, and its members found employment in various white-collar jobs.

Similarly, the lower upper class was largely shattered by war and occupation. The Reich, by taking control of the Polish economy and by integrating it with the German war economy, deprived the Polish bourgeoisie of their enterprises. Many members of this class, as well as members of the landowning class, died in concentration camps. After the war, the nationalization of all enterprises cut off the economic base for a revival of this class.

As noted earlier, the intelligentsia lost about 35 per cent of its members during the war. They were the object of especially severe reprisals, being the class that supplied the nation with leadership in the resistance movement and organized the other classes, giving them ideological direction. In a deliberate attempt to destroy the very roots of Polish national life, the occupation forces set out to exterminate the educated stratum. As a result, losses among the intelligentsia were enormous. For example, of 2,464 university professors and lecturers, 705 perished during the war. Also lost were 848 high school teachers, 3,963 other teachers, 399 artists, and 660 authors and journalists. The medical profession, because of its high percentage of Jews, lost more than one-third of its members. In addition, a considerable number of exiles and displaced persons did not return to Poland after the war. Thus, in 1945, the members of the intelligentsia returned to their work decimated, and deprived of their domiciles, their institutions, and the means of accomplishing their tasks. During the war, there were no Polish universities or high schools, nor any institutions for cultural activities, except those that were underground. The vital forces of the intelligentsia were crushed. Along with the disappearance of the two upper classes, the destruction of the intelligentsia was a most important factor in the disruption of the leadership of the national life which made possible socialist reconstruction and reorientation without any significant resistance. The intelligentsia, as it recovered during the next ten years, changed its social composition and character.

The lower middle class also was almost completely shattered during the war. Its enterprises, integrated into the German war economy, had been reorganized and for the most part shut down. The owners were sent as forced labor to Germany. All Jewish establishments were taken over by the Germans. But a new type of small entrepreneur class emerged during the war and continued to exist for some time after it. It consisted of people who had lost their jobs and now tried to make their livelihoods by running legal, quasi-legal, or illegal enterprises in the gaps of the German war economy. These enterprises were not sound but were calculated to gain as quickly as possible the highest possible profits from black-market operations, smuggling, and so on. It is impossible to ascertain their number. Many of them lasted for only a short time, but many also persisted, and this type of small entrepreneur comprised a considerable part of the lower middle class in the first years following the war. The established middle class — with its way of life, petty bourgeois virtues, and handicraft skills — was reduced in number and unable to impress its features on the new middle class of small entrepreneurs. With its virtual disappearance, the social bases of many political currents in the national life also vanished.

The changes in the peasant and working classes were relatively the smallest. Their social status had not changed, and it had not been possible to deprive them of either property or means of lifelihood because agricultural production and labor continued to be in demand. Thus, even though these two classes had also suffered from repression and forced labor in Germany, both their basic composition and their internal structure were fundamentally unaffected. Hence, at the end of the war, these two classes were in a position to become the principal reservoir of social forces in the process of reconstruction and subsequent expansion. Even if there had been no change in the social and political regime, these classes would have been the principal source of new elites.

It can thus be seen that the war was a great turning point in Poland's social history, disrupting the continuity of the social structure and eliminating the traditional leading social forces, thereby opening the way for radical social change. The social classes that had traditionally supplied the leading elites were unable to reconstitute themselves, and so the new elites had to come from the working class, the peasantry, and the lower ranks of the intelligentsia. It has been sufficiently shown in the history of various nations that it takes at least two or three generations to form a social background such as will give elites the necessary skills in leadership and the art of government and provide them with political insight and foresight.

The new Polish leading groups were formed within the new ruling party, which had Marxist-Leninist ideology as its basic outlook and source of directives in political activities. They were inclined to see the national interests in ideological perspective. This is a very important factor, for the previous political parties and their leading groups had always seen national affairs in the light of their own class interests. The disappearance of the upper social class and the rise of a new social differentiation and stratification made the ideological outlook even more important in the interpretation of national political aims. Ideological loyalty was proclaimed the first concern of the professional political apparatus. A politician can view his activity in either a national, a local, a class, an ideological, or a personal perspective. Every new political elite, in any country and at any time, is inclined to be more ideologically oriented than the old elites, who are more experienced and sophisticated in their outlook and have a more instrumental approach. The members of new elites may also be less resistant to the temptations of power and less inclined to identify personal interests with public interests. All these phenomena emerged in Poland's political life after the war.

Other elements of the macrostructure also changed. After the war, the new state became nationally homogeneous. The German, Ukrainian, and Byelorussian minorities were, according to international agreements, transferred to their respective countries. The remnants of the Jewish community that had survived the barbaric Nazi extermination numbered about 300,000, and many of these left Poland in several waves of emigration to Western Europe and Israel. The position of the Jews in Polish society had essentially changed. Because of their low social status in interwar Poland (as in other East European countries), the Jews had constituted a high percentage of the Polish Communist party, and after the establishment of the communist government, they constituted a high percentage of the new ruling group. Especially during the Stalinist period, the most influential members of the Politburo — as well as the leading members of the Central Committee, Foreign Service, Foreign Trade, and Security Police — were of Jewish origin. After the defeat of Stalinism in 1956, many of them left Poland.

The society also became homogeneous in respect to religion, with Roman Catholics now making up more than 98 per cent of the population. The remainder included mainly small numbers of various Protestant denominations, a small Jewish religious community, and members of the Orthodox faith.

Most significant were the demographic changes. In 1939, Poland had over 35 million inhabitants. The census in February 1946 found within the new frontiers a population of 23.93 million. However, the natural increase was rapid after the war. In 1938, it was 10.7 per thousand; in 1947, it had risen to 14.9; in 1950, it was 19.1; and, in 1953, it reached the postwar peak of 19.5. Only in 1958 did it begin to drop, decreasing to 17.9, after which it steadily went down, coming to 10 per thousand in 1965. The natural increase was strikingly high in the western territories, where in towns like Szczecin and Zielona Góra it reached 30 per thousand. As a consequence, the population in 1966 had again reached 31.811 million, and had only an insignificant percentage of minorities (about 1.2 per cent).

Thus, the problem of integration became quite different from what it had been between the two world wars. The sharp class difference had disappeared, as had ethnic and religious differences. There were still some problems of mutual adaptation among Poles coming from the various parts of Poland and on the part of repatriates returning from other countries. But the population now had the same language, the same national identity and allegiance, and essentially the same cultural tradition and set of national values. Therefore, the regional differences could be overcome by the influence of a strongly centralized set of institutions (such as the school system) and under the impact of such newly developed mass media as radio and television, as well as the press and magazines. [. . .]

Changes in Traditional Social Classes

In the twenty-three years of postwar history, the macrostructure of Polish society has been changed by two essential processes: the transformation in respect to the traditional social classes and the emergence of a new differentiation and stratification due to the functioning of the socialized economy and the new political order. The second process is the more important one. The change affecting the traditional social classes is only a process of transition. It does not create a new structure. It affects only the traditional class characteristics such as level of income and other differences and inequalities. But to a great extent, this process has been regarded by Polish politicians, journalists, and social scientists as the most important one, because the revolution had been made in order to change the class system. The intent of the social revolution consisted in the abolition of this class order. Therefore, the changes within the system have been regarded as the most important effect of the revolution. [. . .]

The Upper Classes

The changes in the traditional classes will be discussed first. As already noted, the two upper classes were not permitted to reconstitute themselves after the disaster of World War II. The landowning class lost its estates. The members of this class who remained in the country took various white-collar and intellectual jobs, according to their education. Many stayed abroad. But the taking away of the economic basis does not at all mean the complete disappearance of the class as a social reality. The families, with their social circles, informal institutions, cultural values, patterns of behavior, and established ways of life still remained. The 'reality' of a class is complicated and durable. The elements that disappeared irrevocably were the landowning classes' political influence, economic role, and means of influencing public life and policies. But their cultural influence persisted, and many of their traditional ways of thinking and behavior were taken over by the newly rising groups, because these were the only models of behavior of people in higher positions existing in the national life. The new groups, rising to leadership in politics and the economy, brought with them, of course, many habits, beliefs, and ideological characteristics of their own social – peasant or working – class. But, voluntarily or not, they had to accede to some generally accepted ways of life and behavior recognized as proper for people in higher positions. Through this mechanism of social continuity many elements of the traditional gentry culture were accepted by the new intelligentsia, new economic managers, and new political officials in their roles of 'cultured men'. It will take a longer time to evolve a new social culture in which the traditional elements of gentry culture will be transformed. Thus, the cultural heritage of the landowning class left its mark in the first postwar decades and will be only slowly transformed by new customs and habits.

No study has been made up to this time in Poland (although materials are being gathered) as to the fate and fortunes of the aristocratic and landed gentry families that for hundreds of years had shaped the destinies of the nation. This class, which has disappeared, was proud and chivalrous but politically unable to maintain its commonwealth (built up in the fifteenth century), to transform it into a modern nation and win the race for power with its neighbors, and finally to defend it and prevent its fall.

A similar fate met the second-ranked upper class, the Polish business class – or 'bourgeoisie', to use the French term. This class did not have such deep traditions as did the gentry. It arose in the nineteenth century and its composition included a very high percentage of minorities. It never played an independent role in Polish history, and its economic rule in inter-war Poland was a very short one. This upper middle class never exercised as much influence in Poland as it did, for example, in Holland. Its intellectual accomplishments and value systems were never dominant nor regarded as the highest in the national culture. The intellectuals and higher circles of the intelligentsia were, for the most part, inclined to accept the gentry culture as its own. And, to some degree, the aristocratic disdain toward the *nouveaux riches* was shared by the lower classes. Moreover, the upper middle class never rose to a position of leadership and did not supply Poland with a political elite having sufficient wisdom, foresight, and political skill to prevent the disaster of 1939. This business class also had many links with international economic organizations – a fact that had some influence on its politics.

It is rather surprising that the two leading classes should have gone from national life without leaving a visible gap in the society. The loss of a highly educated intelligentsia was felt more than the loss of the upper classes. And, although the contribution of the business class to the national cultural heritage was much smaller than that of the landowning class, a single legacy must nevertheless be stressed: the political and economic realism of this class, the ideology of 'organic work' – that is, the ideology of hard work, a thrifty way of life, high respect for skills and 'good work', and sober and unromantic calculation of possibilities in politics and the economy as the way to welfare and international recognition. This lesson is one that the Poles failed to learn in the nineteenth century, and one that the socialists had to adopt from their 'class enemy' in order to be able to carry out the plans of socialist construction. Other elements of this class also remained in Polish society: traditions and methods of business administration, managerial skills, economic experience, and so on – all of which played an essential role in the first years of postwar reconstruction, when many prewar owners and managers were put into positions as directors of socialized enterprises. By 1948 and 1949, however, they had been replaced.

With these two upper classes relegated to oblivion, there remained four other traditional classes: the intelligentsia, the workers, the peasants, and the class of urban and small producers or private entrepreneurs. What kinds of changes took place in these classes and what factors brought them about?

Trends of Change

One of the first changes was that of numerical composition: a decrease in the peasant class and a rapid increase of white-collar employees and manual workers. Then there were shifts in the vocational and professional structure of these classes and changes in the level of their education. Before long there were changes in outlook and value systems that were brought about by education, mass culture, industrialization, and urbanization. The economic and political transformations in the lives of these classes must be stressed. In a market economy, class interests are secured in the interplay of economic forces on the market, and the basic processes of distribution of national income according to different social classes and groups are thus maintained. In a planned economy, distribution of national income is decided by the top economic institutions, and the traditional social classes have very little influence on these decisions.

The political functions of the classes are likewise essentially changed. In a capitalist society, with its characteristic political system, the political interests of the various classes are presumably secured by political parties representing these interests, and these parties may assume political power in elections. In contemporary Poland, the group in power is stabilized and the social classes have little influence on the execution of power, the government being a so-called 'dictatorship of the proletariat'. These limitations on the traditional economic and political functions of social classes result in a kind of political atrophy on the part of the traditional social classes, primarily in respect to class consciousness, the feeling of class solidarity, and class interests. Then, under the continued influence of a socialized and planned economy, the traditional class differences begin to lose their significance. There is a general equalization in standard of living. The higher classes, with their high incomes, no longer exist. The lowest classes with the lowest income also disappear. The differences in wages and salaries are significantly less pronounced than were the differences in income in the interwar society. Life chances are also equalized, with free education, free medical care, free access to cultural life, guaranteed jobs, and so forth. The extremely high rate of social mobility has mixed the social classes. More than 50 per cent of the new intelligentsia who have a higher education come from worker and peasant families. High percentages of the new ruling groups also come from the classes of workers, peasants, and the lower intelligentsia or lower middle class.

The Intelligentsia

Now, beginning with the intelligentsia, let us take a closer look at what remained of the traditional social classes. The intelligentsia suffered high losses during the war, and its reconstitution on the new basis is astonishing. Many factors contributed to this, the most important being the rapidly expanding school system that followed the industrialization and development of the planned economy. In the years between the wars the institutions of higher education turned out a total of about 85,000 graduates. From 1945 to 1966, over 405,000 earned diplomas in higher education. The social composition of the graduates has also changed: about 35 per cent now come from worker families, about 20 per cent from the peasant stratum, some 40 per cent from the intelligentsia, and the rest from the lower middle class and the old upper classes. Of particular significance is the great increase in the class of nonmanual workers. As noted earlier, the national economy in 1938 employed some 700,000 white-collar workers, professionals, and other educated people. In 1965 the corresponding number employed in the socialized and private economy was over 2,600,000. This nonmanual class has shown the most rapid increase and continues to grow faster than the class of manual workers.

Table 16.1: Educational Background, Intelligentsia (percentages)

Field of Study	1937-8	1960-1	1965-6
Technical sciences	10.9	34.4	26.7
Agriculture	8.1	11.6	10.7
Law and economics	40.6	17.7	21.3
Humanities and other social sciences	16.2	9.0	14.9
Science	7.4	8.0	10.3
Medical sciences	15.9	16.8	13.4
Fine arts	0.9	2.5	2.7

Source: *Statistical Yearbook of Education* (Warsaw: Central Statistical Office, 1967), p.401.

The educational background that these members of the intelligentsia have is shown in Table 16.1. We see here a radical drop in the percentage of graduates in law and a rise in the number of graduates in technology and science. This trend toward technical education is also clearly visible in secondary education, with the number of pupils in vocational schools rising from 207,500 in the 1937-8 school year to 1,671,000 in 1965. This is a typical trend for countries in the industrialization and modernization stage. The trend can be seen even more strikingly if we compare the number of students enrolled in the various fields of study (see Table 16.2), rather than the number of graduates. As the admissions to institutions of higher education are also planned and the numbers of students admitted to various fields of study are established centrally, the government can try to harmonize the foreseeable demand in the national economy for manpower that has a higher education with the numbers of students admitted to institutions of higher education. Without entering here into the question of how far such methods of educational planning can be effective, I wish to emphasize only that the government can, in this way, decide the changes in the professional structure of the whole intelligentsia class. The figures in Table 16.2 illustrate the planned efforts of the government to educate a body of manpower that is highly trained and equipped with the technological and practical knowledge necessary to industrialize the country and to run its economy. All this has changed the traditional type of educated man in Poland. In the interwar society, the most highly valued education was a general one — a wide knowledge of the humanities and the knowledge of Latin and Greek was regarded as the mark of the educated and cultured man. In some respects, the English gentleman was the 'model' for the Polish man of letters, who highly appreciated broad, nonprofessional, amateurish, dilettante, cultivated intellectualism. This type of education was most valued in the higher social circles of the intelligentsia among those coming from the 'good' gentry families. Some of the intellectual traditions and pretensions of this intelligentsia have been adopted by the newcomers from the lower classes who see in them symbols of their own 'social advancement'. But, in general, the older type of educated man has given way to the technically minded professional who is proud of his practical skills. Thus, the social functions of the educated stratum have also changed.

Table 16.2: Enrolment of Students, Various Fields of Study

Field of Study	1937-8		1966-7	
	(in figures)	(percentages)	(in figures)	(percentages)
Technical sciences	7,593	15.6	96,975	35.3
Agriculture	3,273	6.6	26,295	9.6
Law and economics	17,838	36.0	53,950	19.7
Humanities and other social sciences	8,557	17.3	36,940	13.5
Science	4,475	9.0	29,450	10.7
Medical sciences	5,750	11.6	55,910	9.4
Fine arts	2,208	4.5	4,951	1.8
Total	49,543	100.0	274,471	100.0

Source: *Statistical Yearbook of Education* (Warsaw: Central Statistical Office, 1967), pp.398,400.

Another factor changing these functions is the feminization of the educated stratum. By 1964, of the 310,400 employees in the socialized economy with a higher education, 101,100, or almost one-third, were women. Of the 598,200 employees with a secondary vocational education, 296,800 were women. And of the 313,700 employees with a secondary general education, 170,500, or over 50 per cent, were women. This growth in the percentage of women employed in the professions and in other occupations that require secondary or higher education has, of course, had many social consequences. Studies of some professions have shown that feminization influences the level of professional performance, its aspiration levels and values, and its social prestige. These factors are very clearly seen in the teaching profession. Teachers in Poland traditionally were the civic leaders in their local communities, but this role is rapidly declining with the feminization of the profession. The same is true for other professions. The feminization of the medical profession is especially regarded as having serious consequences. Over 40 per cent of medical doctors (in 1965, 17,594 out of 39,613), over 90 per cent of the dentists, and over 75 per cent of the pharmacists are women. This feminization has influenced trends in specialization, in professional performance, in social status, and in the prestige of the medical profession. Thus, feminization has changed the profession's traditional role as a leading class in the society. [. . .]

Manual Workers

We have dwelt [. . .] on changes in the intelligentsia because this class is a set of categories becoming more and more significant for the development of Polish society. A second class, playing an equally important part in contemporary developments, is that of the manual workers. According to Marxist theory, this is the basic class of the new socialist order, which means a class that has a vested interest in its own maintenance and development and whose very activity contributes to its existence. (In the same way, the class of entrepreneurs is 'basic' to the existence of the capitalist order.)

[. . .] Here we shall concentrate on the sociological characteristics of manual workers as a social class. The first question to be asked is: in what respect does the status of workers change in a socialist society? Most significant, from the ideological point of view, is the fact that the workers become 'the socialist co-owners of socialized property'. This means that the enterprises in which the workers are employed are now state property, and the profits are reinvested or used for the welfare of the whole population. This idea contributes to the equalization of the life chances of all social classes, giving the workers the right to free education, free medical care, inexpensive housing in state-owned apartments, and any other social measures that will bring about a pronounced equalization of life conditions. It also permits the elimination of unemployment. A point to be stressed is that socialization of the principal branches of the economy, outside of agriculture, has brought about full employment and full access to secondary and higher education for every able and sufficiently motivated worker's child. Moreover, workers' children have profited from certain privileges extended to them in respect to admission to secondary schools and institutions of higher education. The economic status of workers also gives them access to the cultural facilities, libraries, theaters, and museums, and offers them the opportunity to enjoy subsidized recreation. The rise in the prestige of skilled work has already been noted. There is also an increasing participation of workers in the Sejm and People's Councils. In 1965, about 13 per cent of the deputies in the Sejm were workers, and in the urban People's Councils they constituted 28.9 per cent of the council members.

But in spite of these changes in social status, the workers are still hired labor. The socialist revolution does not change the relation of the worker to the machine, nor does it change his position within the technological system of the factory. It changes his position in the social and economic system of the industry or factory. But his relation to the machine and the organizational system of work requires his subordination to the foreman and the management of the factory. He receives wages according to the quantity and quality of work performed, and he must obey the principles and regulations of work discipline. Thus, the status of workers is to some degree inconsistent, being at the same time that of hired laborers and that of co-owners of the means of production.

In order to overcome this discrepancy between the ideologically determined role and the position that results from the functioning of the technological system of the factory, the institution of Workers' Councils was developed in the 1950s. These councils give the workers a certain scope of participation in management. The Workers' Councils are seen as the nucleus of workers' self-government, which is supposed to become the basic institution of the realized socialistic economic order. They are meant to prevent the rise of a highly specialized category of managerial officials who, within the economic organization, might gain unlimited control. The functioning of these councils, which initially gave rise to much hope, seems not, in their first decade, to justify this hope, although it is largely impossible to foresee what the future might bring. The continuing scientific and technological revolution — as it brings about radical changes in the composition, level of education, and standard of living of the workers — may also enable them to participate more fully and effectively in the institution of self-government in factories.

Changes in the social status of workers are due to many causes, among which education is especially significant. [. . .] Preparation for the manual worker's occupation is now mostly the task of the school system, with the traditional method of apprenticeship being replaced by vocational school training. The vocational schools, moreover, not only impart technical knowledge but increasingly provide a general education. This has become necessary inasmuch as the vocational education of the skilled worker must prepare him for his entire working life, that is, for about the next forty years of his life. During this period, the worker must be prepared to adjust to steady changes in technology and methods of work organization, to shifts in jobs, and so forth. His education in the vocational school must give him knowledge and skills that are in some ways in advance of the contemporary state of technology, and it must also give him the necessary flexibility to enable him to make future adjustments. Consequently, it is the view of educators that an increasing emphasis on general education in labor-force training is the best preparation for changing tasks. This approach has consequences other than purely vocational ones. It equips the workers for a greater degree of participation in the representative culture of the nation, diminishes the differences between educated and workers' strata, and enables workers to participate more fully in social and political activities outside of factories.

The political education of the workers is also significant. In vocational schools, in youth organizations, and in cultural institutions, they are given preparation for their future role as social activists. It is important to stress the point that there has been a change in the image of workers. [. . .] The workers are supposed to participate in the social, political, and cultural functions of the enterprise, and it is this participation that slowly but steadily transforms the workers into an educated and socially active stratum.

The last twenty-three years have been years of transition. In the first period of postwar industrialization, masses of the unskilled rural population moved into newly opened factories. Thus, the whole process of change in the nature of the working class was dominated by the influx of peasants, and some sociologists in Poland were commenting on the workers 'becoming boorish'. But in the 1960s, a transformation became evident. The new workers have had not only the full eight years of elementary school but also two or three years of vocational schooling. In factories they are using their opportunities to participate in social, political, and cultural activities. Through their organizations they have gained influence in some matters of management and collective life in the factories. They also are being better prepared to participate in social and political institutions outside of the factories, such as People's Councils. This, then, is the basic trend shaping the character of the working class.

One could speak of 'reorientation' of the workers' class activities and class consciousness. In the nineteenth century, the working class in Poland, as in other European countries, was formed by the capitalist enterprise, by the class struggle for economic and political objectives; the 'new' workers at that time developed their class consciousness by participation in trade unions, in strikes, and in organizations of workers' solidarity. They felt the opposed interests of workers and entrepreneurs and saw that the image of their position in the factory was reflected in the society. In contemporary Poland, the class consciousness of the workers is being developed by a different set of factors. The class struggle for political and economic objectives changed with the introduction of the new political order and planned economy. The trade unions became part of the political establishment. The struggle for economic objectives is carried out by the trade unions within the planning institutions. The activity of workers is being reoriented toward other social aims in fulfilling the social, paternalistic, and political aims of enterprises. The worker sees his life not as a struggle against the management or against the political order, but as a means of fulfilling the plans and achieving the planned targets. A set of new institutions has been created in order to direct his activity to cultural and educational aims. Every worker can attend evening classes or take correspondence courses in secondary education and, afterward, in higher education. All this has made this process of 'reorientation' a social reality.

But the process did not go on without tensions and conflicts. The majority of workers brought up in the prewar society were unable to adjust well to the changing conditions. Also, the rigorous requirements necessitated by reconstruction and the rapid tempo of industrialization brought forth a natural protest on the part of workers. Beginning in 1956, a wave of strikes swept over the country. But the period of unrest and protest ended in the early 1960s. Some unrest may still persist, as the planned rate of growth is high and the standard of living is increasing slowly, slower than the rising expectations. Still, if there are no major setbacks, such as war or some other catastrophe, the process of reorientation in the development of the working class will continue, and will be the most important factor shaping the character of this class in the future. [. . .]

The Peasantry

[. . .] The peasantry constitutes the largest reservoir of the population, and as an economic force it was relatively less damaged by the war than other sectors of the population. The rural population, after the war, was therefore able to repopulate the destroyed cities, supply the labor force necessary for industrialization, resettle the western territories, and send considerable numbers of students to the expanded system of secondary and advanced schools. But the most important problem facing both the peasants and the government was that of incorporating the privately operated farms and the traditional stratum of peasantry into the socialist, integrally planned economy.

According to Marx's classic theory, the peasantry — or perhaps more accurately, the farmers — had not constituted an independent and 'basic' social force in any historically known type of society. In feudal society, although they were the most numerous and oppressed, they were unable to change the social order, which finally was transformed by the rising class of capitalist entrepreneurs and a middle class. In the nineteenth century, farmers were still the most numerous but were, nevertheless, without any possibility of gaining political power and assuming authority in European countries. Marx compared peasants to a 'sack of potatoes', unable to organize as a politically coherent *Klasse für sich* ['Class in itself'] . Thus, he and his followers regarded the peasantry as a passive social mass incapable of any revolutionary, effective action and one that could only be led by an active revolutionary force, such as politically organized workers.

Lenin and other Russian revolutionaries, when preparing and carrying out the revolution in Russia, tried to get the support of the peasant masses by promising them land reform and participation in a democratic government. They hoped that, after the revolution and the establishment of the socialist state, the peasantry would be absorbed by the rising industrialized economy to create conditions similar to those in highly industrialized Western countries, where the percentage of the labor force employed in agriculture is low and the traditional peasantry has been transformed into a middle-class type of farmer-entrepreneur. But the anticipated transformation took longer than was expected, and the socialist planned economy had great difficulties in finding methods of manipulating the farmers' economic decisions so as to harmonize their economic activities with the socialized sector. Finally, Stalin took drastic measures through collectivization, which incorporated agriculture into the socialized sector and subordinated the peasants directly to the economic institutions of the state. The results of this step were far from those hoped for, and the shock of collectivization brought about a sharp drop in productivity that was overcome only after many years.

The situation in Poland was in some respects similar to that in Russia after the revolution, but it was also very different. The similarity was in the numerical strength of the Polish peasantry, which comprised more than 52 per cent of the population, and the differences lay in their social and political traditions. The Polish peasantry was politically organized, even though they were unable to assume power in interwar Poland. Then, too, they were deeply religious and Catholic, which was in opposition to socialist ideology. Finally, their fanatical traditionalism and their regarding the farm not as an enterprise but as a patrimony to be passed on to the next generation had proved to be a factor of national strength and national existence during the nineteenth century. For this reason, in the first period of postwar development, the government tried to gain the support of the peasants by land reform, that is, the parcelization of large estates among former agricultural workers and small farmers. The economic model for this transitional period was based on the principle of close cooperation of three sectors: state-owned enterprises, cooperative enterprises, and private enterprises. The central planning and managing institutions were supposed to manipulate economic decisions of all socialist, cooperative, and private entrepreneurs and to harmonize their activities. Thus, land reform was the initial factor that led to changes in the composition and internal organization of the peasantry. The second factor was the drive toward collectivization, which began after 1948 when Gomułka and his group were removed by Stalinists. The drive toward collectivization, which met with bitter resistance by the peasants, was linked with industrialization and a broadened access to the school system, both of which resulted in a massive exodus of the rural population to the towns and cities. The failure and subsequent renouncement of collectivization meant that the government had to look for other ways and means of manipulating the peasants' economic decisions within the planned economy. A set of institutions and measures, such as contracts, bonuses for products especially important to the economy, and taxes, were applied to this purpose. The consequences of all these factors are considered below.

The land reform had allotted some 6,070,100 hectares to 1,068,400 peasants and agricultural laborers. It created 347,100 new farms in old territories, with an average area of 6.9 hectares, and allotted 254,400 farms with an average area of 1.9 hectares. Thus, great numbers of farm laborers formerly employed on prewar estates or on larger farms had become independent farmers. At the same time, in the newly acquired western and northern territories, 466,800 peasants were settled, which essentially changed the rural districts of the central Polish provinces. Thus, in the first few years after 1944 and 1945, the peasant stratum was considerably strengthened by the elimination of the agricultural proletariat, by the enlargement of small holdings, by the elimination of hidden unemployment, and by the increase in the number of farms.

But before the peasants could reap the fruits of all this, a heavy burden was put on their shoulders: the reconstruction of the devastated economy, followed by rapid industrialization. In order to meet the costs of both, the government was forced to encumber agriculture with heavy taxes and the obligatory delivery of agricultural products at prices lower than the usual market prices. These delivered products were sold to the town population at market prices, and the 'profit' was used to finance the reconstruction and industrialization. It was during this time that the rural exodus began.

The changes in agricultural property between 1950 and 1960 are shown in Table 16.3. Although in the first postwar years the structure of agriculture was strengthened by enlargement of farms and other results of land reform, in the next decade there was a rapid process of fragmentation. This fragmentation was brought on by the drive for collectivization, along with an ideological struggle against the 'rural capitalists', that is, the rich farmers employing hired labor. To avoid persecution, the rich farmers divided their farms into smaller ones and distributed them to their children. Moreover, industrialization, which provided an abundance of jobs outside agriculture, led to the rise of small-sized farms whose owners were employed in various jobs in other branches of the economy, while the farms were run by the wives and children as a source of additional income. Only after 1960 was this inefficient type of fragmentation stopped by law.

Table 16.3: Changes in Agricultural Property

Farm Area (in hectares)	Number of Farms			
	1950		1960	
	(in thousands)	(percentages)	(in thousands)	(percentages)
0.1-0.5	199.7	6.3	345.8	9.6
0.5-2	621.6	19.6	825.6	23.0
2-3	375.5	11.8	428.5	12.0
3-5	616.3	19.5	663.8	18.5
5-7	477.5	15.1	475.1	13.3
7-10	449.9	15.7	460.9	12.9
10-15	246.3	7.8	282.3	7.9
15-20	92.7	2.9	66.2	1.8
Over 20	39.9	1.3	35.9	1.0
Total	3,119.4	100.0	3,584.1	100.0

Source: *Statistical Yearbook of Poland* (Warsaw: Central Statistical Office, 1966), p.245.

The combination of all these factors — land reform, collectivization, industrialization, access to schools and a rising educational level, followed by renunciation of collectivization and the applying of economic methods for linking private farms with the planned economy — led to the division of the traditionally relatively coherent peasant class into several categories. The most important and numerically greatest of these categories is that of the farmers who operate their own farms and make their entire living from them. As noted earlier, about 85 per cent of tillable land is in the hands of private farmers, and in 1960 there were some 3,584,000 such farms. About 2,500,000 of these were operated by farmers who had no additional sources of income and were not employed in any other occupation. This category is still the most traditional part of the peasantry in Poland. But in the years since 1960, the picture of these farmers has become quite different from the one they presented in the early postwar years, to say nothing of the late 1930s. Most significant has been the transformation of the traditional types of peasants into professionally oriented and economically minded farmer-entrepreneurs. The same process that took place in Western Europe in the nineteenth century occurred in Poland under the impact of industrialization and an expanded educational system. When, in 1956, the government renounced the policy of collectivization and created a system of incentives, which linked the peasants with the rest of the socialized economy and aimed at raising the productivity of farms, the process of transforming traditional peasants into modern farmers got its necessary impetus. Also contributing to this transformation was the development of a mass culture that penetrated the villages with the mass circulation of the press, with radio and television sets, and with a rising level of education. In order to stop the excessive exodus from villages, the government had to take several measures toward raising the standard of living in rural districts, including the organization of recreational and cultural institutions similar to those in urban areas.

All this contributed to the 'farmerization' of the traditional peasantry, transforming it into a class of entrepreneurs controlled and led by the institutions of central planning. Through channels of agricultural institutions and organizations and by employing a set of incentives and other instruments of planned policy, these central institutions direct the economic decisions of rural entrepreneurs in such a way that maximum income is achieved, while at the same time the towns and industries are supplied with the necessary agricultural products. A system of agricultural schools, of various organizational patterns, was developed to give farmers the necessary training and to push mechanization and rational methods of farming.

The second numerically large category is that of the peasant-workers, whose number (which is constantly changing) is estimated at about 900,000. This extremely important category includes all owners of private farms who are simultaneously employed in such branches of the economy outside agriculture as industry, mining, construction, and transportation. Sociologists refer to them as people living in two environments. They operate their farms and live in villages or agricultural suburbs, but at the same time they are employed as manual workers in industrial or other enterprises where they are exposed to the impact of a technological, highly rationalized system of organization. There they learn, and have to adjust to, the requirements of formal organization, and to this extent they become a part of the modernized labor force, giving up the traditional rural ways of thinking and behaving. They also become involved in the social and political activities of workers' organizations. They receive an income that they can invest in their farms or use for raising their standards of housing, clothing, and so forth. They are powerful transmitters of urban ways of life to the countryside, and their children, as a rule, receive a vocational secondary education. Usually peasant-workers operate small farms under 2 hectares in size, but some 150,000 of them get a higher income from their farms than from employment in towns and regard themselves primarily as farmers. The latter use the additional income to enlarge and modernize their farms. All these worker-farmers are commuters, and only a small percentage of them spend the whole week in town, returning to their farms just on weekends. As a link between farmers and workers, they are bringing about interpenetration and unification of the two, which have traditionally been sharply separated classes.

A third category of contemporary peasants is the peasant-white-collar employee. This category consists of farm owners who are simultaneously employed in certain white-collar jobs in rural or township Peoples' Councils, in economic or administrative institutions, or as clerks in other branches of the economy. They differ from peasant-workers in several respects. They have, as a rule, a somewhat higher level of education. They have been influenced by the traditional way of life of the intelligentsia. They have connections with administrative state institutions and sometimes belong to the rural political elite. This category came into being during the drive toward collectivization, when the peasants lost interest in farming and when, at the same time, the newly created system of institutions (administrative and economic) needed great numbers of workers. Some peasants transferred their farms to collective units and took jobs in the new institutions. In 1956, when the collective farm drive was abandoned, they reclaimed their farms but remained in their white-collar jobs. Although not a sizable category, numbering only about 200,000 in 1965, they have had a great impact on life in the villages. These farmer-white-collar individuals imitate the way of life of the urban white-collar class, try to give their children a higher education, and constitute a link between two classes, which in the interwar society were separated, thus contributing to equalization and the removal of differences between traditional social classes. They are more exposed to the influences of the nation's representative culture and the aspirations of the urban intelligentsia than are the peasant-workers. Their 'second environment' is that of the administrative office, and their superiors are their models of behavior.

A fourth category is that of farmers who operate the collective farms. There still are in Poland about 1,220 collective farms, on which some 31,000 families work together. These farms are owned by the members of a co-operative, and are run by a board elected by all the members. Most are highly modernized socialized enterprises that specialize in some profitable kind of agricultural production. As a social category, this group is of less importance among the peasant class, inasmuch as present plans call for no further development of collective farms. The socialized sector in agriculture will continue to be developed by increasing the number and area of state farms, which are owned and operated by the state.

Finally, there is also a small subgroup of farmer-entrepreneurs who try to link their farms with the operation of other kinds of enterprises, such as transportation, artisan workshops, or retail trade shops. They number fewer than 10,000. They are a link between the peasantry and the remaining lower middle class of private entrepreneurs. This type of entrepreneur is a rather curious by-product of the transitional period of socialization of the economy during which the state economic institutions, still not able to satisfy all the needs of the people, permit some degree of private initiative, which is also linked with high profit making.

The process of transfer from agriculture to other branches of the economy still goes on, and the number of farmers in the first category noted above is still decreasing, chiefly through the exodus of children and youth as they are brought into the school system. The number of farmers without successors is steadily growing, their farms being taken over by the government and incorporated into the state-owned farms. Some estimates show that more than 15 per cent of the privately operated farms in the first category are operated by owners over sixty-five years of age and without successors, their children having gone into other careers or occupations. Thus, even on the basis of this short sketch, it is clear that the transformation of the peasantry has been both far-reaching and not altogether as anticipated. But one must conclude that the reorganization and decomposition of the peasant class and the bringing about of its equalization in living standards and in education and its interpenetration with other social classes is one of the most significant processes of change in the traditional class system.

The Class of Private Entrepreneurs

A fourth traditional social class still existing in Polish society is that of private small entrepreneurs. Immediately after World War II, this class reemerged on a new economic basis of some 400,000 privately operated enterprises of all kinds. This number was reduced to some 115,000 during the Stalinist era, but afterward rose again. In 1965 there were in Poland 6,934 private industrial enterprises, 97,828 workshops of so-called industrial artisans, 30,623 construction workshops, 138,515 other artisan shops, and 39,409 retail trade shops, restaurants, transportation enterprises, and so on (the peasants' enterprises excluded), altogether over 311,300 enterprises. [. . .] This is a quite different social class than the pre-World War II lower middle class. Its composition is steadily changing, the principles of operation are not so clearly defined, and some of these enterprises operate on a quasi-legal basis, profiting from the shortcomings and gaps in the socialized sector. This class receives a high income, but has very low prestige and does not participate in political authority. It was barely tolerated in the Stalinist period, but now, with the stabilization of the socialist order, it is accorded a stable place in economic and social life. The Democratic party is its political representative. This class is no longer a political threat to the parties in power, and its enterprises are incorporated into the planned economy by measures similar to those for the private farms – that is, by contracts with state-owned enterprises and by manipulation of prices and salaries, taxes, and so forth. The economic decisions of the private entrepreneurs are regulated by all these measures, and thus the private sector is harmonized with the rest of the national economy.

This is a peculiar social class, living within an economic order that by its very ideology is hostile to private initiative. But as time goes on, some kind of adjustment is emerging, and in my judgment, this class will not disappear with the maturation of the socialist order but will only become more integrated within it. It is a class quite different from the lower middle class in Western societies and, most of all, from the 'new middle class' composed of white-collar workers and other categories described by Mills and other sociologists. It is rather an 'old lower middle class' of independent entrepreneurs who have adjusted to the requirements of an integrally planned economy. It exists as such only in Poland, and its existence, together with that of private agriculture, not only gives a distinctive character to the socialist order in Poland, but also presents an interesting experiment for the future. It shows that the socialist order – and an integrally planned economy – can embrace nonsocialized enterprises and social classes based on private property, but without allowing them unlimited profit making and without their gaining political power through the means of private ownership. It seems possible that this class will develop further and, in spite of being regarded by Marxist ideologues with suspicious eyes, will become an integral part of socialized society.

INDEX

agrarian revolution 127
alcohol consumption: crime and 97,
    100-3, 107, 110
Alletz, Eduard 21
appeasement 184-92
Arnoldi, Bishop 68, 71, 79-87 *passim*
atomic bomb 330
Austria 228; First World War and 164-79

Barnes, Thomas 35
Bebel, A. 159
Bernstein, Eduard 149
Bethmann Hollweg, T. von 166-73
    passim, 178-9, 180, 182-3
Biedermann, Karl 31
Blackwell, Sir Ernely 264
Britain: foreign policy 184-92; Germany
    and 191-2; imperialism 126-7, 134-45,
    185-6; journalism 31-6; public
    opinion 187; reforms 190; USA and
    191
Bukharin, N. 120, 294-300
Bulgaria 180, 324
bureaucracy 302-16 *passim*, 349; in the
    SPD 157-8

canuts 37-64
Chamberlain, Joseph 140
Chateaubriand, René de 16, 19, 21
Churchill, W. 319, 320-33 *passim*
class consciousness 51
class warfare 36
Cobden, R. 276
Cold War 317-33; sphere-of-influence
    319-27; universalism 319-23
Cologne disturbances 78-9
concentration, economic 128-9
conflict 9; between church and state
    78-87; in silk weaving 46-8, 52-63;
    international 349
Cook, Arthur 283-4
crime: violent 102-3, 107-11; industrial-
    isation and 96-8; male and female
    101-2; police 102; poverty and 96-8,
    101, 104; property offences 101,
    103-7; social status and 109-10;
    statistics 99-103; urban rural differ-
    ences 103-5, 107-8; values and 104-6

Curzon, Lord 142

Daily Express 268
developing countries 125-6, 133, 334
Disraeli, B. 189-90

economic growth 129; unequal 133-4
Eisenhower, D. 277
Ense, Karl V. von 27
equilibrium, social 9
European integration 334-52

federalism 341-2
First World War 164-92; Austria 164-79;
    Britain 164-74; British censorship
    259-71; Germany 164-83; Russia
    164-74, 181, 219, 222; Serbia 165-74
    passim
France: newspapers in 12-22; socialism
    in 155
French Revolution (1789) 256-7
Freytag, Gustav 27

General Strike (1926) 282-92
German Catholicism 70, 73
German Social Democratic Party 146-63;
    isolation of 159-60; leadership 157-8;
    Marxists 150-1; organisation 152,
    156-8; policy disagreements 151-4;
    revisionist debate 148-50; *Reichstag*
    delegation 160-1; revolution and 153;
    trade unions and 157
Germany 277, 336-7; agriculture 127;
    Britain and 191-2; Catholic Centre
    Party 147; First World War 164-79;
    Nazi regime 302-4, 309-16; news-
    papers 12, 22-31; publishing 23-4;
    unity of 30; USPD 151
Girardin, Emile de 13-15
Girardin, Saint-Marc 19
Gladstone, W. 188-90
Globe 263-4
Görres, Joseph 65, 69
Gutzkow, Carl 23

Harriman, A. 324-5, 329
Hauranne, Duvergier de 17, 19
Häusser, Ludwig 27